AN INTRODUCTION TO

ISLAMIC LAW

AN INTRODUCTION TO
ISLAMIC LAW

BY

JOSEPH SCHACHT

CLARENDON PRESS · OXFORD

Oxford University Press, Walton Street, Oxford OX2 6DP
Oxford New York Toronto
Delhi Bombay Calcutta Madras Karachi
Petaling Jaya Singapore Hong Kong Tokyo
Nairobi Dar es Salaam Cape Town
Melbourne Auckland
and associated companies in
Beirut Berlin Ibadan Nicosia

Oxford is a trade mark of Oxford University Press

ISBN 0–19–825473

First published 1964
Reprinted 1966, 1971, 1975, 1979
First published as paperback 1982
Reprinted 1986

British Library Cataloguing in Publication Data
Schacht, Joseph
An introduction to Islamic law.
1. Islamic law.
I. Title
340.5'9
ISBN 0–19–825473–3

Library of Congress Cataloging in Publication Data
Schacht, Joseph, 1902–1969.
An introduction to Islamic law.
Reprint. Originally published: Oxford:
Clarendon Press, 1964.
Bibliography: p.
Includes indexes.
1. Islamic law. I. Title.
LAW 340.5'9 82–12509
ISBN 0–19–825473–3 (pbk.)

Printed in Hong Kong

PREFACE

THIS book contains an account of our present knowledge of the history and of the outlines of the system of Islamic law. It is intended for two groups of readers: students of history, social sciences, and comparative law on the one hand, and on the other, students of Arabic who might wish to embark upon this particularly important and attractive branch of Islamic studies. Islamic law provides us with a remarkable example of the possibilities of legal thought and of human thought in general, and with a key to understanding the essence of one of the great world religions. This book is concerned with the unique historical phenomenon of Islamic law as such, and not with the contemporary laws of those countries in the Near East and elsewhere where Muslims live. I am writing as a student of Islam and of that manifestation of Islam which is Islamic law, and not as a lawyer, or a comparative lawyer, or a sociologist. Nevertheless, as a student of the history of Islam, I have tried to refer the development of Islamic law to the development of Islamic society, and to integrate the historical and systematic sections of this book as far as the present state of our knowledge allows. In order to keep my account within reasonable limits, I have had to restrict myself to the history of Islamic law within the orthodox or Sunni community, leaving aside the separate developments of Shiite and Ibāḍī law, and to choose, in the systematic section, the doctrine of one of the orthodox schools of law, the Ḥanafī; I have, however, not hesitated to extend the bibliographies to all orthodox schools and to Shiite and Ibāḍī law.

The bibliography forms an essential part of this book; it is intended for both groups of its potential readers, but I have not aimed at bibliographical completeness. In particular, I have omitted those publications which are now of historical interest only, or do not add substantially to what has been said in the text, or fall short of present scholarly standards; I have been selective, too, with regard to the writings of modern lawyers on technical points of Islamic law as applied in contemporary practice. I trust that the short indications of the main Arabic sources, both in the historical and in the systematic section, will be sufficient for students of Arabic; for the sake of other readers of this book, I have referred to translations of Arabic texts to the widest possible extent. Those publications which in my opinion are particularly useful for further study of the subjects in question have been marked by an asterisk, and those which I consider indispensable, by a dagger; it goes without saying that these indications do not imply any derogatory comment on the other titles included in the bibliography.

I have covered substantially the same field in two previous publications, *Esquisse d'une histoire du droit musulman*, Paris, 1953, for the historical section, and *G. Bergsträsser's Grundzüge des islamischen Rechts*, Berlin and Leipzig, 1935, for the systematic section. The present book, not merely a restatement but the result of continuous work on the subject over a number of years, is intended to supersede both. I should like to acknowledge the courtesy of the Middle East Institute in Washington in allowing me to draw on the text of my contribution to the volume *Law in the Middle East*.

J. S.

February 1964

PREFACE TO THE SECOND IMPRESSION

In this second impression, I have made only very few minor changes, but have brought the bibliography up to date.

J. S.

July 1965

CONTENTS

1

INTRODUCTORY

THE sacred Law of Islam[1] is an all-embracing body of religious duties, the totality of Allah's commands that regulate the life of every Muslim in all its aspects; it comprises on an equal footing ordinances regarding worship and ritual, as well as political and (in the narrow sense) legal rules. It is with these last that this book is concerned. This restriction is historically and systematically justified;[2] it must, however, be kept in mind that the (properly speaking) legal subject-matter forms part of a system of religious and ethical rules.

Islamic law is the epitome of Islamic thought, the most typical manifestation of the Islamic way of life, the core and kernel of Islam itself. The very term *fiḳh*, 'knowledge', shows that early Islam regarded knowledge of the sacred Law as the knowledge *par excellence*. Theology has never been able to achieve a comparable importance in Islam; only mysticism was strong enough to challenge the ascendancy of the Law over the minds of the Muslims, and often proved victorious. But even at the present time the Law, including its (in the narrow sense) legal subject-matter, remains an important, if not the most important, element in the struggle which is being fought in Islam between traditionalism and modernism under the impact of Western ideas. Apart from this, the whole life of the Muslims, Arabic literature, and the Arabic and Islamic disciplines of learning are deeply imbued with the ideas of Islamic law; it is impossible to understand Islam without understanding Islamic law.

Islamic law is a particularly instructive example of a 'sacred law'. It is a phenomenon so different from all other forms of law—notwithstanding, of course, a considerable and inevitable number of coincidences with one or the other of them as far as

[1] *sharīʿa, sharʿ*, the sacred Law; *fiḳh*, the science of the *sharīʿa*; *faḳīh* (pl. *fuḳahāʾ*), the specialist in *fiḳh*.

[2] Cf. below, pp. 112, 200 f.

subject-matter and positive enactments are concerned—that its study is indispensable in order to appreciate adequately the full range of possible legal phenomena. Even the two other representatives of a 'sacred law' which are historically and geographically nearest to it, Jewish law and Canon law, are sensibly different.

Both Jewish law and Canon law are more uniform than Islamic law. The history of Jewish law, it is true, shows a break between the law of a sovereign state and that of the Dispersion, but the spirit of the legal matter in the later parts of the Old Testament is already very close to that of the Talmud. Islam, on the other hand, represented a radical breakaway from Arab paganism; Islamic law is the result of a scrutiny, from a religious angle, of legal subject-matter which was far from uniform, comprising as it did the various components of the laws of Arabia and numerous elements taken over from the peoples of the conquered territories. All this was unified by being subjected to the same kind of scrutiny the impact of which varied greatly, being almost non-existent in some fields, and in others originating novel institutions. This inner duality of legal subject-matter and religious norm is additional to the outward variety of legal, ethical, and ritual rules which is typical of a 'sacred law'. Jewish law was buttressed by the cohesion of the community, reinforced by pressure from outside; its rules are the direct expression of this feeling of cohesion, leading to the rejection of all dissentients. Canon and Islamic law, on the contrary, are dominated by the dualism of religion and state, where the state is not, in contrast with Judaism, an alien power but the political expression of the same religion. But their antagonism took on different forms; in Christianity it was the struggle for political power on the part of a tightly organized ecclesiastical hierarchy, and Canon law was one of its political weapons. Islam, on the other hand, was never a 'Church', Islamic law was never supported by an organized power, consequently there never developed a real trial of strength; there merely existed a discordance between the sacred Law and the reality of actual practice of which the regulations framed by the state formed part, a gap more or less wide according to place and time, now and then on the point of being closed but continually reasserting itself.

There were two important changes of direction within the

history of Islamic law; one was the introduction at an early date of a legal theory which not only ignored but denied the existence in it of all elements that were not in the narrowest possible sense Islamic, and which reduced its material sources to the Koran and the example of the Prophet;[1] the second, which began only in the present century, is modernist legislation on the part of contemporary Islamic governments, which does not merely restrict the field in which the sacred Law is applied in practice but interferes with the traditional form of this law itself.[2] Again this interference does not take the form of a struggle for power between competing organizations, it poses itself not in the terms of replacing the sacred by a modern secular law but of renovating its traditional form, and the postulate that Islam as a religion ought to regulate the sphere of law as well, remains unchallenged.

Neither is Islamic law uniform at any point of its development. From the outset the subject-matter out of which it was created varied from place to place, and these geographical differences account for much of the divergencies between the ancient schools of law. Some of the later schools of law perpetuated some of their predecessors, while other later schools arose from differences in the principles and methods of legal reasoning. The sects of the Ibāḍīs and of the Shiites, too, developed their own legal systems. Within orthodox Islam, however, the strongly pronounced 'catholic instinct' of Islam led to the recognition of the four surviving later schools as equally valid alternate interpretations of the sacred Law.

Islamic law came into being and developed against a varied political and administrative background. The lifetime of the Prophet was unique in this respect; it was followed by the turbulent period of the Caliphs of Medina (9–40 of the hijra, A.D. 632–61). The rule of the Umayyads, the first dynasty in Islam (41–132 of the hijra, A.D. 661–750), represented, in many respects, the consummation of tendencies which were inherent in the nature of the community of the Muslims under the Prophet. During their rule the framework of a new Arab Muslim society was created, and in this society a new administration of justice, an Islamic jurisprudence, and, through it, Islamic law itself came into being. The Umayyads were

[1] Cf. below, Chapter 9.

[2] Cf. below, Chapter 15.

overthrown by the ʿAbbāsids, and the early ʿAbbāsids attempted to make Islamic law, which was then still in its formative period, the only law of the state. They were successful in so far as the *ḳāḍīs* were henceforth bound to the sacred Law, but they did not succeed in achieving a permanent fusion of theory and practice, of political power and sacred Law. There followed the gradual dismemberment of the Islamic Empire to which it is, in the nature of things, difficult to assign definite dates but which was well on its way about the year 300 of the hijra or about A.D. 900. Now Islamic law profited from its remoteness from political power; it preserved its stability and even provided the main unifying element in a divided world of Islam. The modern period, in the Western sense of the term, saw the rise of two great Islamic states on the ruins of the previous order, the Ottoman Empire in the Near East and the Mogul Empire in India; in both empires in their hey-days (the sixteenth and the seventeenth century respectively) Islamic law enjoyed the highest degree of actual efficiency which it had ever possessed in a society of high material civilization since the early ʿAbbāsid period. The symbiosis, in the wake of Western political control, of Islamic law and of Western laws in British India and in Algeria (starting in the eighteenth and in the nineteenth century respectively), gave birth to two autonomous legal systems, Anglo-Muhammadan law and *Droit musulman algérien*. Finally, the reception of Western political ideas in the Near East has provoked, in the present century, an unprecedented movement of modernist legislation.

Although Islamic law is a 'sacred law', it is by no means essentially irrational; it was created not by an irrational process of continuous revelation but by a rational method of interpretation, and the religious standards and moral rules which were introduced into the legal subject-matter provided the framework for its structural order. On the other hand, its formal juridical character is little developed; it aims at providing concrete and material norms, and not at imposing formal rules on the play of contending interests. It has, therefore, not easily lent itself to the technical treatment applied to it by modern lawyers in the majority of contemporary Islamic states. It possesses a pronounced private and individualistic character; it is, in the last resort, the sum total of the personal privileges and duties of all individuals. One of the most striking features of traditional Islamic law is the casuistical method which is closely connected with the structure of its legal concepts, and both are the outcome of an analogical, as opposed to an analytical, way of thinking which pervades the whole of it. Islamic law represents an extreme case of a 'jurists' law'; it was created and developed by private specialists; legal science and not the state plays the part of a legislator, and scholarly handbooks have the force of law. This became possible because Islamic law successfully claimed to be based on divine authority, and because Islamic legal science guaranteed its own stability and continuity. The traditionalism of Islamic law, typical of a 'sacred law', is perhaps its most essential feature. These considerations on the nature of Islamic law will be developed in greater detail in the last chapter of this book.[1]

The scholarly investigation of Islamic law is still in its beginnings. This comes partly from the infinite variety and complexity of the subject, partly from its position on the borderline between Islamic and legal studies, and partly from two unexpected developments which have occurred in the present generation; on the one hand, our ideas concerning the early history of Islamic law have undergone a considerable change and whole new horizons have been opened for research, and on the other, modern legislation in a number of Islamic countries has added, after a long period of near-immutability, a new and, as yet, unfinished chapter to its more than millenary history.

[1] Cf. below, Chapter 26.

HISTORICAL SECTION

2

THE PRE-ISLAMIC BACKGROUND

1. THE legal institutions of Arabia in the time of Muhammad were not altogether rudimentary. There was, first, the customary law of the majority of the Arabs, the Bedouins, which, though primordial in character, was by no means simple in its rules and in their application. It is known to us to a limited extent, and in its general character rather than in its details, through pre-Islamic and early Islamic poetry and through the tales of the tribes. The comparable conditions which have survived among the Bedouins of modern times enable us to control the information of the literary sources. Whereas investigation of cases and evidence are dominated by sacral procedures, such as divination, oath, and curse, the positive law of the ancient Arabs is decidedly profane, matter-of-fact, and informal; even their penal law is reduced to questions of compensation and payment.

2. Mecca, however, was a trading city in (admittedly modest) commercial relations with South Arabia, Byzantine Syria, and Sassanian Iraq; the city of Ṭā'if was another centre of long-distance trade, and Medina was the chief town of an intensively cultivated group of oases of palm-trees with a strong colony of Jews, probably mostly Arab converts. It is likely that these and perhaps other towns in Arabia possessed laws more highly developed than those of the Bedouins. We can form some idea of the character of commercial life in Mecca and of the kind of law which it presupposes, including the technique of loans with interest. An important source of information on commercial law and practice in Mecca in the time of Muhammad is provided by the Koran, in its extensive use of commercial technical terms, many of which are legally relevant. This customary commercial

law of Mecca was enforced by the traders among themselves, in much the same way as was the Law Merchant in Europe. There are some traces of agricultural contracts, which may be postulated for Medina, too. It must not be assumed, however, that the outlines of the Islamic law of property, contracts, and obligations formed already part of the customary law of the pre-Islamic Arabs; the reasoning on which this assumption was based has been invalidated by more recent research into the history of Islamic law.

3. The law of personal status and family, of inheritance, and criminal law were dominated, both among the Bedouins and among the sedentary population, by the ancient Arabian tribal system. This system implied the absence of legal protection for the individual outside his tribe, the absence of a developed concept of criminal justice and the reduction of crimes to torts, the responsibility of the tribal group for the acts of its members, and therefore blood feuds, mitigated by the institution of blood-money. All these features and institutions, more or less deeply modified by Islam, have left their traces in Islamic law.

The relations of the sexes in pre-Islamic Arabia were characterized not so much by polygamy, which certainly existed, as by the frequency of divorce, loose unions, and promiscuity, which sometimes make it difficult to draw a line between marriage and prostitution. There were differences in the law of family and marriage between Mecca and Medina, and no doubt other places as well. Slavery and concubinage with slave women were taken for granted.

4. The absence of an organized political authority in Arab society, both Bedouin and sedentary, implied the absence of an organized judicial system. This does not mean that private justice or self-help prevailed in settling disputes concerning rights of property, succession, and torts other than homicide. In these cases, if protracted negotiation between the parties led to no result, recourse was normally had to an arbitrator (*ḥakam*). The arbitrator did not belong to a particular caste; the parties were free to appoint as *ḥakam* any person on whom they agreed, but he was hardly ever the chief of the tribe. A *ḥakam* was chosen for his personal qualities, for his reputation, because he belonged to a family famous for their competence in deciding disputes, and above all, perhaps, for his supernatural powers which they

parties often tested beforehand by making him divine a secret. Because these supernatural powers were most commonly found among soothsayers (*kāhin*), these last were most frequently chosen as arbitrators. The parties had to agree not only on the choice of an arbitrator, but on the cause of action, the question which they were to submit to him. If the *ḥakam* agreed to act, each party had to provide a security, either property or hostages, as a guarantee that they would abide by his decision. The decision of the *ḥakam*, which was final, was not an enforceable judgment (the execution had indeed to be guaranteed by the security), but rather a statement of right on a disputed point. It therefore became easily an authoritative statement of what the customary law was, or ought to be; the function of the arbitrator merged into that of a lawmaker, an authoritative expounder of the normative legal custom or *sunna*. The arbitrators applied and at the same time developed the *sunna*; it was the *sunna*, with the force of public opinion behind it, which had in the first place insisted on the procedure of negotiation and arbitration. This concept of *sunna* was to become one of the most important agents, if not the most important, in the formation of Islamic law.

5. The technical terminology of the customary law of the pre-Islamic Arabs has, as is only natural, to a considerable extent survived in the technical terminology of Islamic law. The converse, however, is not the case, and Islamic legal terms must not without positive proof be assumed to go back to the pre-Islamic period. No comprehensive study of pre-Islamic legal terminology has been undertaken so far. Ancient technical terms have often acquired, in Islamic law, a modified, more narrowly defined, or even definitely different meaning, as have *ajr* and *rahn*; or they have lost their connexion with former symbolic acts, as has *ṣafḳa*; or they have become isolated, archaic survivals, as has *ʿuhda*; or they refer to institutions which Islamic law does not, or does not fully, recognize, as do *maks*, *ʿumrā*, and *ruḳbā*; or they have completely dropped out of use as technical terms, as has *malasā* (the reverse of *ʿuhda*).

6. It is doubtful whether the customary law of pre-Islamic Arabia contained elements of foreign origin; if it did, they do not seem to have survived into Islamic law.[1] Through their

[1] The foreign elements which do exist in Islamic law entered into it in the first century of the hijra.

contacts with the Byzantines on the Syrian frontier the pre-Islamic Arabs came indeed to know a number of Graeco-Latin terms and institutions, most of which were military and administrative, though some belong to the sphere of law. In this way the Greek term for robber, ληστής, entered the Arabic language as a loan-word, *liṣṣ* (with variants *laṣt*, *liṣt*, and *luṣt*), but although the Koran, and after it Islamic law, punishes the crime of highway robbery, the term for it, *ḳaṭʿ al-ṭarīḳ*, is a post-Koranic development, and robbery was in any case not regarded as a crime by the pre-Islamic Arabs. Again, the Arabic verb *dallas*, 'to conceal a fault or defect in an article of merchandise from the purchaser', is derived from Latin *dolus*; the word entered Arabic through the channel of commercial practice at an early date, but it did not become a technical term for fraud in early Islamic law.[1]

The use of written documents is well attested for the pre-Islamic period and for the time of Muhammad, and it continued without interruption into Islamic law, although its theory took no notice of it. The Arabs were familiar with the use of written documents in the surrounding countries of sedentary civilization, and the practice seems to have come to them both from Syria and from Iraq.

The legal institutions of ancient South Arabia, which belong to a different civilization, hardly seem to have influenced those of the (Northern) Arabs. On occasion, however, they enable us to establish or confirm the pre-Islamic character of certain institutions, such as the rule of two witnesses and the contract of *muḥāḳala*.

[1] The term *arabūn* (and variants), from Greek ἀρραβών, 'earnest money, *arrha*', notwithstanding the great antiquity of the institution in the laws of the Near East, is attested in Arabic not earlier than the second century of the hijra, when the institution was rejected by Islamic law.

3

MUHAMMAD AND THE KORAN

1. MUHAMMAD had emerged in Mecca as a religious reformer, and he protested strongly when his pagan countrymen regarded him as merely another soothsayer (*kāhin*). Because of his personal authority he was invited to Medina in A.D. 622 as an arbiter in tribal disputes, and as the Prophet he became the ruler-lawgiver of a new society on a religious basis, the community of Muslims, which was meant to, and at once began to, supersede Arabian tribal society. Muhammad's rejection of the character of a *kāhin* brought with it the rejection of arbitration as practised by the pagan Arabs, inasmuch as the arbitrators were often soothsayers (sura iv. 60). Nevertheless, when he acted as a judge in his community, Muhammad continued to act in the function of a *ḥakam*, and the Koran prescribed the appointment of a *ḥakam* each from the families of the husband and of the wife in the case of marital disputes (sura iv. 35). Whenever the Koran speaks of the Prophet's judicial activity (sura iv. 105 and elsewhere), the verb *ḥakama* and its derivatives are used, whereas the verb *ḳaḍā*, from which the term *ḳāḍī* was to be derived, refers in the Koran regularly not to the judgment of a judge but to a sovereign ordinance, either of Allah or of the Prophet. (It also occurs in connexion with the Day of Judgement, but then it denotes a judgment only in the figurative sense.) In a single verse both verbs occur side by side (sura iv. 65): 'But no, by thy Lord, they will not (really) believe until they make thee an arbitrator (*yuḥakkimūka*) of what is in dispute between them and find within themselves no dislike of that which thou decidest (*ḳaḍayta*), and submit with (full) submission.' Here the first verb refers to the arbitrating aspect of the Prophet's activity, whereas the second emphasizes the authoritative character of his decision. This isolated instance is the first indication of the emergence of a new, Islamic idea of the administration of justice. Muhammad attached indeed great importance to being

appointed by the believers as a *ḥakam* in their disputes, though the insistence of the Koran on this point shows that the ancient freedom in the choice of a *ḥakam* still prevailed; Muhammad, too, reserved to himself the right of the ancient *ḥakam* to refuse to act (sura iv. 59; v. 42; xxiv. 48–51). His position as a Prophet, however, backed in the later stages of his career in Medina by a considerable political and military power, gave him a much greater authority than could be claimed by an arbitrator; he became a 'Prophet-Lawgiver'. But he wielded his almost absolute power not within but without the existing legal system; his authority was not legal but, for the believers, religious and, for the lukewarm, political.

2. The legislation of the Prophet, too, was an innovation in the law of Arabia. Generally speaking, Muhammad had little reason to change the existing customary law. His aim as a Prophet was not to create a new system of law; it was to teach men how to act, what to do, and what to avoid in order to pass the reckoning on the Day of Judgement and to enter Paradise. This is why Islam in general, and Islamic law in particular, is a system of duties, comprising ritual, legal, and moral obligations on the same footing, and bringing them all under the authority of the same religious command. Had religious and ethical standards been comprehensively applied to all aspects of human behaviour, and had they been consistently followed in practice, there would have been no room and no need for a legal system in the narrow meaning of the term. This was in fact the original ideal of Muhammad; traces of it, such as the recurrent insistence on the merits of forgiveness, in a very wide meaning of the word, are found in the Koran,[1] and the abandonment of rights is consequently treated in detail in Islamic law. But the Prophet eventually had to resign himself to applying religious and ethical principles to the legal institutions as he found them.

Thus we find in the Koran injunctions to arbitrate with justice, not to offer bribes, to give true evidence, and to give full weight and measure.[2] Contracts are safeguarded by commands to put them in writing, to call witnesses, to give

[1] Sura ii. 263; iii. 134; iv. 149; xvi. 126; xxiv. 22; xlii. 37, 40, 43; lxiv. 14.

[2] Sura iv. 58; v. 42; vi. 152. — ii. 188. — ii. 283; iv. 135; v. 8; xxv. 72; lxx. 33. — vi. 152; xvii. 35; lv. 8 f.; lxxxiii. 1–3.

securities (*rahn*, as a guarantee and material proof) when there is no scribe available—all pre-Islamic practices which the Koran endorses—or, in general, by the command to fulfil one's contracts and, especially, to return a trust or deposit (*amāna*) to its owner.[1] This command is typical of the ethical attitude of the Koran towards legal matters. Even the prohibitions of a certain game of hazard (*maysir*) and of taking interest (*ribā*),[2] though directly concerned with certain types of legal transactions, are not meant to lay down legal rules regulating the form and effects of these transactions, but to establish moral norms under which certain transactions are allowed or forbidden. The idea that such transactions, if they are concluded notwithstanding the prohibition, are invalid and do not create obligations, does not, as yet, appear in the Koran. It was left to Islamic law to establish, beside the scale of religious qualifications, a second scale of legal validity (see below, pp. 121 f). The same attitude governs the Koranic law of war and booty, and the whole complex of family law. The law of war and booty is primarily concerned with determining the enemies who must be fought or may be fought, how the booty is to be distributed (within the general framework of the rules laid down by pre-Islamic custom), and how the conquered are to be treated. Family law is fairly exhaustively treated in the Koran, albeit in a number of scattered passages (mostly in suras ii and iv); here again the main emphasis is laid on the question of how one should act towards women and children, orphans and relatives, dependants and slaves. The legal effects of an act that conforms to the rules are not mentioned and are, in fact, generally self-evident: for instance that a valid marriage, divorce, &c. takes place; but the legal effects of an act contrary to the rules, for instance the question of civil responsibility, are hardly envisaged either. Technical legal statements attaching legal consequences to certain sets of relevant facts or acts are almost completely lacking, as far as the law of obligations and of family is concerned. They exist, and are indeed almost indispensable, in

[1] Sura ii. 282 f. (cf. xxiv. 33). — ii. 177; iii. 76; iv. 58; v. 1; viii. 27; ix. 4, 7; xvi. 91 f.; xvii. 34; xxiii. 8; lxx. 32.

[2] Sura ii. 219; v. 90 f. — ii. 275–9; iii. 130; iv. 161; xxx. 39. *Ribā* is a special case of unjustified enrichment or, as the Koran expresses it, 'consuming (i.e. appropriating for one's own use) the property of others for no good reason' (*akl amwāl al-nās bil-bāṭil*), which is forbidden in sura ii. 188; iv. 29, 161; ix. 34.

the field of penal law. It is easy to understand that the normative legislation of the Koran incorporated sanctions for transgressions, but again they are essentially moral and only incidentally penal; the prohibition is the essential element, the provision concerning the punishment is a rule of action either for the agents of the newly created Islamic state or for the victim and his next of kin in matters of retaliation. The prohibition of theft is presumed known, and only the punishment is laid down (sura v. 38); conversely, drinking wine (sura ii. 219; iv. 43; v. 90 f.), the *maysir* game of hazard, and taking interest are prohibited without a penalty being fixed (unless it be punishment in Hell).[1] There are provisions concerning retaliation and blood-money, theft, sexual irregularity and false accusation of it, the procedure in these two cases, and highway robbery.[2]

The reasons for Koranic legislation on these matters were, in the first place, dissatisfaction with prevailing conditions, the desire to improve the position of women, of orphans, and of the weak in general, to restrict the laxity of sexual morals and to strengthen the marriage tie,[3] and, while eliminating blood-feuds altogether, to restrict the practice of private vengeance and retaliation; the prohibition of gambling, associated as this was with pagan worship, of drinking wine, and of taking interest constitutes, perhaps, the clearest break with ancient Arabian standards of behaviour. The prohibition of taking interest is no doubt inspired by Muhammad's acquaintance with Jewish doctrine and practice in Medina, rather than by any earlier reaction on his part to the commercial practice of the Meccans; and the extension of the principle of retaliation from homicide to causing bodily harm (sura v. 45) is based on what Muhammad had learned from the Jews about the Old Testament (Exod. xxi. 23–25; Lev. xxiv. 19 f.; Deut. xix. 21). Besides, it had become necessary to deal with new problems which had arisen in family law, in the law of retaliation, and in the law of war because of the main political aim of the Prophet—the

[1] The punishment for drinking wine in Islamic law is based not on the Koran but on traditions from the Prophet.

[2] Sura ii. 178 f.; iv. 92; v. 45; xvi. 126; xvii. 33 — v. 38. — iv. 15 f., 25; xxiv. 2–20. — v. 33 f.

[3] The reforms advocated by Muhammad in this field were more gradual, and the conditions with which he had to contend more intricate than what is assumed by the traditional Muslim interpretation of the Koranic passages in question.

dissolution of the ancient tribal organization and the creation of a community of believers in its stead. This is particularly clear in the encouragement of polygamy by the Koran (sura iv. 3). It is possible that some actual disputes made the need obvious.[1] This second need was, it seems, mainly responsible for the Koranic legislation on matters of inheritance, a subject which is farthest removed from the action of moral principles and most closely connected with the granting of individual rights.[2] Even here the Koranic legislation proceeds, chronologically, from recommending ethical rules of action to laying down definite regulations on how to proceed with regard to the estates of deceased persons, and even in its final enactments preserves the ethical element in the tendency to allot shares in the inheritance to persons who had no claim to succession under the old customary law.

This feature of Koranic legislation was preserved in Islamic law, and the purely legal attitude, which attaches legal consequences to relevant acts, is often superseded by the tendency to impose ethical standards on the believer.

[1] Some regulations were provoked by Muhammad's personal problems, such as the abolition of adoption with its ensuing impediment to marrying the adopted son's wife (sura xxxiii. 5, 37) and the rules concerning false accusation of unlawful intercourse (sura xxiv. 4–20).

[2] Sura viii. 72, 75; xxxiii. 6. — ii. 180–2, 240; iv. 19, 33. — iv. 7–14, 176.

4

THE FIRST CENTURY OF ISLAM

1. THE first three generations after the death of the Prophet (A.D. 632), or, in other words, the first century of Islam, are in many respects the most important, though because of the scarcity of contemporary evidence the most obscure, period in the history of Islamic law. In this period, many distinctive features of Islamic law came into being and nascent Islamic society created its own legal institutions. What little authentic evidence is available shows that the ancient Arab system of arbitration, and Arab customary law in general, as modified and completed by the Koran, continued under the first successors of the Prophet, the caliphs of Medina (A.D. 632–61). The caliphs, it is true, were the political leaders of the Islamic community after the death of the Prophet, but they do not seem to have acted as its supreme arbitrators, and there still remained room, at a slightly later period, for a poet to exhort his audience to choose their arbitrators from the tribe of the Prophet, the Ḳuraysh. In their function as the supreme rulers and administrators, though of course devoid of the religious authority of the Prophet, the caliphs acted to a great extent as the lawgivers of the community; during the whole of this first century the administrative and legislative activities of the Islamic government cannot be separated. This administrative legislation, however, was hardly, if at all, concerned with modifying the existing customary law; its object was to organize the newly conquered territories for the benefit of the Arabs. In the field of penal law, the first caliphs went beyond the sanctions enacted in the Koran by punishing with flogging, for instance, the authors of satirical poems directed against rival tribes, a form of poetic expression common in ancient Arabia. The introduction of stoning to death as a punishment for unlawful intercourse, which does not occur in the Koran and which is obviously taken from Mosaic law, also belongs to this

period.[1] The enforcement of retaliation and blood-money continued to depend on the initiative of the next of kin of the victim. The first caliphs did not appoint *ḳāḍīs* and in general did not lay the foundations of what later became the Islamic system of administration of justice; this is shown by the contradictions and improbabilities inherent in the stories which assert the contrary; the instructions which the caliph ʿUmar is alleged to have given to *ḳāḍīs*, too, are a product of the third century of Islam.

2. Towards the end of the period of the caliphs of Medina the Islamic community was rent by political schisms, and the two 'heterodox' movements of the Khārijīs and of the Shīʿa established themselves beside the 'orthodox' or Sunni majority. Except for the law of inheritance, where the particular beliefs of the 'Twelver' Shiites made necessary a system essentially different from that of the Sunnis from which it is derived, the positive doctrines of Islamic law as adopted by the Khārijīs and by the Shīʿa do not differ from the doctrines of the Sunni schools of law more widely than these last differ from one another. From this it has been concluded that the essential features common to these several forms of Islamic law were worked out before the schism, i.e. earlier than the middle of the first century of Islam. But recent research has shown that the ancient sects of Islam, at the time they hived off from the orthodox community, could not have shared with the majority the essentials of a system of law which did not as yet exist. For some considerable time, and during the second and third centuries of Islam in particular, they remained in sufficiently close contact with the Sunni community for them to take over Islamic law as it was being developed in the orthodox schools of law, making only such modifications as were required by their particular political and dogmatic tenets, and elaborating their own legal theories which, however, are the real bases of their positive doctrines as little as the legal theory of the Sunnis is of theirs (cf. below, p. 115). Certain doctrines which in themselves were not necessarily either Shiite or Sunni became adventitiously distinctive for Shiite as against Sunni law. Examples are the approval of temporary marriage and the doctrine that the concubine who has borne a child to her owner may be sold. The Khārijī and

[1] The punishment for drinking wine, however, was still unsettled under the Umayyads.

the Shīʿa movements represent the two extreme wings of the community of Muslims. Both groups originated in Iraq and were long active there. If their doctrines on technical points of law sometimes agree with each other and diverge from those of the Sunnis, this is because they are based on ancient opinions once current in Iraq which were later abandoned by the Sunnis.

3. At an early period the ancient Arab idea of *sunna*, precedent or normative custom, reasserted itself in Islam. The Arabs were, and are, bound by tradition and precedent. Whatever was customary was right and proper; whatever the forefathers had done deserved to be imitated. This was the golden rule of the Arabs whose existence on a narrow margin in an unpropitious environment did not leave them much room for experiments and innovations which might upset the precarious balance of their lives. In this idea of precedent or *sunna* the whole conservatism of the Arabs found expression. They recognized, of course, that a *sunna* might have been laid down by an individual in the relatively recent past, but then that individual was considered the spokesman and representative, the leader (*imām*) of the whole group. The idea of *sunna* presented a formidable obstacle to every innovation, and in order to discredit anything it was, and still is, enough to call it an innovation. Islam, the greatest innovation that Arabia saw, had to overcome this obstacle, and a hard fight it was. But once Islam had prevailed, even among one single group of Arabs, the old conservatism reasserted itself; what had shortly before been an innovation now became the thing to do, a thing hallowed by precedent and tradition, a *sunna*. This ancient Arab concept of *sunna* was to become one of the central concepts of Islamic law.

Sunna in its Islamic context originally had a political rather than a legal connotation; it referred to the policy and administration of the caliph. The question whether the administrative acts of the first two caliphs, Abū Bakr and ʿUmar, should be regarded as binding precedents, arose probably at the time when a successor to ʿUmar had to be appointed (23/644), and the discontent with the policy of the third caliph, ʿUthmān, which led to his assassination in 35/655, took the form of a charge that he, in his turn, had diverged from the policy of his predecessors and, implicitly, from the Koran. In this connexion, there appeared the concept of the '*sunna* of the Prophet', not yet identified with any set of positive rules but providing a doctrinal link between the '*sunna* of Abū Bakr and 'Umar' and the Koran. The earliest, certainly authentic, evidence for this use of the term '*sunna* of the Prophet' is the letter addressed by the Khārijī leader 'Abd Allāh ibn Ibāḍ to the Umayyad caliph 'Abd al-Malik about 76/695. The same term with a theological connotation, and coupled with the 'example of the forebears', occurs in the contemporary treatise which Ḥasan al-Baṣrī addressed to the same caliph. It was introduced into the theory of Islamic law, presumably towards the end of the first century, by the scholars of Iraq.

4. It would seem natural to suppose that the explicit precepts of the Koran on legal matters were observed from the beginning, at least as far as turbulent Arab society in a time of revolutionary change was amenable to rules. It is indeed obvious that many rules of Islamic law, particularly in the law of family and the law of inheritance, not to mention worship and ritual, were based on the Koran from the beginning, and occasionally this can be positively proved. There are, for instance, two early decisions, which have survived into the later schools of law, concerning a question of divorce; one of them is based on the *textus receptus* of the Koran, and another on a variant reading. As the variant readings were officially abolished during the reign of the Umayyad caliph 'Abd al-Malik (65/685–86/705), it can be concluded that both doctrines had been formulated not later than the middle of the first century of Islam. On the other hand, any but the most perfunctory attention given to the Koranic norms, and any but the most elementary conclusions drawn from them, belong almost invariably to a secondary stage in the development of doctrine. That the thief should have been punished not by having his hand cut off as the Koran prescribes (sura v. 38) and Islamic law maintains, but by flogging as attested by St. John of Damascus (*floruit* between A.D. 700 and 750), merely shows the difficulty of enforcing a penalty which was unknown to the ancient Arabs. But there are several cases in which the early doctrine of Islamic law diverged from the clear and explicit wording of the Koran. One important example which has remained typical of Islamic law is the restriction of legal proof to the evidence of witnesses and the denial of validity to written documents. This contradicts an explicit ruling of the

Koran (sura ii. 282; cf. xxiv. 33) which endorsed the current practice of putting contracts into writing, and this practice did persist during the first century and later, and had to be reconciled with legal theory. The same John of Damascus mentions the insistence on witnesses, and on witnesses only, as a typical custom of the Saracens, and this, too, was probably established sometime about the middle of the first century of Islam.[1]

5. During the greater part of the first century Islamic law, in the technical meaning of the term, did not as yet exist. As had been the case in the time of the Prophet, law as such fell outside the sphere of religion, and as far as there were no religious or moral objections to specific transactions or modes of behaviour, the technical aspects of law were a matter of indifference to the Muslims. This attitude of the early Muslims accounts for the widespread adoption, if regarded from one angle, or survival, if regarded from another, of the legal and administrative institutions and practices of the conquered territories. Outstanding examples are the treatment of tolerated religions, the methods of taxation, and the institutions of *emphyteusis* and of *wakf*.[2] The *wakf* is a good example of the composite nature of the raw material of Islamic law and of the qualitatively new character which its institutions acquired; the *wakf* has one of its roots in the contributions to the holy war which Muhammad had incessantly demanded from his followers in Medina, another in the pious foundations (*piae causae*) of the Eastern Churches, a third in the charities and public benefactions of the early Muslims, and a fourth, which came into prominence later, in the need of the new Islamic society to counteract some of the effects of its law of inheritance. The principle of the retention of pre-Islamic legal practices under Islam was sometimes even explicitly acknowledged, as in this passage of the historian Balādhurī (d. 279/892):

> Abū Yūsuf held that if there exists in a country an ancient, non-Arab *sunna* which Islam has neither changed nor abolished, and people complain to the caliph that it causes them hardship, he is not entitled to change it; but Mālik and Shāfiʿī held that he may change it even if it be ancient, because he ought to prohibit (in similar

[1] For another example, see below, p. 202, n. 2.
[2] On the office of the 'inspector of the market' see below, p. 25.

circumstances) any valid *sunna* which has been introduced by a Muslim, let alone those introduced by unbelievers.[1]

Both opinions presuppose the retention of pre-Islamic legal practices as normal.

Hand in hand with the retention of legal institutions and practices went the reception of legal concepts and maxims, extending to methods of reasoning and even to fundamental ideas of legal science; for instance, the concept of the *opinio prudentium* of Roman law seems to have provided the model for the highly organized concept of the 'consensus of the scholars' as formulated by the ancient schools of Islamic law, and the scale of the 'five qualifications' (*al-aḥkām al-khamsa*; below, p. 121) was derived, albeit at a somewhat later date, from Stoic philosophy. The intermediaries were the cultured non-Arab converts to Islam who (or whose fathers) had enjoyed a liberal education, that is to say, an education in Hellenistic rhetoric which was the normal one in the countries of the Fertile Crescent of the Near East which the Arabs conquered. This education invariably led to some acquaintance with the rudiments of law, which was considered necessary for the orators who were also advocates, and useful for all educated persons. These educated converts brought their familiar ideas, including legal concepts and maxims, with them into their new religion. In fact, the concepts and maxims in question are of that general kind which would be familiar not only to lawyers but to all educated persons. In keeping with this, such parallels as exist between Islamic and Roman law often concern doctrines found in classical Roman (and in late Byzantine) law but not in the legislation of Justinian. This is not an isolated phenomenon. Talmudic and Rabbinic law, too, contains concepts and maxims of classical Roman law which entered it through the medium of popular Hellenistic rhetoric, and the same is the case, as far as can be seen, of Persian Sassanian law which itself came into contact with Talmudic law in Iraq. In Iraq, too, Islamic legal science was to come into being at the turn of the century, when the door of Islamic civilization had been opened wide to the potential transmitters of legal concepts and maxims, the educated non-Arab converts to Islam. That the early Muslim

[1] *Liber expugnationis regionum*, ed. M. de Goeje, Leiden, 1865, p. 448.

specialists in religious law should consciously have adopted any principle of foreign law is out of the question.

In this way concepts and maxims originating from Roman and Byzantine law, from the Canon law of the Eastern Churches, from Talmudic and Rabbinic law, and from Sassanian law, infiltrated into the nascent religious law of Islam during its period of incubation, to appear in the doctrines of the second century A.H.

The following features can with reasonable certainty be regarded as having entered Islamic law in this way: the maxim that 'the child belongs to the marriage bed' (*al-walad lil-firāsh*), which corresponds to the Roman maxim *pater est quem nuptiae demonstrant* and is often referred to, though it has no real part to play in Islamic law; the responsibility of the thief, to whom the Koranic punishment cannot be applied, for double the value of what he stole, an ancient doctrine soon abandoned in Islamic law; the transformation of the old Arabian and Koranic concept of security into that of a security for the payment of a debt which corresponds to the Roman *pignus*; the juridical construction of the contract of *ijāra* in which, following the model of the Roman *locatio conductio*, the three originally separate transactions of *kirā'* (corresponding to *l.c. rei*), *ijāra* proper (corresponding to *l.c. operarum*), and *ju'l* (corresponding to *l.c. operis*) were combined; the three concepts, important in the law of sale, of *makīl*, *mawzūn*, *ma'dūd* which correspond to *quae pondere numero mensura constant*; and the principle, derived from the Canon law of the Eastern Churches, that adultery creates an impediment to marriage, a principle which has only left traces in Sunni law but has been retained in 'Twelver' Shiite and in Ibāḍī (Khārijī) law.

Derived from Jewish law are the method of *ḳiyās*, together with its term which is a loan-word in Arabic, and other methods of legal reasoning, such as *istiṣḥāb* and *istiṣlāḥ*. Sometimes it can be doubtful whether a concept has entered Islamic law directly from Hellenistic rhetoric or by way of Jewish law. The influence of Jewish law is particularly noticeable in the field of religious worship.

From Sassanian law come the office of the 'clerk of the court' (*kātib*), who appears together with the *ḳāḍī* in the second half of the period in question, and the proposal, made in the first half of the second century of Islam, that the caliph should codify the *sunna*, a proposal which, however, did not take root in Islamic law.

6. One of the most distinctive technical features of Islamic law, the juridical construction of contracts, possibly derived from ancient Near Eastern law and might have come to the Muslims through the medium of commercial practice in Iraq. The essential form of a contract in Islamic law consists of offer and acceptance (*ījāb* and *ḳabūl*) where offer and acceptance are taken not in their common and everyday meaning but as the essential formal elements which for the juridical analysis constitute a contract. The offer can always be withdrawn before it has been accepted, but once it has been accepted the contract has been concluded. This juridical construction, however, disagrees with the terminology because *ījāb*, making something *wājib*, means etymologically not 'to offer' but 'to make definite, binding, due', and this reflects a different, unilateral construction of the contract which is well known from other systems of law. It seems, therefore, that a unilateral construction was superseded by the bilateral one, probably at the same period at which the new juridical construction of the contract of *ijāra* (see above, section 5) prevailed. This bilateral construction of contracts is quite isolated among the laws of antiquity,[1] except for one type of the neo-Babylonian contracts of lease and marriage which is attested from the seventh century B.C. onwards until the end of cuneiform literature in the first century B.C. The possibility that this type of contract survived in Babylonia (Iraq), and that the juridical construction of contracts in Islamic law derives from there, calls for further investigation.

[1] Roman law, for instance, has no fixed technical terms for offer and acceptance. It is true that offer and acceptance express the agreement or *consensus* of the parties, but the so-called consensual contracts of Roman law differ essentially from the Islamic concept of contracts. The Koran (sura iv. 29) speaks of 'trade by agreement' (*'an tarāḍ*^{in}), but this is not used as a technical term, as appears from sura ii. 233, and the concept of agreement or *consensus* as such does not enter into the Islamic theory of contracts.

5

THE UMAYYAD ADMINISTRATION AND THE FIRST SPECIALISTS

1. We must now return to the middle of the first Islamic century, when the rule of the caliphs of Medina was supplanted by that of the Umayyads (A.D. 661–750). The Umayyads were not the adversaries of Islam that they were often made out to be by the Arab historians whose writings reflect the hostile attitude of the ʿAbbāsids who in their turn supplanted them. On the contrary, it was the Umayyads and their governors who were responsible for developing a number of the essential features of Islamic worship and ritual, of which they had found only rudimentary elements. Their main concern, it is true, was not with religion and religious law but with political administration,[1] and here they represented the organizing, centralizing, and increasingly bureaucratic tendency of an orderly administration as against Bedouin individualism and the anarchy of the Arab way of life. Islamic religious ideal and Umayyad administration co-operated in creating a new framework for Arab Muslim society, which had been recruited indiscriminately from the Arab tribes and was spread thinly over the vast extent of the conquered territories. In many respects Umayyad rule represents the consummation, after the turbulent interval of the caliphate of Medina, of tendencies which were inherent in the nature of the community of the Muslims under the Prophet. This is the background against which there must be viewed the emergence of Islamic law, of an Islamic administration of justice, and of Islamic jurisprudence.

2. The administration of the Umayyads concentrated on waging war against the Byzantines and other external enemies, on collecting revenue from the subject population, and on paying subventions in money or in kind to the Arab beneficiaries;

[1] They were interested in questions of religious policy and theology in so far as these had a bearing on loyalty to themselves, i.e. on the internal security of the state.

these were the essential functions of the Arab Kingdom. We therefore find evidence of Umayyad regulations, or administrative law, mainly in the fields of the law of war and of fiscal law. The restriction of legacies to one-third of the estate, which goes back to an Umayyad regulation, has a fiscal implication because it meant that when a person died without known next of kin, two-thirds of the estate went to the public treasury.[1] The Umayyads did not interfere with the working of retaliation as it had been regulated by the Koran, but they tried to prevent the recurrence of Arab tribal feuds which threatened the internal security of the state, and they assured the accountancy for payments of blood-money, which were effected in connexion with the payment of subventions.[2] On the other hand, they supervised the application of the purely Islamic penalties, not always in strict conformity with the rules laid down in the Koran.

3. The Umayyads, or rather their governors, also took the important step of appointing Islamic judges or *ḳāḍīs*. The office of *ḳāḍī* was created in and for the new Islamic society which came into being, under the new conditions resulting from the Arab conquest, in the urban centres of the Arab Kingdom. For this new society, the arbitration of pre-Islamic Arabia and of the earliest period of Islam was no longer adequate, and the Arab *ḥakam* was supplanted by the Islamic *ḳāḍī*. This process is exemplified by the half-legendary figure of the so-called *ḳāḍī* Shurayḥ. The traditional opinion asserts, with some variants of detail, that he was the *ḳāḍī* of Kufa over a very long period and died at an incredibly old age. But the historical Shurayḥ was merely a *ḥakam* of the old style among the Arab tribes in the neighbourhood of Kufa. His activity coincided with the establishment and spread of Islam, and his legendary figure reflects the transition from the old to the new form of administration of justice. It was only natural that the *ḳāḍī* took over the seat and wand of the *ḥakam*, but, in contrast with the *ḥakam*, the *ḳāḍī* was a delegate of the governor. The governor, within the limits set

[1] The preference given to the beneficiaries of legacies over the treasury in Ḥanafī law is a later development.

[2] They also seem to have made some effort to mitigate the severity of the ancient Arabian *ḳasāma* by which a person suspected of murder could be put to death on the strength of the affirmatory oath of the next of kin of the victim; cf. below, p. 184, on the Ḥanafī doctrine; the other schools of Islamic law admit in varying degrees the possibility of retaliation on the basis of *ḳasāma*.

for him by the caliph, had full authority over his province, administrative, legislative, and judicial, without any conscious distinction of functions, and he could, and in fact regularly did, delegate his judicial authority to his 'legal secretary', the *ḳāḍī*. The governor retained, however, the power of reserving for his own decision any lawsuit he wished, and, of course, of dismissing his *ḳāḍī* at will. It is to these governors and their delegates, the judges, that John of Damascus refers as the law givers (*νομοθέται*) of Islam.

The jurisdiction of the *ḳāḍī* extended to Muslims only; the non-Muslim subject populations retained their own traditional legal institutions, including the ecclesiastical (and rabbinical) tribunals which in the last few centuries before the Muslim conquest had to a great extent duplicated the judicial organization of the Byzantine state. The Byzantine magistrates themselves, together with the other civil officers, had evacuated the lost provinces at the beginning of the Muslim conquest; but an office of local administration, the functions of which were partly judicial, was adopted by the Muslims: the office of the 'inspector of the market' (*ἀγορανόμος*, in Arabic *'āmil al-sūḳ* or *ṣāḥib al-sūḳ*, a literal translation) who had a limited civil and criminal jurisdiction; it was later, under the early 'Abbāsids, to develop into the Islamic office of the *muḥtasib*. Similarly, the Muslims took over from Sassanian administration the office of the 'clerk of the court' who became an assistant of the *ḳāḍī*; this was well known to the ancient authors.

The earliest Islamic *ḳāḍīs*, officials of the Umayyad administration, by their decisions laid the basic foundations of what was to become Islamic law. We know their names, and there exists a considerable body of information on their lives and judgments, but it is difficult to separate the authentic from the fictitious. Legal doctrines that can be dated to the first century of Islam are rare, but it is likely that some of the decisions which are attributed to those *ḳāḍīs*, and which are irregular by later standards, do indeed go back to that early period. At a slightly later date we can actually see how the tendency to impose an oath on the plaintiff as a safeguard against the exclusive use of the evidence of witnesses grew out of the judicial practice at the beginning of the second century of the hijra. The earliest Islamic *ḳāḍīs* gave judgment according to their own discretion, or 'sound opinion' (*ra'y*) as it was called, basing themselves on customary practice which in the nature of things incorporated administrative regulations, and taking the letter and the spirit of the Koranic regulations and other recognized Islamic religious norms into account as much as they thought fit. The customary practice to which they referred was either that of the community under their jurisdiction or that of their own home district, and in this latter case conflicts were bound to arise. Though the legal subject-matter had not as yet been Islamicized to any great extent beyond the stage reached in the Koran, the office of *ḳāḍī* itself was an Islamic institution typical of the Umayyad period, in which care for elementary administrative efficiency and the tendency to Islamicize went hand in hand. It will become apparent from the subsequent development of Islamic law that the part played by the earliest *ḳāḍīs* in laying its foundations did not achieve recognition in the doctrine of legal theory which finally prevailed, and that the concept of judicial precedent, the authority of a previous judicial decision, did not develop.

The scene was set for a more thorough process of Islamicizing the existing customary law.

4. The work of the *ḳāḍīs* became inevitably more and more specialized, and we may take it for granted that from the turn of the century onwards (*c.* A.D. 715–20) appointments as a rule went to 'specialists', by which are meant not technically trained professionals but persons sufficiently interested in the subject to have given it serious thought in their spare time, either individually or in discussion with like-minded friends. The main concern of these specialists, in the intellectual climate of the late Umayyad period, was naturally to know whether the customary law conformed to the Koranic and generally Islamic norms; in other words, the specialists from whom the *ḳāḍīs* came increasingly to be recruited were found among those pious persons whose interest in religion caused them to elaborate, by individual reasoning, an Islamic way of life. Members of this group (such as Rajā' and Abū Ḳilāba) were among the familiars of the Umayyad caliphs from the last decades of the first Islamic century onwards. These pious persons surveyed all fields of contemporary activities, including the field of law; not only administrative regulations but popular practice as well. They

considered possible objections that could be made to recognized practices from the religious and, in particular, from the ritualistic or the ethical point of view, and as a result endorsed, modified, or rejected them. They impregnated the sphere of law with religious and ethical ideas, subjected it to Islamic norms, and incorporated it into the body of duties incumbent on every Muslim. In doing this they achieved on a much wider scale and in a vastly more detailed manner what the Prophet in the Koran had tried to do for the early Islamic community of Medina. As a result the popular and administrative practice of the late Umayyad period was transformed into the religious law of Islam. The resulting ideal theory still had to be translated into practice; this task was beyond the power of the pious specialists and had to be left to the interest and zeal of the caliphs, governors, *ḳāḍīs*, or individuals concerned. The circumstances in which the religious law of Islam came into being caused it to develop, not in close connexion with the practice, but as the expression of a religious ideal in opposition to it.

This process started from modest beginnings towards the end of the first century of the hijra; a specialist in religious law such as Ibrāhīm al-Nakhaʿī of Kufa (d. 95 or 96 of the hijra, A.D. 713–15) did no more than give opinions on questions of ritual, and perhaps on kindred problems of directly religious importance, cases of conscience concerning alms tax, marriage, divorce, and the like, but not on technical points of law. The same is no doubt true of Ibrāhīm's contemporaries in Medina (see below, p. 31).

The pious specialists owed their authority and the respect in which they were held both by the public and by the rulers, to their single-minded concern with the ideal of a life according to the tenets of Islam, and they gave cautelary advice on the correct way of acting to those of their co-religionists who asked for it. In other words, they were the first *muftīs* in Islam. They often had occasion to criticize the acts and regulations of the government, just as they had to declare undesirable many popular practices, but they were not in political opposition to the Umayyad government and to the established Islamic state; on the contrary, the whole of the Umayyad period, until the civil war which heralded the end of the dynasty, was, at a certain distance, reckoned as part of the 'good old time'; its practice was idealized and opposed to the realities of the actual administration.

6

THE ANCIENT SCHOOLS OF LAW, THE OPPOSITION MOVEMENTS AND THE TRADITIONISTS

1. As the groups of pious specialists grew in numbers and in cohesion, they developed, in the first few decades of the second century of Islam, into the 'ancient schools of law'. This term implies neither any definite organization nor a strict uniformity of doctrine within each school, nor any formal teaching, nor again any official status, nor even the existence of a body of law in the Western meaning of the term. Their members, the 'scholars' (*'ulamā'*) or 'lawyers' (*fuḳahā'*), continued to be private individuals, singled out from the great mass of the Muslims by their special interest, the resultant reverence of the people, and the recognition as kindred spirits which they themselves accorded to one another. The more important ancient schools of law of which we have knowledge are those of Kufa and of Basra in Iraq, of Medina and of Mecca in Hijaz, and of Syria. Our information on the Kufians and on the Medinese is incomparably more detailed than that concerning the Basrians and the Meccans, but the picture gained from the first two schools can be taken as typical. Egypt did not develop a school of law of its own but fell under the influence of the other schools, particularly that of Medina. The differences between these schools were conditioned essentially by geographical factors, such as the difficulties of communication between their several seats, and local variations in social conditions, customary law, and practice, but they were not based on any noticeable disagreement on principles or methods.

The general attitude of all ancient schools of law to Umayyad popular practice and Umayyad administrative regulations was essentially the same, whatever their individual reactions to what they found. Apart from their common basic attitude, there existed at that earliest stage of Islamic jurisprudence a considerable body of common doctrine which was subsequently reduced by increasing differentiation between the schools. This implies not that Islamic jurisprudence at the beginning was cultivated exclusively in one place, but that one place was the intellectual centre of the first theorizing and systematizing efforts which were to transform Umayyad popular and administrative practice into Islamic law. All indications go to prove that Iraq was this centre. The ascendancy of Iraq in the development of religious law and jurisprudence in Islam continued during the whole of the second century. Influences of the doctrine of one school on that of another almost invariably proceeded from Iraq to Hijaz, and not vice versa, and the doctrinal development of the school of Medina often lagged behind that of the school of Kufa. Beyond this the doctrines of the ancient schools of Medina and of Kufa reflect the social conditions prevailing in Hijaz and in Iraq respectively, where the society of Iraq appears as less archaic and more differentiated, but also more rigid in its structure than that of Hijaz.

2. An important aspect of the activity of the ancient schools of law was that they took the Koranic norms seriously for the first time. In contrast with what had been the case in the first century of Islam, formal conclusions were now drawn from the essentially religious and ethical body of Koranic maxims and applied not only to family law, the law of inheritance, and, of course, worship and ritual, but to those branches of law which were not covered in detail by the Koranic legislation. The zenith of the reception of Koranic norms into early Islamic law coincides with the rise of the ancient schools at the beginning of the second century of Islam.

3. The ancient schools of law shared not only a common attitude to Umayyad practice and a considerable body of positive religious law but the essentials of legal theory, not all of which were historically obvious or systematically self-evident. The central idea of this theory was that of the 'living tradition of the school' as represented by the constant doctrine of its authoritative representatives. This idea dominated the development of legal doctrine in the ancient schools during the whole of the second century of Islam. It presents itself under two aspects, retrospective and synchronous. Retrospectively it

appears as *sunna* or 'practice' (*'amal*) or 'well-established precedent' (*sunna māḍiya*) or 'ancient practice' (*amr ḳadīm*). This 'practice' partly reflects the actual custom of the local community, but it also contains a theoretical or ideal element so that it comes to mean normative *sunna*, the usage as it ought to be. This ideal practice, which was presumed constant though it in fact developed as Islamic ideas were imposed on the legal subject-matter, was found in the unanimous doctrine of the representative religious scholars of each centre, in the teaching of 'those whom the people of each region recognized as their leading specialists in religious law, whose opinions they accepted, and to whose decisions they submitted'.

It is only the opinion of the majority that counts; small minorities of scholars are disregarded. This consensus (*ijmā'*) of the scholars, representing the common denominator of doctrine achieved in each generation, expresses the synchronous aspect of the living tradition of each school. How this consensus works is described by an ancient scholar of Basra in the following terms: 'Whenever I find a generation of scholars at a seat of learning, in their majority, holding the same opinion, I call this "consensus", whether their predecessors agreed or disagreed with it, because the majority would not agree on anything in ignorance of the doctrine of their predecessors, and would abandon the previous doctrine only on account of a repeal [for instance in the Koran, which their predecessors had overlooked] or because they knew of some better argument, even if they did not mention it.' In the result, the decision on what constitutes normative practice is left to the last generation of the representatives of each school of law.

The consensus of the scholars is different from the consensus of all Muslims on essentials. This last, in the nature of things, covers the whole of the Islamic world but is vague and general, whereas the consensus of the scholars is geographically limited to the seat of the school in question, is concrete and detailed, but also tolerant and not exclusive, recognizing, as it does, the existence of other doctrines in other centres. Both kinds of consensus count as final arguments in the ancient schools of law, though the consensus of the scholars is of much greater practical importance and is the real basis of their teaching. It is only natural that the consensus of all Muslims should be regarded as not subject to error; that the consensus of the scholars, too, should be so regarded is not equally obvious, and the whole highly organized concept seems to have been influenced from abroad.

4. Originally the consensus of the scholars was anonymous, that is to say, it was the average opinion of the representatives of a school that counted, and not the individual doctrines of the most prominent scholars. The living tradition of the ancient schools maintained this essentially anonymous character well into the second half of the second century of Islam. Nevertheless, the idea of continuity inherent in the concept of *sunna*, the idealized practice, together with the need to create some kind of theoretical justification for what so far had been an instinctive reliance on the opinions of the majority, led, from the first decades of the second century onwards, to the living tradition being projected backwards and to its being ascribed to some of the great figures of the past. The Kufians were the first in attributing the doctrine of their school to Ibrāhīm al-Nakhaʿī, although this body of elementary legal doctrine had very little to do with the few authentic opinions of the historical Ibrāhīm. It rather represents the stage of legal teaching achieved in the time of Ḥammād ibn Abī Sulaymān (d. 120/738), the first Kufian lawyer whose doctrine we can regard as fully authentic. By a literary convention which found particular favour in Iraq, it was customary for a scholar or author to put his own doctrine or work under the aegis of his master. The Medinese followed suit and projected their own teaching back to a number of ancient authorities who had died in the last years of the first or in the very first years of the second century of Islam. At a later period, seven amongst them were chosen as representative; they are the so-called 'seven lawyers of Medina': Saʿīd ibn al-Musayyib, ʿUrwa ibn al-Zubayr, Abū Bakr ibn ʿAbd al-Raḥmān, ʿUbayd Allāh ibn ʿAbd Allāh ibn ʿUtba, Khārija ibn Zayd ibn Thābit, Sulaymān ibn Yasār, and Ḳāsim ibn Muḥammad ibn Abī Bakr. Hardly any of the doctrines ascribed to these ancient authorities can be considered authentic. The transmission of legal doctrine in Hijaz becomes historically ascertainable only at about the same time as in Iraq, with Zuhrī (d. 124/742) and with his younger contemporary Rabīʿa ibn Abī ʿAbd al-Raḥmān for Medina and with 'Aṭā' ibn Abī Rabāḥ for Mecca.

The process of going backwards for a theoretical foundation of Islamic religious law as it was being taught in the ancient schools did not stop at these relatively late authorities. At the same time at which the doctrine of the school of Kufa was retrospectively attributed to Ibrāhīm al-Nakhaʿī, and perhaps even slightly earlier, that doctrine and the local idealized practice, which in the last resort was its basis, were directly connected with the very beginnings of Islam in Kufa, beginnings associated with Ibn Masʿūd, a Companion of the Prophet. It was, however, not to Ibn Masʿūd himself that reference was made in the first place, but to an informal group of 'Companions of Ibn Masʿūd' who were, in some general way, taken to guarantee the authentic and uninterrupted transmission of the correct practice and doctrine in Kufa. At a secondary stage the general reference to the Companions of Ibn Masʿūd gave rise to a formal and explicit reference to Ibn Masʿūd himself, and a considerable body of early Kufian doctrine was attributed to him. Though this body of doctrine differed in a number of details from the general teaching of the Kufian school which went under the name of Ibrāhīm al-Nakhaʿī, Ibrāhīm appears as the main transmitter of doctrine from Ibn Masʿūd, and many opinions were projected back from Ibrāhīm still farther to Ibn Masʿūd. The historical Ibrāhīm had not had personal contact with the historical Ibn Masʿūd, but some members of the originally anonymous group of Companions of Ibn Masʿūd were later identified as uncles of Ibrāhīm on his mother's side, and they formed a family link between the two authorities. Ibn Masʿūd thus became the eponym of the doctrine of the school of Kufa. The corresponding eponym of the Meccans was Ibn ʿAbbās, another Companion of the Prophet, and references to him, too, alternate with references to the Companions of Ibn ʿAbbās. The two main authorities of the Medinese among the Companions of the Prophet were the caliph ʿUmar and his son ʿAbd Allāh ibn ʿUmar. Each ancient school of law, having projected its doctrine back to its own eponym, a local Companion of the Prophet, claimed his authority as the basis of its teaching. This reference to the Companions of the Prophet was called *taḳlīd*, a term which was to gain a different meaning in the later theory of Islamic law.

5. One further logical step remained to be taken in the

search for a solid theoretical foundation of the doctrine of the ancient schools of law, and it was taken by the Iraqians who, very early in the second century of Islam, transferred the term '*sunna* of the Prophet' from its political and theological into a legal context, and identified with it the *sunna*, the idealized practice of the local community and the doctrine of its scholars. The term expressed an axiom but did not as yet imply the existence of positive information in the form of 'traditions' (which became prevalent later), namely that the Prophet by his words or acts had in any fact originated or approved the practice in question. This originally Iraqian concept of the *sunna* of the Prophet was taken over by the Syrians; their idea of living tradition was the uninterrupted practice of the Muslims, beginning with the Prophet, maintained by the first caliphs and by the later rulers, and verified by the scholars. The Medinese, on the other hand used this concept only rarely, whereas the Iraqians, in their turn, hardly used the term '*amal* for practice.

6. It was not long before various movements arose in opposition to the opinions held by the majorities in the ancient schools of law. In Kufa, for instance, where the name of Ibn Mas'ūd had become attached to the main stream of legal doctrine, any opinions which were put forward in opposition to the traditional doctrine of the majority had to invoke an equally high and possibly even higher authority, and for this purpose the name of the caliph 'Alī, who had made Kufa his headquarters, presented itself easily. The doctrines which in Kufa go under the name of 'Alī do not embody the coherent teaching of any individual group; all we can say is that, generally speaking, they represent opinions advanced in opposition to the living tradition, that is to the contemporary average teaching, of the school of Kufa. (There is no trace of a bias in favour of Shiite legal doctrines in these Iraqian traditions from 'Alī.) One group of doctrines attributed to 'Alī represents crude and primitive analogies, early unsuccessful efforts to systematize; they reflect the opinions of groups or individuals who were ahead of the majority of their contemporaries in Kufa in systematic legal thought. Another group of unsuccessful opinions ascribed to 'Alī shows a rigorous and meticulous tendency, and goes farther than the average doctrine of the Kufians in taking religious and ethical considerations into account. Unsuccessful

Iraqian opinions of this type, attributed to ʿAlī, correspond almost regularly to doctrines attested in Medina, where most of them represent the common opinion. It is in keeping with the relatively retarded development of the Medinese school that a body of doctrines which remained unsuccessful in Kufa, where it could not overcome the already established tradition of a school of law, succeeded to a considerable extent in gaining recognition in Medina. Furthermore, in contrast with the opposition in Kufa, the opposition in Medina already reflected the activity of the Traditionists.

7. The movement of the Traditionists, the most important single event in the history of Islamic law in the second century of the hijra, was the natural outcome and continuation of a movement of religiously and ethically inspired opposition to the ancient schools of law. The schools of law themselves represented, in one aspect, an Islamic opposition to popular and administrative practice under the later Umayyads, and the opposition group which developed into the Traditionist movement emphasized this tendency. The main thesis of the Traditionists, as opposed to the ancient schools of law, was that formal 'traditions' (*ḥadīth*, pl. *aḥādīth*) deriving from the Prophet superseded the living tradition of the school. It was not enough for the ancient schools to claim that their doctrines as a whole were based on the teachings of the Companions of the Prophet who presumably knew the intentions of their master best, or even that their living tradition represented the *sunna* of the Prophet. The Traditionists produced detailed statements or 'traditions' which claimed to be the reports of ear- or eye-witnesses on the words or acts of the Prophet, handed down orally by an uninterrupted chain (*isnād*) of trustworthy persons. Hardly any of these traditions, as far as matters of religious law are concerned, can be considered authentic; they were put into circulation, no doubt from the loftiest of motives, by the Traditionists themselves from the first half of the second century onwards.

The Traditionists were not confined to Medina but existed in all the great centres of Islam where they formed groups in opposition to, but nevertheless in contact with, the local schools of law. They disliked all human reasoning and personal opinion which had become an integral part of the living tradition of the ancient schools and which had, indeed, been a constituent element of Islamic legal thought from its very beginnings. Their own standards of reasoning were inferior to those of the ancient schools, as Shāfiʿī, at the end of the second century, had reason to complain. The traditions which they put into circulation were often systematically difficult. Their general tendency was towards strictness and rigorism, not, however, without exceptions. They were occasionally interested in purely legal issues, for reasons which now escape us, but they were mainly concerned with subordinating the legal subject-matter to religious and moral principles, expressed in traditions from the Prophet. There are, for instance, two traditions put into circulation by the Traditionists in Medina, according to which the Prophet had prohibited outbidding and certain practices which might create an artificial rise or fall in prices. Their aim was to make these practices illegal in the same way as, say, the taking of interest was illegal, so that contracts concluded in defiance of the prohibition would be invalid. These particular traditions, however, did not prevail with the Medinese, who, in common with the Iraqians, minimized them by interpretation, and the effort of the Traditionists to change the doctrine of the ancient schools of law remained unsuccessful in this case.

Initially the ancient schools of law, the Medinese as well as the Iraqians, offered strong resistance to the disturbing element represented by the traditions which claimed to go back to the Prophet.[1] It has often been presumed *a priori* that it was the most natural thing, from the first generation after the Prophet onwards, to refer to a real or alleged decision of his whenever a new problem presented itself. This was not the case. Traditions from the Prophet had to overcome strong opposition, and the polemics against them and in their favour extended over most of the second century of the hijra. At the same time it is obvious that once the authority of the Prophet, the highest after the Koran, had been invoked, the thesis of the Traditionists, consciously formulated, was certain of success, and that the ancient schools had no real defence against the rising tide of traditions from the Prophet. The best they could do was to minimize their import by interpretation, and to embody their

[1] The extreme opposition to the Traditionists is represented by the Muʿtazila (cf. below, p. 64, n. 2).

own attitude and doctrines in other alleged traditions from the Prophet, but this meant that the Traditionists had gained their point. Though the ancient schools of law were brought to pay lip-service to the principle of the Traditionists, they did not, however, necessarily change their positive legal doctrine to the full extent desired by this latter group. The Traditionists were sometimes successful in bringing about a change of doctrine, and when this happened the doctrine of the minority in opposition became indistinguishable from that of the majority of the school, so that it is not always possible to determine whether a particular doctrine originated in Traditionist circles or within the ancient schools of law; but they often failed, and we find whole groups of 'unsuccessful' Medinese and Iraqian minority doctrines expressed in traditions from the Prophet. It goes without saying that the interaction of legal doctrines and of traditions must be regarded as a unitary process, the several aspects and phases of which can be separated only for the sake of analysis. All this introduced inconsistencies into the teachings of the ancient schools of law, and these schools accepted traditions from the Prophet as authoritative only as far as they agreed with their own living tradition. The next step was to be taken by Shāfiʿī at the end of the second century of the hijra.

7

EARLY SYSTEMATIC REASONING; LAWYERS OF THE SECOND CENTURY

1. Parallel with the tendency of the early specialists and the ancient schools of law to Islamicize, to introduce Islamic norms into the sphere of law, went the complementary tendency to reason and to systematize. Reasoning was inherent in Islamic law from its very beginnings. It started with the exercise of personal opinion and of individual judgement on the part of the first specialists and *ḳāḍīs*. It would be a gratuitous assumption to regard the discretionary decision of the specialist or magistrate as anterior to the use of rudimentary analogy and the striving after coherence. Both elements are found intimately connected in the earliest period which the sources allow us to discern. Nevertheless, all this individual reasoning, whether purely discretionary and personal or inspired by an effort at consistency, started from vague beginnings, without direction or method, and moved towards an increasingly strict discipline.

Individual reasoning in general is called *ra'y*, 'opinion', in the particular meaning of 'sound, considered opinion'. When it is directed towards achieving systematic consistency and guided by the parallel of an existing institution or decision it is called *ḳiyās*, 'analogy', parity of reasoning. When it reflects the personal choice and discretionary opinion of the lawyer, guided by his idea of appropriateness, it is called *istiḥsān* or *istiḥbāb*, 'approval' or 'preference'. The term *istiḥsān* therefore came to signify a breach of strict analogy for reasons of public interest, convenience, or similar considerations. The use of individual reasoning in general is called *ijtihād* or *ijtihād al-ra'y*, and *mujtahid* is the qualified lawyer who uses it. These terms are to a great extent synonymous in the ancient period, and remained so even after Shāfiʿī. *Ra'y* and *istiḥsān* stem directly from the advisory, cautelary activity of the early specialists.

The oldest stage of legal reasoning is represented by Iraqian doctrines, either discretionary decisions or crude and primitive conclusions by analogy. An old conclusion of this kind, which has survived in the Ḥanafī doctrine, was to demand a fourfold confession from the culprit before he incurred the *ḥadd* punishment for unchastity, by analogy with the four witnesses prescribed for this case by the Koran (sura xxiv. 4). This was originally merely the result of systematic reasoning, and not based on any tradition. The Iraqian opposition exaggerated the underlying tendency towards caution, and put into circulation a tradition to the effect that ʿAlī had demanded a fivefold confession, but this doctrine remained unsuccessful. The original Iraqian doctrine spread into Hijaz and was put there under the aegis of the Prophet in a group of traditions. Nevertheless, the doctrine did not prevail in the school of Medina. The underlying conclusion by analogy provoked another, to the effect that the *ḥadd* punishment for theft could be applied only after a twofold confession from the culprit, by analogy with the two witnesses required in this case. This doctrine was again expressed in a tradition from ʿAlī, and a number of Iraqians, including the *ḳāḍī* of Kufa, Ibn Abī Laylā, a contemporary of Abū Ḥanīfa, held it. Abū Ḥanīfa, however, argued that if a twofold confession were required, the first confession would already create a civil debt, and no *ḥadd* could take place after a civil debt had been incurred even if a second confession were made, and the doctrine that a single confession was sufficient in the case in question prevailed in the Ḥanafī school.

The minimum value of stolen goods, for the *ḥadd* punishment to be applicable, was fixed by some Iraqians, by a crude analogy with the five fingers, at five dirhams. The generally accepted doctrine in Iraq, however, fixed it arbitrarily at ten dirhams, and this has remained the Ḥanafī doctrine. This doctrine has to be regarded as the original opinion, and the analogical reasoning as a refinement which was finally unsuccessful. The minimum value of stolen goods provided the starting-point for fixing, by a crude analogy, the minimum amount of the nuptial gift (*mahr*) which was an essential element of the contract of marriage. Here, too, the original Iraqian decision was discretionary: 'We think it shocking', they said, 'that intercourse should become lawful for a trifling amount', and therefore 'Ibrāhīm al-Nakhaʿī disapproved of a nuptial gift of less than forty, and once he said of less than ten dirhams'. This discretionary decision was later modified, not for the better, by a crude analogy, according to which the use of part of the body of the wife by the husband ought not to be made lawful for an amount less than that legalizing the loss of a limb through the *ḥadd* punishment for theft, and the minimum amount of the nuptial gift was fixed at ten dirhams. This reasoning was expressed in a tradition from ʿAlī. The last words of the statement attributed to Ibrāhīm are intended to put this later doctrine under his authority. A certain Iraqian who held that the minimum value of stolen goods for purposes of *ḥadd* was five dirhams, consistently fixed the minimum *mahr* at five dirhams too. The Medinese recognized originally no minimum amount of *mahr*; only Mālik, followed by the Mālikī school, adopted the principle of the analogical reasoning of the Iraqians, and starting from his own minimum value of stolen goods for the application of the *ḥadd*, which was $\frac{1}{4}$ dīnār = 3 dirhams, fixed the minimum *mahr* at the same amount. At the same time the Iraqians had found this crude analogy unsatisfactory, and fell back on the authority of traditions which had appeared in the meantime in favour of their doctrine, and this has remained the doctrine of the Ḥanafī school.

2. The results of this early systematic reasoning were not seldom expressed in the form of legal 'puzzles', or in the form of legal maxims or adages which were sometimes rhyming or alliterative. Some typical adages are: 'the child belongs to the marriage bed' (cf. above, p. 21); 'there is no divorce and no manumission under duress' (*lā ṭalāḳ wa-lā ʿatāḳ fī ighlāḳ*); 'profit follows responsibility' (*al-kharāj bil-ḍamān*); 'the security takes the place of that for which it is given' (*al-rahn bi-mā fīh*, Iraqian; for the Ḥanafī doctrine, which is different, see below, p. 140), and, in favour of the opposite doctrine, 'the security is not forfeited' (*al-rahn lā yaghlaḳ*, Medinese). These maxims became a favourite mode of expressing legal doctrines, often, no doubt, with a didactic purpose, in a rough-and-ready form; others may have been originally popular proverbs and sayings. They are not uniform as to provenance and period, but many were formulated in the first half of the second century of the hijra, and they reflect a stage when legal doctrines were not yet systematically expressed in traditions, though most of them

gradually acquired the form of traditions. The possibility that some adage or other may even go back to the pre-Islamic period cannot be excluded *a priori*, but this must be positively proved—as has been done, so far, for one particular maxim (*al-walā' lil-kubr*, concerning the transmission of the right of the patron, *mawlā*, by inheritance) which reflects an archaic rule of agnatic succession.

The element of personal discretion and individual opinion in Islamic law was prior to the growth of traditions, particularly of traditions from the Prophet, but because of the success of the main thesis of the Traditionists, most of what had originally been discretionary decisions and the result of individual reasoning by the scholars was put into the mouth of the Prophet. A significant example of this is provided by the rules relating to the ancient contract of *muzābana*, the exchange of dried dates for fresh dates on the tree. This contract contravened the Koranic prohibition of *ribā*, 'excess', and was therefore generally rejected. But in order to enable poor people, who did not themselves possess palm-trees, to acquire fresh dates from the time they began to ripen, certain scholars allowed the exchange of strictly limited quantities of dried dates for estimated equal quantities of fresh dates on the tree. This was originally a discretionary decision (*istiḥsān*), of the same kind as Ibrāhīm al-Nakhaʿī's discretionary opinion on the minimum amount of the nuptial gift. Both opinions, the uncompromising prohibition and the exception made for limited quantities, were put into the form of traditions from the Prophet, and in order to make the exception acceptable, the transaction envisaged by it was called by a technical term of its own, *bayʿ al-ʿarāyā*. This enabled the ancient schools as well as the Traditionists to harmonize the two groups of traditions, and the original discretionary element was eliminated from the doctrine.

3. The literary period of Islamic law begins about the year 150 of the hijra (A.D. 767), and from then onwards the development of technical legal thought can be followed step by step from scholar to scholar. For Iraq, successive stages are represented by the doctrine which must be credited to Ḥammād (d. 120/738), and by the doctrines of Ibn Abī Laylā (d. 148/765), of Abū Ḥanīfa (d. 150/767), of Abū Yūsuf (d. 182/798), and of Shaybānī (d. 189/805) respectively. The Syrian Awzāʿī

(d. 157/774) represents an archaic type of doctrine, and Mālik (d. 179/795) the average doctrine of the school of Medina in his time. During the whole of the second century of Islam, technical legal thought developed very rapidly from its beginnings, which were crude and primitive conclusions by analogy. It tended, first, to become more and more perfected. There is, secondly, an increasing dependence on traditions, as a greater number of traditions came into being and came to be accepted as authoritative. Thirdly, material considerations of a religious and ethical kind, which represented one aspect of the process of Islamicizing the legal subject-matter, tended to merge into systematic reasoning, and both tendencies became inextricably mixed in the result. All three tendencies culminated in Shāfiʿī (d. 204/820). The following examples are intended to illustrate the general trend of development.

Concerning a man who is married to more than four wives and adopts Islam, the earliest and seemingly most natural solution, that he may choose those four wives to whom he wishes to remain married, was that adopted by Awzāʿī. It was also expressed in a tradition from the Prophet. Mālik followed the same doctrine but specified that the Koranic prohibition (sura iv. 23) of marital relationships with two sisters simultaneously or with mother and daughter applied also here and limited the possible choices. The early Iraqians introduced systematic refinements. Abū Ḥanīfa declared: 'If the man was married to all his wives by one contract, and they all become Muslims, he becomes separated from all his wives.' Abū Yūsuf adduced systematic reasoning in favour of this doctrine and added: 'But if he was married by successive contracts, the first four marriages remain valid'; for this detail he also referred to Ibrāhīm Nakhaʿī. The tradition in favour of the first doctrine was still 'irregular', and therefore unacceptable, in the time of Abū Yūsuf. Shaybānī, however, knew already a greater number of traditions from the Prophet and could not disregard them; but he retained the doctrine of Abū Ḥanīfa and Abū Yūsuf with regard to persons who had been members of tolerated religions; the result is very inconsistent. Shāfiʿī, under the spell of the traditions, returned completely to the oldest doctrine and supplied a good systematic argument.

It was an ancient Arab custom that the victors took the

womenfolk of their conquered enemies as concubines without caring much whether they were married women or not. This rough-and-ready practice continued in Islam, and Awzāʿī states correctly: 'Such was the practice of the Muslims, and thus decrees the Koran' (sura iv. 24). The Medinese accepted this practice unreservedly and merely drew the logical conclusion by formulating the legal principle that captivity (in the sense in which Islam recognized it; below, p. 127) dissolved the marriage tie. The Iraqians, however, reasoned that captivity as such did not dissolve the marriage tie, and consequently tried to introduce certain safeguards. Awzāʿī was partly influenced by Iraqian legal thought and, while endorsing the practice, regarded the marriage of captives as continuing valid after captivity, with the result that his doctrine became inconsistent. Abū Yūsuf criticized Awzāʿī's inconsistency, and Shāfiʿī's doctrine is still more thoroughly systematic than that of Abū Yūsuf. At the same time, Awzāʿī, Abū Yūsuf, and Shāfiʿī represent three successive stages of growing formal dependence on traditions.

The Koran says in sura xxiv. 33: 'And those in your possession who desire a writing, write it for them if you know any good in them, and give them of the wealth of Allah which He has given you.' The hearers were supposed to know the details of the transaction referred to, and strict interpretation of the passage suggests that it was not identical with the contract of manumission by *mukātaba* such as was elaborated later by the ancient lawyers in the second century of Islam. Their earliest efforts were arbitrary, such as the decision that the *mukātab* slave becomes free as soon as he has paid half the stipulated amount, or the decision, attributed to ʿAṭāʾ and probably authentic, that he becomes free as soon as he has paid three-quarters. Presumably authentic, too, is the information that ʿAṭāʾ considered it obligatory on the master to conclude a *mukātaba* contract with his deserving slave although ʿAṭāʾ agreed that he had no traditional authority for this doctrine; in other words, the implications of the Koranic passage began to be considered in the time of ʿAṭāʾ. Technically more polished are the opinions that the *mukātab* slave becomes free as soon as he has paid off his value—this seems to have been the current doctrine of the school of Kufa at one time; or that he becomes free *pro rata* of his payments—this doctrine seems to have been connected with the Iraqian opposition; or that he becomes free immediately, and the payments due from him are ordinary debts. Finally, the systematically most consistent doctrine that the *mukātab* remained a slave as long as part of the stipulated sum was still unpaid prevailed in Iraq and in Medina, and it was projected back to certain Companions of the Prophet and finally to the Prophet himself, but all this is later than the simple reference, in Medina, to two of the ancient authorities of the school. Even after the final doctrine on the *mukātab* had prevailed, some concessions in favour of a defaulting *mukātab* were made; but they were subsequently reduced, though not completely eliminated, in the interest of stricter systematic consistency.

4. The opinions of Awzāʿī, in Syria, represent, as a rule, the oldest solutions adopted by Islamic jurisprudence. The archaic character of his doctrine makes it likely that he, who was himself a contemporary of Abū Ḥanīfa, conserved the teaching of his predecessors, who are nothing more than names to us, in the generation before him. When the doctrine which goes under his name was formulated, the Islamicizing and systematizing tendencies of earliest Islamic jurisprudence had, it is true, already begun to operate, but they were still far from having penetrated the whole of the raw material offered by ancient practice. His systematic reasoning, though explicit, is on the whole rudimentary; it is overshadowed by his reliance on the 'living tradition' which he identifies with the '*sunna* of the Prophet'. In this concept of *sunna* and in other respects, Awzāʿī's doctrine comes nearest to that of the ancient Iraqians.

The date of Mālik's death is only a few years earlier than the dates of the deaths of Abū Yūsuf and of Shaybānī, but Mālik's technical legal thought is considerably less developed than that of his Iraqian contemporaries. His reasoning, on the whole, is comparable to that of Awzāʿī, particularly in the dependence of both on the (idealized) practice, the 'living tradition', the consensus of the scholars. It was Mālik's aim to set forth the accepted doctrine of the school of Medina, and this was to a great extent founded on the individual reasoning of its representatives. In combining extensive use of reasoning with dependence on the 'living tradition', Mālik seems typical of the Medinese. In the majority of cases we find Mālik's own reasoning inspired by material considerations, by practical expediency, and by the tendency to Islamicize. Mālik's *Muwaṭṭa'*, the record of his teachings which was written down by his disciples in several closely related versions, enables us to discern the actual practice in Medina in the second half of the second century of Islam.[1]

In Iraq it is not generally possible to distinguish between the common doctrine of the Kufians in the time of Ḥammād and Ḥammād's individual opinions, but a considerable progress in the discussion of technical legal problems between Ḥammād and Ibn Abī Laylā, a *ḳāḍī* of Kufa, one generation later, is obvious. Ibn Abī Laylā's technical reasoning, though generally clumsy and short-sighted, is far from rudimentary; the striving for systematic consistency, the action of general trends and principles, pervade his whole doctrine. A rigid formalism is perhaps the most persistent typical feature of his legal thought. Ibn Abī Laylā's practical, common-sense reasoning often takes material, and particularly Islamic ethical, considerations into account. Connected with this is his regard for contemporary practice. There are numerous traces of his activity as a *ḳāḍī* in his doctrine, last but not least his conservatism, so that he represents an earlier stage in the development of Islamic jurisprudence than his contemporary, Abū Ḥanīfa.

In contrast with Ibn Abī Laylā, Abū Ḥanīfa seems to have played the part of a theoretical systematizer who achieved considerable progress in technical legal thought. Not being a *ḳāḍī*, Abū Ḥanīfa was less restricted than Ibn Abī Laylā by considerations of day-to-day practice; at the same time he was less firmly guided by the realities of administration of justice. There is so much new, explicit legal thought embodied in his doctrine that an appreciable part of it was found defective and was rejected by his disciples. His legal thought is not only more broadly based and more thoroughly applied than that of his older contemporaries but technically more highly developed, more circumspect, and more refined. A high degree of reasoning, often somewhat ruthless and unbalanced, with little regard for practice, is typical of Abū Ḥanīfa's legal thought as a whole.

The doctrine of Abū Yūsuf, by and large, presupposes the doctrine of Abū Ḥanīfa, whom he regarded as his master. The most prominent peculiarity of Abū Yūsuf's own legal thought is

[1] For an example, see below, p. 79.

that he is more dependent on traditions than Abū Ḥanīfa, because there were more authoritative traditions from the Prophet in existence in his time, and compared with this dependence on traditions, Islamic ethical considerations of a material kind are less important. Secondly, the doctrine of Abū Yūsuf often represents a reaction against Abū Ḥanīfa's somewhat unrestrained reasoning, although, in diverging from his master, he occasionally abandoned the more perspicacious or more highly developed doctrine. Finally, a remarkable feature of Abū Yūsuf's doctrine is the frequency with which he changed his opinions, not always for the better. Sometimes the contemporary sources state directly, and in other cases it is probable, that Abū Yūsuf's experience as a *ḳāḍī* caused him to change his opinion. Abū Yūsuf represents the beginning of the process by which the ancient Iraqian school of Kufa was replaced by that of the followers of Abū Ḥanīfa.

Shaybānī, the great disciple both of Abū Ḥanīfa and of Abū Yūsuf, depends on traditions even more than Abū Yūsuf does. This shows itself not only in changes of doctrine but in his habit of duplicating his systematic reasoning by arguments taken from traditions, and in the habitual formula 'We follow this' by which he almost invariably rounds off his references to traditions even when he does not, in fact, follow them. Shaybānī used his personal opinion to the extent common in the ancient schools of law, but most of his reasoning that appears in this guise is in fact strict analogy or systematic reasoning. To this extent Shaybānī prepared the way for Shāfiʿī's rejection, on principle, of discretionary decisions and his insistence on strict analogy or systematic reasoning. Systematic reasoning of a high quality is the feature most typical of Shaybānī's technical legal thought. Shaybānī was the great systematizer of the Kufian doctrine. He was also a prolific writer, and his voluminous works, in which he consciously continued the doctrinal tradition of Abū Ḥanīfa and Abū Yūsuf, became the rallying-point of the Ḥanafī school which emerged from the ancient school of Kufa.

5. In Shāfiʿī, who considered himself a member of the school of Medina although he made the essential thesis of the Traditionists prevail in Islamic law, legal reasoning reached its zenith. Explicit legal reasoning, most of it of a superior quality, occupies a much more prominent place in Shāfiʿī's doctrine

than in that of any of his predecessors, even if we take differences of style and of literary form into account. When Shāfiʿī wrote, the process of Islamicizing the law, of impregnating it with religious and ethical ideas, had in the main been completed. We therefore find him hardly ever influenced in his conscious legal thought by material considerations of a religious or ethical kind, such as had played an important part in the doctrines of Awzāʿī, Mālik, Ibn Abī Laylā, and Abū Ḥanīfa. We also find him more consistent than his predecessors in separating the moral and the legal aspects, whenever both arise with regard to the same problem. In this respect, Shāfiʿī did not carry out the programme of the Traditionists who had tried to identify the categories 'forbidden' and 'invalid'. On the other hand, Shāfiʿī's fundamental dependence on traditions from the Prophet, in which he followed the Traditionists, implied a different, formal way of Islamicizing the legal doctrine. In theory, Shāfiʿī distinguished sharply between the argument taken from traditions and the result of systematic thought. In his actual reasoning, however, both aspects are closely interwoven; he shows himself tradition-bound and systematic at the same time, and we may consider this new synthesis typical of his legal thought.

Shāfiʿī recognized in principle only strict analogical and systematic reasoning (*ḳiyās*, *ijtihād*, also *ʿaḳl* 'reason' or *maʿḳūl* 'what is reasonable', in a narrow technical sense), to the exclusion of arbitrary opinions and discretionary decisions (*ra'y* and *istiḥsān*, which Shāfiʿī uses as synonyms), such as had been customary among his predecessors. This is one of the important innovations by which his legal theory became utterly different from that of the ancient schools. His legal theory is much more logical and formally consistent than that of his predecessors, whom he blames continually for what appears to him as a mass of inconsistencies. It is based on the thesis of the Traditionists that nothing can override the authority of a formal tradition from the Prophet. In accepting this Shāfiʿī cut himself off from the natural and continuous development of doctrine in the ancient schools of law, and he adopted a principle which, in the long run, could only lead to inflexibility. Also the positive solutions which Shāfiʿī proposes are often, sociologically speaking, less advanced than those advocated by the contemporary Iraqians and Medinese; his systematic legal thought, dominated as it was by a retrospective point of view, could hardly be productive of progressive solutions.

For Shāfiʿī, *sunna* is no longer the idealized practice as recognized by representative scholars; it is identical with the contents of formal traditions from the Prophet, even though such a tradition be transmitted by only one person in each generation. According to Shāfiʿī, one must not conclude, as the ancient schools of law did, that the Companions of the Prophet knew the intentions of their master best and would therefore not have held opinions incompatible with them. This led him to reject the *taḳlīd* as practised in the ancient schools. The opinions held and practices inaugurated by persons other than Companions of the Prophet were of course, in Shāfiʿī's eyes, of no authority whatsoever. This new concept of *sunna*, the *sunna* of the Prophet embodied in formal traditions from him, superseded the concept of 'living tradition' of the ancient schools. Traditions from the Prophet could not even be invalidated by reference to the Koran. Shāfiʿī took it for granted that the Koran did not contradict the traditions from the Prophet, and that the traditions explained the Koran; the Koran had therefore to be interpreted in the light of the traditions, and not vice versa. The consensus of the scholars, which expressed the living tradition of each ancient school, also became irrelevant for Shāfiʿī; he even denied the existence of any such consensus because he could always find scholars who held divergent opinions, and he fell back on the general consensus of all Muslims on essentials. The thesis that 'everything of which the Muslims approve or disapprove is good or bad in the sight of Allah' had been formulated shortly before Shāfiʿī. Shāfiʿī developed it further, but the principle, as he formulated it, that the community of Muslims would never agree on an error, was put into the form of a tradition from the Prophet only towards the middle of the third century of the hijra. Shāfiʿī held that, whatever the extent of the knowledge of individual scholars, the community of Muslims as a whole had preserved the traditions from the Prophet in their totality, so that none of them were lost, and the consensus of the Muslims could not contradict the *sunna* of the Prophet as Shāfiʿī understood it. All this left no room for the discretionary exercise of personal opinion, and human reasoning had to be restricted to making correct inferences and drawing systematic conclusions from the traditions. Shāfiʿī was so serious in his main contention that he declared himself prepared to abandon any doctrine of his by which he might unwittingly have contradicted a tradition from the Prophet.

These, in short, were the principles of Shāfiʿī's legal theory. It was a ruthless innovation which it took him some time to elaborate, so that his writings retain numerous traces of the development of his ideas and some unsolved inconsistencies. But notwithstanding all this, Shāfiʿī's legal theory is a perfectly coherent system, superior by far to the theory of the ancient schools, and he became the founder of the *uṣūl al-fiḳh*, the discipline dealing with the theoretical bases of Islamic law. It was the achievement of a powerful mind, and at the same time the logical outcome of a process which had begun much earlier. The development of legal theory in the second century of Islam was dominated by the struggle between two concepts: that of the common doctrine of the community, and that of the authority of the traditions from the Prophet. The doctrine of the ancient schools of law represented an uneasy compromise; Shāfiʿī vindicated the thesis of the Traditionists, and the later schools had no choice but to accept his essential thesis.

We must now take up the external development of Islamic law where we left it at the end of the Umayyad period.

8

ISLAMIC LAW UNDER THE FIRST 'ABBĀSIDS; LEGISLATION AND ADMINISTRATION

1. WHEN the Umayyads were overthrown by the 'Abbāsids in 132 of the hijra (A.D. 750), Islamic law as we know it had acquired its essential features; the need of Arab Muslim society for a new legal system had been filled. The early 'Abbāsids continued and reinforced the Islamicizing trend which had become more and more noticeable under the later Umayyads. For reasons of dynastic policy, in order to differentiate themselves and their revolution from the ruling house which they had superseded, the 'Abbāsids exaggerated the differences, and in conscious opposition to their predecessors proclaimed their programme of establishing the rule of God on earth. As part of this policy they recognized the religious law, as it was being taught by the pious specialists, as the only legitimate norm in Islam, and they set out to translate their ideal theory into practice. They regularly attracted specialists in religious law to their court and made a point of consulting them on problems that might come within their competence. A long treatise which Abū Yūsuf wrote at the request of the caliph Hārūn al-Rashīd on public finance, taxation, criminal justice, and connected subjects has come down to us. But just as the pious specialists who had formed the vanguard of the Islamicizing tendency under the Umayyads had been ahead of realities, so now the early 'Abbāsids and their religious advisers were unable to carry the whole of society with them, particularly as the caliphs themselves were not always very sincere in their professed eagerness to translate the religious ideal into practice. It soon appeared that the rule of God on earth as preached by the early 'Abbāsids was but a polite formula to cover their own absolute despotism. They were thus unable to achieve a permanent

fusion between theory and practice, and it was not long before their successors lacked not only the will but the power to continue the effort.

2. What the early 'Abbāsids did achieve was the permanent connexion of the office of *ḳāḍī* with the *sharī'a*, the sacred Law. This, too, had been prepared under the Umayyads, but under the 'Abbāsids it became a fixed rule that the *ḳāḍī* had to be a specialist in the *sharī'a*. He was no more the legal secretary of the governor but was normally appointed by the central government and, once appointed and until he was relieved of his office, he was to apply nothing but the sacred Law, without interference from the government. But this independence remained theoretical. With its increasing despotism, the temporal power became more and more unwilling to tolerate the existence of any truly independent institution; the *ḳāḍīs* were not only subject to dismissal at the whim of the central government, but had to depend on the political authorities for the execution of their judgments. This was particularly important in the administration of criminal justice.

During the Umayyad period, when the *ḳāḍīs* were the legal secretaries of the governors, they or the governors themselves exercised whatever criminal justice came within the competence of the administrative authorities. But when, under the early 'Abbāsids, the office of *ḳāḍī* was separated from the general administration and became bound to Islamic law in substance and procedure, the formal rules of evidence of this last made it impossible for the *ḳāḍī* to undertake a criminal investigation, and his inability to deal with criminal cases became apparent. Consequently the political powers stepped in and transferred the administration of the greater part of criminal justice to the police (*shurṭa*),[1] and it has normally remained outside the sphere of practical application of Islamic law. Nevertheless, the office of *ḳāḍī* in this its final form proved to be one of the most vigorous institutions evolved by Islamic society.

The centralizing tendency of the early 'Abbāsids which was responsible for the appointment of the *ḳāḍīs* by the central government also led to the creation of the dignity of Chief *Ḳāḍī* (*ḳāḍi l-ḳuḍāt*). It was originally an honorific title given to

[1] This term, which originally denoted the guard of a general or governor, is probably derived from Latin *cohort(em)*.

the *ḳāḍī* of the capital, whom the caliphs would normally consult on the administration of justice. The *ḳāḍī* Abū Yūsuf was the first to receive this title, and the caliph Hārūn not only solicited his advice on financial policy and similar questions, as mentioned above, but used to consult him on the appointment of all *ḳāḍī*s in the Empire. The Chief *Ḳāḍī* soon became one of the most important counsellors of the caliph, and the appointment and dismissal of the other *ḳāḍī*s, under the authority of the caliph, was the main function of his office. It has been suggested that the office of Chief *Ḳāḍī*, which notwithstanding its historical importance has always been somewhat neglected by the theorists of Islamic law, is of Persian origin and the translation, into an Islamic context, of that of the Zoroastrian *Mōbedhān Mōbedh*. Its introduction by the early ʿAbbāsids certainly coincided with the introduction of strong Persian elements into ʿAbbāsid government, and ancient Arab writers themselves have pointed out the parallels between the two institutions.

An institution which the early ʿAbbāsids, and perhaps before them the later Umayyads, borrowed from the administrative tradition of the Sassanian kings, was the 'investigation of complaints' (*naẓar fil-maẓālim*). It was a prerogative of the absolute monarch by which the caliphs themselves or, by delegation, ministers or special officials and later the sultans, heard complaints concerning miscarriage or denial of justice or other allegedly unlawful acts of the *ḳāḍī*s, difficulties in securing the execution of judgments, wrongs committed by government officials or by powerful individuals (cf. below, p. 160, on *ghaṣb*), and similar matters. Very soon formal Courts of Complaints were set up. The more important lawsuits concerning property, which in theory would have come within the jurisdiction of the *ḳāḍī*, tended to be brought before the Courts of Complaints too, so that their jurisdiction became, to a great extent, concurrent with that of the *ḳāḍī*s' tribunals. The very existence of these tribunals, which were established ostensibly in order to supplement the deficiencies of the jurisdiction of the *ḳāḍī*s, shows that much of the administration of justice by the *ḳāḍī* had broken down at an early period.

At the same time at which the *ḳāḍī*s' tribunals found themselves superseded, to a considerable degree, by the Courts of Complaints, they had also to accommodate themselves to the continued jurisdiction of the 'inspector of the market', whose office had continued into Islam from Byzantine times. The early 'Abbāsids, while maintaining his functions, superficially Islamicized this office by entrusting its holder with discharging the collective obligation, enjoined in the Koran,[1] to 'encourage good and discourage evil', making him responsible for enforcing Islamic morals and behaviour in the community of Muslims, and giving him the Islamic title of *muḥtasib* (his office is called *ḥisba*). In addition to his ancient powers of enforcing traffic, building, sanitary, and trading regulations and deciding disputes arising from them, it was now part of his duties to bring transgressors to justice and to impose summary punishments which came to include the flogging of the drunk and the unchaste and even the amputation of the hands of thieves caught in the act; but the sincere eagerness of the rulers to enforce these provisions of the *sharī'a* commonly made them overlook the fact that the procedure of the *muḥtasib* did not always satisfy the strict demands of Islamic law. These several aspects of the institution of the *ḥisba* exemplify the nature and extent of the adoption of the ideal doctrine of the sacred Law under the early 'Abbāsids. The institution itself has survived, in some Islamic countries at least, into the present, and so has the right of every Muslim, notwithstanding the presence or absence of an officially appointed *muḥtasib*, to come forth as a private prosecutor or 'common informer'.

3. Under the Umayyads the administration of justice had been left to the provincial governors and their legal secretaries, the *ḳāḍīs*, and the administrative and legislative activity of the central government, and of the provincial governors, too, had originally lain outside of, and was only gradually brought into, the orbit of nascent Islamic law. Under the 'Abbāsids, however, when the main features of the *sharī'a* had already been definitely established, when Islamic law had come to be recognized, in theory at least, as the only legitimate norm of behaviour for Muslims, and when the *ḳāḍīs*, bound to apply this law, were appointed by the central government under the direct authority of the caliph, the caliph himself had to be incorporated into the system. This was done not by attributing to him the right to legislate; it would have been difficult to acknowledge this right

[1] suras iii. 104, 110, 114; vii. 157; ix. 71, 112; xxii. 41; xxxi. 17.

of the ruler in a system of religious duties which had been formulated not on the basis of, but in a certain opposition to, the practice of the government, and which was fast falling under the influence of the Traditionists. Even speaking of the caliphs of Medina, themselves Companions of the Prophet, Shāfiʿī (who upheld the thesis of the Traditionists) could say: 'A tradition from the Prophet must be accepted as soon as it becomes known, even if it is not supported by any corresponding action of a caliph. If there has been an action on the part of a caliph and a tradition from the Prophet to the contrary becomes known later, that action must be discarded in favour of the tradition from the Prophet.' The solution which was adopted was to endow the caliph with the attributes of a religious scholar and lawyer, to bind him to the sacred Law in the same way in which the *ḳāḍīs* were bound to it, and to give him the same right to the exercise of personal opinion (*ijtihād al-raʾy*) as was admitted by the schools of law. The explicit theory of all this was formulated only much later, but the essentials were expressed in two traditions dating from the end of the second century of the hijra, which retrospectively put the doctrine into the mouth of the Umayyad caliph ʿUmar ibn ʿAbd al-ʿAzīz in the following terms: 'No one has the right to personal opinion (*raʾy*) on points settled in the Koran; the personal opinion of the caliphs concerns those points on which there is no revelation in the Koran and no valid *sunna* from the Prophet; no one has the right to personal opinion on points settled in a *sunna* enacted by the Prophet.' And: 'There is no Prophet after ours, and no holy book after ours; what Allah has allowed or forbidden through our Prophet remains so for ever; I am not one who decides but only one who carries out, not an innovator but a follower.'

According to this doctrine, which was consciously adopted very early under the ʿAbbāsids, the caliph, though otherwise the absolute chief of the community of Muslims, had not the right to legislate but only to make administrative regulations within the limits laid down by the sacred Law. This doctrine, which was projected back into the preceding period, effectively concealed the fact that what was actually legislation of the caliphs of Medina, and particularly of the Umayyads, had to a great extent, directly by being approved and indirectly by provoking contrary solutions, entered into the fabric of Islamic law. The adoption of the theory in question did not even lead to a clear division between legislation and administration for the future. The later caliphs and the other secular rulers often had occasion to enact new rules. But although this was in fact legislation, the rulers used to call it administration, and they maintained the fiction that their regulations served only to apply, to supplement, and to enforce the *sharī'a*, and were well within the limits of their political authority. This fiction was maintained as much as possible, even in the face of contradictions with and encroachments on the sacred Law.

The discretionary power of the sovereign which enables him, in theory, to apply and to complete the sacred Law and, in practice, to regulate by virtually independent legislation matters of police, taxation, and criminal justice, all of which had escaped the control of the *ḳāḍī* in early 'Abbāsid times, was later called *siyāsa*. This *siyāsa* is the expression of the full judicial power which the sovereign had retained from the Umayyad period onwards and which he can exercise whenever he thinks fit. Owing to the ambiguity explained in the preceding paragraph, its existence is admitted even by the strict theory of Islamic law. *Siyāsa* means, literally, 'policy', and it comprises the whole of administrative justice which is dispensed by the sovereign and by his political agents, in contrast with the ideal system of the *sharī'a*, the religious law of Islam, which is administered by the *ḳāḍī*. The application of *siyāsa*, in the nature of things, often touches the *naẓar fil-maẓālim*, and both terms are, to a certain extent, used as synonyms. The *ḳāḍī*s, too, are obliged to follow the instructions which the ruler may give them in exercise of his power of '*siyāsa* within the limits assigned to it by the *sharī'a*' (*siyāsa shar'iyya*). In fact, until the modern period when legal modernism led to far-reaching interference with Islamic law itself, the Islamic rulers were generally content with legislating on matters which fell outside the competence of the *ḳāḍī*s. The most important examples of this kind of secular law are the *siyāsa* of the Mamlūk sultans of Egypt which applied to the military ruling class, and the *ḳānūn-nāme*s of the Ottoman sultans.

As a result of all this, a double administration of justice, one religious and exercised by the *ḳāḍī* on the basis of the *sharī'a*, the other secular and exercised by the political authorities on the basis of custom, of equity and fairness, sometimes of arbitrariness, of governmental regulations, and in modern times of enacted codes, has prevailed in practically the whole of the Islamic world.

4. This was how Islamic law actually grew and, one might almost be tempted to say, was fated to grow, out of seeds which had been sown well before ʿAbbāsid times.[1] In the first years of ʿAbbāsid rule, however, an unsuccessful effort was made to introduce the idea of codification and legislation. The author of this proposal was the Secretary of State, Ibn al-Muḳaffaʿ, an Iranian convert to Islam, who was put to death in 139/756. In a treatise or memorandum which he wrote in the last few years of his life for the caliph Manṣūr, he deplored the wide divergencies in jurisprudence and in administration of justice which existed between the several great cities (and even their several quarters), and between the main schools of law. These divergencies, he said, either perpetuated different local precedents or came from individual reasoning which was sometimes faulty or pushed too far. He suggested therefore that the caliph should review the different doctrines, codify and enact his own decisions in the interest of uniformity, and make this code binding on the *ḳāḍīs*. This code ought to be revised by successive caliphs. The caliph and the caliph alone, Ibn al-Muḳaffaʿ asserted, had the right to decide at his discretion; he could give binding orders on military and civil administration, and generally on all matters on which there was no precedent, but he must base himself on Koran and *sunna*. This *sunna*, however, Ibn al-Muḳaffaʿ realized, was based not on authentic traditions from the Prophet and the caliphs of Medina, but to a great extent on administrative regulations of the Umayyad government. Therefore, he concluded, the caliph was free to determine and codify the *sunna* as he thought fit.

Ibn al-Muḳaffaʿ wrote at a time when the ʿAbbāsid government was attempting to make Islamic law the only law of the

[1] How much all this was the natural outcome of conditions which existed already at the end of the Umayyad period becomes evident from the fact that the theory and practice of the law in Islamic Spain, where an escaped member of the Umayyad family founded an independent principality six years after the ʿAbbāsid revolution (138/756), was to all intents and purposes identical with that in the ʿAbbāsid empire. Only a few of the ʿAbbāsid innovations did not immediately percolate into Islamic Spain, such as the title *muḥtasib* for the old *ʿāmil al-sūḳ*, and the office of the *ḳāḍi l-ḳuḍāt*, to which the institution of the *ḳāḍi l-jamāʿa* bears only a superficial resemblance.

state, but when that law itself was still in its formative period. The revolutionary propaganda which had brought the ʿAbbāsids to power had made extravagant claims for the divine kingship of the 'cousins of the Prophet'. Though the ʿAbbāsids, once they had attained their goal, quickly dissociated themselves from the more extremist of their adherents, the plea of Ibn al-Muḳaffaʿ for state control over law (and, incidentally, over religion too) was in full accord with the tendencies prevailing at the very beginning of the ʿAbbāsid era. But this was no more than a passing phase, and orthodox Islam refused to be drawn into too close a connexion with the state. The absolute power which the caliphs, and later the governors, sultans, &c., exercised over the appointment and dismissal of the *ḳāḍīs* could not replace their lack of control over the law itself. The result was that Islamic law became more and more removed from practice, but in the long run gained more in power over the minds than it lost in control over the bodies of the Muslims. Hardly forty years after Ibn al-Muḳaffaʿ wrote his memorandum for Manṣūr, Abū Yūsuf composed his treatise for Hārūn; a comparison of the two documents shows well the speed with which Islamic law developed during the second century of the hijra.

9

THE LATER SCHOOLS OF LAW AND THEIR 'CLASSICAL' THEORY

1. IN the early 'Abbāsid period, too, the ancient schools of law, which had the main reason for their separate existence in geography, transformed themselves into the later type of school, based on allegiance to an individual master. The religious specialists of each geographical unit in the central parts of the Islamic world had developed a certain minimum agreement on their doctrines, and by the middle of the second century of the hijra many individuals, instead of working out independent doctrines of their own, began to follow the teaching of a recognized authority in its broad outlines, while reserving to themselves the right to differ from their master on any point of detail. This led in the first place to the forming of groups or circles within the ancient schools of law. Thus there existed within the Iraqian school of Kufa the 'followers of Abū Ḥanīfa', a group which included Abū Yūsuf and Shaybānī, but, in addition, Abū Yūsuf had followers of his own. Similarly, within the school of Medina, and particularly in its dependency which was Egypt, there were 'followers of Mālik' who regarded the book of their master, the *Muwaṭṭa'*, as their authoritative work. They were originally only a fraction of the Medinese, just as the followers of Abū Ḥanīfa were only part of the Kufians. But the extensive literary activity of the followers of Abū Ḥanīfa, particularly of Shaybānī, in Iraq, and of the followers of Mālik in North Africa,[1] together with other factors, some of them accidental, brought it about that the bulk of the ancient school of Kufa transformed itself into the school of the Ḥanafīs, and the ancient school of Medina into the school of the Mālikīs, and the ancient schools of Basra and of Mecca, respectively, became merged in them. Another group of Kufians, and perhaps

[1] The *Mudawwana*, the origins of which go back to within one decade from Mālik's death, is the great corpus of their doctrine.

of Iraqians generally, formed the school of Sufyān Thawrī (d. 161/778), which counted followers for several centuries. The ancient school of the Syrians, too, transformed itself into the school of Awzāʿī which had a somewhat shorter span of life. This transformation of the ancient schools of law into 'personal' schools, which perpetuated not the living tradition of a city but the doctrine of a master and of his disciples, was completed about the middle of the third century of the hijra (*c.* A.D. 865). It was the logical outcome of a process which had started within the ancient schools themselves but was precipitated by the activity of Shāfiʿī.

Shāfiʿī, whose life spanned the second half of the second century, started as a member of the school of Medina, and continued to regard himself as one, even after he had adopted the essential thesis of the Traditionists and tried to convert to it the adherents of the ancient schools, particularly the Medinese, through vigorous polemics. He did his best to represent his new doctrine as one which followed naturally from their own premises and which, therefore, they ought to accept, but adopting the thesis of Shāfiʿī meant, nevertheless, breaking with the school of Medina or, for that matter, with any of the ancient schools. It did not mean joining the ranks of the pure Traditionists because, as Shāfiʿī himself had realized, their standards of reasoning were inferior to those of the ancient schools, quite apart from the fact that their interests were less technically legal. Any legal specialist, therefore, who became converted to Shāfiʿī's thesis became a personal follower of Shāfiʿī, and in this way Shāfiʿī became the founder of the first school of law on an exclusively personal basis, certainly with a common doctrine, but a doctrine which had once and for all been formulated by the founder. Shāfiʿī might well protest that it was not his intention to found a school, that his opinions counted for nothing, and that he was prepared to amend them if he found himself unwittingly contradicting a reliable tradition from the Prophet; already a direct disciple of his, Muzanī (d. 264/878), had composed his *Mukhtaṣar* as an 'extract from the doctrine of Shāfiʿī and from the implications of his opinions for the benefit of those who may desire it, although I must warn them that Shāfiʿī forbade anyone to follow (*taḳlīd*) him or anyone else'. The term *taḳlīd*, which in the usage of the ancient schools had denoted the formal reference to Companions of the Prophet, had come to mean reliance on the teaching of a master. The doctrinal movement started by Shāfiʿī has always been known as the Shāfiʿī school, and it soon took its place beside the Ḥanafī and the Mālikī schools.[1]

2. Shāfiʿī's effort to supersede the ancient schools of law by a new doctrine based on the thesis of the Traditionists failed, but he succeeded in making this thesis, which was indeed the logical outcome of the search for an irrefutable Islamic basis of the *sharīʿa*, prevail in legal theory. Whereas the Ḥanafīs and the Mālikīs, who continued the ancient schools of Kufa and of Medina, did not change their positive legal doctrine appreciably from what it had been when Shāfiʿī appeared, they finally adopted, together with the Shāfiʿīs, a legal theory of traditionist inspiration. This 'classical' theory of Islamic law, or doctrine of the *uṣūl al-fiḳh*,[2] which was established during the third century of the hijra (ninth century A.D.), was in many respects more elaborate than Shāfiʿī's own theory, and differed from it in one essential aspect. Shāfiʿī, in order to be able to follow the traditions from the Prophet without reservation, rejected the principle of the consensus of the scholars, which embodied the living tradition of the ancient schools, and restricted his own idea of consensus to the unanimous doctrine of the community at large. The classical theory returned to the concept of the consensus of the scholars, which it considered infallible in the same way as the general consensus of the Muslims. But it had to take into account the status which Shāfiʿī had meanwhile won for the traditions from the Prophet, and it extended the sanction of the consensus of the scholars to Shāfiʿī's identification of the *sunna* with the contents of traditions from the Prophet. The main result of Shāfiʿī's break with the principle of 'living tradition' thus became itself part of the 'living tradition' at a later stage. The price that had to be paid for this recognition was that the extent to which traditions from the Prophet were in fact accepted as a basis of law was in the future to be determined by the consensus of the scholars, which left the representatives of each school free to determine it for themselves (by interpretation, and so forth), and Shāfiʿī's attempt to erect the traditions

[1] The Arabic term for a 'school' of religious law is *madhhab* (pl. *madhāhib*).
[2] In contrast with the *uṣūl*, 'roots', positive law is called *furūʿ*, 'branches'.

from the Prophet, instead of the living tradition and the consensus, into the highest authority in law was short-lived in its effect. The fact that the Shāfiʿī school itself had to accept this modification of the legal theory of its founder shows the hold which the idea of consensus had gained over Islamic law. It follows that the common legal theory, the discipline of the *uṣūl al-fiḳh*, has little relevance to the positive doctrine of each school.

As a result of the development described so far, the classical theory teaches that Islamic law is based on four principles or 'roots' (*uṣūl*, pl. of *aṣl*): the Koran, the *sunna* of the Prophet which is incorporated in the recognized traditions, the consensus (*ijmāʿ*) of the scholars of the orthodox community, and the method of reasoning by analogy (*ḳiyās*). (See further below, pp. 114 f.)

The essentials of this theory and, in particular, the fully developed concept of the consensus of the scholars occur already in the work of Ṭabarī (d. 310/923). Whereas Shāfiʿī had called Koran and *sunna* the 'two principles' and considered *ijmāʿ* and *ḳiyās* subordinate to them, Ṭabarī recognizes three *uṣūl*: Koran, *sunna* as expressed in traditions from the Prophet, and *ijmāʿ*, which for him is absolutely decisive; beside these he places *ḳiyās* (avoiding this technical term in relation to his own doctrine and using circumlocutions, such as 'parallel', 'similarity', or 'amounting to'). The later Ḥanbalīs (see below, p. 63), too, whilst treating *ḳiyās* as a recognized principle, avoid putting it formally on the same level as the other *uṣūl*, although *istiḥsān* and *istiṣlāḥ* (see the following paragraph) are admitted to the rank of 'controversial principles'. The final admission of *ḳiyās* to the 'classical' group of four *uṣūl* is the result of a compromise, on the lines envisaged by Shāfiʿī, between the old, unrestricted use of *ra'y* (or *istiḥsān*) and the rejection of all human reasoning in religious law (see below, sections 4 and 5).

3. Although the later schools of law shared the essentials of this classical theory, traces of the different doctrines of the ancient schools have survived in some of them to a greater or lesser extent. The old unfettered use of personal opinion (*ra'y*), for instance, continued to be recognized as legitimate by the Ḥanafīs under the name of 'approval' or 'preference' (*istiḥsān*) in cases where the strict application of analogy would have led

to undesirable results. (Cf. below, p. 204.) This does not mean that the followers of the Ḥanafī school are, or have been for more than a thousand years, at liberty to use their own discretionary judgement, any more than the adherents of any of the other schools; it means merely that the official doctrine of the school is in a number of cases based not on strict analogy but on the free exercise of personal opinion on the part of the school's earliest authorities. Mālik and other early authorities of the Mālikī school, too, are known to have exercised *istiḥsān* in a number of cases; the Mālikī school, however, prefers the method of *istiṣlāḥ*, 'having regard for the public interest (*maṣlaḥa*)', a consideration which differs only in name and not in kind from the reasoning of the Ḥanafīs and to which essentially the same qualification applies. The Shāfi'īs and the Ḥanbalīs (see below, section 4), too, use *istiṣlāḥ*. The exact definition of *ijmā'* has always remained somewhat controversial. The Mālikīs recognize, beside the general consensus of the scholars, the consensus of the (ancient) scholars of Medina (*ijmā' ahl al-Madīna*), the town of the Prophet and, according to them, the true home of his *sunna*. This doctrine perpetuates the ancient idea of a local, geographical consensus.

In the later Middle Ages, when Morocco had become the most active centre of the Mālikī school where it developed in relative isolation, a number of features became prominent there which were not shared by the other schools, and not even by Mālikī doctrine in other countries. Most of these features fall under the heading of 'judicial practice' (*'amal*). The concept of *'amal* had been prominent in the theory of the ancient school of Medina, and the 'practice of Medina' continued to play a minor part in the legal theory of the Mālikī school. Now in Morocco, from the end of the ninth/fifteenth century onwards, 'judicial practice', as opposed to the strict doctrine of the school, found a recognized place in the system, and it was set down in special works. The later Mālikī school in Morocco took more notice than the other schools of law of the conditions prevailing in fact, not by changing the ideal doctrine of the law in any respect, but by recognizing that the actual conditions did not allow the strict theory to be translated into practice, and that it was better to try to control the practice as much as possible than to abandon it completely, thus maintaining a kind of protective zone around the *sharīʿa*. Later Mālikī doctrine in Morocco upheld the principle that 'judicial practice prevails over the best attested opinion', and it allowed a number of institutions rejected by strict Mālikī doctrine. This Western Mālikī *ʿamal* is not customary law; it is an alternative doctrine valid as long as it is felt advisable to bring custom within the orbit of the *sharīʿa*, and it mirrors, on a different plane, its predecessor, the *ʿamal* of Medina.

If later Mālikī doctrine in the West thus took limited notice of custom and actual practice, it remains, nevertheless, true that Islamic law, including the Mālikī school, ignores custom as an official source of law. Custom (*ʿurf*, *ʿāda*) is recognized as a restrictive element in dispositions and contracts (below, pp. 126, 144, 155) and as a principle in interpreting declarations; it also serves occasionally as the basis of *istiḥsān* (below, pp. 152, 155, 157) or *istiṣlāḥ*. Besides, custom and customary law have co-existed with the ideal theory of Islamic law, while remaining outside its system, in the whole of the Islamic world. As a point of historical fact, custom contributed a great deal to the formation of Islamic law, but the classical theory of Islamic law was concerned not with its historical development but with the systematic foundation of the law, and the consensus of the scholars denied conscious recognition to custom.[1]

4. The legal doctrine as it had been elaborated by Shāfiʿī did not satisfy the uncompromising Traditionists. It was derived, it is true, from traditions from the Prophet, but with the help of a highly developed method of analogical and systematic reasoning. The Traditionists, on their part, preferred not to use any human reasoning in law and chose, as much as possible, to base every single item of their doctrine on a tradition from the Prophet, 'preferring a weak tradition to a strong analogy', as their opponents put it pointedly. Although the number of individual traditions went on increasing, they were still very far from covering every individual type of case, and the Traditionists were in fact unable to do without reasoning. But the reasoning which they used was of a cautelary nature, concerned with moral issues,

[1] Occasional references to the abstract principle that the Law changes with a change in custom or in conditions, or that it takes custom into account, should not be overrated in their import as far as positive law is concerned; they envisage either the kind of consideration which has been mentioned in the text or the confirmation of existing customs by Koran and *sunna*, &c.

and differing widely from the systematic legal thought which had been brought to technical perfection by Shāfiʿī and which the Traditionists disliked.[1] This becomes apparent in the oldest legal texts inspired by traditionist doctrine, which contain the teachings of the prominent traditionist Ibn Ḥanbal (d. 241/855) and were compiled by his disciples in the same way in which the disciples of Mālik had edited the teachings of their master. They mark the beginnings of the Ḥanbalī school which, it should be noted, never absorbed its parent movement as completely as the Ḥanafī and Mālikī schools absorbed theirs. For some time Ibn Ḥanbal and his adherents were regarded by the followers of the other schools not as real 'lawyers' but as mere specialists on traditions. Nevertheless, the Ḥanbalīs became one of the recognized schools, and although they were never numerous, they counted among their adherents a surprisingly high proportion of first-class scholars in all branches of Islamic learning. The Traditionists of the third century of the hijra do not seem to have shown much interest in legal theory except for the general idea of the authority of traditions, but when the scholars of the Ḥanbalī school, much later, came to elaborate a complete system of doctrine, they, too, had to adopt the 'classical' legal theory which was based not on traditions but on consensus, and they recognized analogical reasoning (but cf. above, p. 60). It was left to the great independent Ḥanbalī thinker Ibn Taymiyya (d. 728/1328), to whom we shall have to return later (below, p. 72), to reject the all-embracing function of the consensus of the scholars, and at the same time to affirm the necessity of analogical reasoning of an improved kind.

5. About the same time that the movement of the Traditionists gave rise to the Ḥanbalī school, Dāwūd ibn Khalaf (d. 270/884) founded the Ẓāhirī school of law, the only school which owed its existence to and took its name from a principle of legal theory. It was their principle to rely exclusively on the literal meaning (*ẓāhir*) of the Koran and the traditions from the Prophet and to reject as contrary to religion not only the free exercise of personal opinion which had been customary before Shāfiʿī, but even the use of analogical and systematic reasoning which Shāfiʿī had retained. For instance, the Koran forbids

[1] A certain interest in technical legal problems is, however, noticeable in the elaborate chapter headings of Bukhārī (on whom see below, pp. 226 f.).

interest, and many traditions relate that the Prophet forbade an excess in quantity and a delay in delivery in the barter or sale of gold, silver, wheat, barley, and dates. The other schools extended this prohibition by analogy beyond the five commodities mentioned, either to all goods that were sold by weight or measure as the Ḥanafīs do, or to all foodstuffs that could be preserved, and so on. The Ẓāhirīs, however, refused to extend the ruling to commodities other than those mentioned in traditions. In this particular case the Ẓāhirī school seems less exacting, but in others it appears much stricter than the other schools; it applies an abstract principle without regard for the consequences. It was not so much abstract thought which the Ẓāhirīs rejected as the technical methods of legal reasoning which they considered subjective and arbitrary. In the last resort they, too, were unable to do without deductions and conclusions from the proof texts, but they tried to represent their conclusions as implied in the texts themselves. Another axiom of the Ẓāhirīs was that the only legally valid *ijmāʿ* was the consensus of the Companions of the Prophet. It was this Ẓāhirī thesis that the Ḥanbalī Ibn Taymiyya later took over in a mitigated form.[1] The legal thought of the Ẓāhirīs, which we know mainly through the writings of Ibn Ḥazm (d. 456/1065), has certain points of resemblance with the doctrine of the Ḥanbalīs and of the Traditionists in general, but essentially it goes back to a literalist attitude which can be found among the Khārijīs, as far back as the first century of Islam, and in the theological movement of the Muʿtazila, in the second century.[2]

Ibn Tūmart (d. 534/1130), the founder of the religious and political movement of the Almohads in North Africa, held that religious law should be based on the Koran, the *sunna*, and the *ijmāʿ*, which last he restricted to the consensus of the Companions of the Prophet, but in establishing the *sunna* he gave the practice of the people of Medina preference over traditions, so that the practice of Medina became his decisive argument, and

[1] Cf. below, p. 72, on the rejection of *taḳlīd* which is common to them too.

[2] The Muʿtazila were extreme opponents of the Traditionists. They insisted on basing their system of religious doctrine exclusively on the Koran, and used the method of literal interpretation, together with systematic reasoning, in order to discredit traditions. Although they did not elaborate a system of legal doctrine of their own, they often discussed problems of legal theory and of positive law from their particular point of view.

Mālik's *Muwaṭṭa'* one of his authoritative books; he also admitted *ḳiyās* within very narrow limits. At the same time he was strongly opposed to the system of positive law (*furū'*) as it had been worked out in the Mālikī school and was exclusively studied under the Almoravids (below, p. 86) in North Africa in his time, and to the systems of the other schools of law as well. In particular, he repudiated the authority of the *mujtahids* (below, p. 71), the great masters of the established schools, against whom he asserted his own authority as 'infallible *imām*' (*imām ma'ṣūm*); he declared their disagreements inadmissible, and regarded the practice of *taḳlīd* with regard to them as ignorance. This legal theory of Ẓāhirī inspiration was paralleled, at least under the third Almohad ruler, Abū Ya'ḳūb Yūsuf (558/1163–580/1184), by an administration of justice on Ẓāhirī lines, closely supervised by the ruler himself, but the movement does not seem to have developed a technical legal literature of its own.

6. There were several other 'personal' schools of law, such as those of Abū Thawr (d. 240/854) and of Ṭabarī (d. 310/923), not to mention a number of more or less independent scholars, particularly in the early period. But since about 700 of the hijra or A.D. 1300 only four schools of law have survived in orthodox Islam, the Ḥanafī, the Mālikī, the Shāfi'ī, and the Ḥanbalī schools.

The Ḥanafī school is well represented in Iraq, its home country, and in Syria. It spread early to Afghanistan, the subcontinent of India,[1] and Turkish Central Asia. It became the favourite school of the Turkish Seljukid rulers and of the Ottoman Turks, and it enjoyed exclusive official recognition in the whole of the Ottoman Empire, a status which it has preserved in the *ḳāḍīs*' tribunals even of those former Ottoman provinces where the majority of the native population follows another school, such as Egypt.

The Mālikī school spread westwards from its first centres, Medina and Egypt, over practically the whole of North Africa and over Central and West Africa as far as it is Muslim; it was also predominant in medieval Muslim Spain where it had superseded the school of Awzā'ī at an early date. The Muslims of the eastern coastal territories of Arabia, as far as they

[1] Where there are minorities of Shiites.

are not Ḥanbalīs (Wahhābīs) or Sectarians (Ibāḍīs who represent the one surviving branch of the Khārijīs,[1] or Shiites), are Mālikīs too.

The Shāfiʿī school started from Cairo, where Shāfiʿī spent the last years of his life. It prevails in Lower Egypt, in Hijaz, in south Arabia as far as it is not Zaydī Shiite, and in most of East Africa as far as it is Muslim. There are a considerable number of Shāfiʿīs in Iraq. In the Middle Ages the school was well represented in Persia too, before that country became 'Twelver' Shiite. There are also Shāfiʿīs in some districts of central Asia and in some coastal regions of India. Finally, the Shāfiʿī school is followed by almost all Muslims in Indonesia, in Malaya, and in the rest of South-East Asia.

The Ḥanbalī school did not at once succeed, in the same way as the other surviving orthodox schools of law, in prevailing in any extensive territory, but it had followers in many parts of the Islamic world, including Persia before it became Shiite. Its two great centres were Baghdad, the home town of Ibn Ḥanbal, and, somewhat later, Damascus, where the activity of the Ḥanbalī reformer Ibn Taymiyya (d. 728/1328; cf. below, p. 72), whose teachings are, however, not typical of the Ḥanbalī school as a whole, is one of the highlights of a brilliant period in the history of the school.

From the eighth/fourteenth century onwards the Ḥanbalī school declined and seemed on the verge of extinction, when the puritanical movement of the Wahhābīs of the twelfth/eighteenth century, and especially the Wahhābī revival in the present century, gave it a new lease of life. The religious founder of this movement, Muḥammad ibn ʿAbd al-Wahhāb (d. 1201/1787), was influenced by the works of Ibn Taymiyya. Whereas the Ḥanbalī school had always been regarded by orthodox Islam as one of the legitimate schools of law, the intolerant attitude of the earlier Wahhābīs towards their fellow Muslims caused them for a long time to be suspected as heretics, and they have come to be generally considered orthodox only since their political successes in the present generation. The Ḥanbalī school is officially recognized in Saudi Arabia, and the inhabitants of Najd, the eastern half of that country, are practically all

[1] Other groups of Ibāḍīs are found in Algeria (the Mzab), Tunisia (the island of Djerba), and Libya (the Djebel Nefūsa).

Ḥanbalīs; there are also groups of them, of varying size, in Hijaz, in the principalities on the Persian Gulf, and in the subcontinent of India.

7. In their relationship to one another, the orthodox schools of law have, notwithstanding acts of fanaticism, particularly on the part of the populace and of the rulers in the high Middle Ages, generally practised mutual toleration. This attitude goes back to the time of the ancient schools of law which had accepted geographical differences of doctrine as natural. The maxim that disagreement (*ikhtilāf*) in the community of Muslims was a sign of divine indulgence had already been formulated in the second century of the hijra, though it was put into the mouth of the Prophet only much later. This mutual recognition was not incompatible, and did indeed go together with vigorous polemics and the insistence on uniformity of doctrine within each geographical school. The opportunity for disagreements on questions of principle arose only from the time of Shāfiʿī's systematic innovation onwards. In this particular case, the several schools arrived at a compromise, and generally speaking the consensus, which acted as the integrating principle of Islam, has succeeded in making innocuous those differences of opinion that it could not eliminate. The four schools, then, are equally covered by *ijmāʿ*, they are all deemed to translate into individual legal rules the will of Allah as expressed in the Koran and in the *sunna* of the Prophet; their alternative interpretations are all equally valid, their methods of reasoning equally legitimate; in short, they are equally orthodox. The same held true of the other schools of law as long as they existed; before about A.D. 1300, not only four but up to seven schools were regarded as the equally valid interpretations of the sacred Law; but once a school had ceased to exist, the consensus came into action again and it was no longer permissible to adhere to those schools which once had been on an absolutely equal footing with the others. This is a telling example of the way in which consensus acts in reducing differences progressively. The success of some schools and the extinction of others were brought about partly by the growing weight of consensus itself, and partly by external circumstances, such as the favour or disfavour of princes and a more or less favourable geographical situation for attracting students and making their doctrines known. Even within the

individual schools and in their relationship to one another consensus acts as an integrating principle. Not only will the recognized doctrine of each school,[1] through the elimination of stray opinions, become more and more uniform and settled down to the most minute details as time goes on; it also happens not infrequently that a school which, from its own premises, would have to regard an act as indifferent or permissible, prefers in fact to classify it as commendable or reprehensible, so as not to diverge too far from those other schools which regard it as obligatory or forbidden.

[1] The individual Muslim may join the school of his choice or change his allegiance without any formality; he may even, for the sake of convenience or for any reason of his own, with regard to any individual act or transaction adopt the doctrine of a school other than that which he habitually follows. This procedure is called *taḳlīd,* in a sense which is derived from the later meaning of this term. If he does this, however, he ought to follow the doctrine of the chosen school in all respects until the act's completion, and ought not to combine the doctrines of more than one school (this is called *talfīḳ*). The Modernists have disregarded this last rule.

10

THE 'CLOSING OF THE GATE OF INDEPENDENT REASONING' AND THE FURTHER DEVELOPMENT OF DOCTRINE

1. IN the first few decades of ʿAbbāsid rule, Islamic law, with the active help of the government, seemed at last on the point of dominating the practice. But it was denied this success; the administration of the state and religious law drew apart again, and the increasing rigidity of the *sharīʿa* itself prevented it from keeping pace with actual practice. This development calls for two parallel surveys: one of the later development of Islamic law in itself, and the other of the relation between theory and practice.

2. The early ʿAbbāsid period saw not only the rise of the schools of law but the end of the formative period of Islamic law, of which the formation of the schools was itself a symptom. The whole sphere of law had been permeated with the religious and ethical standards proper to Islam; Islamic law had been elaborated in detail; the principle of the infallibility of the consensus of the scholars worked in favour of a progressive narrowing and hardening of doctrine; and, a little later, the doctrine which denied the further possibility of 'independent reasoning' (*ijtihād*) sanctioned officially a state of things which had come to prevail in fact. To the earliest specialists in religious law, the search for legal rulings had been identical with the exercise of their personal opinion (*ijtihād al-raʾy*), of their own judgement on what the law ought to be. They based themselves on the rudimentary guidance available in the Koran and in the practice of the local community of Muslims, and applied the standards so gained to the administrative practice and customary law prevailing in Arabia and in the recently conquered territories. The questions as to who was a qualified scholar and who had the right to independent exercise of his own opinion

had not yet arisen. It was open to anyone sufficiently interested to embark upon this kind of speculation on religious law. This freedom to exercise one's own judgement independently was progressively restricted by several factors, such as the achievement of a local, and later of a general, consensus, the formation of groups or circles within the ancient schools of law, the subjection of unfettered opinion to the increasingly strict discipline of systematic reasoning, and last but not least the appearance of numerous traditions from the Prophet (and from his Companions), traditions which embodied in authoritative form what had originally been nothing more than private opinions. Thus the field of individual decision was continually narrowed down, but nevertheless, during the whole of the formative period of Islamic law, the first two and a half centuries of Islam (or until about the middle of the ninth century A.D.), there was never any question of denying to any scholar or specialist of the sacred Law the right to find his own solutions to legal problems. The sanction which kept ignoramuses at bay was simply general disapproval by the recognized specialists. It was only after the formative period of Islamic law had come to an end that the question of *ijtihād* and of who was qualified to exercise it was raised.

The first indications of an attitude which denied to contemporary scholars the same liberty of reasoning as their predecessors had enjoyed are noticeable in Shāfiʿī, and from about the middle of the third century of the hijra (ninth century A.D.) the idea began to gain ground that only the great scholars of the past who could not be equalled, and not the epigones, had the right to 'independent reasoning'. By this time the term *ijtihād* had been separated from its old connexion with the free use of personal opinion (*ra'y*), and restricted to the drawing of valid conclusions from the Koran, the *sunna* of the Prophet, and the consensus, by analogy (*ḳiyās*) or systematic reasoning. Shāfiʿī had been instrumental in bringing about this change, but he did not hesitate to affirm the duty of individual scholars to use their own judgement in drawing these conclusions. By the beginning of the fourth century of the hijra (about A.D. 900), however, the point had been reached when the scholars of all schools felt that all essential questions had been thoroughly discussed and finally settled, and a consensus gradually established itself to the effect that from that time onwards no one might be deemed to have the necessary qualifications for independent reasoning in law, and that all future activity would have to be confined to the explanation, application, and, at the most, interpretation of the doctrine as it had been laid down once and for all. This 'closing of the door of *ijtihād*', as it was called, amounted to the demand for *taḳlīd*, a term which had originally denoted the kind of reference to Companions of the Prophet that had been customary in the ancient schools of law, and which now came to mean the unquestioning acceptance of the doctrines of established schools and authorities. A person entitled to *ijtihād* is called *mujtahid*, and a person bound to practise *taḳlīd*, *muḳallid*.

Under the rule of *taḳlīd* as it was finally formulated, the doctrine must not be derived independently from Koran, *sunna*, and *ijmā'*, but it must be accepted as it is being taught by one of the recognized schools which are, of course, themselves covered by consensus. Again, the official doctrine of each school is to be found not in the works of the old masters, even though these had been qualified in the highest degree to exercise *ijtihād*, but in those works which the common opinion of the school recognizes as the authoritative exponents of its current teaching. These are now generally handbooks dating from the late medieval period, and subsequent works derive their authority from them. The recognized handbooks contain the latest stage of authoritative doctrine that has been reached in each school, but they are not in the nature of codes; Islamic law is not a corpus of legislation but the living result of legal science.

The transition from the régime of *ijtihād* to the régime of *taḳlīd* occurred, of course, only gradually, and this is reflected by the theory of several degrees of *ijtihād* in descending order; the very authors of the authoritative handbooks are generally denied even the lowest degree of *ijtihād* and are considered merely *muḳallids*. The final doctrine of a school may sometimes differ from, and in the nature of things inevitably goes far beyond, the opinions held by its founder or founders. The details of the growth of doctrine within each school, though amply documented by the existing works, still remain a subject for scholarly investigation. Even during the period of *taḳlīd*, Islamic law was not lacking in manifestations of original thought in which the several schools competed with and influenced one another. But this original thought could express itself freely in nothing more than abstract systematic constructions which affected neither the established decisions of positive law nor the classical doctrine of the *uṣūl al-fiḳh*. Most of these theoretical developments, too, which are quite independent of Koran, *sunna*, and *ijmāʿ*, and which represent the most technically juridical part of Islamic legal thought, still remain to be investigated.

3. The rule of *taḳlīd* did not impose itself without opposition, however. In later generations also there were scholars who held that there would always be a *mujtahid* in existence, or who were inclined to claim for themselves that they fulfilled the incredibly high demands which the theory had, by then, laid down as a qualification for *ijtihād*. But these claims, as far as positive law was concerned, remained theoretical, and none of the scholars who made them actually produced an independent interpretation of the *sharīʿa*. Other scholars did not so much claim *ijtihād* for themselves as reject the principle of *taḳlīd*. This was the case of Dāwūd ibn Khalaf, the founder of the Ẓāhirī school (d. 270/884; above, p. 63), of Ibn Tūmart, the founder of the Almohad movement (d. 524/1130; above, p. 64), and of the eminent Ḥanbalī, Ibn Taymiyya (d. 728/1328), followed by his disciple, Ibn Ḳayyim al-Jawziyya (d. 751/1350). These scholars considered it unauthorized and dangerous to follow blindly the authority of any man, excepting only the Prophet, in matters of religion and religious law. (This applies, of course, only to scholars and not to laymen.) The theoretical rejection of *taḳlīd* became one of the tenets of the Ẓāhirī school, though in practice it left its individual adherents hardly more freedom of doctrine than did the other schools.

Ibn Taymiyya did not explicitly advocate the reopening of the 'door of *ijtihād*', let alone claim *ijtihād* for himself; but as a consequence of his narrowly formulated idea of consensus he was able to reject *taḳlīd*, to interpret the Koran and the traditions from the Prophet afresh, and to arrive at novel conclusions concerning many of the institutions of Islamic law. The Wahhābīs, who constitute the great majority of the present followers of the Ḥanbalī school, have adopted, together with Ibn Taymiyya's theological doctrines, the whole of his legal theory, including his rejection of *taḳlīd*; but at the same time they have retained, unchanged, Ḥanbalī positive law as it had been developed in the school before Ibn Taymiyya, apparently without being troubled by the resulting inconsistency.

Parallel with and partly influenced by the Wahhābīs there arose, from the eighteenth century onwards, individuals and schools of thought who advocated a return to the pristine purity of Islam, such as the movement of the Salafiyya, who may conveniently be called Reformers, and others, from the last decades of the nineteenth century onwards, who laid the emphasis on renovating Islam by interpreting it in the light of modern conditions, and who may conveniently be called Modernists. Both tendencies, which to a certain degree overlap, reject traditional *taḳlīd*. Some Modernists, in particular, combine this with extravagant claims to a new, free *ijtihād* which goes far beyond any that was practised in the formative period of Islamic law; but neither type of movement has produced any results worth mentioning in the field of positive religious law.[1] The recent reshaping of institutions of the *sharīʿa* by secular legislation in several Islamic countries takes its inspiration from modern constitutional and social ideas rather than from the essentially traditional problem of the legitimacy of *ijtihād* and *taḳlīd*. This Islamic legislative modernism will be discussed below, Chapter 15.

4. Whatever the theory might say on *ijtihād* and *taḳlīd*, the activity of the later scholars, after the 'closing of the door of *ijtihād*', was no less creative, within the limits set to it by the nature of the *sharīʿa*, than that of their predecessors. New sets of facts constantly arose in life, and they had to be mastered and moulded with the traditional tools provided by legal science. This activity was carried out by the *muftīs*. A *muftī* is a specialist on law who can give an authoritative opinion on points of doctrine; his considered legal opinion is called *fatwā*. The earliest specialists, such as Ibrāhīm Nakhaʿī, were essentially *muftīs*; their main function was to advise interested members of the public on what was, in their opinion, the correct course of action from the point of view of the sacred Law. This cautelary and advisory element is still clearly discernible in the work of Mālik. From the beginning, the specialists had formed groups of like-minded amateurs, and in the time of Shāfiʿī a class of

[1] The operative words here are religious law, as opposed to secular legislation.

professionals had emerged. Shāfiʿī informs us that the knowledge of the details of religious law was beyond the reach of the general public, and was not even found among all specialists. The members of the public had been in need of specialist guidance from the very beginnings of Islamic law, and this need grew stronger as the law became more technical and its presentation more scholastic. The practical importance of the sacred Law for the pious Muslim is much greater than that of any secular legal system for the ordinary law-abiding citizen. It comes into play not only when he has to go to the courts; it tells him what his religious duties are, what makes him ritually clean or unclean, what he may eat or drink, how to dress and how to treat his family, and generally what he may with good conscience regard as lawful acts and possessions. There was thus a constant need of specialist guidance on these questions.

From the start the function of the *muftī* was essentially private; his authority was based on his reputation as a scholar, his opinion had no official sanction, and a layman might resort to any scholar he knew and in whom he had confidence. In order, however, to provide the general public, and also government officials, with authoritative opinions on problems of religious law, Islamic governments from some date after the final establishment of the schools of law have appointed scholars of recognized standing as official *muftīs*. (The chief *muftī* of a country is often called *Shaykh al-Islām*.) But their appointment by the government does not add to the intrinsic value of their opinions, they have no monopoly of giving *fatwās*, and the practice of consulting private scholars of high reputation has never ceased. A *ḳāḍī*, too, may consult a scholar when he is in doubt, and official *muftīs* are often attached to *ḳāḍīs*' tribunals. Parties to a lawsuit before the *ḳāḍī* will arm themselves with *fatwās* as authoritative as possible, though the *ḳāḍī* is not bound to accept any of them.

The doctrinal development of Islamic law owes much to the activity of the *muftīs*. Their *fatwās* were often collected in separate works, which are of considerable historical interest because they show us the most urgent problems which arose from the practice in a certain place and at a certain time. As soon as a decision reached by a *muftī* on a new kind of problem had been recognized by the common opinion of the scholars as correct, it was incorporated in the handbooks of the school. On the other hand, the judgments given by the *ḳāḍīs* had no comparable influence on the development of Islamic law after the end of its formative period in early 'Abbāsid times, essential though the contribution of the earliest *ḳāḍīs* had been to laying its foundations.

5. It will have become clear from the preceding paragraphs that Islamic law, which until the early 'Abbāsid period had been adaptable and growing, from then onwards became increasingly rigid and set in its final mould. This essential rigidity of Islamic law helped it to maintain its stability over the centuries which saw the decay of the political institutions of Islam. It was not altogether immutable, but the changes which did take place were concerned more with legal theory and the systematic superstructure than with positive law. Taken as a whole, Islamic law reflects and fits the social and economic conditions of the early 'Abbāsid period, but has grown more and more out of touch with later developments of state and society.

11

THEORY AND PRACTICE

1. WE can distinguish three different kinds of legal subject-matter, leaving aside the cult and ritual and other purely religious duties, according to the degree to which the ideal theory of the *sharīʿa* succeeded in imposing itself on the practice. Its hold was strongest on the law of family (marriage, divorce, maintenance, &c.), of inheritance, and of pious foundations (*wakf*); it was weakest, and in some respects even non-existent, on penal law, taxation, constitutional law, and the law of war; and the law of contracts and obligations stands in the middle.

We have seen that the political authorities took over the administration of criminal justice at an early period. As regards taxation, only lip-service was paid to the *sharīʿa* and its modest demands, and Islamic law regarded all other taxes as illegal impositions.[1] As regards constitutional law, the state as envisaged by the theory of Islamic law is a fiction which has never existed in reality, and the law of war was deduced from a one-sided picture of the wars of conquest, and was hardly ever applied in practice.

On the other hand, the institutions concerning the *statut personnel* (i.e. marriage, divorce, and family relationships), inheritance, and *wakf*, have always been, in the conscience of the Muslims, more closely connected with religion than other legal matters, and therefore generally ruled by Islamic law. This religious character of the law of family and inheritance is not a coincidence; the greater part of Koranic legislation is concerned with these matters. Nevertheless, we find that even in the field of marriage, divorce, and family relationships actual practice has been strong enough to prevail over the spirit, and in certain cases over the letter, of religious law, either de-

[1] The technical term for this kind of tax is *maks*, which meant 'market-dues' in pre-Islamic Arabia, but they were not recognized in Islamic law. They existed in south Arabia too; cf. A. F. L. Beeston, *Qahtan*, i (below, p. 219).

pressing the position of women or raising it. In addition, numerous groups of converts to Islam have retained their original law of inheritance, mostly to the disadvantage of women. Special rules concerning real estate, of which only a few rudiments exist in the *sharīʿa*, have been elaborated in detail, on the bases provided by Islamic law, and they vary according to place and time; these complements to the *sharīʿa* often diverge from strict theory. The institution of *waḳf*, becoming an important part of the law of real estate, has been popular in most, though not all, Islamic countries; here, too, practice has often led to developments which did not agree with strict Islamic law, for instance, in the early Ottoman period. Customary penal law, often incorporating the principle of monetary fines and administered by village, tribal, and similar authorities rather than by governments, forms part of the customary law of numerous groups of Muslims; this kind of customary law was even codified in writing.

The customary law of the contemporary Bedouins deserves special mention because, though influenced by Islamic law, it goes back in the last resort to the customary law of the pre-Islamic Arabs and enables us to control the information which literary sources give us on this last. Among the tribesmen of Yemen and of south Arabia in general this tribal customary law is called, *a potiori*, *ḥukm* (*aḥkām*) *al-manʿ*, or *al-manʿa*, 'provisions of protection', 'sanctions', and in Dhofar and Oman, *ḥukm al-ḥawz* (from *ḥawz*, the tribal law-man), and it is consciously and openly opposed to the *sharīʿa*. Religiously inclined persons therefore call it *ḥukm al-ṭāghūt*, 'provisions of the idol, or idols', after sura iv. 60. Here, too, there exist written codifications of this customary law, as well as hostile references to it in the writings of the representatives of the *sharīʿa*.

In the vast field of the law of contracts and obligations the *sharīʿa* had to resign an ever-increasing sphere to practice and custom. The theory of the sacred Law did not fail to influence practice and custom considerably, albeit in varying degrees at different places and times, but it never succeeded in imposing itself on them completely. This failure resulted chiefly from the fact that the ideal theory, being essentially retrospective, was from the early ʿAbbāsid period onwards unable to keep pace with the ever-changing demands of society and commerce.

It may be said that, as far as popular conscience is concerned, the sacred Law is observed, even in the field of purely religious duties, to the extent to which custom demands it, so that essential duties are often neglected, non-essential practices faithfully observed, and even formalities which are unknown to the *sharīʿa* imposed by custom. In the field of the law of property, for instance, the right of pre-emption was eagerly adopted by popular custom in numerous Islamic countries, although Islamic law itself approves its exclusion by the use of evasions (*ḥiyal*).

2. The law of contracts and obligations was ruled by a customary law which respected the main principles and institutions of the *sharīʿa*, but showed a greater flexibility and adaptability, supplementing it in many respects.[1] It developed, for instance, the sale of real property with the right of redemption (*bayʿ al-wafāʾ*, *bayʿ al-ʿuhda*); this aims at avoiding the irrevocable alienation of land but is not admissible in strict Islamic law either as a sale or as a pledge. It also used the *suftaja* and *ḥawāla* as a bill of exchange beyond the limits set to it by Islamic law; this made real banking activities, not only by Jewish bankers but by Muslim merchants, possible in the Middle Ages. Several institutions of this customary commercial law were transmitted to medieval Europe through the intermediary of the law merchant, the customary law of international trade, as is attested by medieval Latin *mohatra*, from Arabic *mukhāṭara*, a term for the evasion of the prohibition of interest by means of a double sale (see the following section), by the French term *aval*, from Arabic *ḥawāla*, for the endorsement on a bill of exchange, by the term *cheque*, from Arabic *ṣakk*, 'written document', and by the term *sensalis* (*sensale*, *Sensal*), from Arabic *simsār*, 'broker'.

3. The customary commercial law was brought into agreement with the theory of the *sharīʿa* by the *ḥiyal* (sing. *ḥīla*) or 'legal devices', which were often legal fictions. The *ḥiyal*, which are not confined to commercial law but cover other subject-matters as well, can be described, in short, as the use of legal means for extra-legal ends, ends that could not, whether they themselves were legal or illegal, be achieved directly with the means provided by the *sharīʿa*. The 'legal devices' enabled

[1] Islamic law does not recognize the liberty of contract (below, p. 144).

persons who would otherwise, under the pressure of circumstances, have had to act against the provisions of the sacred Law, to arrive at the desired result while actually conforming to the letter of the law. For instance, the Koran prohibits interest, and this religious prohibition was strong enough to make popular opinion unwilling to transgress it openly and directly, while at the same time there was an imperative demand for the giving and taking of interest in commercial life. In order to satisfy this need, and at the same time to observe the letter of the religious prohibition, a number of devices were developed. One consisted of giving real property as a security for the debt and allowing the creditor to use it, so that its use represented the interest; this transaction forms a close parallel to the sale with the right of redemption (above, section 2). Another, very popular, device consisted of a double sale (*bay'atān fī bay'a*), of which there are many variants. For instance, the (prospective) debtor sells to the (prospective) creditor a slave for cash, and immediately buys the slave back from him for a greater amount payable at a future date; this amounts to a loan with the slave as security, and the difference between the two prices represents the interest; the transaction is called *mukhāṭara* (above, section 2) or, more commonly, *'īna*. Euphemistically, it is also called *mu'āmala*, 'transaction', and the money-lender *tājir*, 'trader', because traders also acted as money-lenders. This custom prevailed in Medina as early as in the time of Mālik. There were hundreds of these devices, extending over all fields of the law of contracts and obligations, many of them highly technical, but all with a scrupulous regard for the letter of the law.[1] The acknowledgement plays a very important part in the construction of numerous *ḥiyal*, because it creates an abstract debt and is therefore particularly suitable for bringing about legal fictions. (cf. below, p. 151).

Evasions and other devices are not unknown to other legal systems, including Jewish and Canon law, and legal fictions in particular played a considerable part in Roman law and elsewhere. But their function in Roman law was to provide the

[1] A special branch of *ḥiyal* consists of evasions of obligations undertaken under oath or dispositions made dependent on the fulfilment of a condition (below, pp. 117, 159); they take advantage of the tendency of Islamic law to interpret declarations restrictively in this case, so that there are numerous possibilities of avoiding the incidence of the undesirable obligation or disposition.

legal framework for new requirements of current practice with the minimum of innovation; in Islamic law it was to circumvent positive enactments.[1] The giving and taking of interest corresponded indeed with a requirement of commercial practice, but a requirement that the Koran, and Islamic law after it, had explicitly and positively banned. The legal devices represented a *modus vivendi* between theory and practice: the maximum that custom could concede, and the minimum (that is to say, formal acknowledgement) that the theory had to demand. The recognition of the validity of the *ḥiyal* by the theory of Islamic law was facilitated, on the one hand, by the heteronomous and irrational side of the *sharīʿa*, which called for observance of the letter rather than of the spirit (cf. below, p. 204), and, on the other, by the principle that the law, and the *ḳāḍī* in his judgment, are concerned with the outward aspect of things only and not with questions of conscience and hidden motives (cf. below, p. 123). The first and simplest *ḥiyal* were presumably thought out by the interested parties who felt the need for them, the merchants in particular, but it was quite beyond them to invent and apply the more complicated ones; they had to have recourse to specialists in religious law, and these last did not hesitate to supply the need. Once the system of religious law had been elaborated, the religious zeal of the first specialists was gradually replaced and superseded by the not less sincere, not less convinced, but more technical, more scholastic, interest of professionals who took pride in inventing and perfecting small masterpieces of legal construction. The inventors of *ḥiyal* had to calculate the chances of legal validity to a nicety if the *ḳāḍī*, who was bound to the sacred Law, was not to upset the real effects of the business transaction which their customers, the merchants, had in mind, effects which depended upon the validity of every single element in an often complicated series of formal transactions. The activity of the authors of *ḥiyal*, catering for the practice, shares this advisory and cautelary character with that of the early specialists who first elaborated the theory of Islamic law. The early specialists warned their contemporaries against acts incompatible with the Islamic way of life; the authors of *ḥiyal* helped

[1] There are also fictitious actions, brought by agreement of the parties in order to have a claim or right confirmed by the *ḳāḍī*; they are not necessarily connected with *ḥiyal* but are used, for instance, in order to have the validity of a *waḳf* confirmed

theirs not to conclude contracts which would be considered invalid by the fully developed system of Islamic law.

There are certain differences of degree in the attitudes of the several schools of law towards the *ḥiyal*. The Ḥanafīs are the most favourably inclined. Abū Yūsuf and Shaybānī composed treatises dealing with *ḥiyal*, and the treatise of Shaybānī has survived. Another such book, which is attributed to Khaṣṣāf (d. 261/874) but was presumably written in Iraq in the fourth century of the hijra (tenth century A.D.), enables us to discern, through the thin veil of its legally unobjectionable forms, the realities of practice in that place and time. Shāfiʿī (and the first few generations of his school after him) regarded the *ḥiyal* as forbidden or reprehensible, although he had to recognize them as legally valid; but the success of the *ḥiyal* literature of the Ḥanafīs brought about, from the fourth century of the hijra onwards, both the production of books of *ḥiyal* by Shāfiʿī authors, of which that of Ḳazwīnī (d. 440/1048 or soon afterwards) has survived, and the distinction of *ḥiyal* which are allowed and which form the great majority, from those which are reprehensible or forbidden. The Mālikīs seem to have paid less attention to the subject, but the doctrine of the school admits some *ḥiyal* and rejects others. The Traditionists, in keeping with their general approach to questions of religious law, rejected *ḥiyal*, and the section on *ḥiyal* in Bukhārī's *Ṣaḥīḥ* (below, p. 226) contains a sustained polemic against them, with quotations from otherwise unknown early treatises on *ḥiyal*. The Ḥanbalī scholar Ibn Taymiyya, in a special work of his, attacked and declared invalid the *ḥiyal* in general and the so-called *taḥlīl* ('making lawful') in particular; this last aims at removing the impediment to remarriage between the former husband and wife after a triple repudiation by arranging for the marriage of the woman to another husband with the understanding that this marriage would be immediately dissolved after (real or pretended) consummation. Ibn Taymiyya's disciple, Ibn Ḳayyim al-Jawziyya, however, distinguished *ḥiyal* which were lawful, by which a lawful end was to be achieved by lawful means, from those which were forbidden, and which he declared invalid; the first group comprises numerous devices in the field of commercial law. The Ḥanafīs, on their part, whilst they state that *ḥiyal* which cause prejudice to another are forbidden, and are loth to suggest *ḥiyal* which comprise acts that are in themselves reprehensible, let alone forbidden, are not really concerned with the moral evaluation of *ḥiyal* in detail, and they take their being legally valid for granted. According to them many *ḥiyal* are not even reprehensible, for instance those which aim at evading the incidence of the right of pre-emption; and the device of *taḥlīl* has been widely practised, by Ḥanafīs, Mālikīs, and Shāfi'īs, down to the present generation.

4. A further feature of customary commercial law, and of Islamic law as applied in practice as a whole, was its reliance on written documents.[1] We have seen that Islamic law, at a very early period, diverged both from an explicit ruling of the Koran and from current practice by denying the validity of documentary evidence and restricting legal proof to the oral evidence of witnesses. Written documents, however, proved so indispensable in practice that, notwithstanding their persistent neglect in theory, they remained in constant use, became a normal accompaniment of every transaction of importance, and gave rise to a highly developed branch of practical law with a voluminous literature of its own, the beginnings of which go back to the second century of the hijra (eighth century A.D.). Theory continued to reason as if there were no documents but only the oral testimony of witnesses, possibly helped by private records of their own; practice continued to act as if the documents were almost essential and the 'witnessing' only a formality to make them fully valid; and the professional witnesses came, in fact, to exercise the functions of notaries public. Again, the authors of the practical books of legal formularies were themselves specialists in religious law; they and the professional witnesses themselves acted as legal advisers to the parties concerned and provided forms of documents for all possible needs of the practice and safeguards against all possible contingencies, documents which had only to be 'witnessed' in order to become legally valid. Finally, even strict theory deigned to recognize the existence of written documents and to admit them as valid evidence once they had been attested by qualified witnesses, the Mālikīs to the widest extent, the Ḥanafīs and the

[1] Documents are called *ṣakk*, pl. *ṣukūk*, or *wathīḳa*, pl. *wathā'iḳ*, or *dhukr*, pl. *adhkār*, also *dhukr ḥaḳḳ*, pl. *adhkār ḥuḳūḳ*. The branch of legal science which deals with documents is called the science of *shurūṭ* (pl. of *sharṭ*), 'stipulations'.

Ḥanbalīs with some hesitation, whereas the Shāfiʿīs continued to regard them strictly as accessories; but the actual use of written documents was equally extensive among the adherents of all schools. In the modern period, during which the application of Islamic law and the organization of its tribunals have been increasingly modified by independent Islamic governments, written documents have been generally admitted as valid proof, and sometimes the competence of the *ḳāḍīs* has even been restricted to cases in which documentary evidence is produced.

Written documents often formed an essential element of *ḥiyal*. The more complicated *ḥiyal* normally consisted of several transactions between the parties concerned, each of which was perfectly legal in itself, and the combined effect of which produced the desired result. Each transaction was, as a matter of course, recorded and attested in a separate document. Taken in isolation, a document recording a single transaction or an acknowledgement made by one of the parties might be used by the other party to its exclusive advantage and for a purpose contrary to the aim of the whole of the agreement. In order to prevent this happening, the official documents were deposited in the hands of a trustworthy person (*thiḳa*) or intermediary, together with an unofficial covering document which set out the real relationship of the parties to each other and the real purport of their agreement. (This kind of document is technically called *muwāḍaʿa*, 'understanding'.) The intermediary, then, acting on the contents of the covering document, handed to each party only those papers which they were entitled to use at any given stage, and prevented an unauthorized use of any document by producing, if necessary, the document of a compensating transaction or acknowledgement which had been prepared and attested beforehand for this very purpose.

The whole phenomenon of customary commercial law is of considerable importance for the legal sociology of Islam in the Middle Ages.

5. The works on *ḥiyal* and the works on *shurūṭ* belong to a well-defined branch of Ḥanafī legal literature, together with works on *waḳf*, on legacies, on the minutes (*maḥḍar*) and written judgments (*sijill*) of the *ḳāḍīs* and the duties of the *ḳāḍī* (*adab al-ḳāḍī*) in general, and, at a certain distance, on maintenance. All these subjects are of importance for the application of Islamic

law in practice, and they tend to appear in combination among the works of a series of highly esteemed Ḥanafī authors over several centuries.

6. We must think of the relationship of theory and practice in Islamic law not as a clear division of spheres but as one of interaction and mutual interference, a relationship in which the theory showed a great assimilating power, the power of imposing its spiritual ascendancy even when it could not control the material conditions. This asserted itself not only in the *ḥiyal* and in the *shurūṭ*, but in the later Mālikī *ʿamal* (above, p. 61 f.), in the institutions of the *naẓar fil-maẓālim* and of the *muḥtasib*, in the Ottoman *ḳānūn-nāme*s, and in numerous other ways. Also, Islamic governments in the past have always appointed *ḳāḍī*s and provided them, in principle, with the necessary means of execution; and the functions of the *ḳāḍī* extended far beyond the mere administration of justice.

Thus a balance established itself in most Islamic countries between legal theory and legal practice; an uneasy truce between the *ʿulamāʾ* ('scholars'), the specialists in religious law, and the political authorities came into being. The *ʿulamāʾ* themselves were conscious of this; they expressed their conviction of the ever-increasing corruption of contemporary conditions (*fasād al-zamān*), and, in the absence of a dispensing authority, formulated the doctrine that necessity (*ḍarūra*) dispensed Muslims from observing the strict rules of the Law. Whereas traditional Islamic governments were unable to change it by legislation, the scholars half sanctioned the regulations which the rulers in fact enacted, by insisting on the duty, already emphasized in the Koran (sura iv. 59, 83, and elsewhere), of obedience to the established authorities. As long as the sacred Law received formal recognition as a religious ideal, it did not insist on being fully applied in practice.

The *sharīʿa* could not abandon its claim to exclusive theoretical validity and recognize the existence of an autonomous customary law; its representatives, the *ʿulamāʾ*, were the only qualified interpreters of the religious conscience of the Muslims. It possessed an enormous prestige and an unquestioned ascendancy, so much so that the idea that law must be ruled by religion has remained an essential assumption of the Modernists, who otherwise do not hesitate to interfere deeply with the traditional doctrine of Islamic law. But the laws which rule the lives of the Muslim peoples have never been coextensive with pure Islamic law, although this last has always formed an important ingredient of them.[1] These conditions have prevailed in all parts of the Islamic world since the early Middle Ages.

[1] Hostile references to practice in works of Islamic law are an important source of information on it for the Middle Ages.

12

PURIST REACTIONS

1. THE general and normal conditions described in the preceding chapter were occasionally disturbed by violent religious reform movements, such as that of the Almoravids in north-west Africa and Spain from about 447/1055 to 541/1146, that of the Fulānīs or Fulbe in West Africa, including Northern Nigeria, in the nineteenth century, and that of the Wahhābīs in Arabia in the nineteenth and again in the present century. The Almoravids and the Fulānīs were Mālikīs, the Wahhābīs, as mentioned before, Ḥanbalīs. All these movements made it their aim, in the states which they set up, to enforce Islamic law exclusively, to abolish the double system of administration of justice, and to outlaw customary and administrative law. In the past the effects of these religious reform movements on the observance of the *sharīʿa* have usually tended to wear off, until presently a new equilibrium between theory and practice has established itself.

2. A British colonial protectorate was established over the Fulānī sultanate and emirates of Northern Nigeria in 1900, at a time when Islamic law in that region was still near its highest degree of practical application. Custom, if not entirely eradicated, had been pushed into the background, and the only existing tribunals were those of the *ḳāḍīs* who were competent in all matters, including penal law. Only the customary land law remained valid and was enforced by the councils of the sultan and of the emirs, and the occasional exercise of *siyāsa* by the rulers, parallel with the application of the *sharīʿa* by the *ḳāḍī*, was taken for granted. Its natural respect for Islamic religion caused the British administration to identify 'native law and custom', the maintenance of which had been promised when the protectorate was established, with the pure theory of Mālikī Islamic law, as far as the Muslims of Northern Nigeria

were concerned.[1] The colonial administrators were also inclined to prefer a formal and explicit doctrine, such as is provided by Islamic law, to changeable and badly defined customs. The *'ulamā'*, from whom the *ḳāḍīs* were recruited, did not fail to take advantage of these favourable conditions, the rulers themselves came to repudiate the exercise of *siyāsa*, and in the later years of the British protectorate, in the absence of any desire on the part of the British administration to interfere with the law applicable to the Muslim populations, pure Islamic law acquired an even higher degree of practical application than before. This has often been the effect of a colonial administration.

3. Ḥanbalī Islamic law is to its full extent applied in Saudi Arabia by *ḳāḍīs*' tribunals (and in Najd, the eastern part of the country, directly by the governors, too). King Ibn Saud in 1346/1927 conceived the project of having a code of Islamic law elaborated; this code was to be based not on the Ḥanbalī doctrine only, but following the thought of Ibn Taymiyya, each particular norm was to be taken from that school whose doctrine on the point in question appeared to be most solidly based on Koran and *sunna*. Under the protests of the Ḥanbalī *'ulamā'*, however, he had to abandon the project, and Saudi Arabian regulations of 1347/1928 and 1349/1930 make it obligatory on the *ḳāḍīs* to apply the recognized texts of the Ḥanbalī school. Beside the *sharī'a* (according to Ḥanbalī doctrine) stand the administrative regulations of the government which, in fact, have the force of law although, in order to avoid the appearance of a secular legislation, they are called *niẓām* 'ordinance', or *marsūm* 'decree', and not *ḳānūn* which has become the technical term for the secular laws of the Islamic countries in the Near East. An Ordinance on Commerce was promulgated in 1350/1931, and commercial courts were set up in Jeddah, Yanbu', and Dammam, but they were abolished again and their functions taken over by the Ministry of Commerce established in 1954.[2] The penal law of the *sharī'a* is not formally but materially affected by the ordinances on Work and Workmen, on Motor Vehicles, and others. Under the first, claims of

[1] Slavery and the *ḥadd* punishments of mutilation, stoning, and crucifixion were, however, abolished, but not the punishment of flogging, which used to be carried out in a very mild way in Northern Nigeria.

[2] The Ordinance on Commerce is based on the Ottoman Code of Commerce, but all references to interest have been expunged.

'compensation' for accidents at work are decided by the Ministry of Finance, whilst the *ḳāḍī* declares himself incompetent to deal with these matters but gives judgment on questions of blood-money concurrently; under the second, the police investigate and decide on the guilt, if any, of the driver, and the *ḳāḍī* then allots the blood-money on the basis of their decision; numerous ordinances provide for monetary fines and imprisonment as punishments which, should the occasion arise, are imposed together with those prescribed by the *sharīʿa*. Finally, in 1373/1954, a Court of Complaints (*dīwān al-maẓālim*) was established.

In Yemen, Imām Yaḥyā tried to enforce pure Islamic law (according to the Zaydī Shiite doctrine), against the opposition of the people.

4. The example of Afghanistan shows that purism in the sphere left to Islamic law may exist together with the restriction of its application in practice by customary law. Tribal customs prevail in that country, and the *sharīʿa* (according to Ḥanafī doctrine) is subsidiary to them. But when King Amanullah in 1924 tried to introduce a Penal Code which, too, out of respect to the *sharīʿa* was called *niẓām-nāme* and not *ḳānūn*, and the innovations of which amounted to nothing more than the introduction of monetary fines and the restriction of the discretion of the *ḳāḍī* with regard to the *taʿzīr* by introducing a graded system of punishments, he was forced by the *ʿulamāʾ* to replace it by an amended version which amounted to its repeal.

13

ISLAMIC LAW IN THE OTTOMAN EMPIRE

1. Of essentially the same kind, though sensibly different in their effects, were the efforts of established Islamic states (later than the early ʿAbbāsid period) to subject the actual practice to the rule of the sacred Law. The most remarkable and, for a time, the most successful of these efforts was made in the Ottoman Empire.

The Islamization of the Ottoman Turks was an event of far-reaching importance in the history of Islamic law. Having entered Islam recently, and being free from the restraints of history, they took Islam more seriously than those peoples who had professed it for a long time. At the beginning, mystical and antinomian tendencies prevailed among them, customary and administrative law predominated, and institutions incompatible with the *sharīʿa* were taken for granted, such as the *devshirme*, the periodical forced levy of children from the Christian subjects for recruitment into the standing army and their forced conversion to Islam, fiscal measures such as a tax on brides (*ʿarūs resmi*), and the system of land tenure (see below). These particular features, and others, survived into the following period.

2. Early in the sixteenth century, however, Islamic orthodoxy, represented by the *ʿulamā*ʾ, the Islamic scholars, and in particular the specialists in Islamic law, emerged victorious. The Ottoman sultans, particularly Selim I (1512–20) and Süleymān I (1520–60), and their immediate successors, were more serious than the first ʿAbbāsids in their desire to be 'pious' rulers, and they endowed Islamic law, in its Ḥanafī form, which had always been the favourite of the Turkish peoples, with the highest degree of actual efficiency which it had ever possessed in a society of high material civilization since early ʿAbbāsid times. They based the whole administration of justice on the *sharīʿa*, they even made the smallest unit of their civil administration coextensive

with the *kaḍā'*, the district in which a *kāḍī* was competent, and put the local chief of police, the *subashî*, under the orders of the *kāḍī*; they provided for a uniform training of scholars and *kāḍīs* and organized them in a graded professional hierarchy; and they endowed the Grand Mufti, the *muftī* of Istanbul who was at the head of the hierarchy and bore the title of *Shaykh al-Islām*, with a special authority. He became one of the highest officers of state, and he was charged with assuring the observance of the sacred Law in the state and with supervising the activity of the *kāḍīs*. On all important occasions he was consulted on whether the action envisaged by the government was in keeping with the *sharī'a*. The office reached the zenith of its power under Süleymān I, particularly in the person of Abul-Su'ūd (Grand Mufti from 952/1545 until his death in 982/1574).

Abul-Su'ūd succeeded in bringing the *kānūn*, the administrative law of the Ottoman Empire, into agreement with the *sharī'a*. Supported by Süleymān, he completed and consolidated a development which had already started under Meḥemmed II (see below, section 3). Already before his appointment as Grand Mufti he had begun, on the orders of the sultan, to revise the land law of the European provinces and to apply to it the principles of the *sharī'a*. The uncompromising application of these principles, however, proved impracticable, and Abul-Su'ūd finally arrived at a workable compromise between the Islamic concept of *wakf* and the Ottoman fiscal institution of *tapu*. On the other hand, Abul-Su'ūd reformulated, consciously and in sweeping terms, the principle that the competence of the *kāḍīs* derived from their appointment by the sultan and that they were therefore bound to follow his directives in applying the *sharī'a*. These directives, which were thirty-two in number in the time of Abul-Su'ūd, took two forms: instructing the *kāḍīs* to follow one of several opinions admitted by the Ḥanafī authorities, and withdrawing certain matters from their competence. *Kāḍīs* had always been appointed each for a certain circumscription, or even to hear, within their respective circumscriptions, certain classes of causes only (for instance, causes concerning marriage or succession). It was therefore nothing unprecedented when Sultan Süleymān in 1550, at the suggestion of Abul-Su'ūd and in order to secure uniformity of judgments (cf. below, p. 138), instructed the *kāḍīs* not to hear actions which without a valid grond had not been brought for more than fifteen years. This introduced, in fact, a period of prescription, or statute of limitation, of fifteen years, which became typical of Islamic law as applied in the Ottoman Empire. The restriction of the competence of the *ḳāḍīs* became a favourite device of the modernists for introducing material changes into Islamic law (see below, p. 106), although this idea was far from the minds of the Ottomans.

3. The Ottoman sultans distinguished themselves not only by their zeal for the sacred Law but by their legislative activity; Süleymān I himself bears the appellation of *Ḳānūnī* (which refers, it is true, not exclusively to his legislative activity but to his care for an efficient administration in general). In perfect good faith they enacted *ḳānūn*s or *ḳānūn-nāme*s which were real laws, convinced that in doing so they neither abrogated nor contradicted the sacred Law but supplemented it by religiously indifferent regulations.[1] In fact the very first of these Ottoman *ḳānūn-nāme*s, that of Sultan Meḥemmed II (1451–81), repeatedly refers to Islamic law and freely uses its concepts. It treats, among other matters (office of the Grand Vizier, court ceremonial, financial ordinances), of penal law; it presupposes that the *ḥadd* punishments are obsolete and replaces them by *ta'zīr*, i.e. beating, and/or monetary fines which are graded according to the economic position of the culprit. In fact, these provisions go beyond merely supplementing the *sharī'a* by the *siyāsa* of the ruler, and amount to superseding it. The so-called *ḳānūn-nāme* of Süleymān I, which in its major parts seems to have been compiled previously under Bāyezīd II (1481–1512), shows a considerable development along these lines; it treats in greater detail of military fiefs, of the position of non-Muslim subjects, of matters of police and penal law, of land law, and of the law of war. In the field of penal law, a considerable place is given to bodily punishments, such as emasculating the seducer, hanging incendiaries and certain thieves and housebreakers, cutting off the hands of forgers and coiners 'where it is customary', and, as an alternative to fines, of thieves (which

[1] The Ottomans were not the first to introduce either the technique or the term, both of which are attested for the states of the Mamlūks in Syria and Egypt and of the Aḳ-Ḳoyunlu in northern Mesopotamia before their time, but they developed the practice considerably.

revives this particular *ḥadd* punishment), and the use of torture when there is circumstantial evidence of theft or receiving.

The supervision of public morals was the responsibility of the *ḳāḍī*s; numerous instructions concerning these matters were issued to them, and they had them carried out by the *subashî* or chief of police, whilst the *muḥtasib* supervised trade and industry on their behalf.

4. The legal order in the Ottoman Empire in the sixteenth century was far superior to that prevailing in contemporary Europe, if only because of its uniformity, but the subsequent decadence of the empire could not fail to affect it adversely. The efforts at reform which had started with energy under Maḥmūd II (1808–39) led unavoidably to a conflict with the *sharīʿa*; in the *Khaṭṭ-i sherīf* of Gülhane (end of 1839), enacted by Maḥmūd's successor ʿAbdülmejīd (1839–61), the Muslims and non-Muslims were for the first time uniformly called 'subjects'. In the following decade there began the legislation of the *Tanẓīmāt* after European models; its first important manifestation was the Code of Commerce (1850), and one legal subject-matter after another was withdrawn from the orbit of Islamic law.

The *sharīʿa* was, however, not officially abandoned as yet; on the contrary, Ottoman Turkey is the only Islamic country to have tried to codify and to have enacted as a law of the state parts of the religious law of Islam. This is the *Mejelle* (with its full title *Mejelle-i aḥkām-i ʿadliyye*; in modern Turkish orthography *Mecelle*), which covers the law of contracts and obligations and of civil procedure in the form of articles, and was promulgated as the Ottoman Civil Code in 1877. According to the explanatory memorandum, its purpose was to provide the recently created (secular) tribunals with an authoritative statement of the doctrine of Islamic law and to obviate (without forbidding it) recourse to the works of Islamic jurisprudence which had proved difficult and impracticable. Strict Islamic law is by its nature not suitable for codification because it possesses authoritative character only in so far as it is taught in the traditional way by one of the recognized schools. The experiment of the *Mejelle* was undertaken under the influence of European ideas, and it is, strictly speaking, not an Islamic but a secular code. It was not intended for the tribunals of the *ḳāḍīs*, and was in fact not used in them as long as they existed in Turkey, and it contains certain modifications of the strict doctrine of Islamic law, particularly in the rules concerning evidence.[1] Nevertheless, the *Mejelle* was one of the official codes of the Ottoman Empire; it remained in force (subject to subsequent legislation) in the territories, and later states, which were detached from the Ottoman Empire after 1918, where it was applied as the 'civil law' by modern secular tribunals, until it was replaced by new civil codes in Lebanon (1932), Syria (1949), and Iraq (1953), and it is still the basis of the 'civil law' of Cyprus (detached already in 1878), Israel, and Jordan.[2]

5. In Turkey itself, not only the *Mejelle* but the whole of Islamic law and the tribunals of the *ḳāḍīs* were abolished in 1926, and the same happened in Albania in 1928. In the Muslim parts of Yugoslavia (Bosnia and Herzegovina), too, the *Mejelle* was abolished, although the institution of pre-emption was retained, but Islamic law has continued in some respects to be applied to Muslims in matters of *statut personnel*, legacies, and *waḳf*, all this by secular tribunals. In Greece, too, Islamic law, administered by *muftīs*, has remained applicable to Muslims in matters of *statut personnel*, inheritance, and *waḳf* in the territories ceded by the Ottoman Empire in 1913.

[1] For instance, all the other traditional qualifications are required of a witness and his evidence, but not the quality of being a Muslim (arts. 1684 ff.).

[2] See the bibliographies on these countries, below, pp. 255 ff. The *Mejelle* was never in force in Egypt. On the Ottoman family law of 1917 see below, p. 103.

14

ANGLO-MUHAMMADAN LAW AND *DROIT MUSULMAN ALGÉRIEN*

1. ANOTHER important though less lasting effort to apply the whole of Islamic law in practice was made in India under the Mogul emperor Awrangzīb ʿĀlamgīr (1067/1658–1118/1707) as part of the orthodox reaction against the ephemeral religious experiment of the emperor Akbar. Here, too, the Ḥanafī doctrine was followed, and an enormous compilation not of *fatwās* but of extracts from the authoritative works of the school was made by order of the emperor whose name it bears, the so-called *Fatāwā al-ʿĀlamgīriyya*. This instance of a prince appearing officially as a sponsor of a work of religious law is wellnigh unique.[1] The prevalence of the *sharīʿa* in practice, inaugurated by ʿĀlamgīr, lasted well into the period of British control in India.

2. When the East India Company in 1772 decided to claim sovereign rights and the power of jurisdiction outside its 'factories', they found not only the *statut personnel*, the inheritances, and the whole of the civil law of the Muslims, but penal law as well ruled by the *sharīʿa*. The *sharīʿa*, though successively modified, remained the basis of criminal law, applicable to all inhabitants in Bengal and other Muslim parts of British India until 1862. The Islamic law of evidence was not entirely abolished until 1872. As regards the law of family and inheritance and other matters sanctioned by religion (which included *waḳf*, gifts, and *shufʿa* or pre-emption), the continued validity of the *sharīʿa* for Muslims was guaranteed by a regulation of 1772, which has substantially remained in force until this day. From the early nineteenth century onwards, 'Twelver' Shiite law was applied to the 'Twelver' Shiites. According to strict

[1] A precedent was the *Fatāwā al-Tātārkhāniyya*, compiled by order of Tātārkhān (d. soon after 752/1351), a nobleman at the court of Muḥammad II Ṭughlāḳ (726/1324–752/1351).

theory, the whole of Islamic law, including the rest of civil law, penal law, and the law of evidence, ought to be regarded as sanctioned by religion, but no significant voice of dissent was raised when Islamic law in these last fields was superseded by codes of British inspiration in the course of the nineteenth century. This, from the systematic point of view, was an important departure, of much greater importance than the silent ignoring of the relevant sections of Islamic law which had taken place in most Islamic countries from the early Middle Ages onwards. It showed that the idea of a secular law had for the first time been accepted by the leaders of an important community of Muslims.

In 1772, too, British magistrates replaced the *ḳāḍīs* in British India, and until 1864 they were assisted by *mawlawīs* or Muslim scholars, who were in fact *muftīs* and whose duty it was to state the correct doctrine of Islamic law for the benefit of the magistrate.[1] In fact, for the time being things went on much as before, only what would formerly have been the decision of the *ḳāḍī* now became a report to the magistrate which he might or might not think fit to implement. Without any judicial function, and mainly as keepers of registers of marriages for purposes of evidence, *ḳāḍīs* have survived on a customary basis until the present time. As time went on the magistrates (judges) in the Muslim parts of British India came to be increasingly recruited from the Indian Muslims themselves. But the whole judiciary was trained in English law, and English legal concepts, such as the doctrine of precedent, and general principles of English common law and equity inevitably infiltrated more and more into Islamic law as applied in India. Last but not least, the jurisdiction of the Privy Council as a final court of appeal could not fail to influence, much against its intentions, the law itself.

3. In this manner, more than by positive legal changes which were few,[2] Islamic law in British India, which later

[1] The *mawlawīs* were, in the nature of things, purists, and under their advice the first British magistrates were inclined to reject written evidence. Occasionally these magistrates even went so far as to apply the *ḥadd* punishment of cutting off the hand for theft.

[2] e.g. the early suppression of slavery, the suppression of legal incapacities, including the disability to inherit, on the grounds of difference of religion, in 1850, and the prohibition of child marriages in 1929 by making them (not invalid but) a criminal offence.

became Pakistan and the Republic of India, has developed into an independent legal system, substantially different from the strict Islamic law of the *sharīʿa*, and properly called Anglo-Muhammedan law. Out of this law there has grown a new Anglo-Muhammadan jurisprudence, the aim of which, in contrast with Islamic jurisprudence during the formative period of Islamic law, is not to evaluate a given body of legal raw material from the Islamic angle, but to apply, inspired by modern English jurisprudence, autonomous juridical principles to Anglo-Muhammadan law. This law, and the jurisprudence based on it, is a unique and a most successful and viable result of the symbiosis of Islamic and of English legal thought in British India.[1]

The most important single act in the closing years of British rule in India was the Shariat Act of 1937, which abolished the legal authority of custom among the Muslims of British India almost completely and imposed upon them the official doctrine of the *sharīʿa* as modified by statute and interpreted by Anglo-Indian jurisdiction. Notwithstanding the ascendancy of the *sharīʿa*, inheritance in particular had continued to be ruled by custom, often excluding women, among numerous communities of Muslims; the act in question aimed at correcting this.[2] To enforce the pure theory of the *sharīʿa* against the custom in a country in which the *sharīʿa* was in any case applied only in part and deeply anglicized even in its central chapters, the *statut personnel*, was an act of deliberate archaism and purism.[3]

4. The application of English legal reasoning to institutions of Islamic law occasionally led to difficulties, as in the case of *waḳf*. An essential feature of the Ḥanafī *waḳf* is the permanence of its purpose, and if the beneficiaries are, for instance, the descendants of the founder, the poor or some other permanent purpose must be appointed as subsidiary beneficiaries. The Privy Council, however, held in 1894 that the ultimate reversion

[1] A similar though more short-lived interaction of English law and of the Ottoman *Mejelle* took place in Palestine under the British Mandate. Cf. the bibliography on Palestine and Israel, below, p. 255.

[2] The Act did not apply to agricultural land; in Pakistan, the Punjab Muslim Personal Law Application Act of 1948 made the Islamic law of inheritance applicable to this too, but it has often been circumvented.

[3] On the Dissolution of Muslim Marriages Act of 1939, see below, p. 104.

to the poor was illusory, and that this kind of 'family *wakf*' had to be treated as 'simple gifts of inalienable life-interests to remote unborn generations of descendants'[1] which were forbidden in Islamic law and therefore invalid. This decision, which invalidated a fundamental institution of Islamic law of great practical importance, created such dismay in India that the legislature had to step in and pass the Mussalman Wakf Validating Act of 1913, which restored the doctrine of Islamic jurisprudence concerning the family *wakf*. But as this Act was not retroactive, the Privy Council in 1922 could still hold that family *wakfs* created before 1913 were invalid, and it had to be made retroactive by another Mussalman Wakf Validating Act of 1930. Only recently, in 1956, a Pakistan Commission on Islamic family law, under the influence of modernist legislation concerning *wakf* in the countries of the Near East (below, p. 103), expressed the opinion that the Act of 1913 had outlived its usefulness and should be repealed, but no legislative action has been taken so far.

Anglo-Muhammadan law did not apply to the Muslims in the British possessions in East Africa, but the East African Court of Appeal from 1946 onwards and the Privy Council from 1952 onwards have held themselves bound by the decision of 1894 concerning family *wakfs*, whereas the Acts of 1913 and 1930 applied only to India and not to East Africa. Legislative measures, parallel to the Indian Acts, taken in Zanzibar and in Kenya (also in Aden) have proved unavailing against the settled intention of the courts, and representative Muslims of those territories petitioned for relief in 1958.

5. The development of Islamic law under French legal influence in Algeria was in some respects parallel to its development under British influence in India, but widely different in its results. In the greater part of Algeria, the *ḳāḍīs* continued to apply Islamic law according to Mālikī doctrine in those matters which customarily fell under their competence.[2] The French administration even extended the sphere of application of Islamic law against custom beyond what had been the case

[1] I have compressed this quotation from the judgment in the famous case *Abul Fata* v. *Russomoy* (22 *Law Reports*, Indian Appeals, 76).

[2] A Bill of 1959 proposed to abolish the tribunals of the *ḳāḍīs* and to unify the administration of justice in the hands of the (secular) civil courts, following the adoption of a similar measure in Egypt in 1955 (below, p. 103).

under the Turks. This is comparable to what happened in Northern Nigeria under British administration. Positive legislative changes have been rare in Algeria too. They were mainly concerned with the guardianship of minors and the formalities of marriage and divorce, culminating in an ordinance of 4 February 1959 (with regulations contained in a decree of 17 September 1959) which lays down that the marriage is concluded by the consent of husband and wife, fixes minimum ages for marriage, and decrees that the marriage can be dissolved, other than by death, only by a judicial decision on certain grounds at the demand of husband or wife, or at their joint demand.[1] The final court of appeal is the Muslim Appeals Division (*Chambre de revision musulmane*) of the Court of Appeal in Algiers. The influence of this court on Islamic law in Algeria is comparable to that of the Privy Council on Islamic law in British India. This court has sometimes considered itself obliged to diverge from the strict doctrine of Islamic law when the latter's rules of detail appeared to it incompatible with Western ideas of fairness, justice, or humanity. The court has sometimes seen fit, in giving the grounds for its judgments, to modify the traditional interpretation of the Muslim jurists, but its intentions appear with greater clarity and to their full advantage when they are formulated directly and frankly, without being supported by the considerations to which the court itself cannot have attached too much importance.

French case-law or precedents are the major factor which has determined the form in which Islamic law has been applied in Algeria; this case-law (*jurisprudence*), in its turn, has been to a considerable extent influenced by the *doctrine*, the legal thought of the French jurists of Algeria, and in particular of the late Marcel Morand (d. 1932) who in 1906 was commissioned to prepare a Draft Code of Algerian Muslim Law which was published in 1916 (*Avant-projet de code du droit musulman algérien*). The author incorporated in his work several modifications of strict Mālikī law, adopting the doctrines of the Ḥanafī school when these last seemed to him to correspond better with modern ideas. The *Code Morand*, as it is called, has never become law, but it is of great practical importance.[2]

[1] This recalls the Tunisian Code of Personal Status of 1956 (below, p. 108).

[2] On the *Code Santillana* for Tunisia, see below, p. 108.

In this way, Islamic law as applied in Algeria, too, has become an independent legal system, properly called *Droit musulman algérien*. No comparative study of the different ways in which English and French juridical thought have approached the problems of Islamic law has been undertaken so far.

6. In Pakistan (and in the Republic of India) the achievement of independence has not changed the continued validity of Anglo-Muhammadan law. (On recent developments in Pakistan, see below, p. 104 f.) It remains to be seen what the position of Islamic law will be in the Republic of Algeria.

15

MODERNIST LEGISLATION

1. In the Near East, Western influence on Islamic law was not technically juridical, as it was in India, nor of the complex character which it assumed in Algeria, but it asserted itself as a consequence, first of Westernizing tendencies and later of the modernist movement, both of which arose out of the contact of the world of Islam with modern Western civilization. Modernism aims at adapting Islam to modern conditions, by renovating those parts of its traditional equipment which are considered medieval and out of keeping with modern times. Modernist criticism is in the first place directed against Islamic law in its traditional form, not indeed against the concept of a 'religious law', the postulate that Islam as a religion ought to regulate the sphere of law as well, but against the body of doctrine developed by the Muslim scholars of the Middle Ages and its claim to continued validity. A great many leading Modernists are modern lawyers by profession, and though the whole of the modernist movement extends over a variety of fields, its mainspring is the desire to put a new Islamic jurisprudence in the place of the old one.

2. During the nineteenth century, the effects on Islamic law of the contact with the West were upon the whole restricted to the adoption of the Western form of codes subdivided into articles, both in the Ottoman *Mejelle* and in the officially sponsored codification of the Ḥanafī law of family and inheritance (1292/1875) by Muḥammad Ḳadrī Pasha for Egypt.[1] The purpose of this work, too, was to provide the secular tribunals with a convenient means of ascertaining the law applied by the *ḳāḍīs*' tribunals. In contrast with the *Mejelle*, it was never officially enacted, although a project of codification of the law of marriage and divorce, based on it, was published

[1] The codifications of the law of property (1308/1891) and of the law of *waḳf* (1311/1893) are private works by Ḳadrī Pasha.

by the Egyptian Ministry of Justice in 1916. Ḳadrī Pasha's codification of the law of family and inheritance inspired a few similar private efforts in other countries. The production of the *Code Morand* for Algeria and of the *Code Santillana* for Tunisia therefore followed an example given by the two main countries of the Near East.

Modifications of the rules of Islamic law concerning evidence, which correspond to and even go beyond those contained in the *Mejelle*, appear in Egypt for the first time in the *Règlement des Mehkémehs* of 1897 and, to a greater extent, in the *règlements* of 1910 and 1931.[1] These last modifications were substantially adopted by Lebanon in 1943 and by Syria in 1947. From 1880 onwards, too, the administration of *sharī'a* justice was reorganized in Egypt by the creation of a hierarchy of tribunals, the introduction of stages of appeal, and the staffing of the higher tribunals with several judges. This kind of organization of tribunals has been adopted in most of the other Islamic countries (including Saudi Arabia).

3. Only in the present generation has the ground been prepared for legislation by Islamic governments on the law of family, of inheritance, and of *waḳf*, subjects which have always formed part of the central domain of the *sharī'a*. This legislative interference with the central part of Islamic law itself (as opposed to the silent or explicit restriction of its sphere of application by custom or by legislation) presupposes the reception of Western political ideas. Whereas a traditional Muslim ruler must, by definition, remain the servant of the sacred Law of Islam, a modern government, and particularly a parliament, with the modern idea of sovereignty behind it, can constitute itself its master. The legislative power is not any more content with what the *sharī'a* is prepared to leave to it officially or in fact; it wants itself to determine and to restrict the sphere left to traditional Islamic law, and to modify according to its own requirements what has been left. This has led to an unprecedented relationship between Islamic and secular law.

It took modernist jurisprudence some time to find its own

[1] Here, too, the quality of being a Muslim is silently omitted from the list of qualifications required of a witness. Documentary evidence is required in a number of cases.

strength. It was hampered, at the beginning, by the difficulty of justifying itself within the framework of traditional Islamic jurisprudence, which denies the right of *ijtihād* to later generations. It was natural on the part of the *'ulamā'*, the traditional scholars, to confront the Modernists with this argument, and equally natural on the part of these last to try to shake the thesis of their opponents, as though their own aim did not lie outside the field to which it could consistently be held to apply. The whole discussion concerning the legitimacy or lack of legitimacy of a new *ijtihād*, which engaged the energies of many traditional scholars and modernists, has died down in the Near East since the Modernists have not only advocated a new departure in Islamic jurisprudence but actually succeeded in inspiring modernist legislation.

Nowadays a position has been reached in which many Islamic scholars of a traditional background, without necessarily sharing all the opinions of the Modernists, recognize their effort as legitimate and act, in a way, as their advisers; the uncompromising demand of *taḳlīd*, the unquestioning acceptance of the traditional doctrine of one school of law, in particular, have lost much ground. The attitude of these *'ulamā'* is comparable to that of the Mālikī scholars in Morocco in the later Middle Ages who, by recognizing *'amal*, tried to conserve as much as possible of traditional Islamic law in changed social conditions. This has remained the real aim of the traditional scholars, and they react most strongly to any attempt at applying modernist *ijtihād*, which would almost pass without comment in the field of family law, to the religious duties of Islam in the narrow meaning of the term, such as fasting. But from the point of view of strict Islamic law there is no essential difference between the two fields in question. The rearguard action of Islamic law was hardly ever seriously joined in the fields of penal and of constitutional law; in the field of contracts and obligations it was being fought, with varying success, during the whole of the Islamic Middle Ages and until well into the nineteenth century; in the fields of the law of family, of inheritance, and of *waḳf*, where the battle is still going on, it had already been lost in the second decade of the present century, although many of the defenders do not realize it as yet; there remains the last strong position, the religious duties in the narrow meaning of the term, and it is obvious that the chances of the defenders are best here.

4. Modernist legislative interference with Islamic law started modestly with the Ottoman Law of Family Rights of 1917, which was later repealed in Turkey but remained valid in Syria, Lebanon, Palestine, and Transjordan (as they then were),[1] and is still part of the family law of the Muslims in Lebanon and in Israel. Then, from 1920 onwards, the impetus of modernist jurisprudence and of the modernist legislative movement inspired by it, came from Egypt. The most important milestones of this legislation in Egypt have been: the acts No. 25 of 1920 and No. 25 of 1929 on the law of family, No. 78 of 1931 on the organization of the *ḳāḍī*s' tribunals (incorporating further important modifications of the law of family), No. 77 of 1943 on the law of inheritance, No. 48 of 1946 on *waḳf*, No. 71 of 1946 on legacies, No. 180 of 1952 by which the private or family *waḳf*s were abolished, and finally No. 462 of 1955 which abolished the *ḳāḍī*s' tribunals (together with all denominational jurisdictions of personal status) and unified the administration of justice in the hands of the secular courts. A Bill which aims at restricting polygamy and the right of the husband unilaterally to repudiate his wife has been in preparation since 1956, and in 1962 the completion of the drafting of a new Code of Personal Status, incorporating further innovations, was announced. As a result, all those sections of Islamic law which were being applied in practice have been modified in Egypt more or less deeply.

This reshaping of Islamic law by modernist legislation has evoked much interest and inspired similar movements in other countries of the Near East, in the Sudan, Jordan, Lebanon, Syria, Iraq, and Libya, and the laws enacted in those countries occasionally went even further than their Egyptian prototypes. The Egyptian act of 1946 served as a model for the Lebanese law of 1947 on *waḳf*, and a Syrian act of 1949 anticipated the Egyptian act of 1952 in abolishing the private or family *waḳf*s.[2] The Syrian Law of Personal Status of 1953 made the permission to conclude a second marriage dependent on the proved ability of the husband to support a second wife, and a corresponding

[1] But not in Iraq, which had already been occupied by the British forces.

[2] At the same time the Islamic law of inheritance was abrogated in Syria, but this particular measure did not survive the short-lived political régime which enacted it.

Iraqian law of 1959 demanded in addition that there be some 'lawful benefit' involved, both anticipating the Egyptian project of 1956 and the resulting Egyptian Bill of 1961.

Modernist legislators in Iraq were faced by the problem, particular to that country, that its Muslim inhabitants are almost equally divided between Sunnis and 'Twelver' Shiites, whose laws of inheritance differ fundamentally from each other. A draft Code of Personal Law of 1947 which was never enacted had contained, to a large extent, alternative provisions applicable to each of the two groups, not only in the law of inheritance but in the law of family as well. The Law of Personal Status of 1959 unified all provisions and, in the matter of inheritance, adopted a radical and unprecedented solution which was derived from the rules governing the transfer of a kind of leasehold in government land, and diverged greatly both from Sunni and from 'Twelver' Shiite law. A new political régime, however, in 1963 repealed this last innovation and made the 'Twelver' Shiite law of inheritance applicable to all Iraqian Muslims.

The influence of Near Eastern legal modernism extended even to British India, where it appeared in the Dissolution of Muslim Marriages Act of 1939. This act, generally speaking, adopts the doctrines of the Mālikī school on points on which they are considered to be more in keeping with modern ideas than those of the Ḥanafī school which prevails among the Muslims of the Indian subcontinent. The whole act is typical of modernist legislation in the Near East, but it is hardly in keeping with the development of Anglo-Muhammadan law which had followed an independent course so far, nor even with the tendency underlying the Shariat Act of 1937 (cf. above, p. 96).

5. The development of modernist legal thought in Pakistan has remained under the shadow of the problem of *ijtihād*. This is not surprising, because the concept of *ijtihād* has much exercised the minds of scholars in that part of the Islamic world for the last few hundreds of years. Under the spell of this problem, modernist legal thought in Pakistan has shown itself more conditioned by the traditional system, even though in a negative way, than has the corresponding thought in the Near East. The division between the traditionalist and the modernist wings

in Pakistan, where the first piece of modernist legislation was enacted only very recently, has perhaps remained more uncompromising than it has become in the countries of the Near East. A commission was appointed to inquire whether modifications of 'the existing laws governing marriage, divorce, maintenance and other ancillary matters among Muslims' were desirable; it presented its report in 1956, and some of its recommendations concerning the law of marriage and divorce, which, though supported by a greatly different reasoning, were closely similar to legislative measures enacted in the Near East, were adopted in the Muslim Family Law Ordinance of 1961.[1] But the majority of its members had been chosen from among modernist thinkers, and the solitary traditionalist on it presented a minority report which contradicted the conclusions of the majority in all essentials. The coexistence of two opposing trends of thought in Pakistan appears, too, from the fact that, almost contemporaneously with the report of the commission on the reform of family law, there appeared in 1954 the report of another commission on *zakāt*, which proposed the reintroduction of the Islamic alms-tax, long lapsed in practice except in the form of voluntary distributions to the poor, as a fiscal ordinance of the government. There had even been, in 1952, an abortive attempt to appoint a committee of '*ulamā*' who were to approve all proposed legislation, and the constitution of 1962 provided for an Advisory Council of Islamic Ideology. All this was part of the wider discussion of the Islamic character of the constitution of Pakistan.

6. Modernist legislation does not, generally speaking, arise out of a genuine public demand. There exist the two well-defined groups of the '*ulamā*', who are for the greater part traditionalists, and of the Modernists, many of whom are modern lawyers. Modernist legislation is imposed by a government whenever the Modernists have succeeded in gaining its sympathy and the government feels strong enough to overcome the resistance of the traditionalists. Modernist Islamic legislation therefore often appears somewhat haphazard and arbitrary. In Jordan, for instance, a Law of Family Rights, based mainly on the Ottoman law of 1917, was enacted in 1927, but a law of

[1] The recommendations concerning the law of *wakf* (see above, p. 97) have not been given legal sanction so far.

1943 repealed it in favour of the traditional doctrine of the law of family. This, in its turn, was repealed by the Jordanian Law of Family Rights of 1951, some provisions of which, inspired by previous Egyptian legislation, anticipated those of the Syrian Law of Personal Status of 1953. It is difficult to believe that social conditions and public opinion in Jordan should have moved in two opposite directions between 1927 and 1951, and should have been in advance of those in Syria for some time.

7. The method used by the modernist jurists and legislators in the Near East savours of an unrestrained eclecticism which goes beyond combining the doctrines of more than one recognized school (*talfīḳ*; above, p. 67 n. 1); any opinion held at some time in the past is apt to be adopted, without regard to its historical and systematic context. Materially, the Modernists are bold innovators; formally, they try to avoid the semblance of interfering with the essential content of the *sharīʿa*. Rather than changing the positive rules of traditional Islamic law outright, they take advantage of its principle that the ruler has the right to restrict the competence of the *ḳāḍīs* with regard to place, time, persons, and subject-matter, and to choose, among the opinions of the ancient authorities, those which the *ḳāḍīs* must follow (cf. above, p. 91). The ideas and arguments of the Modernists come from the West, but they do not wish to abolish Islamic law openly as Turkey has done. The postulate that law, as well as other human relationships, must be ruled by religion has become an essential part of the outlook of the Muslims in the Arab countries of the Near East.

8. This legislative interference with traditional Islamic law in the Arab Near East is accompanied by the seemingly opposite desire to create a modern law of contracts and obligations on the basis of Islamic jurisprudence.

When modern secular codes, mainly derived from French law, were introduced in Egypt in 1883, certain institutions of Islamic law, such as pre-emption (*shufʿa*), the transfer of debts (*ḥawāla*), the stipulated right of cancellation (*khiyār al-sharṭ*), the contract for delivery with prepayment (*salam*), as well as the rule that debts arising out of a sale of intoxicating liquor are unenforceable, were retained in the civil law of Egypt; even the settlement of a private prosecution for causing bodily harm by payment of blood-money, though hardly ever resorted to in practice, is still envisaged in the Code of Criminal Procedure of 1950. The Lebanese Codes of (Real) Property of 1930 and of Obligations and Contracts of 1932 contain similar provisions.

Now something much more ambitious is suggested: adopting not the positive solutions of strict Islamic law but the general formal principles which were elaborated by the early scholars, and deriving from them a new, modern law. Those who advocate this are to a great extent persons who have been in favour of a modernist reshaping of Islamic law in those fields in which it is still being applied in practice. They also advocate a unified jurisdiction, merging the *ḳāḍīs*' tribunals into the secular courts. The common aim underlying this programme of 'secular Islamic legislation' and the modernist reshaping of Islamic law is to express modern ideas, which have come from the West, in a traditional medium.

The only tangible results of the programme in question so far, apart from the abolition of the *ḳāḍīs*' tribunals in Egypt in 1955 and in Tunisia in 1956, have been an introductory article in the Egyptian Civil Code of 1948, which mentions 'the principles of Islamic law', together with custom and natural justice, as rules to follow in cases in which the code itself gives neither an explicit nor an implicit directive, and the corresponding introductory articles (with slight differences in the relative placing of these several elements) in the Syrian Civil Code of 1949, the Iraqian Civil Code of 1953, and the Civil Code of Libya of 1954. Whatever the explanatory note of the Egyptian code may say, Islamic law has not become one of its constituent elements to any considerably greater degree than it had been in its predecessor. The civil codes of Syria and of Iraq do not essentially differ from the Egyptian code in this respect, although the influence of Islamic law is somewhat more noticeable in the Iraqian code. The Syrian Constitution, in its versions of 1950 and of 1953, has even declared that Islamic law should be the main source of legislation, but this provision has had no practical effect so far.[1]

9. A legislation based directly on Islamic jurisprudence, but destined to be applied by secular tribunals, had much earlier been introduced, under French auspices, in Tunisia. There

[1] This was imitated in the constitution of Kuwayt of 1962 which declares that the *sharī'a* is 'an essential source of legislation'.

the late David Santillana (d. 1931) produced on behalf of the Commission for the Codification of the Laws of Tunisia the draft (*avant-projet*) of a Civil and Commercial Code, as far back as 1899. This *Code Santillana*, as it is called, accentuates the features common to Islamic and to Roman law, and part of it was enacted in 1906 as the Tunisian Code of Obligations and Contracts.

In Tunisia, too, a Mālikī Grand Mufti, when he became Minister of Justice in 1947, appointed a commission and charged it with elaborating a code of the Islamic law of family which should aim at harmonizing the doctrines of the Mālikī and of the Hanafī schools, both of which enjoyed equal status in Tunisia. This project, which actually fell within the sphere of traditional Islamic jurisprudence rather than that of modernist legislation, came to nothing for political reasons.[1]

Finally, by legislation enacted in 1956, Tunisia has put herself in the forefront of the movement of legislative modernism. First of all, the so-called public *waḳf*s were abolished, and their assets became the property of the state, a measure more far-reaching than the abolition of the so-called private *waḳf*s in Syria and in Egypt;[2] secondly, and following on the Egyptian act of the year before, the separate jurisdiction of the *ḳāḍī*s' tribunals was abolished; and thirdly, a Tunisian Code of Personal Status was enacted. Although the code has retained some typically Islamic institutions, such as the nuptial gift or 'dower', and foster-parentship as an impediment of marriage, and although it still agrees in many details with the doctrine of one or the other of the two schools of Islamic law recognized in Tunisia, it cannot be regarded, even under the most accommodating interpretation, as being merely an adaptation of traditional Islamic law. Polygamy was prohibited and made a criminal offence; marriage is concluded by the consent of bridegroom and bride; and divorce can be pronounced only by a court of law (*a*) at the request of one of the spouses on the grounds specified in the code, (*b*) in the case of mutual consent, (*c*) at the request of one of the spouses, in which case the court fixes the indemnity due to one spouse by the other. The wife, there-

[1] A similar initiative in Saudi Arabia was defeated by the traditional Ḥanbalī scholars (above, p. 87).

[2] The private *waḳf*s, too, were abolished in Tunisia in the same year.

fore, has essentially been made the equal of the husband with regard to monogamy and divorce, as she has been made, too, with regard to matrimonial régime. The section of the code on the law of succession still reproduced the traditional doctrine almost without change; but a law of 1959 introduced important changes in favour of the daughter and the son's daughter, and added a whole 'book' on legacies. Although any suggestion of abolishing Islamic law was carefully avoided by the Tunisian authorities, their recent legislation differs, objectively speaking, from traditional Islamic law as much as does the 'secular' Civil Code of Turkey.

10. In Morocco the administration of Islamic law, as far as it was customarily applicable, continued on traditional lines, with due respect for Moroccan *ʿamal* (above, p. 61 f.), well into the present century. The withdrawal of matters of civil, commercial, and penal law from the competence of the *ḳāḍī*s was taken for granted, and the Berber tribes followed their customary law, to the exclusion of the *sharīʿa*, even in matters of the law of family and inheritance. The continued validity of customary law for the Berber tribes, occasionally admitted by sultans in the past, was confirmed by a *dahir* (*ẓahīr*, decree) of 11 September 1914, but tribunals of customary law were given a formal legal basis only by a *dahir* of 16 May 1930; this, however, met with strong criticism on political grounds, though not on the part of the populations directly concerned. A *dahir* of 14 March 1938 regulated the guardianship of minors, and by drawing on the Ḥanafī doctrine introduced a mild measure of modernist legislation. Then, in 1957 and 1958, the *Mudawwana* or Code of Personal Status and Inheritance was enacted in instalments. The commission charged with drafting this *Mudawwana* laid stress not only on the Mālikī principle of *istiṣlāḥ* but on the recognized method of later Islamic jurisprudence in Morocco, of giving preference to a juridically less-sound doctrine if it agrees with *ʿamal*, and it appears from their statements that they saw their task as creating a new Moroccan *ʿamal*. This Moroccan legislation, although provoked and influenced by Near Eastern legislative modernism, stands in the tradition of Islamic legal thought particular to that country, and by frankly distinguishing between 'the best attested traditional doctrine' and *ʿamal*, its authors have been spared the central

ambiguity inherent in much of Near Eastern legal modernism.[1]

11. In Iran, where the officially recognized form of Islamic law is that of the 'Twelver' Shiites, the modern legislative movement started later than in Turkey and in the Arabic-speaking countries, and its results, as far as they concern the *sharīʿa*, have therefore been, in some respects, more conservative, and in others more far-reaching, than those achieved elsewhere at identical times. The bulk of relevant Iranian legislation was enacted between 1926 and 1938; in particular, the first part of the Iranian Civil Code dates from 1928, and the second part from 1935. This code contains also the law of family and of inheritance. The regular jurisdiction is that of the secular tribunals; the *ḳāḍī*s are competent in a restricted number of cases concerning marriage, divorce, and guardianship, and in those lawsuits which can be decided only by the formal rules of evidence of the *sharīʿa*;[2] but all these cases must first be referred to the tribunals of the *ḳāḍī*s by the secular tribunals. The modern law of family diverges only rarely from traditional Shiite law; also the law of contracts and obligations and of inheritance, all matters which normally come before the secular tribunals only, follows the *sharīʿa* closely but has silently dropped institutions which are considered obsolete, such as slavery. The constitution of 1907 provided for a committee of *ʿulamāʾ* who were to decide whether any proposed legislation was or was not in keeping with the *sharīʿa*, but this provision has had no effect in practice.[3]

12. The situation in which the modernist lawyers of Islam find themselves resembles essentially that which prevailed at the end of the first and at the beginning of the second century of the hijra. Islamic jurisprudence did not grow out of an existing law, it itself created it; and once again, it has been the modernist jurists who prepared, provoked, and guided a new legislation. It had been the task of the early specialists to impose Islamic standards on law and society; the real task which confronts the contemporary jurists, beyond their immediate

[1] Already in 1930 a prominent scholar of traditional formation, who later became Moroccan Minister of Justice, discussed the question of 'renovating' Islamic jurisprudence in a most discerning way.

[2] This last provision has become largely ineffective through the increasing reliance on documentary evidence in procedure.

[3] On a similar abortive attempt in Pakistan see above, p. 105.

aim of adapting traditional Islamic law to modern conditions, is to evaluate modern social life and modern legal thought from an Islamic angle, to determine which elements in traditional Islamic doctrine represent, in their view, the essential Islamic standards. What interests the student of the history of Islamic law most is not which measures of detail may have been adopted temporarily here and there, but the extent to which the various doctrinal and historical backgrounds of the several Islamic countries may have influenced their reactions to the issue in question. But the interest and importance of traditional Islamic law, which has existed for more than a thousand years and is still eagerly studied all over the Islamic world, is not affected by these changes. It still casts its spell over the laws of contemporary Islamic states: in the states of traditional orientation, such as Saudi Arabia, as the law of the land; and in the states of modernist orientation as an ideal influencing and even inspiring their secular legislation.

SYSTEMATIC SECTION

16

THE ORIGINAL SOURCES

1. THE chapters which follow contain the substance of the doctrine of the religious law of Islam concerning those subject-matters which are legal in the narrow meaning of the term, and according to the fully developed doctrine of the Ḥanafī school. Worship and ritual, and other purely religious duties, as well as constitutional, administrative, and international law, have been omitted, the first because they developed under different conditions and in close connexion with the dogma, the second on account of its essentially theoretical and fictitious character and the intimate connexion of the relevant institutions with the political history of the Islamic states rather than with the history of Islamic law. Among the several schools of law of the main body of orthodox Muslims the Ḥanafī school has been chosen because of its historical importance and wide distribution. The account which follows is based on the *Multaḳa l-Abḥur* of Ibrāhīm al-Ḥalabī (d. 956/1549), one of the latest and most highly esteemed statements of the doctrine of the school, which presents Islamic law in its final, fully developed form without being in any way a code. The other orthodox schools, and the Ibāḍīs and the Shiites, too, possess similar authoritative works.

2. The development of the style, method, and contents of the works of Islamic law reflects the development of legal doctrine. Every work covers only those cases which it explicitly discusses and which are evidently similar; every new case represents a new problem which calls for a new decision. The several works and even, more so, the several schools, differ from one another not only by their principles and tendencies but by the groups of cases which they consider. The greater number

of cases and decisions in a later work as compared with a similar older one represents, generally speaking, the outcome of the discussion in the meantime. Whereas the decisions express the tendencies of the several authors and of their schools, the cases themselves reflect, in principle, the influx of new subject-matter. This aspect of Islamic legal literature, which in its later period was dominated by the production of commentaries, supercommentaries, glosses, extracts, further commentaries, and so on, offers a wide field for future investigation.

3. The works of Islamic law start invariably with the ritual duties; the other subjects are arranged in more or less obvious groups on traditional lines regardless of any system, with differences from school to school and occasional variations within a school. The order in which the subjects are treated is sometimes justified by specious reasonings. The several modes of arrangement are in any case connected and go back to the very beginnings of Islamic legal literature in the second century of the hijra (eighth century A.D.). The influence of foreign models has been suggested but not yet been proved.

None of the modern systematic distinctions, between private and 'public' law, or between civil and penal law, or between substantive and adjective law, exists within the religious law of Islam; there is even no clear separation of worship, ethics, and law proper. The single chapters of the works of Islamic law fall, it is true, in the main under one or the other of those headings as far as the subject-matter is concerned, but there is continual overlapping and, above all, the concept of any systematic distinction is lacking.[1] At the utmost we notice that specific concepts are proper to certain fields, for instance that the right or claim of Allah (*ḥaḳḳ Allāh*) as opposed to a private claim (*ḥaḳḳ ādamī*) is proper to a special section of penal law, or that special rules apply to proxy in the sphere of worship, or that liability to a *ḥadd* punishment is incompatible with incurring a civil obligation (above, p. 38).

In the present book, however, the subject-matter has been arranged not according to the traditional order as exemplified by the *Multaḳa 'l-Abḥur*, but according to the broad systematic

[1] It is irrelevant in this context that the distinctions in question do exist for the modern jurists, for whom the Ottoman *Mejelle* is a civil code, or for those scholars with a traditional background who have been influenced by modernist thought.

divisions of modern legal science, certainly not with any idea of imposing alien categories on Islamic law, but in order to enable the reader to appreciate its doctrines against the background of modern legal concepts, and to throw into relief not only what is peculiar to it but also what is missing there.

4. Important or difficult parts of Islamic law have often been treated in separate works, particularly the law of succession (*farā'iḍ*), and several subjects which were directly relevant to the administration of the sacred Law in practice, such as *waḳf*, legal devices (*ḥiyal*), written documents (*shurūṭ*), and the duties of the *ḳāḍī* (*adab al-ḳāḍī*); numerous monographs treat of the particularly intricate subjects of liability and of appreciation of evidence. The administration of justice in general is discussed in the works on the *aḥkām sulṭāniyya*, the government and administration of the Islamic state (below, p. 230 f.). There are further numerous treatises on *ḥisba*, the office of the *muḥtasib*, the 'inspector of the market', and on Mālikī *'amal*. An important group of works deals with the problem of distinguishing between seemingly parallel but systematically distinct cases (*furūḳ*), and with the systematic structure of positive law in general (*ashbāh wa-naẓā'ir, ḳawā'id*). Special works deal with the definition of technical terms. There are, further, comparative accounts of the doctrines of several schools (*ikhtilāf*, 'disagreement'); the older ones reflect the discussions between the several schools, the later ones are simple handbooks. Finally, the works on the *ṭabaḳāt*, the 'classes' or generations of lawyers, which supplement the general biographical sources, give biographical and bibliographical information on the scholars belonging to each school, and occasionally important extracts from their writings.

5. A separate branch of legal learning is the discipline of the *uṣūl al-fiḳh*, the 'roots' or principles from which Islamic law is derived, in other words, Islamic legal theory, the development of which has been traced in the first part of this book. In its final, classical form it recognizes four official bases: the Koran, the *sunna* of the Prophet, the consensus (*ijmā'*) of the scholars, and reasoning by analogy (*ḳiyās*), that is to say, two material sources, a method, and a declaratory authority. It follows that this last, the *ijmā'*, is the decisive instance; it guarantees the authenticity of the two material sources and determines their correct interpretation. The methods of interpretation and

deduction, including the theory of repeal of one verse of the Koran, or of one *sunna* of the Prophet, by another,[1] questions of *ijtihād* and *taḳlīd*, *istiḥsān* and *istiṣlāḥ*, and similar subjects form the main contents of the numerous works on *uṣūl*. All this amounts essentially to a retrospective systematizing and justification of the existing positive doctrines. Theories of *uṣūl* can be said to have led to the elaboration of complete systems of positive law only in the cases of Shāfiʿī and of Dāwūd al-Ẓāhirī. The works on *uṣūl* treat also of certain general concepts which permeate the whole of the subject-matter of positive law, such as those discussed in the following chapter and in chapter 18, section 1.

[1] Repeal, *naskh;* the repealing passage is called *nāsikh,* the repealed one *mansūkh.*

17

GENERAL CONCEPTS

1. *Intention and declaration.* A fundamental concept of the whole of Islamic religious law, be it concerned with worship or with law in the narrow sense, is the *niyya* (intent). It applied originally to acts of worship; the religious obligation is discharged not by outward performance as such but only if it is done with a pious intent. But Islamic orthodoxy insisted on the performance, and *niyya*, from being a state of mind, became an act of will directed towards performing a religious duty; it must, as a rule, be explicitly formulated, at least mentally. An act of worship without *niyya* is invalid, and so is the *niyya* without the act. The *niyya* thus comes near to the concept of animus aimed at producing legal effects, and expressed in a declaration of intention. But the declaration in Islamic law is not merely a manifestation of will; it has a value of its own and under certain circumstances can produce legal effects even without or against the will. There is a general tendency underlying many decisions of detail, though it is not a principle applicable to each individual case, that a declaration made in explicit, formal terms (*ṣarīḥ*, *expressis verbis*) is legally valid even if the *niyya* is lacking, but a declaration made implicitly or by 'allusion' (*kināya*) only if the *miyya* is present. In addition, the declaration is often valid even when its import is not understood. This tendency originates in the idea of the magical effect of the right word, and leads to formalism; the evidence of witnesses, for instance, is valid only if preceded by a derivative of the root *sh-h-d* 'to give testimony'. But this formalism has a rational basis; in order to create a *mufāwaḍa* (unlimited mercantile partnership), for instance, either this term must be used or every single legal effect mentioned. On the other hand, even a very imperfect declaration accompanied by *niyya* is regarded as legally valid whenever possible; only a very faulty one is invalid even if the *niyya* is present. By means of a complicated network of casuistry all possible forms

of declaration are tested as to whether they are valid on their own, or only if accompanied by *niyya*, or not at all. Similarly, ambiguous (*mubham*) declarations are scrutinized as to their particular meanings. This investigation often amounts to determining whether a given declaration is compatible with the existence of a certain *niyya* claimed afterwards by the person who made it, that is to say, interpreting the wording without regard to the *niyya*. The interpretation is not strictly objective; there is a tendency to restrict the effect of the declaration, to mitigate the resulting religious and legal obligation, particularly in the case of an undertaking under oath with a self-imposed penalty, such as repudiation of one's wife or manumission of one's slaves, for non-fulfilment, which amounts to a conditional repudiation or manumission (cf. below, p. 159). This tendency often affords the possibility of evading the resulting obligation.

The declaration is not defined narrowly; Islamic law recognizes also the conclusive act or 'gesture' (*ishāra maʿhūda*), not as a general principle but in a number of individual cases. Silence as such cannot replace a declaration of consent (*riḍā*), except in a few special cases; for instance, when the guardian for the purpose of marriage asks the consent of the virgin bride to a proposed marriage, her silence (or laughing, or quiet crying) is regarded as *riḍā*. The idea that silence is consent when speaking out is obligatory occurs only rarely. Writing is accepted unconditionally only from a mute person, from others, in theory at least, only with considerable reservations. (For the practice, see above, pp. 82 f.)

Among the defects of declarations, error is taken into a limited account in their casuistic interpretation. Error in a confession plays a somewhat more important part in criminal law. As regards fraud, there is little inclination to protect the victim; it manifests itself only in the case of 'grave deception' (*ghabn fāḥish, laesio enormis*). The doctrine of duress (*ikrāh*) is more developed. What is envisaged in the first place is the threat (*tahdīd*); it is recognized only if the one party is in a position to carry it out and the other party fears that this may actually happen. The effects of duress in civil and those in criminal law, how far it invalidates a declaration and how far it diminishes responsibility, are not distinguished. The effect in civil law is that the threat of death, severe beating, and long imprisonment makes the declaration voidable (by *khiyār*, *optio*); exceptions, however, are made mainly in favour of desirable transactions, such as manumission of slaves and adoption of Islam. The effects in criminal law are discussed casuistically; the effect of duress, whenever it is recognized, is not only to remove the penal sanction, but to make the act itself allowed; if it is not recognized, the penalty (*ḥadd*) is applied in full. For instance, drinking wine under the threat of death or mutilation is permissible, and the refusal to do so would be sinful. Conversely, apostasy from Islam is a sin and martyrdom meritorious, but it is allowable to feign apostasy under duress. (This simulation, *taḳiyya*, plays an important part in Shiite religious law.)

2. *Term and condition.* Among the several set terms laid down by Islamic law the most important are the waiting-periods imposed on a woman after the termination of her marriage (called *ʿidda*) and on a female slave after a change of owner (called *istibrāʾ*); there are also set terms for negative and positive prescription and the presumption of death. Technical rules are laid down for interpreting the terms and periods mentioned by the parties in their declarations, particularly in contracts of hire and lease. Generally speaking, the term (*ajal*) must be certain (*maʿlūm*).

Conditions (*sharṭ*, pl. *shurūṭ*), in the wider meaning of the term, are the general prerequisites for the validity of a legal act, and in particular an act of worship (for ritual prayer, for instance, they are ritual purity, covering one's nakedness, facing the direction of the Kaaba, and *niyya*), as opposed to its essential elements (*rukn*, pl. *arkān*). Another group are the 'conditions implied in the nature of the transaction' (*shurūṭ yaḳtaḍīha l-ʿaḳd*, *condicio iuris*) and the 'conditions intimately connected with the transaction' (*shurūṭ mulāyima* or *muwāfiḳa*), e.g. in a contract of surety: 'if you buy such and such a thing from *X*, I stand security for the price'. A further group are the requirements for the incidence of a religious or legal duty (*shurūṭ wujūb*), such as the payment of the alms-tax. Related to this is the enjoinment (*modus*) by which the occurrence of a legal effect is made dependent on the fulfilment of an imposed stipulation, e.g. 'I buy this slave for you on condition that you manumit him.' Finally, there is the condition in the narrow meaning of the term.

Terms and conditions in the several transactions are discussed casuistically and have given rise to numerous evasions. A group apart consists of those transactions which by their nature imply a term, such as the sale with future delivery (*salam*), or a condition, such as the undertaking under oath. The stipulation of a term is inadmissible in transactions which aim at immediate transfer of ownership (*tamlīk fil-ḥāl*), the stipulation of a condition in the case of an exchange of monetary assets (*muʿāwaḍa māliyya*). Therefore both are excluded in the case of sale and of division; the stipulation of a term but not of a condition is admitted in contracts of hire and lease, but conversely in the case of donation and of marriage; both are admitted in the case of repudiation, manumission, and legacy. The several contracts of association are treated differently; the stipulation of a term but not of a condition is admitted in the *muzāraʿa* and the *musāḳāt* (special contracts of lease of agricultural land with profit-sharing), conversely in the *shirka* (mercantile partnership); both are admitted in the *muḍāraba* (sleeping partnership). If the stipulation of a condition is excluded, an invalid condition makes the whole transaction invalid, but not if it is admitted.

A particular case is the suspense, abeyance (*wuḳūf*) of rights and legal effects (which then are in abeyance, *mawḳūf*), for instance the marriage of the slave pending the master's consent, some rights of the missing, untraceable person, and most of the rights of the apostate; conversely, the share of a son in the inheritance is set aside for the unborn child of a deceased person. All these rights depend on a condition being realized, namely the consent of the master, the return of the missing person, the repentance of the apostate, and the live birth of the child, respectively.

3. *Agency*. Declaration by proxy (through a messenger, *rasūl*) is not clearly distinguished from procuration; for instance, if the messenger has seen the object bought, it is contested whether the right of rescission after inspection has lapsed. As to representation proper, the sphere of worship is, for once, clearly distinguished from the sphere of law in the narrow sense. Proxy in worship (*niyāba*; *nāʾib*, the deputy in matters of worship) is admitted in religious duties concerning property, but not in those concerning the person; the emphasis is on charging another with the fulfilment of an obligation. In the sphere of

law in the narrow sense, the emphasis is on conferring powers of disposal on another (*wakāla*, procuration; *muwakkil*, the principal; *wakīl*, the deputy, agent, proxy in legal affairs); the presence or absence of the principal may be relevant. In the exchange of monetary assets (*muʿāwaḍa māliyya*) the *wakīl* acts as a principal (*aṣīl*) and has the corresponding rights and duties; in other transactions, such as relinquishment of a claim, or marriage, his part is legally that of a messenger; but even in the first case the rights of ownership are transferred directly to the *muwakkil*. Exceptions from the general rules are recognized in favour of certain effects considered desirable; for instance, if a slave has been given the mandate to buy himself from his master on behalf of the mandant and he buys himself on his own behalf, the contract is valid; and if a wife has been given the mandate to repudiate herself, it cannot be withdrawn. An unlimited mandate is possible; it is given by using the words: 'act at your discretion'. Normally, however, it is limited, and its contents must be clearly defined. The deputy is then bound by this instruction, and his function approaches that of the messenger; this makes it possible to appoint persons who do not have full legal capacity. Conversely, the power of disposal of the deputy may exceed that of the mandant; a Muslim cannot buy or sell wine, but he can instruct a non-Muslim to do it on his behalf (this, however, is contested). The object of a contract of service (*ijāra*; below, p. 155) cannot form the object of a mandate; and as there is no distinction between civil law and criminal law as such, the appointment of a deputy to exact corporal punishments (*ḥadd* and *ḳiṣāṣ*), which are construed as claims against a third person, is explicitly excluded.

The effects of a procuration as regards third parties are not treated separately from its effects as between mandant and deputy, nor is the right to represent clearly distinguished from the duty to carry out a mandate; but professional brokers (*simsār*) are obliged to collect the claims of their mandants.

The legal guardian (*walī*)[1] and the guardian appointed by testament (*waṣī*) are at the same time agents and/or executors.

4. *Validity, nullity, and religious qualifications.* Islamic law

[1] *Walī* is the nearest male relative of his female relations, and of his minor male relations; he is the holder of parental authority, and, in particular, he gives his female relatives in marriage.

recognizes, first, the following scale of religious qualifications (*al-aḥkām al-khamsa*, 'the five qualifications'): (1) obligatory, duty (*wājib*, *farḍ*); Islamic law distinguishes the individual duty (*farḍ ʿayn*), such as ritual prayer, fasting, &c., and the collective duty (*farḍ kifāya*), the fulfilment of which by a sufficient number of individuals excuses the other individuals from fulfilling it, such as funeral prayer, holy war, &c.; (2) recommended (*sunna*,[1] *mandūb*, *mustaḥabb*); (3) indifferent (*mubāḥ*), to be distinguished from *jā'iz*, allowed, unobjectionable (see below); (4) reprehensible, disapproved (*makrūh*); (5) forbidden (*ḥarām*); the opposite of this is *ḥalāl*,[2] everything that is not forbidden.

There exists, secondly, a scale of legal validity, the widest concept in which is *mashrūʿ*, recognized by the law, corresponding with it. According to the degree of this correspondence, a transaction is (1) *ṣaḥīḥ*, valid, if both its nature (*aṣl*) and its circumstances (*waṣf*) correspond with the law; (2) *makrūh*, reprehensible, disapproved, if its *aṣl* and its *waṣf* correspond with the law, but something forbidden is connected with it; (3) *fāsid*, defective, if its *aṣl* corresponds with the law but not its *waṣf*; (4) *bāṭil*, invalid, null and void. *Aṣl* and *waṣf* correspond approximately to *rukn* and *sharṭ* (above, section 2). This second scale is less developed than the first. Transactions which are *ṣaḥīḥ* or *makrūh* produce their legal effects, and *ṣaḥīḥ* is therefore often used in the sense of legally effective, so as to cover both categories. Synonyms of *ṣaḥīḥ* in this wider meaning are *lāzim* and *wājib*,[3] binding, and *nāfidh*, operative, the first two of which emphasize the subjective, and the third the objective, effects. The distinction between *fāsid* and *bāṭil*, which is not recognized to the same extent, or not at all, by the other schools of Islamic law, is often not clearly made; the idea of *fāsid* comes near to that of 'voidable', though it is not identical with it, and *fāsid* contracts, even if they are not voided, sometimes have only restricted legal effects. To be distinguished from the quality as *fāsid* is the right of rescission (*khiyār*, *optio*), the right to cancel (*faskh*) or to ratify (*imḍā'*) a contract within a stipulated time; this right can be granted by law or stipulated by contract (cf. below, p. 152).

[1] *Sunna* in this sense must be distinguished from *sunna* as the 'normative practice' of the community or the example of the Prophet.

[2] Used only of things and of persons, e.g. one's wife or female slave, not of acts.

[3] With a meaning different from that of *wājib*, 'obligatory'.

Both scales of qualifications apply concurrently to the same set of facts. This appears most clearly with regard to acts that are unobjectionable; they are *jā'iz* from the religious and therefore *ṣaḥīḥ* and *wājib* from the legal point of view. If the safe-conduct given by an individual Muslim is declared *jā'iz*, this means not only that, subjectively speaking, he is not forbidden to give it, but that, objectively speaking, it is unobjectionable and therefore valid; and conversely that, objectively speaking, it is unobjectionable and therefore, subjectively speaking, permitted. Or if a contract of sale has been concluded in conformity with all provisions of the law, it is not only permitted and unobjectionable but valid and binding. The same correspondence is obvious in the concept of *ijāza*, the 'declaration that something is *jā'iz*', approval (*ratihabitio*), such as the approval of the act of an unauthorized agent (*fuḍūlī*); the principal declares that he does not object to the act of the *fuḍūlī* in question and that it is therefore valid. The concept of *jā'iz* is typical of the way in which the legal subject-matter is subjected to religious scrutiny; it comprises everything that does not provoke a religious objection. The fusion of valid and invalid with allowed and forbidden respectively, was facilitated by the fact that both pairs of concepts were coextensive in the field of worship. In the field of law in the narrow sense, it is true, this was not completely the case. Not only are there situations to which only one of the two pairs of concepts can be meaningfully applied, it seems occasionally that the same act is at the same time to be qualified as valid and as forbidden. Closer scrutiny, however, shows that the two predicates refer to separate acts or to separate aspects of the situation. For instance, a sale concluded at the time of the call to the Friday prayer is *makrūh* in the sense of the second scale of qualifications; it is legally effective but its conclusion at that particular time is forbidden. Or if the political authority appoints a *ḳāḍī* who is not *'adl*, or if the *ḳāḍī* accepts the evidence of a witness who is not *'adl*, these acts constitute breaches of duty which are forbidden, but the appointment and the judgment based on the evidence in question are nevertheless valid. The quality as *makrūh* does not prevent the legal effects from taking place; it only, in special cases, creates an additional liability for tort, e.g. if a loan for use is terminated prematurely; or it enables the public authorities to interfere, e.g. by forcing the speculator on rising prices of food to sell. There are degrees even within the sphere of *ḥarām*; a transaction qualified as *ḥarām* is not always *bāṭil* but occasionally only *fāsid*, and sometimes even *ṣaḥīḥ* (cf. below, p. 146).

Similar to the distinction between the religious sphere and the sphere of law proper is that between *ḳaḍā'*, the judgment given by the *ḳāḍī*, *forum externum*, and *diyāna*, the conscience, *forum internum*,[1] particularly in interpreting defective declarations which, when accompanied by the relevant *niyya*, may be valid before the conscience but not before the *ḳāḍī*. Conversely, 'legal devices' or evasions are considered valid if they conform to the letter of the law, regardless of the underlying motives. To the sphere of *diyāna* belong the kindred concepts of *tanazzuh*, *wara'*, religious scruple, and *iḥtiyāṭ*, precaution. So it may happen that a wife is considered repudiated once before the *ḳāḍī*, but twice in order to allay the religious scruple, i.e. if the former husband and wife want to be quite sure that they do not commit a sin, they ought to consider themselves separated twice.

[1] Alternative terms are *ẓāhir* and *bāṭin*, the 'outward' and the 'inward' state.

18

PERSONS

1. *Capacity and responsibility.* Legal capacity begins, generally speaking, with birth. The unborn child can inherit and receive a legacy; if it is a slave it can be manumitted, it can also be bequeathed by legacy but not sold; all this becomes effective, in principle, only if it is born within six lunar months from the occurrence in question. For causing an abortion, a special indemnity (called *ghurra*), different from blood-money, is to be paid; this devolves, by a curious fiction, upon the legal heirs of the child. Legal capacity ends with death. The missing person (*mafḳūd*), some of whose rights are in abeyance (above, p. 119), is declared dead only after 90 or even 120 lunar years have elapsed since his birth.

The concept of responsibility is subsumed under that of legal capacity (*ahliyya*), within which are distinguished the *ahliyyat al-wujūb* and the *ahliyyat al-adā'*. The *ahliyyat al-wujūb*, 'capacity of obligation', is the capacity to acquire rights and duties; the *ahliyyat al-adā'*, 'capacity of execution', is the capacity to contract, to dispose, and therefore also validly to fulfil one's obligations; it can be either full or restricted, and is harmonized with the *ahliyyat al-wujūb* by considering the 'qualification' (*ḥukm*), the essential character of the obligation.

The highest degree of legal capacity is that of the free Muslim who is sane (*'āḳil*) and of age (*bāligh*); he is fully responsible (*mukallaf*). Majority is determined by physical indications, by the declaration of the youth in question, or, failing this, by reaching the age of fifteen lunar years. The *mukallaf* has the capacity to contract and to dispose (*taṣarruf*), he is bound o fulfil the religious duties, and he is fully subject to criminal law, being capable of deliberate intent (*'amd*). The insane (*majnūn*) and small children (*ṭifl*) are wholly incapable but can incur certain financial obligations; the idiot (*ma'tūh*) and the minor (*ṣabī*, *ṣaghīr*) have, in addition, the capacity to conclude purely advantageous transactions and to accept donations and charitable gifts; 'intelligent', 'discriminating' minors (*ṣabī yaʿḳil, mumayyiz*) can, further, adopt Islam, enter a contract of manumission by *mukātaba* if they are slaves, and carry out a procuration. As regards a major who is irresponsible (*safīh*), for instance a spendthrift, it is contested whether he is subject to interdiction (*ḥajr*), or capable in principle and only put under the protective supervision of the authorities until he reaches the age of twenty-five lunar years.

Higher demanda are made of the witness who must also be 'of good character' (*ʿadl*), i.e. must not have committed grave sins[1] and must not persevere in small ones. The opposite of *ʿadl* is the sinner (*fāsiḳ*); between both stands the *mastūr*, the person of whom nothing is known to his disadvantage. But the quality of being *ʿadl* is a religious and not a legal requirement; the *ḳāḍī* must not accept the evidence of a *fāsiḳ*, but if he does, his judgment based on it is nevertheless valid. The *ḳāḍī*, too, must be *ʿadl* and possess, in addition, the necessary qualities of character and the necessary knowledge; similarly, if a *fāsiḳ* is appointed *ḳāḍī*, his appointment is valid, and if a *ḳāḍī* who has been *ʿadl* becomes *fāsiḳ*, his appointment does not become invalid.

A quality of importance in penal law is the quality of *muḥṣan*, applicable only to free persons and having two strictly different meanings: a *muḥṣan* in the sense of being a free person who has never committed unlawful intercourse is protected, by penal provisions, against *ḳadhf* (below, p. 179); and a *muḥṣan* in the sense of a free person who has concluded and consummated a valid marriage with a free partner is subject to a more severe punishment, stoning to death, if he or she should afterwards have illegal intercourse. These rules are directly based on the Koran and on traditions, respectively.

Islamic law does not recognize juristic persons; not even the public treasury (*bayt al-māl*) is construed as an institution, its owner is the Muslim community, i.e. the sum total of individual Muslims. As regards the *waḳf* or *ḥabs* (pious foundation, mortmain), it is construed as the withdrawal from circulation of the substance (*ʿayn*) of a property owned by the founder and the

[1] Unless he has repented of them; but he must never have been punished for *ḳadhf* (below, p. 179).

spending of the proceeds (*manfa'a*) for a charitable purpose; there is no unanimous doctrine on who becomes the owner of the substance. An essential feature is the permanence of its purpose, which may be anything not incompatible with the tenets of Islam; therefore, if the beneficiaries are, for instance, the descendants of the founder, the poor or some other permanent purpose must be appointed as subsidiary beneficiaries in case the original beneficiaries should die out.[1] Objects of a *waḳf* are mostly immovables, but also movables in so far as this is customary, e.g. books. There are detailed rules concerning the administration of the *waḳf* and its use for a purpose other than that designated by the founder.

The capacity to dispose can be extended or restricted, by *idhn* or *ḥajr* respectively. The *idhn* ('permission') can be granted to a minor by the father or other legal guardian, but not with regard to purely disadvantageous transactions (e.g. divorce, manumission, acknowledgement). The term *ḥajr* ('restriction', interdiction) denotes both the status and the act of imposing it; the minor and the slave are normally, and the small child and the insane necessarily, in the status of *ḥajr*. As an act, *ḥajr* is required in order to revoke the *idhn*; it is pronounced by the authorities against the irresponsible *muftī* who teaches the public reprehensible tricks, against the ignorant physician who is a danger to his patients, and against the bankrupt transport contractor (this is singled out because the transaction in question, *ijāra*, is based on payment in advance).

2. *Legal position of women.* The legal position of women is not unfavourable. The woman is, it is true, considered inferior to the man, she has less rights and duties from the religious point of view. If she commits apostasy she is not executed but forced, by imprisonment and beatings, to return to Islam. As regards blood-money, evidence, and inheritance, she is counted as half a man; she does not belong to the *'āḳila* (below, p. 186). Also with regard to marriage and divorce her position is less advantageous than that of the man; on certain grounds, the husband has the right of correction. But as regards the law of property

[1] In modern terminology, this, the so-called private or 'family' *waḳf* (*waḳf ahlī* or *dhurrī*), is distinguished from the so-called public or 'charitable' *waḳf* (*waḳf khayrī*) which is immediately destined for some public or charitable purpose. In strict Islamic law, however, the private *waḳf*, too, is considered a charity, and the same rules apply to both kinds of *waḳf*.

and obligations, the woman is the equal of the man; the matrimonial régime is even more favourable to her in many respects. She may even act as a *ḳāḍī* in certain matters.

3. *Legal position of slaves* (*raḳīḳ*, slaves in general; *ʿabd* or *mamlūk*, the male slave; *ama* or *jāriya*, the female slave; *ḥurr*, the free person). From tle religious point of view the slave is considered a person, but being subject to his master he is not fully responsible; he is at the same time a thing (*chose*, *res*). The effects of slavery are mitigated (*a*) by restrictions on its origin, (*b*) by the legal rights of the slave, and (*c*) by facilities for and the recommendation of manumission.

(*a*) Slavery can originate only through birth or through captivity, i.e. if a non-Muslim who is protected neither by treaty nor by a safe-conduct falls into the hands of the Muslims. Sale of free persons into slavery for debt is unknown.

(*b*) The slave has rights as a person; in particular, he or she can get married. The male slave may marry up to two female slaves; the female slave may also marry a free man who is not her owner, and the male slave a free woman who is not his owner. The marriage of the slave requires the permission of the owner; he can also give the slave in marriage against his or her will. The permission implies that the owner becomes responsible with the person (*raḳaba*) of the slave for the pecuniary obligations which derive from the marriage, such as nuptial gift, and maintenance; if the owner defaults, the slave can be compulsorily sold in order to provide the cover. Minor slaves are not to be separated from their near relatives, and in particular their parents, in sale (cf. below, p. 152). The unmarried female slave is at the disposal of her male owner as a concubine, but no similar provision applies between a male slave and his female owner. The children of a female slave follow the status of their mother, except that the child of the concubine, whom the owner has recognized as his own, is free with all the rights of children from a marriage with a free woman; this rule has had the most profound influence on the development of Islamic society.

The slave is less protected than the free man by criminal law; it is true that retaliation for the intentional killing of a slave takes place even against a free man,[1] but there is no retaliation

[1] This is an important point of difference between the schools of law; the Mālikīs, Shāfiʿīs, and Ḥanbalīs hold the opposite view.

for bodily harm caused to a slave; the person guilty of *ḳadhf* against a slave is not liable to the *ḥadd* punishment but only to a 'discretionary punishment' (*ta'zīr*) because the slave is not *muḥṣan* (above, section 1). Apart from this, the protection of the slave does not go beyond that of property in general. There is no protection of the slave against his owner in criminal law because retaliation, blood-money, &c. are private claims which are vested in the owner himself; the slave has no capacity to sue in this case. But the authorities must ensure that the owner fulfils the religious duties towards his slave; he must not overwork him and must give him sufficient rest; the slave of a persistent offender can be sold compulsorily. On the other hand, the criminal responsibility of a slave is less than that of a free man; he is not stoned to death for unlawful intercourse because he is not *muḥṣan*, he is only punished by half the number of lashes applicable to a free man who is not *muḥṣan*; for drinking wine, and for *ḳadhf*, too, he is liable to half the number of lashes applicable in the case of a free man; he is subject to retaliation only for intentional killing, not for causing bodily harm.

The slave has no capacity to dispose, but he can carry out a procuration; his statement is accepted to the same extent as is that of the free man in pecuniary transactions, and if he is *'adl*, also in some religious matters, but he cannot be a witness. He has the right to claim maintenance from his owner. The pecuniary liability for torts (*jināyāt*; below, p. 186 f.) caused by the slave is borne by the owner, but he can surrender the slave instead (*daf'*, *noxae deditio*); conversely, he can, in certain circumstances, redeem (*fidā'*) the slave who has become liable with his person. In certain cases the master is not responsible for the acts of his slave; a liability then emerges only if the slave later becomes free, for instance for the culpable loss of a deposit handed to the slave, or for the loan for use or the loan of money given to him. The *peculium* of the slave is not recognized, but its existence in fact is often taken into consideration.

The owner can confer the capacity to dispose upon his slave, whether for a single transaction, such as getting married, or in general, for trade; a slave who has received this last permission is called *ma'dhūn*. This permission does not include unilaterally disadvantageous transactions, such as donations, neither does it include non-pecuniary transactions, such as concluding a marriage or redeeming one's own person from retaliation. The transactions concluded by the *ma'dhūn* engage the stock-in-trade handed over to him by the owner, and his own person; if he runs into debt, the owner must either surrender him so that he may be sold to pay off the debt, any uncleared debt reviving if the slave becomes free, or the owner must pay it on his behalf. The same rule applies to the pecuniary liability of the *ma'dhūn* for torts and to his liability for pecuniary obligations deriving from marriage (in contrast with the rule applicable to the ordinary slave). The permission is revoked either by law, e.g. if the owner becomes insane, or by *ḥajr* on the part of the master.

(*c*) Manumission (*'itk* or *i'tāḳ*) is recommended by religion; it is in certain cases prescribed as a religious expiation (*kaffāra*) and is often the self-imposed penalty for non-fulfilment of an undertaking under oath. The slave becomes free by law if he becomes the property of a person who is his *maḥram*, i.e. related to him within the forbidden degrees. The *umm walad*, the female slave who has borne a child to her owner which he has recognized, becomes free by law on his death; the owner therefore can dispose of her only by manumission or by the contract of *mukātaba*; he cannot surrender her and becomes liable to the amount of her value instead; but he can give her in marriage without her consent. Manumission is favoured by law in cases of doubt; if there is an imperfect expectancy of manumission, the slave is given the possibility of acquiring his freedom by work (*sa'y* or *si'āya*), e.g. if he is joint property and one owner manumits his share. There are several special forms of manumission, first the manumission with effect at the death of the owner (*tadbīr*), to be distinguished from a legacy; a slave manumitted in this form (*mudabbar*) has the same legal position as the *umm walad* (but see below, p. 170). Further, the sale of the slave to himself; in this case the slave becomes free immediately and owes the price to his former master. Finally, the contract of *mukātaba* by which the slave (*mukātab*) acquires his freedom against a future payment, mostly by instalments; he becomes free immediately as far as the power of disposition of the owner is concerned, and after performance of the contract as far as his substance (*raḳaba*) is concerned; he has the same capacity to dispose as the *ma'dhūn*, and the owner cannot give him in marriage without his consent. The *mukātaba* can be revoked if the slave defaults, either by agreement or by the *ḳāḍī* on application of the master. The ownership of the possessions of the *mukātab* is in abeyance, and according to the performance or non-performance of the contract it is retrospectively attributed either to one or to the other. The *mukātab* has the expectancy of, but not a claim to, assistance from the proceeds of the alms-tax. All this has the consequence that the slave has to a great extent the capacity to sue his master.

The manumitted slave remains to his former master in the strictly personal relation of clientship (*walā'*; both patron and client are called *mawlā*); this has certain effects in the law of marriage and of inheritance.

The position of slaves is therefore not intolerable; the Islamic law of slavery is patriarchal and belongs more to the law of family than to the law of property. Apart from domestic slaves, Islamic law takes notice of trading slaves who possess a considerable liberty of action, but hardly of working slaves kept for exploiting agricultural and industrial enterprises. The last were found, indeed, only infrequently in Islamic society. The legal rules concerning slavery reflect, on the whole, actual conditions.

4. *Legal position of non-Muslims.* The basis of the Islamic attitude towards unbelievers is the law of war; they must be either converted[1] or subjugated or killed (excepting women, children, and slaves); the third alternative, in general, occurs only if the first two are refused. As an exception, the Arab pagans are given the choice only between conversion to Islam or death. Apart from this, prisoners of war[2] are either made slaves or killed or left alive as free *dhimmīs* (see what follows) or exchanged for Muslim prisoners of war, at the discretion of the *imām*; also a treaty of surrender is concluded which forms the legal basis for the treatment of the non-Muslims to whom it applies. It is often called *dhimma*, 'engagement', 'obligation', 'responsibility', because the Muslims by it undertake to safeguard the life and property of the non-Muslims in question, who are called *dhimmīs*. This treaty necessarily provides for

[1] Islamic law does not allow forced conversion.

[2] Islamic law does not, on principle, envisage war between Muslims but only the holy war; prisoners of war are therefore by definition unbelievers.

the surrender of the non-Muslims with all duties deriving from it, in particular the payment of tribute, i.e. the fixed poll-tax (*jizya*) and the land-tax (*kharāj*), the amount of which is determined from case to case.[1] The non-Muslims must wear distinctive clothing and must mark their houses, which must not be built higher than those of the Muslims, by distinctive signs; they must not ride horses or bear arms, and they must yield the way to Muslims; they must not scandalize the Muslims by openly performing their worship or their distinctive customs, such as drinking wine; they must not build new churches, synagogues, and hermitages; they must pay the poll-tax under humiliating conditions. It goes without saying that they are excluded from the specifically Muslim privileges, but on the other hand they are exempt from the specifically Muslim duties; in principle, non-Muslims follow the rules of their own religions with regard to what is lawful for them. In particular, they are not subject to the prohibition of wine and pork, and can therefore trade in them. Neither offences against individual Muslims, including even murder, nor refusal to pay the tribute, nor transgression of the other rules imposed upon the non-Muslims, are considered breaches of the treaty; only joining enemy territory or waging war against the Muslims in their own country are regarded as such.

A non-Muslim who is not protected by a treaty is called *ḥarbī*, 'in a state of war', 'enemy alien'; his life and property are completely unprotected by law unless he has been given a temporary safe-conduct (*amān*); this can be validly given by any Muslim, man or woman, who is *mukallaf*. He is then called *musta'min*, and his position resembles in general that of the *dhimmī*, except that he is not obliged to pay tribute for a year; should he remain in Islamic territory longer, he is made a *dhimmī*.

The former burning question as to who is to be considered an unbeliever (*kāfir*) has found a tolerant solution; the heretic is regarded as an unbeliever only if he denies an essential element of Islam. Within the unbelievers a distinction is made, in descending order of privilege, between the followers of revealed religions who believe in a prophet and possess a scripture (*ahl*

[1] The *kharāj* remains a charge on the land, even if its owner adopts Islam or it otherwise becomes the property of a Muslim.

al-kitāb), the Zoroastrians, and the pagans; the children of a mixed marriage between unbelievers belong to the higher religion. A Muslim may marry a woman belonging to the *ahl al-kitāb* (their children are, of course, Muslims), but not one of the *ahl al-kītāb* a Muslim woman. For the rest, the Muslim and the *dhimmī* are equal in practically the whole of the law of property and of contracts and obligations. But the *dhimmī* cannot be a witness, except in matters concerning other *dhimmīs* (even if they belong to different religions); he cannot be the guardian of his child who is a Muslim, although a *dhimmī* woman has the right to the personal care of her child who is a Muslim; he cannot be the executor of a Muslim; he cannot be the owner of a Muslim slave and is, if necessary, forced by the authorities to sell him. In criminal law, the *dhimmī* is liable to *ḥadd* punishments and to 'discretionary punishment' (*ta'zīr*) as far as they are not specifically Muslim, therefore not to the *ḥadd* for drinking wine and to the more severe punishment for illegal intercourse of the *muḥṣan*. The *dhimmī* is protected by penal law to the same extent as the Muslim; but because of his lesser criminal responsibility, he is protected against *ḳadhf* not by *ḥadd* but only by *ta'zīr*. The *dhimmī* is the equal of the Muslim with regard to retaliation.[1] Finally there are cases in which there exists a negative equality; neither the Muslim nor the *dhimmī* can enter a *mufāwaḍa* (unlimited mercantile partnership) with the other, neither belongs to the *'āḳila* of the other, and the difference of religion and the difference of domicile, be it the Islamic state (*dār al-Islām*) or any country within enemy territory (*dār al-ḥarb*), exclude inheritance (though not legacies) between any two persons.

The majority of rules pertaining to the *dhimmī* which are discussed in the sources are concerned with the effects of his conversion to Islam, particularly with regard to situations which are possible without, but not within, Islam (e.g. marriage to more than four wives, marriage within the prohibited degrees, ownership of wine or pork). Occasionally, if conversion to Islam of a *dhimmī* entails a legal loss for another *dhimmī* (e.g. the conversion of the wife of a *dhimmī*), this last is offered Islam

[1] The other schools of Islamic law, however, do not make a Muslim liable to retaliation for the murder of a *dhimmī*, the Shāfi'īs and the Ḥanbalīs absolutely, and the Mālikīs in most cases.

so that he may conserve his rights. The convert becomes a *mawlā*, i.e. he needs an Arab patron (also called *mawlā*), in the same way as a manumitted slave, but he is free to choose his patron by a contract of clientship (*muwālāt*). Conversion from Islam to another religion, on the contrary, is considered apostasy and is subject to penal sanctions.

To sum up, Islamic law interferes with non-Muslims only in so far as Muslims, too, are concerned directly, and very occasionally indirectly, for instance in so far as the punishment of theft constitutes a religious interest of the Muslims. Apart from this, non-Muslims are left complete legal freedom provided no Muslim, and this includes the tribunal of the *ḳāḍī*, is concerned; freedom in matters of religion is guaranteed explicitly. This is the basis of the factual legal autonomy of the non-Muslims, including their own jurisdictions, which was extensive in the Middle Ages, and has prevailed in part until the present generation.

19

PROPERTY

1. *Objects of property.* Islamic law does not strictly define the object of property as a tangible thing (*chose*, *res*). The thing (*ʿayn*), it is true, is opposed to the claim or debt (*dayn*), but the usufruct (*manfaʿa*, pl. *manāfiʿ*) of things that can be used forms a separate category; as opposed to *manfaʿa*, the thing itself is also called *raḳaba*, substance. The usufruct is, in a certain way, regarded as a thing; the use is not a *ius in re aliena* but a property of usufruct. Then, however, usufruct is not merely assimilated to the other things but made the subject of special transactions; the contract of *ʿāriyya* (loan of non-fungible things) is defined as the gratuitous transfer of usufruct, the contract of *ijāra* (hire and lease) as the sale of usufruct, but they are nevertheless separate contracts. In the case of 'things that increase' (*māl nāmī*; *namāʾ*, the accession) the usufruct includes the proceeds (*ghalla*), including the proceeds of letting or hiring out. The proceeds can also become the object of separate rights of property, e.g. by legacy which confers a right *in rem*; these rights then do not include the right of direct use.

The thing as object of legal transactions, *res in commercio*, is called *māl*, but its opposite is not simply the *res extra commercium*, but there are several graded categories.

(*a*) things which are completely excluded from legal traffic, which cannot be objects of property, and the sale of which is null and void (*bāṭil*), e.g. a free person, animals not ritually slaughtered (*mayta*), and blood;

(*b*) things in which there is, in fact, no ownership (which are *ghayr mamlūk*), that is to say (1) things which are not under individual control (are not in custody, *ḥirz*), or which are public property (*milk al-ʿāmma*), such as air and water, big rivers and public roads; everyone is entitled to use them in a way which does not cause prejudice to the public, and no one can dispose of them; (2) the *waḳf* (above, p. 125 f.); according to another opinion, the *waḳf* is the property of Allah; (3) things that are 'not known' (*ghayr maʿlūm*), such as birds in the air, to which are assimilated things which are not in actual possession, such as a runaway slave (*ābiḳ*); in order to exclude uncertainty (*gharar*), Islamic law refuses the power to dispose of the right of ownership;

(*c*) things in which there is no separate ownership, that is to say (1) things which do not, or do not yet, exist independently, such as the flour in the corn or the milk in the udder; (2) constituent parts, such as a beam in the roof, but this is not worked out consistently, because the upper story of a house can be a separate property; this category merges into that of things which exist independently but usually belong to another thing, such as the key of a house; unless the contrary is stipulated, these follow the principal thing to which they belong;[1]

(*d*) those slaves in whom there is only a restricted ownership, particularly the *umm walad*, the *mudabbar*, and the *mukātab*;

(*e*) things which are objects of property but on the disposal of which there are restrictions, and in particular (1) things of trifling value; the minimum value of *māl* is 1 dirham; (2) holy things, such as the soil of Mecca the sale of which is reprehensible; (3) things which are ritually impure, such as wine and the pig; (4) other things without market value (*māl ghayr mutaḳawwim*), the sale of which is *fāsid*;

(*f*) finally, things which are not in actual possession and the recovery of which cannot be expected (*māl ḍimār*), such as things which have been lost, usurped, or confiscated.

This system is not set out as a whole but its categories are discussed piecemeal in connexion with the several transactions; also the legal effect, whether the transaction becomes *bāṭil* or *fāsid*, is often left undecided. Occasionally the legal effect differs according to the nature of the transaction; the most important distinction is that certain things cannot be sold, donated, or given as *mahr*, but can be inherited or bequeathed by legacy, e.g. the unborn child of a female slave.

Similar restrictions apply to performances, some of which cannot be paid for and cannot be offered in payment, e.g. the serving of a mare by a stallion.

1 But unless the contrary is stipulated in a contract of sale, the seed does not follow the ground, and the fruit does not follow the tree.

Māl is divided into immovables (*'aḳār*) and movables (*māl manḳūl*, *māl naḳlī*), and into fungibles (*mithlī*) and non-fungibles (*ḳīmī*). Fungibles are again divided into things that can be measured (*makīl* or *kaylī*) or weighed (*mawzūn* or *waznī*) or counted (*ma'dūd mutaḳārib*, i.e. 'homogeneous', belonging to the same kind), categories which are of importance in connexion with the prohibition of *ribā*. On the basis of traditions concerning this prohibition, wheat, barley, dates, and salt belong to the category of *makīl*, gold and silver to the category of *mawzūn*; apart from this, custom (*'urf*) decides to which category any given commodity belongs.

2. *Ownership and possession.* Ownership, the right to the complete and exclusive disposal of a thing, is called *milk*, possession *yad*, the owner *mālik* or *rabb*, the possessor *dhul-yad*. Islamic law does not distinguish between possession and *detentio*. *Milk* and *mālik* are used not only of property rights *in rem* but of rights to usufruct, or of the right to intercourse in marriage or concubinage, whereas *yad* can also denote the authority of the husband in marriage, or of the father. Categories of possession proper are fiduciary possession (*yad amāna*) and, above all, legitimate and illegitimate possession (*yad muḥiḳḳa* and *yad mubṭila*), this last, for instance, in the case of usurpation. Among the many cases in which ownership and possession are distinct, the most important is that of the *mukātab* slave; he has left the possession but not the ownership of his master.

The acquisition of ownership may be original or derivative. (*a*) Original acquisition occurs in the first place through occupancy (*istīlā'*) of things that have no owner (*res nullius*). In this connexion arises the question of expectancy. If someone sets up a net in order to catch birds, he has the expectancy of the property of the birds caught; but if he sets up a net in order to dry it, anyone who takes the birds caught in it acquires the property, even though he takes them from land belonging to another. Also, the owner of the ground has an exclusive right in trees that grow in it, and in its alluvion. As regards precious metals, a distinction is made between the mine (*ma'din*) and the treasure (*rikāz*); of both, as well as of the booty (*ghanīma*) taken from the enemy in war, one-fifth is to be paid to the public treasury. The mine belongs to the owner of the ground, to the finder only if the ground has no owner; the treasure belongs in either case to the finder (at least according to the doctrine of Abū Yūsuf). But this applies only if the treasure dates from pre-Islamic times; a treasure dating from Islamic times is not ownerless but has only left the possession of its owner and is regarded as found property (*luḳaṭa*). Ownership can never be acquired by finding; the finder is only entitled to make a charitable gift (*ṣadaḳa*) of the found object when the legal term for giving public notice has elapsed without result; if he is poor, he is entitled to use the object himself; but it is better to hold it on trust (as *amāna*), which implies the intention of returning it to the owner; if this is lacking, its retention becomes usurpation. The acquisition of the proceeds (*istighlāl*) is an essential part of the right of ownership.

The questions of specification and of commixtion and confusion are treated not from the point of view of property, but partly from that of usurpation and partly from that of deposit; Islamic law lays the emphasis on establishing the kind and extent of liability involved. The original owner is therefore often given the choice either of claiming compensation pure and simple, or of claiming the return of the object itself with a compensatory payment on his part for an increase in value or with a compensatory payment by the usurper for a decrease in value; another consideration is that specification creates property in a usurped object if its name and its main uses are changed thereby. There is a difference of opinion concerning the confusion of two quantities of the same species, but if it happens without an act of the usurper, joint ownership (*ishtirāk*) in proportion to the two quantities is created. Usurpation further creates ownership if the usurper has made the object inaccessible and has been made liable for its value; through the payment of the value he acquires ownership from the time of the usurpation, but even then the original owner may, in certain circumstances, assert his right of ownership should the usurped object become accessible again.

Several kinds of original acquisition of ownership are of importance for the law of procedure. In proving ownership, preference is given to the proof of kinds of acquisition which cannot be repeated, such as weaving, milking, shearing, over those which can be repeated, such as building (because the house can have collapsed in the meantime), planting, sowing. Acquisitive prescription is not recognized as such; its effects are, however, achieved by the procedural rule that no claim of ownership in land against the possessor can be entertained, under certain conditions, after a number of years (30 or 33 or 36 are sometimes mentioned) has passed without this claim being made.

(*b*) Derivative acquisition of ownership occurs (1) through transfer of ownership by transfer of possession, i.e. by delivery (*taslīm*) and taking possession (*ḳabḍ*; *tasallum*, taking delivery; *istīfā'*, receiving; *taḳābuḍ*, taking possession reciprocally). This kind of acquisition of property occurs in connexion with a number of obligations. *Taslīm* and *ḳabḍ* do not necessarily effect transfer of ownership in all circumstances, e.g. not in the case of a sale with the right of rescission; the reasoning that this is because the full intention of transferring ownership is lacking is, however, absent from Islamic law.

(2) Derivative acquisition of ownership occurs further through transactions which by themselves create rights *in rem*, i.e. create ownership without taking possession. The most important of these is the legacy which creates ownership and not merely a claim against the heirs. Contracts, too, are on occasion regarded as conferring by themselves rights *in rem*; Islamic law does not make a clear distinction (see below, pp. 141, 152).

(3) The pledge, pawn (*rahn*), occupies a special position, because possession is taken but the ownership is not transferred; transfer of ownership occurs only under certain conditions as an effect of the contract.

Cessation of ownership occurs normally through transfer; this may occur against the will of the owner, as in the case of usurpation when the usurper acquires ownership. An important particular case is apostasy from Islam; here the cessation of ownership is at first in abeyance and becomes definite only when the apostate (*murtadd*) dies or leaves the Islamic state without returning to Islam.

Joint ownership (*mushā'*, or, seen in its obligatory aspect, *sharikat māl*, association in property) is treated in detail, particularly with regard to land and to slaves. It arises, as a rule, from inheritance, also from confusion (intentional and unintentional), and from the acquisition of proceeds by a partnership. Joint property created by confusion is subject to a limitation of disposal; the share can be sold other than to the partner (*sharīk*) only with his consent, because in this case each partner is the individual owner of a fraction of the component parts of the object which in actual fact cannot be separated from the fraction owned by the other. Joint property is of two kinds, according to whether it can be divided or not. Division (*ḳisma*) is the normal case. It can often be enforced without the consent of the other partners, but not if it would reduce the use that could be made of the resulting parts. There are numerous material rules on the procedure to be followed by the *ḳāḍī* who carries out the division. If the object itself is not divided, its use is distributed, either by space so that, for instance, each partner inhabits certain rooms of a house, or, if this is not possible, by time so that, for instance, each partner inhabits the house for a month, or uses the services of the slave for a day.

The protection of ownership, much pronounced in Islamic law, manifests itself, among other rules, in the protection of bona fide acquisition; if an object is vindicated, claimed by a third party (*istiḥḳāḳ, istirdād*), the party who has sold it becomes liable for the *darak*, the default in ownership, to the amount of the price paid. Another consequence is that the owner can make the hirer directly responsible for the loss of an object which the depositary has hired out. But the concept of protection of possession is absent from Islamic law. Possession confers a prejudice as to ownership; if possession itself is in dispute, claims are decided in a casuistic manner; the person who wears a garment prevails over him who holds its sleeve. Occasionally the special rules of the law of evidence result in putting the possessor in a less advantageous position; if both the possessor and a 'stranger' (*khārij*) produce a proof of ownership of the same kind, the proof of the 'stranger' is, under certain conditions, given preference because he is the claimant and therefore charged with the onus of proof, a fact which gives his proof a prior claim to be heard.

3. *Pledge, pawn* (*rahn*). The contract of pledging a security demands offer and acceptance; it becomes binding (*lāzim*) when possesion of the pledge is taken. The contract has an obligatory aspect which is emphasized in Islamic law; the pledgee is liable for the pledge, to the amount either of its value or of the debt secured, whichever is less, but if it gets lost through

his fault (*taʿaddī*), to the amount of its value; he is also obliged to return it when the debt is paid. The aspect *in rem* of this contractual relationship becomes evident, for example, by the transfer of possession inherent in it; disposal of it by the pledgor (debtor) is absolutely excluded; he has not even the right to demand its surrender for sale in order to pay the pledgee (creditor); the transfer of possession can be replaced by depositing the pledge, by agreement, with a trustee, a 'person of good character' (*ʿadl*); the pledgee has the right to sell it when the debt is due in order to pay himself out of the proceeds. The pledge presupposes the existence of a debt; it cannot be given in connexion with a fiduciary relationship (*amāna*), e.g. deposit or loan of non-fungible objects, responsibility for *darak*, suretyship for the person, retaliation, pre-emption, &c. The pledge is, in principle, a collateral security; the debt remains in existence in so far as it is not covered by the sale of the pledge, and any credit balance which remains after the sale of the pledge is held by the pledgee in trust (*amāna*) for the pledgor. In exceptional cases only, the destruction or the loss of the pledge wipes out the debt, e.g. if a slave who has been given as a pledge commits a tort and is surrendered or redeemed by his owner, the pledgor. The pledgor retains the ownership of the pledge, he is therefore also the owner of any accessions, such as the young of animals, the fruit of trees, but these, too, become part of the pledge; expenses which are necessitated by the pledge itself are to be paid by the pledgor, and expenses which arise from the retention of the pledge by the pledgee are to be paid by the latter; the pledge cannot be used by either. The concept of mortgage is unknown in Islamic law.

Different from the pledge is the retention (*ḥabs*) of a thing in order to secure a claim connected with it; the law grants this right *in rem* (lien) in a number of special cases, e.g. the *ḥabs* of a thing for the wages for work done on it, or of a thing bought by procuration for the price, or of found property (and even, under certain conditions, of illegally appropriated property) for necessary expenses made for it. It is contested whether the liability of the lienor is the same as that of the pledgee or more extensive.

4. *Immovables* (including the *iura in re aliena* which arise only in this connexion). The law of real estate shows minor

divergencies from the general law of property. The concept of a thing as a separate entity is to some degree set aside; separate ownership in the upper story of a building is possible; this is regarded not as a servitude or easement but as a real right of property; when the upper story has collapsed it cannot be sold. Separate ownership is possible, too, in single rooms or apartments of a house. No taking of possession is necessary for the transfer of ownership in the case of sale (this is, however, contested); the contract of sale is not purely obligatory. This leads to stricter rules of evidence in the proof of ownership. Vindication of real property requires, as a rule, the proof that the defendant is the possessor, and still higher demands are made if an inheritance of real property is vindicated. Usurpation of immovables affects only the usufruct.

Public property (*milk al-ʿāmma*) as such, as distinguished from the related concepts of the public treasury and the *waḳf*, is greatly restricted in scope; it exists, for instance, in a thoroughfare, whereas the blind alley is the joint property of the abutters. The use of public property is to a certain degree free to every person; he may even erect a booth, &c. on it, as long as it does not cause prejudice to the public, but every person can sue for its removal. Land in the vicinity of an inhabited place is reserved for its inhabitants, as a kind of common, for pasturage, estovers, &c.

The occupancy of real property takes the form of cultivating waste land (*iḥyāʾ al-mawāt*); this is land which is not put to use and has no determined owner, be it a Muslim or a *dhimmī*; the licence of the *imām* to do so is necessary. The occupied land is marked by an enclosure; the occupant is obliged to cultivate it within three years; should he fail to do so, the licence lapses. Special cases in which, according to the prevailing opinion, the licence of the *imām* is not required, are the digging of a well and the planting of a tree in waste land; the occupant acquires around it a reserved zone of a diameter which varies according to circumstances.

To the law of real estate belong restrictions of ownership in favour of the neighbour, deriving from the duty of avoiding acts which are likely to disturb the neighbour in the exercise of his ownership. This gives right only to personal claims, not to interference with the property of another.

There is further the right of pre-emption (*shufʿa*), the right to substitute oneself for the buyer in a completed sale of real property (which includes the upper story of a building). It is granted by law and cannot be bought. Entitled to its exercise are, in the following order, (1) the co-owner, (2) the owner of a servitude in the property, and (3) the owner of an adjoining property. The exercise of *shufʿa* is precluded by a number of grounds, for instance if the person who would be entitled to it has himself made a bid, and the use of evasions in order to prevent its incidence is approved by the majority of scholars.[1] It is exercised in stages, the first being the immediate raising of the claim to it before witnesses, as soon as the entitled party comes to know of the sale; failure to do so is considered an abandonment of the claim.

Servitudes in real property are the right of passage, the right to let flow or to pour out water, and, conversely, the right to draw water or to water one's animals, and others. The right to build an upper story, in contrast with those just mentioned, adheres not to the property but to the person of the owner of the existing upper story; therefore the upper story itself can be sold, but not the right to build it.

Expropriation in the public interest exists only within very narrow limits.

The theory of Islamic law has thus developed only a few rudiments of a special law of real estate; conditions of land tenure in practice were often different from theory, varying according to place and time, and here the institution of *waḳf* has become of great practical importance.

5. *Water.* Questions of irrigation have always been particularly important in the Near East. The origin of the provisions of Islamic law concerning rights in water must be looked for not in Arabia, where there are no perennial streams, but in Iraq, a country of artificial irrigation from time immemorial.

Big rivers, such as the Euphrates and the Tigris, are not private property; small watercourses and canals are the joint property of the owners of the adjoining land. This has numerous obligatory effects, in particular the duty of maintenance by dredging,

[1] One such device consists of making a charitable gift of one room to the prospective buyer, who thereby becomes a co-owner, and then selling him the rest of the house.

and the rule against making unilateral changes in drawing the water; as far as this diverges from pre-existing rights, it requires the consent of all co-owners. The division of the use of the water between the several owners is assured either by mechanical devices (distributors or runnels with inlets of fixed size) or by the allocation of fixed periods of time. This right to use water can be separated from the land to which it belongs, not by sale but by legacy. Although the water in such a canal is privately owned, every one has the right to drink from it, to use it for performing the ritual ablution, &c., but he must not trespass on the land of another without the permission of the owner, except in a case of necessity. Full private property in water exists only if it is in custody, i.e. in a container.

20

OBLIGATIONS IN GENERAL

1. *Preliminaries.* Unjustified enrichment and risk are both rejected on ethical grounds; this prohibition pervades the whole of the law, but shows its effects most clearly in the law of obligations, and this is why these subjects are treated in the present chapter. Several obligations have been treated or will be treated in other contexts: the obligations deriving from proxy (above, p. 119 f.), those deriving from slavery (above, pp. 127 ff.), those deriving from a change of religion (above, p. 132 f.), those deriving from joint ownership (above, p. 138 f.), those deriving from pledging a security (above, p. 139 f.), those deriving from the matrimonial régime and from the duty of maintenance (below, p. 167 f.), and those deriving from torts and crimes (below, pp. 181 ff.; see also p. 160).

2. *Types of contract.* Islamic law does not recognize the liberty of contract, but it provides an appreciable measure of freedom within certain fixed types. Liberty of contract would be incompatible with the ethical control of legal transactions. A means of achieving it exists in the abstract obligation (*dayn muṭlaḳ*) which is based on the acknowledgement of a debt without regard to its cause of origin. This can be used to ensure a valuable consideration for any kind of performance, even though it be not envisaged by the types of contract provided, but it has not been used constructively in elaborating the doctrine. It was widely used, however, in practice, particularly as an element of legal devices. The concept of custom plays an important part in the law of obligations, but its function is essentially restrictive because transactions are allowed only in so far as they are customary (*muta'ārif*). There is nothing corresponding to the *bonae fidei obligatio* of Roman law.

There exists no general term for obligation; the nearest approximation to it is *dhimma*, 'care as a duty of conscience'; the debtor has the performance 'in his care'. A claim or debt, primarily of money but also of fungible things in general, is called *dayn*. It may be, or may have become, due or matured (then it is called *dayn ḥāll*), or it may be due at a future date (then it is called *dayn ilā ajal*). The most common ground for an obligation arising is the contract (*'aḳd*); this is the field of pecuniary transactions (*mu'āmalāt*). The conclusion of the contract is essentially informal; only the literal meanings of certain technical terms, such as *ṣafḳa*, 'striking hand upon hand', for concluding a contract, reflect former symbolic acts.

The contract is a bilateral transaction, and it requires an offer (*ījāb*) and an acceptance (*ḳabūl*), both made normally in the same meeting (*majlis*, 'session') of the contracting parties; the withdrawal (*rujū'*) of the offer before the acceptance is made is possible, and so is the stipulation of the right of rescission (*sharṭ al-khiyār*). One category of contracts is the exchange of monetary assets or rights (*mu'āwaḍa māliyya*, contracts *do ut des*). Bilateral, too, and therefore concluded by offer and acceptance, are pecuniary transactions without a countervalue (*'iwaḍ*), such as the donation or the loan of non-fungible objects. Offer and acceptance can be expressed in the form of compliance with an order, e.g. by the words 'sell me' and 'I sell you herewith'. Acceptance is not required in the case of unilateral dispositions with immediate legal effect, e.g. repudiation, manumission, or acquittance of a debtor. (These dispositions are called *taṣarruf nājiz* or *taṣarruf munjaz*.)

3. *Unjustified enrichment* (*faḍl māl bilā 'iwaḍ*). It is a general principle of Islamic law, based on a number of passages in the Koran, that unjustified enrichment, or 'receiving a monetary advantage without giving a countervalue', is forbidden, and that he who receives it must give it to the poor as a charitable gift. This applies, for instance, to reletting a hired object for a greater sum, or to reselling a bought object, before payment has been made for it, for a higher price. Special cases are the giving and taking of interest, and other kinds of *ribā*, literally 'increase', 'excess'. *Ribā* is defined as 'a monetary advantage without a countervalue which has been stipulated in favour of one of the two contracting parties in an exchange of two monetary values'. The prohibition applies to objects which can be measured or weighed and which, in addition, belong to the same species. Forbidden are both an excess in quantity and a delay in performance. If only one of these two conditions is

realized (e.g. in an exchange of cloth of a certain kind for cloth of the same kind, which is not measured or weighed, or of wheat for barley, which do not belong to the same species), an excess in quantity is allowed, but a delay in performance remains forbidden. Similar rules apply to usufruct; therefore the hire of two objects, one for the other, is allowed only if they do not belong to the same species.

The prohibition of a delay in the exchange of goods which are subject to the rules concerning *ribā* finds its logical complement in the general prohibition of an exchange of obligation for obligation (*bayʿ al-dayn bil-dayn*), and the prohibition of unjustified enrichment is further strengthened by the prohibition of combining two contracts, of concluding one contract as part of another (*ṣafḳa fī ṣafḳa*), because this could lead to the stipulation of a monetary advantage without giving a countervalue.[1]

A contract concluded in contravention of the rules concerning *ribā* is *fāsid*. If two unequal quantities of the same species are exchanged, the contract is valid as far as the smaller quantity and its equivalent are concerned, and the excess quantity must be returned.

The whole prohibition applies in the first place to sale and barter, but also to the amicable settlement. It is directed against speculation in food and in precious metals, and against any transactions which are tantamount to giving and taking interest, including some old-fashioned ones, such as supplying the seed in exchange for a larger amount of corn from the harvest. The casuistry surrounding the prohibition enables us to discern some types of transaction in actual use during the early period of Islamic law, such as the exchange of animal for meat, of wheat for flour, of dried dates for fresh dates on the tree (the so-called *muzābana*), a similar contract concerning corn (the so-called *muḥāḳala*), &c.

4. *Risk* (*gharar*, literally 'hazard'). Starting from the Koranic prohibition of a certain game of hazard (*maysir*), Islamic law insists that there must be no doubt concerning the obligations undertaken by the parties to a contract. The object of the

[1] Under this rule, a contract of sale in which a non-fungible object is pledged as a security for the price would be *fāsid* because pledging a security is a separate contract; it is, however, admitted as valid by *istiḥsān*.

contract, in particular, must be determined (*ma'lūm*, 'known'; opposite *majhūl*, 'unknown'). This requirement is particularly strict as regards objects which can be measured or weighed, which are subject to the prohibition of *ribā*; no undetermined quantity (*juzāf*) is permissible here, not even if the price of a unit of weight or measure be stated. For the same reason it is forbidden to sell dates which are still unripe, to be delivered when they have ripened, because it is unknown whether they will ripen at all. The price, too, and the countervalue in general must be determined; the kind of coins in which payment is to be made must be mentioned; but it is permissible to sell for a countervalue which is present and is shown, even though it be not defined. Similar rules apply to the values exchanged in other contracts, e.g. the usufruct and the rent in a contract of lease. The same is true of any stipulated term, but a distinction is made according to the nature of the contract, and vague expressions which are rejected in the *salam* contract are admitted in the contract of suretyship. From this requirement and from the prohibition of *ribā* together derives the requirement in the case of goods which are subject to the rules concerning *ribā*, that possession must be taken and their weight or measure checked before they are resold. These rules are aimed at all kinds of gambling, one of the great passions of the ancient Arabs, and here, too, the old sources of Islamic law enable us to discern some of the aleatory transactions in which this passion found expression in the early Islamic period (the so-called *mulāmasa*, *munābadha*, and *ilḳā' bil-ḥajar*). There are only two exceptions from the general prohibition of aleatory transactions: (1) in favour of prizes for the winner or winners of horse races, on account of their importance as a training for the holy war, and (2) for the winner or winners of competitions concerning knowledge of Islamic law.

5. *Liability* (*ḍamān*; *ḍāmin*, liable). Questions of liability form one of the most intricate subject-matters in the Islamic law of obligations. Liability may arise from the non-performance of a contract (especially if the performance would have consisted in handing over an object, in cases where the object has perished so that the performance has become impossible), or from tort (*ta'addī*, literally 'transgression'), or from a combination of both. The depositary and other persons in a position of trust (*amāna*;

such a person is called *amīn*) are not liable for accidental loss, but they lose this privileged position through *ta'addī*, illicit acts which are incompatible with the fiduciary relationship, such as using the deposit, whether the loss is caused by the unlawful act or not. The concept of *ta'addī*, however, is not restricted to the doctrine of liability, it means tort in general; in other words, liability arising from non-performance of a contract is reduced to liability arising from a tort—a trace of archaic legal reasoning. Islamic law nevertheless distinguishes liability for the effect of an unlawful act or delict as such from liability for an act contrary to a contract, and it discusses both kinds of liability whenever they happen to arise concurrently.

6. *Extinction of obligations*. The normal case is the fulfilment (*īfā'*), especially the payment (*ḳaḍā'*) of a debt; the debt can also be set off against a claim. The acquittance (*ibrā'*) of the debtor by the creditor likewise extinguishes the debt; it must be unconditional and not subject to the stipulation of a term, but it can take place in the form of a legacy. It has the same effect as the relinquishment (*isḳāṭ*) of a claim. Both forms of remission must be distinguished from the cancellation (*faskh*) of a contract and from the amicable settlement (*ṣulḥ*). The *faskh* brings about a condition as if a contract had never existed; it can be produced unilaterally, by *khiyār* (below, p. 152 f.). In its turn it must be distinguished from the reversal (*iḳāla*) of a sale, which is regarded as a new sale.

The *ṣulḥ* is not only procedural, although its aim is the elimination of dispute; it is always possible as an agreement of the parties to modify an existing obligation by which the creditor, for a consideration (*badal*), waives his original claim. If the debtor acknowledges his original obligation, the *ṣulḥ* amounts to replacing a concrete debt by an abstract one; in this case the rules relating to *ribā* must be taken into account. If the debtor does not acknowledge the original obligation, the *ṣulḥ* is a separate transaction. The *ṣulḥ* is not confined to the law of obligations; claims arising from the law of slavery, family law, and penal law can also be settled by it (but not, of course, *ḥadd* punishments).

Another way of extinguishing an obligation is by transforming it into a new one by the *ḥawāla*, literally 'transfer'. This is, in the first place, a mandate to pay, i.e. I owe something to *A* and charge *B* to pay my debt. It can also be an assumption of my debt by *B*. The practical prerequisite in both cases is that I have a claim against *B* which is equal to or higher than the claim of *A* against me. This is not necessarily a debt, it can also be a claim for the return of an object, e.g. a deposit or something taken by usurpation. Normally, therefore, the *ḥawāla* amounts to an assignment; I assign to *A* a claim of mine against *B*, in order to satisfy a claim of *A* against me. But the existence of a claim of *A* against me is not a necessary prerequisite, and the *ḥawāla* then amounts to a mandate to collect, i.e. I charge *A* to collect my claim against *B*. The element common to all cases is merely that an obligation of *B* towards *A* is created. The acceptance of the *ḥawāla* by *A* extinguishes my obligation; it revives only if *B* dies bankrupt or (in the absence of legal evidence) denies the existence of the *ḥawāla*. Performance of *B* towards *A* extinguishes my claim against him only if the *ḥawāla* was concluded with specific reference to this obligation, not if it was unconditional.

One of the practical advantages of this institution is that it enables me to make payments in another place through *B*. Its effect is the same as that of the *suftaja* or bill of exchange. This is defined as 'a loan of money in order to avoid the risk of transport'; I lend an amount to *B*, in order that he may pay it to *A* in another place. The difference between *ḥawāla* and *suftaja* is that the obligation of *B* towards me, which in the case of the *ḥawāla* is normally supposed as already existing, is, in the case of the *suftaja*, created on purpose by a payment which I make to *B*, and this can be construed only as a loan of money; the transaction is reprehensible, because it is a loan of money from which I derive, without giving a countervalue, the advantage of avoiding the risk of transport, but it is not invalid. In practice, I buy from *B* a draft on the place in question. Historically, the origin of the bill of exchange can be traced to the *suftaja* and *ḥawāla*.

7. *Plurality of persons in one contracting party*. Islamic law considers the existence of an obligatory relationship with more than one creditor, debtor, buyer, lessee, guarantor, &c. Occasionally a joint relationship comes into being; e.g. each of two buyers is entitled to take possession and to pay the price; then he has a claim against the other for his share in the price, and

the right to secure it by retaining the object. Occasionally, too, joint action is required, e.g. on the part of two proxies; and if there are two depositaries, one must give a mandate to the other. Generally, however, each acts for himself; e.g. each of two creditors is entitled to conclude an amicable settlement, but this engages his share only and the other creditor has the choice of joining in the transaction or not. All this is discussed casuistically, in detail, but general principles hardly emerge.

21

OBLIGATIONS AND CONTRACTS IN PARTICULAR

1. *Acknowledgement* (*iḳrār*). The acknowledgement has a procedural and a material aspect. It is one kind of legal evidence, and although it is in theory weaker than the evidence of witnesses, can be withdrawn in criminal proceedings involving a *ḥadd* punishment, and requires confirmation by the party concerned if it is used to establish a family relationship (e.g. by acknowledging that a person is one's son or brother), it is in practice the most conclusive and uncontrovertible means of creating an obligation on the part of the person who makes it. If a contract of sale, for instance, is proved by the evidence of witnesses, a number of pleas are open to the buyer in rebuttal of a claim for payment of the price; but *A*'s acknowledgement that he owes the sum in question to *B* cannot be withdrawn or qualified by a subsequent plea. The importance of the *iḳrār* is that it creates an abstract obligation without regard to the cause of its origin. An acknowledgement of debt made during mortal illness ranks, it is true, not together with the other debts but immediately after them, and it is not considered, as other unilaterally disadvantageous transactions during mortal illness are, a legacy which would be restricted to one-third of the estate. If someone makes an acknowledgement in the following terms, 'I have usurped this thing from *A*, no, from *B*', he owes the thing to *A* and its value to *B*, because the withdrawal (*rujūʿ*) of the first acknowledgement in favour of *A* (by the word 'no') is invalid, and the thing owed to *B* on the strength of the second acknowledgement is regarded as having been destroyed by the first acknowledgement, so that its value takes its place.

2. *Sale* (*bayʿ*; *shirāʾ*, the purchase). The contract of sale forms the core of the Islamic law of obligations, the categories of which have been developed in most detail with regard to this contract, and other commutative or synallagmatic contracts,

although regarded as legal institutions in their own right, are construed on the model of *bayʿ* and sometimes even defined as kinds of *bayʿ*. Sale is an exchange of goods or properties (*māl*); it therefore includes barter and exchange. As far as sale in the narrow sense is concerned, one distinguishes the object which is being sold from the price (*thaman*) and the value (*ḳīma*); each is the countervalue (*ʿiwaḍ*) of the other. As the price consists of fungible things (normally gold or silver), whereas the object which is being sold is, generally, a non-fungible thing, the rules applicable to both are not quite identical; the vendor, for instance, is allowed to dispose of the (fungible) price even before he has taken possession. The contract of sale becomes complete (*tāmm*) by reciprocally taking possession (*taḳābuḍ*); this terminology shows that it is not regarded as purely obligatory. A stipulation to the advantage or disadvantage of one of the parties, which is extraneous to the purpose of the contract, e.g. that the buyer should manumit the slave which he buys, is invalid and makes the contract *fāsid*. If someone buys leather on condition that the seller should make it into shoes, the contract would be *fāsid* under this rule; but because it is the generally adopted procedure, the contract is admitted as valid by *istiḥsān*.[1] A *fāsid* sale conveys, even after the two parties have taken possession, only a 'bad ownership' (*milk khabīth*) and is liable to cancellation until the object is resold. Reprehensible, but not invalid, are, among others, a sale concluded at the time of the call to the Friday prayer and a sale of slaves by which a minor is separated from his near relatives; should minor children be separated from their parents the sale is, according to some authorities, invalid.

The right of rescission (*khiyār*, *optio*) is the right unilaterally to cancel (*faskh*) or to ratify (*imḍā'*) a contract, and in particular a contract of sale; if it is not exercised within the proper time limit, the sale is complete (*tāmm*), with a somewhat different meaning of the term. It can be conferred by law, or agreed upon by the contracting parties. The buyer has the right of rescission at the time at which he sees the object which he has bought, the act of 'seeing' not to be taken too narrowly (*khiyār al-ru'ya*); also in the case of a defect, i.e. everything that causes a reduction in price among traders (*khiyār al-ʿayb*), or lack of a

[1] See also above, p. 146, n. 1.

stipulated quality. The defect gives only the right of rescission, not of abatement; this last arises only if the return of the object of the sale has become impossible, either by its loss or by the occurrence of a new defect after delivery but before recognition of the first defect (in which case return is possible only with consent of the seller), or by increase in value (such as the dyeing of cloth). If the seller delivers less than the stipulated quantity, the buyer has the choice between rescission of the sale and abatement of the price in proportion. The buyer loses the right of rescission if, for instance, he kills or manumits the slave for a consideration, or consumes the food that he has bought. The waiver of the *khiyār al-ʿayb* by the buyer in a contract of sale is possible; the resulting absence of obligation is called *barāʾa*. The buyer can stipulate the right of choosing from among several objects (*khiyār al-taʿyīn*), and by agreement of the contracting parties there can be conferred on one or on both or on a third party the general right of rescission (*khiyār al-sharṭ*) during a period of not more than three days (according to the prevailing opinion).

A special kind of sale, although regarded as a separate kind of contract, is the *salam*, the ordering of goods to be delivered later for a price paid immediately. The term *raʾs al-māl*, 'capital', which is used to denote the price in this contract, shows the economic meaning of the transaction: the financing of the business of a small trader or artisan by his clients. The object of the *salam* is mostly fungible things, but it cannot be gold or silver. Because of its closeness to the subject of the prohibition of *ribā*, the contract of *salam* has been carefully worked out and is subject to numerous special rules. Its counterpart, delayed payment (*nasīʾa*, the delay) for goods delivered immediately, is also possible, but this kind of sale plays a minor part in Islamic law. The name 'sale on credit' (*bayʿ al-ʿīna*) is given *a potiori* to an evasion of the prohibition of *ribā* which is based on this transaction and is reprehensible; for instance, *A* (the creditor) sells to *B* (the debtor) some object for the sum of capital and interest, payable at some future date, and immediately afterwards buys the same object back for the capital payable at once. This amounts to an unsecured loan; on another form of *ʿīna* which provides a security for the loan, see above, p. 79.

Islamic law discusses, with much technical detail, the *tawliya*, resale at the stated original cost, the *waḍīʿa*, resale with a rebate on the stated original cost, and the *murābaḥa*, resale with a stated surcharge which represents the profit. The main consideration is the exclusion of dishonest, unjustified enrichment, but the exact part which these transactions played in the economic life of early Islamic society is not always clear.

Islamic law prohibits the archaic contracts of *muzābana* and *muḥāḳala* (see above, p. 146), but makes an exception in favour of the sale, or barter, of a strictly limited quantity of dried dates for the same estimated quantity of fresh dates on the tree (*bayʿ al-ʿarāyā*; cf. above, p. 40).

Barter of commodities hardly plays a part in Islamic law, but money-changing (*ṣarf*) and, in general, dealing in precious metals receive detailed attention on account of the prohibition of *ribā*. The exchange of precious metals is regarded as 'sale of price for price' (*bayʿ thaman bi-thaman*), and each is a consideration for the other. A consequence of the rules concerning *ribā* is that an exchange of gold for gold and silver for silver is possible only in equal quantities, without regard to differences in quality and to workmanship, so that a golden cup equals its weight in coins of gold; but this particular difficulty can easily be avoided by payment in the other precious metal. A rich casuistry, including many economically impossible cases, has been developed on the subject.

3. *Hire and lease* (*ijāra*; *ujra*, the hire, rent; *ajr*, the wage). The contract of *ijāra* is the sale of a usufruct, and the rules relating to a contract of sale, such as those of *khiyār al-ruʾya*, *khiyār al-ʿayb*, *khiyār al-sharṭ*, *faskh*, and *iḳāla* (but not *shufʿa*), apply to it, too. A defect which occurs after the conclusion of the *ijāra* entitles the hirer or renter to cancel it, if the defect prevents or reduces the possibility of use, e.g. the illness of a hired slave, or the collapse of a rented house. The hirer or renter is further entitled to cancel the *ijāra* if he has a valid excuse (*ʿudhr*), particularly if the purpose of the contract is obviated; this is defined very broadly, so that even the hire of a mount can be cancelled if the hirer renounces the journey. The *ijāra* is also cancelled by the death of one of the contracting parties. In the case of a defective *ijāra* the 'fair wage or rent' (*ajr* or *ujrat al-mithl*) is applicable.

Islamic law distinguishes two kinds of *ijāra*, for a period or for carrying out a task. The period must be determined; it is not possible to hire or rent for a stated amount per month. A special case of *ijāra* for a period is the lease of agricultural property. It is forbidden to stipulate that the lessee should undertake work from which the lessor, too, derives advantage, such as dredging canals; if the crop has not yet been harvested when the lease expires, it continues for the fair rent until the crop has ripened; the lease of one agricultural property for another is forbidden because it would amount to *ribā*. Allowed are, on the contrary, albeit not unanimously, the special contracts of *muzāra'a* and *musāḳāt*, where the rent consists of a percentage of the produce; the *muzāra'a* is the lease of a field, the *musāḳāt* the lease of a plantation of fruit trees or vines.

Services can be hired either for a period or by a contract for work (*ajīr*, the hired servant; *ajīr khāṣṣ*, the employee; *ajīr mushtarak*, the self-employed artisan). An archaic contract which is tolerated, by *istiḥsān*, because it is customary, is the hire of a wet-nurse for her food and clothing. There are special forms of *khiyār* if the artisan has carried out the work contrary to the contract; the employer has the choice either of refusing acceptance of the work and demanding compensation for his material, or of accepting the work and paying the 'fair' but not more than the stipulated wage. With regard to liability in this case, it is contested whether the artisan is in the privileged position of a depositary (above, p. 147 f.); apart from this, there exists a special kind of liability for what the artisan destroys by working on it; in most cases the employer has the choice either of paying the wage and demanding compensation for the completed work, or of not paying the wage and demanding compensation for his material. On the retention of a thing by the artisan for wages due for work done on it, see above, p. 140.

The contract of manufacture (*istiṣnā'*), on the other hand, is merely a *salam* contract; it is valid only in so far as it is customary.

4. *Society*. The concept of corporation does not exist in Islamic law (neither does that of a juristic person; cf. above, p. 125); only the *'āḳila* can be regarded as a rudimentary form of corporation. There is also no freedom of association, and only certain kinds of society (*sharika* or *shirka*; *sharīk*, the partner), or more specifically of mercantile partnership (*sharikat 'aḳd*), as

opposed to joint ownership (*sharikat māl*), are permitted. This mercantile partnership falls within the sphere of the procuration (*wakāla*). Two partners only are generally envisaged.

Islamic law distinguishes the following kinds of partnership. (*a*) the unlimited mercantile partnership (*mufāwaḍa*), with full power and liability of each partner; it amounts to a mutual procuration and suretyship, and is possible only with equal shares. It engages the whole property of both partners, excepting only food and clothing for themselves and their families, which each buys separately; there exists therefore no separate social capital. It is not possible between free men and slaves, Muslims and *dhimmīs*, &c.

(*b*) The limited liability company (*sharikat ʿinān*), which amounts to a mutual procuration; each partner is responsible to third persons for his own transactions, and he has the right of recourse against the other partner to the amount of his share. This kind of partnership engages only the capital which has been brought in, and it can be restricted to certain kinds of transactions. The shares of the partners can be different, and if both do not do the same amount of work, their shares in the profit may differ from their shares in the capital.

(*c*) The partnership of artisans (*sharikat al-ṣanāʾiʿ wal-taḳabbul*), for the joint pursuit of a trade or of connected trades.

(*d*) The credit co-operative (*sharikat al-wujūh*), without capital; it consists of pooling the credit of the partners for buying goods on credit, reselling them, and sharing the profit.

The sleeping partnership (*muḍāraba*), which has common features with the *muzāraʿa* and the *musāḳāt*, is not a society proper; it consists of a fiduciary relationship (*amāna*) and a procuration, and becomes a partnership only as far as the profit is concerned. The sleeping partner (*rabb al-māl*) bears the loss. A defective *muḍāraba* is treated as if it were a hire of services; it becomes defective if it is stipulated that a fixed sum, instead of a percentage of the profit, shall be the share of one of the partners, if it is stipulated that the working partner shall bear the loss, or if the profit cannot be determined exactly, e.g. if it is stipulated that the working partner shall live in a house belonging to the sleeping partner, so that the notional rent of the house becomes part of the profit. How far the expenses are borne by the working partner and how far by the partnership is laid down in detail. When a profit is followed by a loss, the procedure in certain cases is the same as if the profit had been distributed already, so that the working partner is not affected by the loss. When the *muḍāraba* is dissolved, the working partner may still exchange gold for silver after notice of dissolution has been given, if the working capital was silver, and vice versa. This is admitted by *istiḥsān* because it is customary; in strict *ḳiyās* he would be entitled only to sell the remainder of the merchandise because both precious metals are regarded equally as price. The *muḍāraba* has become an important device for circumventing the prohibition of *ribā*.

5. *Deposit* (*wadīʿa*). The deposit is the commission given by the owner to another to hold his property in safe custody; it is a fiduciary relationship (*amāna*). The safe-keeping must be assured by the depositary himself or by a member of his family. The depositary's refusal to return the deposit, his denial that a deposit exists, and its confusion with his own property, are usurpation and engender liability; other kinds of 'transgression' (*taʿaddī*; above, p. 147 f.), particularly using the deposit, engender liability too. The effects of these other kinds of *taʿaddī* in the case of a deposit are different from those in the cases of hire and lease and of the loan of non-fungible objects; in the case of a deposit, liability ceases when the *taʿaddī* ceases, but in the case of the other contracts it continues until the termination of the contractual relationship.

6. *Loan of non-fungible objects* (*ʿāriyya, commodatum*). *ʿĀriyya* is defined as putting another temporarily and gratuitously[1] in possession of the use of a thing, the substance of which is not consumed by its use. It is distinguished as a separate contract from the loan of money and of other fungible objects which are intended to be consumed (this is the *ḳarḍ, mutuum*). The borrower may, generally speaking, lend the borrowed thing to a third party, but he must not hire it out or give it as a security. The owner may at any time demand the return (*rujūʿ*) of the thing which he has lent, but he may become liable for damages, for instance if he prematurely demands the return of a field which he has lent for a long period and the borrower has planted on it.

7. *Donation* (*hiba*). A donation becomes complete (*tāmm*) only through taking possession as fully as possible under the

[1] Any stipulated reward would be unjustified enrichment.

circumstances; this requires, generally speaking, the permission of the donor. A special case is the donation on condition of giving a countervalue; having been a donation in the first place, it becomes a sale after the countervalue has been given. It is possible to revoke (*rujūʿ*) a donation before the donee has taken possession; after he has taken possession, this is strongly reprehended and excluded in a number of cases, one of which is that a countervalue has been given. Should the object of the donation or the countervalue be vindicated, the return of the countervalue or of the object, respectively, may be claimed under certain conditions.

The charitable gift (*ṣadaḳa*) is treated as a donation, except that it cannot be revoked.

Archaic forms of donation are (*a*) donation for life (*ʿumrā*); Islamic law treats it as an unconditional donation; (*b*) donation with the stipulation that the object becomes the property of the surviving party (*ruḳbā*); it is invalid on account of uncertainty, but some authorities treat it in the same way as the *ʿumrā*.

8. *Suretyship* (*kafāla*; *kafīl*, the guarantor; *aṣīl*, the principal debtor). Suretyship in Islamic law is the creation of an additional liability with regard to the claim, not to the debt, the assumption not of the debt but only of a liability, and it has its origin in procedure. It is of two kinds, suretyship for the person (*kafāla bil-nafs*) and suretyship for the claim (*kafāla bil-māl*).

Standing surety for a person means undertaking the liability for the appearance of the debtor or of his agent in a lawsuit; it is effective only if a lawsuit is possible, and not if the debtor has absented himself and his whereabouts are unknown; it is extinguished by the death of the guarantor or of the debtor; in the case of non-performance, the guarantor is imprisoned.[1]

Suretyship for the claim can be independent or additional to suretyship for the person; if the guarantor stipulates that the debt of the principal debtor be remitted, its effect is that of the *ḥawāla*.

Acceptance by the creditor is necessary in either case of suretyship. Suretyship is possible only in connexion with an already existing claim concerning property; it is therefore not possible in connexion with *ḥadd* punishments, retaliation, and the payment due by the slave under a contract of *mukātaba*; on the other hand, it is possible not only in connexion with debts of

[1] See also below, p. 202.

money but also with unsecured claims to non-fungible objects. The liability of the guarantor can, generally speaking, not go beyond the liability of the debtor; therefore the acquittance of the debtor by the creditor also acquits the guarantor, but not vice versa. An exception is made in the case of suretyship for the debt of a slave for which this last would become liable only when he is manumitted (see above p. 128); then the guarantor is nevertheless liable for immediate payment, because suretyship cannot be made subject to the stipulation of a term, and it obliges with immediate effect. A recourse of the guarantor against the principal debtor is possible only if the latter has asked him to stand surety.

9. *Obligation under oath.* Islamic law regards as an oath (*yamīn*) every statement or undertaking which is emphasized by the words 'by Allah' or by a similar formula; in the case of non-fulfilment of the undertaking a religious expiation (*kaffāra*), which need not be more than fasting on three consecutive days, must be performed, but there is no punishment for perjury concerning the past. Islamic law regards as an oath, too, an undertaking with a self-imposed penalty (above, p. 117) and, in general, a declaration by which a unilateral disposition is made dependent on the occurrence of a certain event, such as 'if I do such and such a thing, or if such and such a thing happens, my wife is repudiated, or my slave is manumitted'. In these cases the disposition becomes effective automatically if the condition on which it was made dependent is fulfilled. This kind of conditional repudiation and manumission has acquired considerable importance in the practice of Islamic law.

10. *Unauthorized agency.* Islamic law does not, on principle, recognize unauthorized agency of a stranger as a source of obligations, but the principal can approve the act of an unauthorized agent (*fuḍūlī*) and thereby make it valid. Expenses made in the interest of a found object or of a foundling (*laḳīṭ*) create an obligation only if they have been made with the permission of the authorities, which, however, can be given afterwards. Correspondingly taking up a found object is merely recommended, obligatory only if its loss is to be feared. As an exception, Islamic law imposes the obligation of paying a reward (*juʿl*) for bringing back a fugitive slave from a distance of more than three days' journey (except between near relatives); this

was originally based on a public offer of reward, but has lost this character and has been fixed at 40 dirhams.

11. *Obligations arising from torts and crimes.* These comprise not only liability for damage to property but liability to retaliation for crimes against the person, and liability for monetary payments in place of retaliation, for which in many cases not the author of the tort but his *ʿāḳila* is responsible, and all give rise to a private claim (*ḥaḳḳ ādamī*). For practical reasons, however, these last will be discussed below, pp. 177 f., 181 ff. There remains the special case of *ghaṣb*.

Ghaṣb, usurpation of the property of another (including the abduction of a free person), is defined as the annulment of legitimate possession by establishing an illegitimate possession. It is a sin, makes the usurper (*ghāṣib*) liable to discretionary punishment, and engenders the obligation of return to the owner in the same place, as well as the highest degree of liability known to Islamic law. The usurper is liable for the loss of the usurped object, even in the case of a usurped slave's dying of a wound inflicted upon him by his owner before the usurpation (because the *ghaṣb* breaks the continuity of the effect of the owner's act), or in the case of a usurped free child's dying of lightning or of a snake bite (because the usurper has by the *ghaṣb* exposed him to the danger). The usurper is equally liable for the acquisition of ownership in the usurped object by specification, commixtion, and confusion, and the owner often has the choice of more than one way of making the usurper responsible. The usurper is further liable for a diminution of value, also indirectly for a delict of the usurped slave, that is to say, the owner is directly responsible but has the right of recourse against the usurper. The usurper is, however, not responsible for the proceeds and for an increase in value, but he is responsible for the the usufruct of a *waḳf*. The person who exercises duress is assimilated to the usurper.

These provisions, which reflect the social conditions in the formative period of Islamic law, in which acts of misappropriation of private property by high-handed action were frequent, not only protect the owner in all transactions in which possession is transferred, but cover those cases of unlawful appropriation which fall outside the very narrow definitions of delicts against property (theft and highway robbery) in penal law.

22

FAMILY

1. *The family* is the only group based on consanguinity or affinity which Islam recognizes. Islam is opposed to tribal feeling, because the solidarity of believers should supersede the solidarity of the tribe. Intermediate groups have left traces only in connexion with succession (the *ʿaṣaba*), with crimes against the person (the *ʿāḳila*), and with the duty of maintenance beyond the limits of the family in the narrow meaning of the term; but these are merely extensions of the family and not groups in their own right.

2. *Marriage* (*nikāḥ*; *zawj*, the husband; *zawja*, the wife) is a contract of civil law, and it shows traces of having developed out of the purchase of the bride; the bridegroom concludes the contract with the legal guardian (*walī*) of the bride, and he undertakes to pay the nuptial gift (*mahr*, *ṣadāḳ*) or 'dower' (in the sense in which the term is used in the Old Testament), not to the *walī* as was customary in the pre-Islamic period, but to the wife herself. The contract must be concluded in the presence of free witnesses, two men or one man and two women; this has the double aim of providing proof of marriage and disproving unchastity. The requirements made of the witnesses for the second aim are lower than those for the first, so that witnesses suffering from legal defects may assure the second aim but not the first. This contract is the only legally relevant act in concluding marriage; privacy (*khalwa*) between husband and wife, and consummation (*dukhūl*) are facts which may have legal effects when the marriage is dissolved, but are not essential for its conclusion. The *walī* is the nearest male relative, in the order of succession (as *ʿaṣaba*), followed by the manumitter and his *ʿaṣaba*, and failing those, the *ḳāḍī*. The *walī* can give his ward in marriage against her will if she is a minor, but when she comes of age she has the right of rescission; some, however, hold that she does not have this right if it was her father or

grandfather who gave her in marriage. (See also above, p. 117.) Similar rules apply if the bridgroom, as a minor, is married by his *walī*. Also the slave woman whom her master has given in marriage against her will has the right of rescission when she becomes free. A free woman who is fully responsible may give herself in marriage, but the *walī* has the right to object if the prospective husband is not of equal birth. The degrees of equality by birth (*kafā'a*), which is demanded only of the man, among the free Muslims are: members of Ḳuraysh, the tribe of the Prophet; other Arabs; and non-Arabs (with subdivisions of these degrees).

The free man may be married to up to four wives simultaneously, the slave to up to two; but the man who is already married to a free wife may not marry a wife who is a slave. There are numerous impediments to marriage, all based on relationship. (On the difference of religion, see above, p. 132).

(*a*) Marriage is forbidden with the *maḥārim* (plural of *maḥram*), the 'non-marriageable persons' *par excellence*, i.e. one's female ascendants and descendants, the (former) wives of one's ascendants and descendants, one's sister and the female descendants of one's sister and brother, one's paternal and maternal aunts and the sisters and aunts of the ascendants, one's mother-in-law and the other female ascendants of one's wife, and one's step-daughter and the other female descendants of one's wife (this last group only if the marriage with the wife was consummated). It is therefore permitted to marry one's first cousins and the half-brother's half-sister (from another marriage).

(*b*) Fosterage (*raḍā'*), i.e. relationship by nursing, is an impediment to marriage of not quite the same extent, the wet-nurse taking the place of the mother. It can combine its effects with those of consanguinity and affinity; for instance, it is forbidden to marry the sister of one's foster-mother. To produce a relationship by nursing, the smallest amount of suckling during the first two and a half years of one's life is sufficient.

(*c*) Forbidden, too, is the 'combination' (*jam'*), i.e. simultaneous marriage with two women who are related to each other within the forbidden degrees by consanguinity, affinity, or fosterage. In this case, only one of the two women is *maḥram*, 'non-marriageable'. The same rule applies to slave women who are in this relationship; they cannot be concubines simultaneously.

To produce affinity which acts as an impediment to marriage, no valid marriage is required, not even intercourse; lustful kissing is sufficient; for instance, if the wife kisses her stepson lustfully, her marriage becomes invalid. Similarly, in the case of 'combination', if the wife suckles her fellow wife, a case not quite impossible under conditions of child marriage and extended suckling, both marriages are, for the time being, invalid until the husband decides in favour of one; these, then, are means of forcing a divorce.

Special stipulations inserted in the contract of marriage, for instance that the husband shall not marry another woman, or that the bride shall be a virgin, are not binding; if the *mahr* has been fixed in consideration of a stipulation of this kind, and it is not fulfilled, the 'fair *mahr*' takes its place; but a conditional repudiation achieves the effect of imposing a stipulation.

Temporary marriage (*mutʿa*), recognized by the 'Twelver' Shiites, is not admitted by the Sunnis, but actual conditions are hardly different on both sides, because of the facility of divorce, the stability of most *mutʿa* marriages among the Shiites, and the possibility of concubinage; among the Sunnis, too, the effect of a *mutʿa* marriage can be achieved by an informal agreement outside the contract of marriage.

The distinction between *fāsid* and *bāṭil* is also made with regard to contracts of marriage. If a *fāsid* marriage is consummated, a *mahr* must be paid to the wife, the wife must keep the waiting period if the marriage is dissolved, and the children born of it are legitimate—all this in contrast with a marriage which is *bāṭil*. Which defects in the contract make a marriage *fāsid* and which *bāṭil*, is decided casuistically, with some controversy on details. Concurrent with this doctrine are two further considerations: the prohibition of unlawful intercourse which applies equally to *fāsid* and to *bāṭil* marriages, and the far-reaching recognition of *shubha* (below, pp. 176, 178) which makes the *ḥadd* punishment for unchastity inapplicable; as a result, the systematic discussions in the sources may seem somewhat complicated.

3. *Divorce*. The normal case is the repudiation (*ṭalāḳ*) of the wife by the husband; it is either revocable (*rajʿī*) or definite (*bāʾin*). The difference depends on the way in which it is formulated; if a normal, regular expression is used, it is revocable,

otherwise (and also if the repudiation is pronounced before consummation of the marriage or for a consideration) it is definite. Therefore, and because repudiation is a disposition with immediate effect, also in order to distinguish between ordinary repudiation and its variant forms, all possible modes of expression are interpreted casuistically. A revocable repudiation does not dissolve the conjugal community and can be withdrawn during the waiting period of the wife; a definite repudiation dissolves the conjugal community, so that a new marriage is necessary if the former husband and wife wish to return to each other. After a husband has repudiated his wife three times (twice, if she is a slave), the former husband and wife can marry again only after the wife has been married to another husband and this marriage has been consummated.[1] The triple repudiation has therefore become the normal form of divorce. The husband ought to pronounce three separate repudiations during three successive states of purity from menstruation of his wife, but it has become customary to pronounce the triple repudiation in one declaration; this is considered an innovation and is forbidden, but is recognized as valid. Conditional repudiation (*ta'līḳ al-ṭalāḳ*), by which repudiation happens automatically if a certain event occurs (above, pp. 117, 159), has become very important in practice. There is also the possibility of *tafwīḍ*, conferring on the wife the power to repudiate herself; this power must, in principle, be exercised in the same meeting (*majlis*) of husband and wife, unless the declaration of *tafwīḍ* declares the contrary; but even a *tafwīḍ* in the form 'you are repudiated whenever you will' is valid.

To the variant forms of repudiation belong the *mubāra'a*, the dissolution of marriage by agreement with mutual waiving of any financial obligations, and, more important, the *khul'*, by which the wife redeems herself from the marriage for a consideration. On the part of the wife, the *khul'* is regarded as an exchange of assets, but on the part of the husband as an undertaking under oath, so that he cannot withdraw an offer of *khul'* which he has made.

A further variant form of repudiation is the *īlā'*, a dissolution of the conjugal community by the oath of the husband to abstain from marital intercourse for four months (two months

[1] On the so-called *taḥlīl*, an evasion of this rule, see above, p. 81.

if the wife is a slave); if the husband keeps the oath it has the effect of a definite repudiation, but it can, as any other oath, be withdrawn against performance of the *kaffāra* or of a self-imposed penalty, as the case may be. Presumably an old form of repudiation which Islam does not recognize as such is the *ẓihār*, the use of the formula 'you are for me (as untouchable) as the back (*ẓahr*; *pars pro toto*, for body) of my mother'; it does not dissolve the marriage but is regarded as an impious declaration which requires a particularly heavy *kaffāra* which, in contrast with the *kaffāra* in other cases, can be enforced by the *ḳāḍī*.

The *tafrīḳ* (literally 'separation', but a real dissolution of marriage) is normally pronounced by the *ḳāḍī*, on his own initiative or at the instance of one of the spouses, exceptionally by the *walī* in exercise of his right of objection or by the wife in exercise of her right of rescission at manumission. Grounds on which the wife may demand dissolution of her marriage by the *ḳāḍī* are the exercise of her right of rescission on coming of age, impotence of the husband, and, according to some authorities only, his lunacy and certain grave chronic diseases. The husband may demand dissolution of the marriage by the *ḳāḍī* in exercise of his right of rescission on coming of age; he can always exercise his right of repudiation.[1] The *ḳāḍī* pronounces *tafrīḳ* on his own initiative in the case of serious impediments to marriage, e.g. the 'combination' of two sisters; in other cases he merely forbids the conjugal community.

Marriage is also dissolved by *liʿān*, which belongs to penal law; the husband affirms under oath that the wife has committed unchastity or that the child born of her is not his, and she, if the occasion arises, affirms under oath the contrary; these affirmations are made in stringent forms of a magical character.

Finally, the marriage ceases if it becomes invalid, either through apostasy from Islam of one of the spouses, or by one of them, being a slave, becoming the property of the other.

The legal position of the wife, under a system of polygamy, concubinage, and repudiation, is obviously less favourable than that of the husband, but she has at least certain possibilities of

[1] The distinction between *ṭalāḳ* and *tafrīḳ* is not purely formal; if *tafrīḳ* takes place before consummation of the marriage for a reason inherent in the wife, no financial obligations from the marriage arise for the husband, in contrast with *ṭalāḳ*. This is of greater practical importance in the other schools of law, where there are more grounds for demanding *tafrīḳ* on the part of the husband (and of the wife).

obtaining a divorce, and her situation is in fact considerably improved by the effects of the matrimonial régime and by the institution of conditional repudiation, wherever it has become customary to pronounce it immediately after the conclusion of the marriage.

Every dissolution of a marriage which has been consummated, even by an 'untrue', i.e. not undisturbed, privacy of husband and wife, entails a waiting period (*ʿidda*) of the wife before she can marry another husband. The *ʿidda* of a pregnant woman lasts until her delivery; if she is not pregnant it lasts four months and ten days if the husband has died and she is a free woman (half that time if she is a slave); in all other cases (also after extra-matrimonial intercourse) it lasts until three menstruations have occurred if she is a free woman or an *umm walad* (two menstruations for other slave women) or, if she does not menstruate, three months (half that time if she is a slave woman other than an *umm walad*). There is an analogous period which must elapse before the owner may begin to have intercourse with a slave woman whom he has bought; it is called *istibrāʾ*, and lasts normally until one menstruation has occurred or, alternately, one month. It is not obligatory but only recommended if the previous owner of the female slave is herself a woman.

4. *Family relationships*. The marital power is far-reaching and includes a limited right of correction; the husband may forbid his wife to leave the house, and may restrict the access even of her own relatives to her. A disobedient wife is liable to correction by the husband and loses her right of maintenance. On the other hand, the wife may refuse, for herself and for her children, to accompany the husband on journeys.

The recognized duration of pregnancy is from six months to two years; this implies that the husband must acknowledge as his own a child born within two years from the dissolution of the marriage, and his refusal to do so would be *ḳadhf*; he may also acknowledge as his own a child born still later. Although the acknowledgement of paternity of a person of unknown origin amounts to an adoption, adoption as such does not exist; it was rejected by the Koran (sura xxxiii. 4 f.). The foundling (*laḳīṭ*) can be claimed by anyone as his offspring; until the contrary is proved he is free and a Muslim, unless he has been found in a non-Muslim quarter; if he is claimed by no one, the person who has found him has restricted parental authority. The right of the mother in the child is stronger than that of the father; she has the right to the care of the child (*haḍāna*), in the case of boys until the age of 7 or 9, in the case of girls until they become of age. It is not a duty but only a right which the mother loses if she concludes a subsequent marriage with a person other than a *maḥram* of the child, i.e. his relative within the prohibited degrees; in this case, and if the mother dies, the right of *haḍāna* is transferred to the nearest female relative, first of the mother, then of the father.

5. *Matrimonial régime*. There is no matrimonial community of goods and no dot or marriage portion (dowry in the Western sense); the wife has the right to the nuptial gift (*mahr*) and to maintenance (*nafaḳa*); this gives her a strong position as against the husband. The wife may leave the fixing of the *mahr* to the husband, which may amount to a waiver. The minimum amount of the *mahr* is ten dirhams; if the amount of *mahr* has not been fixed (also in some cases if the stipulation or the marriage itself is *fāsid*), the 'fair *mahr*' (*mahr al-mithl*), which is determined with regard to the social position and the other qualities of the bride, not of the bridegroom, is payable. It is customary to pay part of the *mahr* immediately and to postpone payment of the rest, but it is possible to stipulate immediate payment or postponement of the whole. The unpaid part beçomes due (1) on the death of one of the spouses in every case, (2) in the case of repudiation if the marriage has been consummated at least by a 'true', i.e. undisturbed, privacy between husband and wife. If repudiation takes place before consummation, the wife has the right to half the stipulated *mahr* (or, if no *mahr* was stipulated, to an indemnity which is called *mut'a*[1] and consists of a set of clothing, on the basis of sura ii. 236). The obligation of the husband to pay the *mahr* in full in the case of repudiation, acts as a powerful limitation of his freedom to repudiate.

The maintenance of the wife comprises food, clothing, and lodging, i.e. a separate house or at least a separate room which can be locked, for the well-to-do also a servant; she is not obliged to bear any part of the expenses of the matrimonial establishment. Her claim to maintenance is suspended if she

[1] To be distinguished from *mut'a* in the sense of temporary marriage.

is a minor, is disobedient (in particular, if she leaves the house unauthorized or refuses marital intercourse), is imprisoned for debt, performs the pilgrimage without her husband, or is abducted (by *ghaṣb*), all cases in which she cannot fulfil her marital duties. If the husband absents himself without providing for the maintenance of the wife, the *ḳāḍī* authorizes her to provide for it by pledging her husband's credit. The claim to maintenance continues during the *ʿidda*, provided the marriage has not been dissolved through a fault of hers (e.g. by kissing her own stepson, or by apostasy from Islam).

On inheritance between spouses, see below, p. 171. The right of the wife to inherit cannot be frustrated by repudiation, because the wife who has been definitely repudiated during the last illness of the husband inherits if he dies during the *ʿidda*. Conversely, the husband inherits if the wife has caused the dissolution of the marriage during her last illness and dies during the *ʿidda*.

The children have a claim to maintenance only if they are poor and, in principle, only against their father. The maintenance of the illegitimate child and of the child whose paternity has been contested by *liʿān* is the responsibility of the mother, that of the foundling the responsibility of the public treasury. The parents have no right of usufruct in the property of their children. The right of the father or grandfather to act on behalf of his children or grandchildren is not unlimited; he cannot conclude unilaterally disadvantageous transactions, such as lending their property as *ʿāriyya*, making an amicable settlement if the opponent produces no evidence, or abandoning the claim to retaliation. A legal guardian who is not the father or grandfather is still further restricted in his powers.

Beyond these cases, only those who are not themselves poor are obliged to provide maintenance. In particular, the sons and daughters must provide equally for the maintenance of their parents. The incidence of the duty of maintenance differs from that of the right of inheritance; it may happen that a person is obliged to provide maintenance without being a legal heir.

23

INHERITANCE

1. *General.* There is no institution of an heir (*heredis institutio*) in Islamic law, and the testament is restricted to making legacies and to appointing an executor and/or guardian. The law of inheritance provides for fixed shares which take precedence over the succession of the next of kin to the residue. There is no universal succession (*successio in universum ius*);[1] out to the estate (*tarika*) are paid, first, the costs of the funeral and, second, the debts; these become immediately due by the death.[2] If the debts equal or exceed the assets of the estate, the assets are distributed among the creditors, if necessary in proportion to their claims. Conversely, claims form part of the estate. Obligations and rights survive to a lesser degree than debts and claims; many contracts are dissolved by death, for instance hire and lease, and in some cases suretyship. With regard to the right of rescission, the *khiyār al-taʿyīn* and the *khiyār al-ʿayb* survive, but not the *khiyār al-ruʾya* and the *khiyār al-sharṭ*. From the remaining assets are further deducted the legacies, which are restricted to one-third of these assets unless the heirs give their approval or do not exist at all. The distinction between debt and legacy is often doubtful but important because the heirs have an interest in having considered as legacies as many dispositions as possible. An important distinction is that the manumission of the *umm walad* is to be debited to the whole of the assets, that of the *mudabbar* to the third. Not only monetary values but also other claims, such as the claim to exact retaliation, can be inherited.[3]

[1] But each heir is considered to have become the owner of his individual portion on the death of the deceased.

[2] On debts arising from an *iḳrār* made during the mortal illness, see above, p. 151.

[3] The waiver of the claim to blood-money by a fatally injured person in a case of *khaṭaʾ* is regarded as a legacy and therefore restricted to one-third of the assets, but the gratuitous waiver of retaliation, which implies the waiver of blood-money. in a case of *ʿamd* is effective without this restriction.

2. *Succession* (*farā'iḍ*, the allotted portions). Grounds of exclusion from succession are the quality of being a slave, having caused the death of the deceased, difference of religion, and difference of domicile (between the Islamic state and a non-Islamic country, as well as between these last). Grounds of qualification as an heir (*wārith*) are consanguinity, marriage, and clientship, in the following order.

(1) those entitled to a fixed share (*farḍ*, *sahm*);

(2) the *'aṣaba*, roughly corresponding to the agnates; unless the shares of the first group cover the whole of the estate, groups (1) and (2) inherit together, the *'aṣaba* taking the residue after the shares of the first group have been deducted; but apart from this, each group excludes the following groups from succession;

(3) the manumitter (who is the patron, *mawlā*, of the person he has manumitted) and, after him, his *'aṣaba*;

(4) if there are no heirs belonging to groups (2) and (3), the heirs belonging to the first group once more, by having their shares increased in proportion so that they cover the whole of the estate;

(5) the *dhawu 'l-arḥām*, roughly corresponding to the cognates;

(6) the patron chosen by a convert to Islam, on conversion, by a contract of clientship (the *mawla 'l-muwālāt*);

(7) relatives who have been acknowledged as such by the deceased, without evidence;

(8) beneficiaries of legacies, without restriction to one-third of the estate, if there are no (other) heirs; this provision, systematically speaking, does not belong here;

(9) the public treasury.

These rules presuppose a patriarchal organization of the family, modified by the inclusion of some cognates in the first and the second group; clientship has precedence over the acknowledgement of relationship, which amounts to an adoption. The right of representation, the concept that a pre-deceased heir is represented by his descendants, does not exist in Sunni law.

The most typical feature of the Islamic law of inheritance is the shares of certain heirs (the first group, above), which are in all essentials laid down in the Koran.

(*a*) The daughter (and if there is no daughter, the son's

daughter) and the full sister (and if there is no full sister, the half-sister on the father's side) receive one-half, provided there are no male relatives of the same degree (see below, on the *ʿaṣaba bi-ghayrih*);[1] if there are several of these female relatives, the daughter and the son's daughter exclude the sister from a share (see below, on the *ʿaṣaba maʿa ghayrih*), two and more daughters the son's daughter, two and more full sisters the half-sister, and they receive together two-thirds (see below, (*e*)).

(*b*) The husband receives one-half if there are no children or son's children, and one-quarter in the contrary case.

(*c*) The wife receives one-quarter if there are no children or son's children, and one-eighth in the contrary case; if there are several wives, they divide this in equal portions.

(*d*) The mother receives one-third if there are no children or son's children and not more than one brother or sister, and one-sixth in the contrary case; but if in the first case husband or wife coexist with the father, the mother receives only one-third of the residue after the shares of husband or wife have been paid.[2]

(*e*) Half-brothers and half-sisters on the mother's side, if there are two or more of them, receive one-third, the males and females dividing it in equal portions; one half-brother or half-sister on the mother's side receives one-sixth. One-sixth is also the share of the father (or, if there is no father, the nearest male or female ascendant in the male line), provided there are children or son's children,[3] of the son's daughter (or son's daughters who divide it in equal portions), provided there is one daughter,[4] and of the half-sister (or half-sisters) on the father's side, provided there is one full sister (and no daughter or son's daughter; see above (*a*)).

These provisions aim at modifying a system of purely agnatic succession, under which only men inherit, in favour mainly of the nearest female relatives,[5] the spouse, and also of the father (or other ascendants). The father, who is qualified under an

[1] See also below, p. 173, n. 1.

[2] In other words, her share is reduced to half the portion of the father.

[3] If there are no children or son's children, the father is treated as *ʿaṣaba*; see below.

[4] This sixth 'completes' the half which is the share of the daughter, by bringing the aggregate up to two-thirds; see above (*a*). The same applies to the share of the half-sister on the father's side; see what follows.

[5] But the daughter's daughter remains excluded.

agnatic system, too, needs to be protected against being completely excluded by existing male descendants, but he is further privileged as against female descendants; if he coexists with these, he takes either his fixed share or the portion of an *aṣaba* or both. It is rare that the concurrence of several shares leads to the exclusion of near male relatives; this can never happen to the descendants and ascendants, but if a woman leaves a husband (share: one-half), the mother (share: one-sixth) and half-brothers on the mother's side (share: one-third), this exhausts the inheritance, and nothing is left over for full brothers.[1] It can even happen that the aggregate of the shares amounts to more than one unit; in this case the shares are reduced in proportion (*ʿawl*). For instance, a woman leaves a husband (share: one-half) and two sisters (share: two-thirds), this amounts to seven-sixths, which are reduced to sevenths.

The second group of heirs, the *ʿaṣaba*, is somewhat wider than that of the agnates proper. It comprises in the first place the *ʿaṣaba bi-nafsih* (' *ʿaṣaba* by themselves, in their own right'), the agnates proper, i.e. men who are connected with the deceased in the male line, in the following order: descendants, ascendants, descendants of the father, descendants of the grandfather, descendants of the great-grandfather, and so on. It comprises, secondly, and *pari passu* with the first, the *ʿaṣaba bi-ghayrih* (' *ʿaṣaba* through another'), i.e. those female relatives whose shares are one-half each (see above (*a*)); they are deemed to become *ʿaṣaba* through their coexisting brothers, and their portions then amount to half the respective portions of their brothers. It comprises, thirdly, the *ʿaṣaba maʿa ghayrih* (' *ʿaṣaba* in conjunction with another'), i.e. the full sister (or sisters) and the half-sister (or half-sisters) on the father's side, if they are not *ʿaṣaba bi-ghayrih* and are excluded from their fixed share by a daughter or son's daughter (above (*a*)). These extensions of the group of agnates, too, aim at protecting near female relatives in cases in which they receive no share, although they are less privileged than the corresponding males.

The nearer relative, in the order mentioned, excludes, generally speaking, the more remote—relatives on the father's

[1] The Mālikīs and the Shāfiʿīs decide that the full brothers divide the third together with the half-brothers on the mother's side in equal portions. There are a few other similar cases.

and the mother's side exclude relatives on the father's side only, and a person entitled to inherit excludes all those who are related to the deceased through him;[1] all female ascendants are excluded by the mother, the female ascendants on the father's side also by the father and by a nearer male ascendant in the male line, but not by a male ascendant of the same degree. He who is himself excluded by having caused the death of the deceased does not exclude others; for instance, his sons are not disqualified. The transfer of the right to inherit from the manumitter to his *'aṣaba* (above, third group) takes place not simply according to the rules of inheritance, but according to a somewhat different, more archaic system. In the fourth group, husband and wife do not take part in the increase of shares. The fifth group comprises persons related to the deceased through a female, and those female relatives who are not *'aṣaba* or entitled to a fixed share; there exists a complicated system of precedence among them.

3. *Testamentary dispositions.* Testamentary dispositions are restricted to appointing an executor and/or guardian (*waṣī*) and to making legacies (*waṣiyya*; pl. *waṣāyā*). The *waṣī* must accept the charge, before or after the death; his main function in the first place is the partition of the inheritance. The *waṣī* who has been appointed by testament is not only an executor but the agent of heirs who are minor or absent, and he administers the inheritance on their behalf; or a separate person may be appointed for this last purpose. His powers as an agent are similar to those of a guardian who is not the father or grandfather; with regard to a major they are more restricted than with regard to a minor, for instance, he is not entitled to sell real property on behalf of a major. If two *waṣī*s have been appointed, each can act severally to some considerable extent. The liability of the *waṣī* is of the restricted, not of the extensive kind; the loss is borne by the estate, in certain cases even if it has occurred to the detriment of one of the heirs after the partition of the inheritance, owing to some non-malicious act of the *waṣī*. The *waṣī* is supervised by the *ḳāḍī* who may, if necessary, himself appoint a *waṣī* or remove him if he is incapable or dishonest.

[1] e.g. the full brothers and sisters and the brothers and sisters on the father's side are excluded by the male descendants and ascendants in the male line. Exceptions have been mentioned above.

The *waṣiyya* creates a right *in rem* and not merely a claim against the heirs. It cannot be made by a minor (or a slave, not even a *mukātab*). Donation, sale for less than the value, manumission, and other unilaterally disadvantageous transactions, if made during a mortal illness, are also regarded as *waṣiyya*; should the sick person not die of it in the end, these transactions are valid as if he had not been ill at all. Grounds of exclusion from a legacy are less strict than those from succession, but the person who has caused the death of the deceased is still excluded, as are the heirs themselves (unless the other heirs give their approval). Legacies must not exceed one-third of the estate; if they exceed it, their total is reduced to one-third, not in proportion but by a complicated system of reckoning based on priorities (unless the heirs give their approval). Legacies are interpreted casuistically with the tendency towards regarding them as valid whenever possible. The legacy can be revoked, either by declaration or by conduct, in particular by alienation of its object or by acts which would create ownership if applied to the property of a third party, such as specification. The legacy becomes void if the legatee dies before the legator. It needs to be accepted after the death of the legator; if the legatee dies after the legator but before he has accepted the legacy, his right is transferred to his heirs without an acceptance by these last being required.

24

PENAL LAW

1. *General survey*. The penalties envisaged by Islamic law consist of two disparate groups which correspond to the two sources from which all penal law is commonly derived, private vengeance and punishment of crimes against religion and military discipline. The first has survived in Islamic law almost without modification. The second group is represented only by crimes against religion, and that in a particular sense; certain acts which have been forbidden or sanctioned by punishments in the Koran have thereby become crimes against religion. These are: unlawful intercourse (*zinā*); its counterpart, false accusation of unlawful intercourse (*ḳadhf*); drinking wine (*shurb al-khamr*); theft (*sariḳa*); and highway robbery (*ḳaṭʿ al-ṭarīḳ*). The punishments laid down for them are called *ḥadd* (plural *ḥudūd*), Allah's 'restrictive ordinances' *par excellence*; they are: the death penalty, either by stoning (the more severe punishment for unlawful intercourse) or by crucifixion or with the sword (for highway robbery with homicide); cutting off hand and/or foot (for highway robbery without homicide and for theft); and in the other cases, flogging with various numbers of lashes. Lashes can also be awarded by the *ḳāḍī* as *taʿzīr* 'chastisement'; this takes the place of the *ḥadd* in cases in which this last is not fully incurred, and it can also be awarded by the *ḳāḍī* at his discretion, starting with as little as a disapproving look or a reprimand, for any unlawful act. The number of lashes in the less-severe *ḥadd* for unlawful intercourse is 100, in the *ḥadd* punishments for false accusation of unlawful intercourse and for drinking wine 80, and in the *taʿzīr* not more than 39 (i.e. less than the lowest *ḥadd* punishment for a slave; according to others, not more than 75, less than the lowest *ḥadd* punishment for a free person). The intensity of the lashes, which is different in each case, and other details of carrying out the punishments, are regulated, too. Imprisonment (*ḥabs*) is not a punishment, except as *taʿzīr*, but

a coercive measure which aims at producing repentance (*tawba*) or ensuring a required performance. There are no fines in Islamic law.

The *ḥadd* is a right or claim of Allah (*ḥakk Allāh*), therefore no pardon or amicable settlement is possible. On the other hand, prosecutions for false accusation of unlawful intercourse and for theft, crimes which include infringing a right of humans (*ḥakk ādamī*), take place only on the demand of the persons concerned, and the applicant must be present both at the trial and the execution. In the case of unlawful intercourse the witnesses play a corresponding part; if they are not present (and, if the punishment is stoning, if they do not throw the first stones) the punishment is not carried out. The religious character of the *ḥadd* punishment manifests itself also in the part played by active repentance (*tawba*); if the thief returns the stolen object before an application for prosecution has been made, the *ḥadd* lapses; repentance from highway robbery before arrest also causes the *ḥadd* to lapse, and any offences committed are treated as ordinary delicts (*jināyāt*) so that, if the person entitled to demand retaliation is willing to pardon, blood-money may be paid instead or the punishment remitted altogether. In the case of offences against religion which are not sanctioned by *ḥadd* punishments (below, section 4), the effects of repentance are even more far-reaching. There is a strong tendency to restrict the applicability of *ḥadd* punishments as much as possible, except the *ḥadd* for false accusation of unlawful intercourse, but this in its turn serves to restrict the applicability of the *ḥadd* for unlawful intercourse itself. The most important means of restricting *ḥadd* punishments are narrow definitions. Important, too, is the part assigned to *shubha*, the 'resemblance' of the act which has been committed to another, lawful one, and therefore, subjectively speaking, the presumption of bona fides in the accused. Duress is recognized to a wide extent, in the case of unlawful intercourse and of drinking wine to the extent that it must be proved that the act was voluntary. Only one *ḥadd* is due for several offences of the same kind that have not yet been punished. There are short periods of limitation, in general one month; in the case of drinking wine, according to the prevailing opinion, the time during which the smell of wine or drunkenness persists. This does not mean that the offence is not punishable any longer, but that the *ḳāḍī* does not accept evidence, if there is a justification for the delay in reporting the offence, such as distance, the period of limitation does not run. Finally, proof is made difficult; in contrast with the acknowledgement concerning other matters, the confession of an offence involving a *ḥadd* can be withdrawn (*rujūʿ*); it is even recommended that the *ḳāḍī* should suggest this possibility to the person who has confessed, except in the case of false accusation of unlawful intercourse; and particularly high demands are made of the witnesses as regards their number, their qualifications, and the content of their statements. These demands are most severe with regard to evidence on unlawful intercourse, on the basis of sura xxiv. 4 which refers to an accusation that had been raised against Muhammad's wife, ʿĀ'isha; in this case four male witnesses are required instead of the normal two, and they must testify as eyewitnesses not merely to the act of intercourse but to 'unlawful intercourse' (*zinā*) as such; correspondingly, a confession of unlawful intercourse, in order to bring about the *ḥadd* punishment, must be made on four separate occasions.[1] A further safeguard lies in the fact that an accusation of unlawful intercourse which is dismissed constitutes *ḳadhf* which itself is punishable by *ḥadd*; for instance, if one of the four required witnesses turns out to be a slave or to be otherwise disqualified from giving valid evidence, or if there are discrepancies between their respective depositions, or if one of them retracts (*rujūʿ*) his evidence, all are, in principle, liable to the *ḥadd* for *ḳadhf*.

The liability of the slave (but not of the woman) to *ḥadd* punishments is less; he is punished with half the number of lashes applicable to a free person, and he is not subject to the penalty of being stoned to death.

The approach of Islamic law to the *jināyāt*, i.e. homicide, bodily harm, and damage to property, is thoroughly different. Whatever liability is incurred through them, be it retaliation or blood-money or damages, is the subject of a private claim (*ḥaḳḳ ādamī*); there is no prosecution or execution *ex officio*, not even for homicide, only a guarantee of the right of private vengeance, coupled with safeguards against its exceeding the

[1] But in the case of other offences sanctioned by *ḥadd* a single confession is sufficient.

legal limits; pardon (*'afw*) and amicable settlement are possible, but repentance has no effect. There is no tendency to restrict liability here, and the whole attitude of Islamic law is the same as in its law of property. (See also above, pp. 148, 160.) The concept of bona fides plays no prominent part, but there is a highly developed theory of culpability which distinguishes, not quite logically, deliberate intent, quasi-deliberate intent, mistake, and indirect causation. The life of the slave is protected in the same way as that of the free person, and on his part he is liable to retaliation for homicide with deliberate intent; in all other respects, with regard to *jināyāt* committed by him and against him, he is treated as property for which the owner is responsible and damage to which creates a liability to the owner.

There is, finally, a small group of provisions which fall under neither of the two main headings.

2. Ḥadd *punishments*

(*a*) Unlawful intercourse (*zinā*). It is defined as intercourse without *milk* or *shubhat milk*; *milk* is the right to it arising from marriage or ownership of a female slave; *shubha* with regard to the wife exists, for instance, in a marriage which is *fāsid* but which the husband might have considered valid; or during the waiting period following the definite dissolution of the marriage, which the husband might have thought similar to the waiting period after a revocable repudiation; and with regard to a female slave if the master has manumitted his *umm walad* but not yet dismissed her, or if he has sold his female slave but not yet delivered her, or if the female slave belongs to one of his ascendants or descendants (or to his wife, but not to his brother), or if he is the part-owner of a female slave. In many of these cases, in which no *ḥadd* takes place, intercourse creates a financial obligation, payment of the 'fair *mahr*' to a free woman and of a compensation (called *'uḳr*) to the owner or the part-owner of a female slave. Whether *ḥadd* is applicable or not is disputed in some cases, even important ones, e.g. if intercourse has taken place with a woman hired for that purpose, or for homosexuality. If in these cases *ḥadd* is not applicable, then at least *ta'zīr* is. The *ḥadd* is stoning to death for the *muḥṣan*, 100 lashes for others (50 for the slave in every case).

(*b*) False accusation of unlawful intercourse (*ḳadhf*). Protected by this *ḥadd* is only the *muḥṣan*, in the other meaning of this term (above, p. 125), not therefore, in particular, a person who has been convicted of *zinā* or of a similar act.[1] Only explicit accusation of unlawful intercourse or, in the case of a woman, impugning the legitimacy of her child, amounts to *ḳadhf*. The punishment is 80 lashes (40 for the slave). Here, too, *ta'zīr* is applicable if the *ḥadd* is not fully incurred, e.g. for false accusation of unlawful intercourse directed against an unbeliever or a slave, who are only technically not *muḥsan*, or for a grave insult of a free Muslim which does not amount to *ḳadhf*, e.g. 'O son of a whore'[2] or 'O sinner (*fāsiḳ*)'; no *ta'zīr* is awarded for expressions such as 'O dog', unless the insult has been directed against a scholar in religious law or a descendant of the Prophet; this last provision is based on *istiḥsān*.

Complementary to the rules concerning *ḳadhf* is the procedure of *li'ān* between husband and wife; it makes the *ḥadd* for *ḳadhf* inapplicable to the husband, the *ḥadd* for *zinā* to the wife (provided she, too, makes the affirmation under oath). The concept of adultery, however, is unknown to Islamic law; the wife has no exclusive right on the person of the husband, and although extra-marital intercourse on her part is neglect of her marital duties, it is punished only as a crime against religion.

(*c*) Drinking wine (*shurb al-khamr*). There are two grounds for punishment, drinking wine in any quantity, and being drunk and incapable from whatever cause. The application of this *ḥadd* is made difficult by the required proof that the act was voluntary; therefore the *ḥadd* cannot be applied, without further proof, to a person found drunk and incapable. The punishment is 80 lashes (40 for the slave).

(*d*) Theft (*sariḳa*). *Sariḳa* occurs if a *mukallaf*, including a slave, takes by stealth something of the value of at least ten dirhams, in which he has neither the right of ownership (*milk*) nor *shubhat milk*, out of custody (*ḥirz*); this last consists either of keeping it in a properly secured place or of the presence of a custodian. The stipulation of *milk* or *shubhat milk* excludes everything that belongs

[1] Also the *ḳadhf* directed against a deceased person who was *muḥṣan* is punishable on the demand of his ascendant or descendant.

[2] Because the term for 'whore', *ḳaḥba*, does not amount to an explicit accusation of unlawful intercourse.

to the class of things in which the absence of the ownership is possible, therefore everything that is found in Islamic territory without an owner such as wood, grass, fishes, birds, as long as the acquisition of ownership in it is not obvious, e.g. wood that has been fashioned into a door; assimilated to this are fruits which have not been harvested and easily perishable things such as meat. The same stipulation excludes things which cannot be objects of property, such as a free person, also wine and musical instruments; assimilated to this are things which on account of their holiness are not *in commercio*, such as copies of the Koran and also books on religious sciences. It finally excludes things of which the culprit is a part-owner, including public property, or to which he has a title, including the counter-value of a claim. The stipulation of stealth excludes open robbery (*nahb*) and snatching things unawares (*ikhtilās*, used of pick-pockets, &c.). The stipulation of custody excludes theft from a near relative (*maḥram*), from a house which the accused had been permitted to enter, and embezzlement (*khiyāna*). The stipulation of 'taking' implies that the object must have been removed from the *ḥirz*; a thief who is caught red-handed within the *ḥirz*, e.g. within the house, is therefore not subject to *ḥadd* according to some, *ḥadd* does not even take place if the thief from inside the *ḥirz* hands the object to an accomplice outside). If there are several thieves, *ḥadd* takes place only if the value of the object, when divided by their number, at least equals ten dirhams. The punishment consists of cutting off the right hand and in the case of a second theft, the left foot; in the case of further thefts, and also if the other hand or other foot are not fully usable, the thief is merely imprisoned until he shows repentance. The *ḥadd* punishment excludes pecuniary liability; only if the stolen object is still in existence is it returnable to the owner.

The great majority of cases in which *ḥadd* for theft is not applicable are not punished by *ta'zīr* but fall under the rules concerning *ghaṣb*.

(*e*) Highway robbery (*ḳaṭ' al-ṭarīḳ*). This crime is regarded as related to theft on one side and to homicide on the other, but it is not subsumed under these, except in the case of active repentance before arrest; the penalties inflicted differ according to the different facts of the case. If only plunder has happened and the value of the loot, when divided by the number of culprits, at least equals the minimum amount required for the *ḥadd* for theft to be applicable, the right hand and the left foot are cut off; if only homicide has happened, execution with the sword takes place, not as retaliation but as *ḥadd*; if both plunder and homicide have happened, execution by crucifixion alive takes place. These punishments are awarded to all accomplices, whatever their individual acts; on the other hand, if one of them is exempt from *ḥadd*, e.g. because he is a minor, the *ḥadd* for highway robbery lapses for all, although each remains criminally responsible for his own individual acts.

3. *Jināyāt* (literally 'offences', sing. *jināya*), i.e. *homicide, bodily harm*, and *damage to property*. The scale of punishments is developed in most detail for homicide (*ḳatl*). There are, on the one hand, degrees of culpability, and, on the other, degrees of legal sanctions, where a distinction is made between retaliation (*ḳiṣāṣ, ḳawad*), expiation (*kaffāra*), and blood-money (*diya*), payable either by the culprit himself or by his *ʿāḳila* (below, p. 186). Islamic law distinguishes:

(*a*) deliberate intent (*ʿamd*; *ḳaṣd*, the aim, purpose), which implies the use of a deadly implement; this entails retaliation but no *kaffāra*; the *walī al-dam*, the next of kin who has the right to demand retaliation, may waive it, either gratuitously (this is the pardon, *ʿafw*) or by settlement (*ṣulḥ*) with the culprit, for the blood-money, or for more, or for less, and then the *kaffāra* must be performed;

(*b*) quasi-deliberate intent (*shibh al-ʿamd*), i.e. an intentional act but without using a deadly implement; this entails the performance of *kaffāra* by the culprit and the payment of the 'heavier' blood-money by his *ʿāḳila*;

(*c*) mistake (*khaṭaʾ*), and cases assimilated to mistake (*mā ujriya mujra l-khaṭaʾ*); these entail the same, but only the normal blood-money;

(*d*) indirect homicide (*ḳatl bi-sabab*), opposed to direct, bodily causation; this entails payment of the normal blood-money by the *ʿāḳila* but no *kaffāra*. Cases (*a*) to (*c*) have the further effect that they exclude the culprit from inheritance from the deceased.

This scheme applies to homicide. If it is a question of bodily harm, case (*b*) is merged into case (*a*), but retaliation takes place only for a few kinds of injuries (see below), and in all other cases normal blood-money or a fixed percentage of it is to be paid, in cases (*a*) and (*b*) by the culprit himself, in cases (*c*) and (*d*) by his *'āḳila*. Damage to property entails in all cases liability of the culprit.

There are a few cases of homicide with *'amd* in which there is no retaliation but the culprit must pay the 'heavier' blood-money: if the ascendant kills his own descendant, and if the master kills his own slave[1] or the slave of his descendant. If there are several culprits and one is exempt from retaliation for this or any other reason, the others are exempt too, but must pay the 'heavier' blood-money. The 'heavier' blood-money must further be paid by him who kills an insane or a minor with *'amd* in self-defence; in this particular case, self-defence is not recognized as such because the insane and the minor are not *mukallaf* and therefore not responsible for their acts. They are also incapable of *'amd* and a homicide committed by them is never more than *khaṭa'*, with the special provision that their *'āḳila* must also perform the *kaffāra* for them and that they are not excluded from inheritance.

As regards the distinction between *'amd* and *shibh al-'amd*, it is discussed with much casuistry which implements are to be regarded as deadly or not so, and which other methods of homicide fall into one or the other category. Burning to death is *'amd*, flogging to death is *shibh al-'amd*, homicide by drowning and strangling are controversial.

In the case of *khaṭa'*, one distinguishes whether it resides in the purpose (*fil-ḳaṣd*), e.g. if someone shoots at a man because he takes him for an animal, or in the act (*fil-fi'l*), e.g. if someone shoots at a target and accidentally hits a man, or whether the act can be assimilated to mistake (*mā ujriya mujra l-khaṭa'*), e.g. when a person turns over in his sleep and suffocates another. The concept of negligence is unknown to Islamic law.

Indirect causation (*tasbīb*) creates liability only if the act in question was unauthorized. If someone digs a well and another falls into it, he is not liable if he did it on his own property, or on the property of another with the permission of the owner, or on public property with the permission of the *imām*. The sphere of authorized acts is very extensive; if someone performs

[1] In this particular case, no blood-money is due either.

the ritual ablution in a blind alley of which he is an abutter and therefore a joint owner and another slips in the water which has been poured out, or if someone builds a bridge on public property, even without the permission of the *imām*, and someone falls through it, no liability arises; if a wall threatens collapse, the owner becomes liable only after the owner of the adjoining threatened property has asked him to demolish it. As regards liability for acts of animals, the person in charge of an animal is liable for the damage caused by certain, in fact by most, acts of the animal; equally liable is he who incites or pricks an animal, without regard to the lawfulness or unlawfulness of his act. On the other hand, if a donkey-driver lets his animal out on hire and because of a non-malicious act on his part the hirer falls from the donkey and dies, contractual liability is in any case excluded, and delictual liability does not arise either. The (unaccompanied) rider, however, is regarded as the direct, and not the indirect, cause of the acts of the animal caused by him; he may therefore become liable to *kaffāra* and be excluded from inheritance.

Occasionally there arises the question who is liable for damage by indirect causation. If a stone from a construction falls on to a public road, the workmen are liable until completion and delivery, the owner only after that; the workmen are not liable for unauthorized acts if their unauthorized character is not obvious to them, e.g. if they dig a well on property which has been designated to them by their employer as his own although he is not in fact the owner. If someone hires a workman to sprinkle water on the public road in front of his shop, the workman would be liable in strict analogy because he knows that the public road is not private property, but it is decided by *istiḥsān* that the employer is liable. Liability for damage caused by an unauthorized construction, &c., on public property does not cease with its sale, but liability for damage caused by a wall on private property that collapses does, even if the seller has been asked to demolish it.[1] Occasionally the party that is liable in the first place is given the right of recourse; if someone ties an animal to a string of animals without the knowledge of the person in charge, this last is liable but has the right of recourse against the person who has tied the animal on; if someone orders

[1] See also below, p. 204.

a minor to kill someone, the *'āḳila* of the minor is liable but has the right of recourse against the person who gave the order.

There is no liability for acts against a person who is not protected, whose blood is *hadr* (or *hadar*; opposite *ma'ṣūm*, inviolable). This is in the first place the *ḥarbī*; further, a person killed or wounded in self-defence (excepting the case mentioned above, p. 182). The limits of self-defence are determined casuistically; in general, it is recognized only in a case of dangerous attack (not, for instance, of an attack with a stick in a city in daytime, in contrast with a similar attack outside a city or at night), also in a case of theft at night if it can be prevented only by attacking the thief, and in forcing access to water in a case of extremity if access to water is denied. There is further no liability, of course, for carrying out the death penalty, or for death caused by carrying out *ḥadd* or *ta'zīr* punishments; also if a man surprises his wife or his female *maḥram* in unlawful intercourse and kills her and/or her accomplice; finally, for suicide and in a few other cases.

If the killer is not known, the ancient procedure of *ḳasāma*, a kind of compurgation, takes place. If the body of a person is found who has obviously been killed, the inhabitants of the quarter, the owner of the house (and his *'āḳila*), the passengers and crew of the boat in which he is found, must swear fifty oaths that they have not killed him and do not know who has killed him; if there are not fifty of them, they must swear more than once. Should they refuse to swear, they are imprisoned until they do. They thereby become free from liability to *ḳiṣāṣ* but must, as *'āḳila*, pay the blood-money. If the body of a killed person is found in the main mosque, the public treasury pays his blood-money; if it is found in open country, his blood is not avenged (*hadr* or *hadar*, in a semantic meaning slightly different from that above).

Entitled to prosecute for homicide (and in the case of *ḳasāma*, entitled to demand the oath and, if there are more than fifty persons eligible to swear it, to designate the fifty who swear) is the *walī al-dam* (literally, 'avenger of the blood'), who is the next of kin (the nearest of the *'aṣaba*) according to the law of succession, or several as the case may be. He carries out retaliation, he may waive it, either gratuitously or by settlement, and he receives the blood-money or may waive his claim to it. An injured person himself has the right to demand retaliation, if applicable, or the payment of the blood-money to himself.

The considerable restriction of blood feuds was a great merit of Muhammad's. According to Bedouin ideas, any member of the tribe of the killer, and even more than one, could be killed if homicide had occurred. Islam allows only the killer himself (or several killers for one slain) to be put to death, and only if he is fully responsible and has acted clearly with deliberate intent; Islamic law further recommends waiving retaliation. The execution is carried out with the sword. Retaliation for bodily harm is restricted to those cases in which exact equality can be assured, e.g. the loss of a hand, a foot, a tooth, &c. If the culprit with *ʿamd* has made two persons lose the same hand, only his corresponding hand is cut off in retaliation, and the proper percentage of the blood-money is paid for the other hand. Retaliation for the loss of an eye takes place only if its seeing power has been destroyed (in this case the same is done to the culprit with a red-hot needle), not if it has been knocked out. Retaliation also takes place for a wound in the head which lays bare the bone.

Retaliation is regarded as full amends for an intentional homicide; if it does not or cannot take place, both *kaffāra* must be performed and blood-money must be paid (see above), but no *kaffāra* is due when no sin was committed.[1] The *kaffāra* consists of the manumission of a Muslim slave or, if the culprit is unable to perform this, in fasting during two consecutive months. The 'heavier' blood-money (*diya mughallaẓa*) amounts to 100 camels of a determined high quality, the 'normal' blood-money (*diya muḥakkaka*) to 100 less valuable camels or 1,000 dīnārs or 10,000 dirhams. The blood-money for a woman is half of that for a man. The full blood-money is to be paid not only for homicide but for grievous bodily harm, particularly the loss of organs which exist singly, e.g. the tongue (also for the loss of the beard and of the head of hair); half the blood-money for the loss of organs which exist in pairs, one-tenth for one finger or one toe, one-twentieth for one tooth; a detailed

[1] According to the Mālikīs (who do not distinguish between *ʿamd* and *shibh al-ʿamd*), every intentional homicide for which retaliation does not or cannot take place is punished by the so-called *ʿuḳūba* ('punishment') which consists of 100 lashes and imprisonment of one year; this punishment is systematically isolated and is neither a *ḥadd* nor a *taʿzīr*.

tariff covers most other wounds. This penalty for wounds is called *arsh*; if no percentage of the blood-money is prescribed, the so-called *ḥukūma* becomes due, i.e. it is estimated by how much the bodily harm in question would reduce the value of a slave, and the corresponding percentage of the blood-money must be paid. A special case is that of causing a miscarriage by hurting a pregnant woman; for this, the so-called *ghurra*, which amounts to 500 dirhams, must be paid; it is deemed to belong to the dead child, and is therefore inherited from it. The same applies to abortion without the father's consent; in this case the *ʿāḳila* of the wife must pay the *ghurra*.

In most cases it is not the culprit himself but his *ʿāḳila* who must pay the blood-money. The payment is made in three yearly instalments, with the provision that each member of the *ʿāḳila* has to pay not more than 3 or 4 dirhams altogether. If the amount is less than one-twentieth of the blood-money, not the *ʿāḳila* but the culprit himself must pay. The *ʿāḳila* consists of those who, as members of the Muslim army, have their names inscribed in the list (*dīwān*) and receive pay, provided the culprit belongs to them; alternatively, of the male members of his tribe (if their numbers are not sufficient, the nearest related tribes are included); alternatively, of the fellow workers in his craft or his confederates; and the *ʿāḳila* of the client, both in the sense of a manumitted slave and of a convert to Islam, is his patron and the *ʿāḳila* of his patron. This institution has its roots in the pre-Islamic customary law of the Bedouins, where the culprit could be ransomed from retaliation by his tribe, and the inclusion of confederates and of clientship seems to be ancient Arabian too. The concept of *ʿākila* was Islamicized by introducing the *dīwān* which replaces tribal relationship, but the adaptation to urban conditions by introducing the fellow workers in a craft was insufficient, and the whole institution fell into disuse at an early date.

Liability for *jināyāt* of a slave stands apart; it is analogous to liability for acts of an animal, with the provision that the owner does not become liable for more than the value of the slave, which is a rule of civil law. The slave is subject to retaliation only for homicide with *ʿamd*, not for causing bodily harm. In other cases of *ʿamd* he is surrendered as property to the claimant, unless this becomes impossible by his or her quality as *umm walad*, *mudabbar*, or *mukātab*, or by his master having alienated him after the commission of the *jināya* but without knowledge of it; then the *arsh* or the value of the slave, whichever is less, must be paid. If it is a case of *khaṭa'*, the master may choose between surrendering the slave or paying the *arsh* or his value, whichever is less. Conversely, the blood-money for a slave is his value but not more than the blood-money for a free person less a token reduction of 10 dirhams.

4. *Special measures*, preventive or punitive, may be taken for reasons of public policy (*siyāsa*), e.g. the banishment (*nafy*) or the imprisonment (*ḥabs*) of a beautiful youth, or the execution of criminals who strangle their victims in a city. Rebels (*bughāt*), i.e. Muslims who refuse to obey the *imām*, are fought only in order to reduce them to obedience and are not subject to any special penal sanction; they are to be fought as clemently as possible, and their property is inviolable. The male apostate from Islam, however, is killed; it is recommended to offer him return to Islam and to give him a reprieve of three days. The woman who commits apostasy is imprisoned and beaten every three days (the female slave by her master) until she returns to Islam. No legal penalties are provided for other offences against religion as such; they will be atoned for in the world to come. Even neglect of ritual prayer, the performance of which is regarded as particularly important, is punished only by *ta'zīr*, unless it is accompanied by a denial of its obligatory character, which would be unbelief and therefore apostasy. There is no punishment for perjury, nor for giving false evidence; it is merely made known publicly (*ta'rīf*), and in certain cases liability for the damage caused arises; according to some authorities only, the false witness is severely beaten and imprisoned.

5. There exists, therefore, *no general concept of penal law* in Islam. The concepts of guilt and criminal responsibility are little developed, that of mitigating circumstances does not exist; any theory of attempt, of complicity, of concurrence is lacking. On the other hand, the theory of punishments, with its distinction of private vengeance, *ḥadd* punishments, *ta'zīr*, and coercive and preventive measures, shows a considerable variety of ideas.

25

PROCEDURE

1. *The judge* (*ḳāḍī*, *ḥākim*). The *ḳāḍī* is a single judge. He is appointed by the political authority, but the validity of his appointment does not depend on the legitimate character of that authority—one of the matter-of-fact features in Islamic law. On the qualities required of the *ḳāḍī*, see above, p. 125; a woman may, in theory, qualify to be a *ḳāḍī* (but see below, section 7). An appointment secured by bribery (*rashwa*) is invalid. To gain one's livelihood from the office of *ḳāḍī* is permissible if it was not stipulated, because if it were stipulated it would be an invalid hire of services. Court costs are unknown in theory. The *ḳāḍī* possesses competence within his jurisdiction (both are called *wilāya*), but this is limitative only with regard to real property, and even this is contested. In fact, the competence of the *ḳāḍī* is limited by the rule that he cannot give judgment against an absent party (*ghā'ib*) who is not represented by a deputy. The *ḳāḍī* cannot give judgment in favour of his near relatives. On the other hand, his competence extends beyond the judicial office, and includes the control of the property of the missing person, the orphan, the foundling, and the person with restricted capacity to dispose, of found objects, pious foundations, and estates of inheritance. His power to dispose goes further than that of the guardian, even than that of the father; he may, for instance, lend the money of an orphan. His approval validates acts of unauthorized agency in these fields. Beyond these fields, too, the *ḳāḍī* is competent, for instance, to authorize the wife to incur debts in satisfaction of her claim to maintenance; if he has not done that, claims for maintenance relating to the past are not actionable. Finally, the *ḳāḍī* is in charge of public welfare in general, e.g. he forces the speculator on rising prices of food (*muḥtakir*) to sell; he is, generally speaking, 'the guardian of those who have no other guardian'.

Of the *ḳāḍī*'s assistants, the most important is the secretary (*kātib*); the judgment is committed to writing (*sijill*, from *sigillum*, the written judgment; *maḥḍar*, the minutes), in two copies, one of which is kept in the records (*dīwān*) of the tribunal. There are, further, the interpreter, the agent (*amīn*, literally 'fiduciary') of the *ḳāḍī*, particularly for the administration of property, the divider of inheritances (*ḳāsim*), the witnesses, and the experts; they must all be *'adl*.

The essence of the Islamic law of procedure consists of instructions to the *ḳāḍī*, whose duty it is to act in a certain way, e.g. to treat both parties equally, not to distort their statements, nor to suggest answers to the witnesses, but beside this, the aspect of validity, too, is recognized. The two aspects, duty and validity, may deviate from each other; the *ḳāḍī* must not accept the evidence of a *fāsiḳ*, but if he does, his judgment based on it is nevertheless valid. The *ḳāḍī* has the duty of giving just judgment, a duty which is enjoined in the Koran, but there is no means of reversing an unjust judgment, because strict Islamic law does not recognize stages of appeal; only the tribunal of *maẓālim* can, in a way, be regarded as an appellate court. This lack is to a certain extent made good through control on the part of the *ḳāḍī*'s successor; when he takes over the records and the prison, he instructs two fiduciaries to check everything, in particular whether the prisoners have been imprisoned justly, i.e. on account of an acknowledgement or confession or of a legal proof; if this is not the case, he has the name of the prisoner published so that any claims may be lodged against him, demands a surety for his person if necessary, and then releases him.

Instead of applying to the *ḳāḍī* it is possible to appoint an arbitrator (*ḥakam*). Only a person qualified to be a *ḳāḍī* may be a *ḥakam*; he is bound to apply Islamic law, and his judgment can be set aside by the ordinary *ḳāḍī* if it does not correspond with the doctrine of the school law of the latter. The judgment of the *ḥakam* is binding only on the parties who have appointed him; he can therefore not give judgment against the *'āḳila* for the blood-money in a case of homicide with *khaṭa'*.

2. *Action in general* (*khuṣūma*, the litigation; *da'wā*, the claim, lawsuit; *mudda'ī*, the claimant, plaintiff; *mudda'ā 'alayh*, the defendant). No action is possible without a claimant, but there is no office of public prosecutions. This principle is limited by the competence of the *ḳāḍī* to take action in matters of public

welfare; also the office of the *muḥtasib*, who in theory is the representative of the community in fulfilling the duty of 'encouraging good and discouraging evil', has in practice become an office of public prosecutions. It is not compulsory to apply to the *ḳāḍī*, and there are possibilities of settling disputes out of court other than the appointment of a *ḥakam*. This, in addition to the rules of substantive law which apply to non-Muslims, gives them, in fact, legal autonomy; as long as no party applies to the *ḳāḍī* he takes no notice.

The first question to be decided is whether the action is admissible ('valid', *ṣaḥīḥ*), and, in particular, whether the defendant is capable of being sued (whether he is *khaṣm*, a term which is also used of the parties to a lawsuit in general); if that is the case, the action takes place in public. The *ḳāḍī* questions the defendant concerning the claim; if he acknowledges it, the lawsuit is decided; if he denies it, the *ḳāḍī* asks the plaintiff to produce his evidence; if he cannot produce evidence or if his witnesses are absent, the *ḳāḍī* orders the defendant, provided the plaintiff demands it, to take the oath, relating to facts only and not to right or wrong; if the defendant takes the oath, the case is dismissed; if he declines to take it (*nukūl*), judgment is given for the plaintiff (it is recommended that the oath be offered to the defendant three times).[1] Only the defendant takes the oath, not the witnesses. Representation by attorney (*wakīl*) is possible, although the normal procedure is to plead in person.

It is sometimes difficult to determine whether the defendant is capable of being sued. The agent who has been given a mandate to buy real property is capable of being sued under a claim of pre-emption as long as he has not delivered the property to the mandant; the possessor of an object is not capable of being sued for delivery if he declares that he holds it in deposit for a third party who is absent, but he is capable of being sued if he declares that he has bought it from a third party who is absent, or if the plaintiff claims that the defendant possesses it by usurpation.

Typical of the action in Islamic law is a very sharp distinction between the parts of the plaintiff (claimant) on whom the onus

[1] According to the other schools of Islamic law, judgment for the plaintiff is given only if he himself takes the oath.

of proof lies, and the defendant whose statement, confirmed by the oath, holds good, that is to say, in whose favour the presumption operates if there is no proof. It is therefore of great importance that these parts should be assigned correctly. Because the stringent rules of Islamic law as regards evidence bring it about that no proof can be offered in many lawsuits, the problem of deciding who is plaintiff and who defendant often amounts to deciding whose statement holds good, in whose favour the presumption operates. It is not always possible to give an unqualified answer to this question; very often each party raises claims against the other, and then both have to take the oath (this procedure is called *taḥāluf*).

3. *Presumptions.* The general principle is that the presumption operates in favour of the party who denies, in contrast to the party who affirms, or claims. In a litigation concerning the usufruct in a contract of *ijāra* this is the lessor, but in a litigation concerning the rent it is the lessee. Simple cases like this are numerous, but even more numerous are the complicated examples which taken in their totality constitute a very intricate subject with a great many differences of opinion between the authorities of the school in question. The following examples are intended to illustrate certain relevant considerations. In the first place, objective probability is taken into account. In litigation concerning the ownership of domestic utensils, the presumption operates in favour of the wife as regards articles destined to be used by women, and vice versa. *A* instructs *B* to buy a slave for 1,000 (dīnārs) and hands the money over to him; the slave whom *B* has bought is worth 1,000 but *A* claims that *B* has paid only 500; then the presumption operates in favour of *B*. But if *A* has not yet handed over the money and the slave is in fact worth only 500, the presumption operates in favour of *A*. In a litigation concerning *mahr* the presumption operates in favour of the husband if the amount stated by him equals the 'fair *mahr*' or is more, and in favour of the wife if the amount stated by her equals the 'fair *mahr*' or is less; if neither is the case, the oath is offered to both parties and if both take it judgment is given for the 'fair *mahr*'. Expediency is taken into account too. If a minor is in the 'possession' (cf. above, p. 136) of a Muslim and of a *dhimmī*, and the Muslim claims him as his Muslim slave but the *dhimmī* claims

him as his son, the presumption operates in favour of the *dhimmī*; being free is to the advantage of the minor, and he can always become a Muslim. Or, by a more technically legal reasoning, the statement itself is regarded as a declaration of intention. For instance, in a litigation concerning *shuf'a* the seller mentions a lower price than the buyer; if it has not been paid yet, the statement of the seller holds good because it can be interpreted as a remission; but if it has been paid, the statement of the buyer holds good because the seller is not an interested party any longer. Similarly, if the husband sends something to his wife and she claims it was a gift, but he claims it was a payment of *mahr*, the presumption operates in his favour because it is he who transfers the ownership. Singularly formal is the principle of regarding the present condition as decisive. If the water of a rented mill ceases to flow and the lessee claims that this has been the case from the beginning of the lease, but the lessor claims that it has only just happened, the statement of the lessor or of the lessee holds good according to whether the water flows at the moment of litigation or not. Concurrently there exists the opposite principle of antedating an event as little as possible. These two principles can come into conflict. A Christian dies and his widow is a Muslim but declares that she adopted Islam after the death of her husband, so that she should be entitled to inherit, but the other heirs contest this; according to the first principle, the presumption operates in favour of the heirs, and this is the prevailing opinion; according to the second principle, it operates in favour of the widow, but although this agrees with objective probability it is the opinion of a minority only. There are cases where a statement holds good only in part. If an 'intelligent' (*mumayyiz*) minor is in the possession of a man and claims to be the slave of another, he is considered the slave of the first.

4. *Evidence* (*bayyina*). By far the most important kind of evidence is the testimony (*shahāda*) of witnesses, so much so that the term *bayyina* is sometimes used as a synonym for 'witnesses'. The acknowledgement is, strictly speaking, not 'evidence' if it is made during the action; in theory it is weaker than the evidence of witnesses, and in order to gain its full effect as the most conclusive and incontrovertible means of creating obligations, it must be proved by the testimony of witnesses. Circumstantial

evidence is not admitted (the isolated case of the *ḳasāma* does not belong systematically to the context of evidence), but the knowledge of the *ḳāḍī* is a valid basis for the judgment. Written documents (*ṣakk*, *wathīḳa*) are ignored by the theory, although the *ḳāḍī* keeps written records; there are no legal acts which must be embodied in a document, and an explicit ruling of the Koran which prescribes written documents in certain cases (sura ii. 282; cf. xxiv. 33) is interpreted as a recommendation. Written documents are merely aids to memory, and their contents are evidence only in so far as they are confirmed by the testimony of witnesses. At the utmost, a written statement can be accepted as a declaration. This is the theory; on the part played by written documents in the practice of Islamic law, see above, p. 82 f.

Two men or one man and two women, who possess the quality of *ʿadl*, are required as witnesses (*shāhid*, pl. *shuhūd*) in a lawsuit;[1] a greater number of witnesses does not lend additional value to their testimony. (For special rules on criminal procedure, see below, section 7.) Outside a lawsuit, less stringent demands are made, down to one person who is not a fully qualified witness. For instance, if a slave delivers an object and declares that it is a donation of his master, it is lawful to accept it; or if a minor declares that he has permission to buy an object, it is lawful to sell it to him. Even in a lawsuit the evidence of two women only is accepted as valid concerning matters of which women have a special knowledge, such as birth, virginity, &c. Whether the witnesses are in fact *ʿadl* must be established by inquiry. Unbecoming, despicable acts, such as playing backgammon or entering a public bath without a loin-cloth, do not nullify the quality of *ʿadl* but nevertheless enable the *ḳāḍī* to reject the testimony of the person in question. (The same ruling applies to blind persons.) The relevant time is that of giving evidence, not of witnessing the event on which evidence is given. In order to prove that a person is incompetent to give evidence, it is not sufficient to say 'he is a sinner', but details must be given, or it must be proved that the party in whose favour he is to testify has himself acknowledged that he is not *ʿadl*, or that he has been hired. Also incompetent to give

[1] The other schools of law accept also the evidence of one man together with the oath of the plaintiff in lawsuits concerning property and obligations.

evidence are near relatives of the party in whose favour and personal enemies of the party against whom evidence is to be given. The witness can testify only to what he has seen himself, except in matters such as family relationship or death. The testimony of both witnesses must be identical; in certain well-defined cases only small divergencies are tolerated, for instance if one testifies with regard to 1,000 (dīnārs) and the other with regard to 1,100. But if two witnesses testify that *A* killed *B* on a certain day in Mecca, and two others that he killed him on the same day in Kufa, both testimonies are invalid. The testimony of *dhimmīs* in matters concerning other *dhimmīs* is accepted.

If the defendant is absent, the *ḳāḍī* may send a copy of the evidence to the *ḳāḍī* in whose district the defendant is living, but this must be accompanied by witnesses who can testify not only on the authenticity but on the contents of the document. If the primary witnesses do not or cannot appear, indirect evidence, i.e. evidence concerning their testimony (*shahāda ʿalā shahāda*) can be submitted; two witnesses must testify on the deposition of each of the primary witnesses, but the secondary witnesses can be the same for each of them, so that two altogether are sufficient.

The technical rules concerning evidence have sometimes surprising consequences. In the example of the purchase of a slave, for instance, the statement of the seller as to the price is not taken into account at all, and in the example of litigation concerning *shufʿa* it is not taken into account if the price has been paid, because he is now a 'stranger' (*khārij*, *ajnabī*) and not an interested party, and is not sufficient as a witness. Valid evidence can, in fact, normally be secured only if the transaction was concluded in the presence of recognized witnesses. This is the starting-point for the institution of professional witnesses (*ʿudūl*, pl. of *ʿadl*) or 'notaries'.

If evidence is given, it is admitted only in so far as it does not necessarily contradict the assertions of the party who produces it; each party is bound by his own assertions. If someone claims to have received an object as a donation and produces evidence that he bought it at a later date, the evidence is admitted because the donor may have repudiated the donation and the donee may have had to buy the object; if he produces evidence that he bought it at an earlier date, it is not admitted because the claim of a donation implies the acknowledgement that the object was the property of the donor before. Also, if someone claims that a house is his property and produces evidence of a specific acquisition of ownership, for instance by purchase or inheritance, the evidence is admitted, but not if he claims a specific acquisition of ownership and produces evidence of simple ownership only.

5. *Consideration of evidence and judgment.* The emphasis of the Islamic law of procedure lies not so much on arriving at the truth as on applying certain formal rules. The *ḳāḍī* must not, it is true, give judgment against his own knowledge, and other provisions, too, show concern for establishing the facts, but, generally speaking, the formal rule of procedure is observed for its own sake. If in the example of litigation concerning *mahr* both parties take the oath, judgment is given for the 'fair *mahr*'. If the parties to a sale dispute the amount of the price and both take the oath, the sale is annulled at the demand of one of them. The procedure in the case of *liʿān*, if both husband and wife take the oath, reveals a similar attitude.

If both parties produce evidence, the number of the witnesses produced by each, beyond their minimum number, is irrelevant. There is no examination of the witnesses, or of the likelihood of their testimony being true. There are only two possibilities: one of the two testimonies is given preference, in analogy with the doctrine of presumptions, or *tahātur*, the conflict of equivalent testimonies, takes place.

The rule followed in the first case is that the evidence of the party who has not the benefit of the presumption is given preference; this is a consequence of the general rules concerning the burden of proof. If both the possessor and a 'stranger' produce evidence of simple ownership, the evidence of the latter is given preference because the burden of proof rests on him. But if the evidence of the possessor is more valuable because it is more specific, e.g. evidence of acquisition of ownership by purchase, this last is given preference. Another consideration that is used to decide which of two testimonies is to be given preference, often with surprising results, is that of their respective dates.

Tahātur takes place, for instance, if each of two parties proves that he has bought the same object from the other; the solution of this case is a matter of dispute. If each of two parties has more than three beams supported by the dividing wall of their adjoining houses, the wall is adjudicated to both as common property. The same judgment is given if both prove possession of the same piece of real property; but if one can prove the factual exercise of control, e.g. that he has dug on it, his evidence is given preference. If there are several claimants, and each produces evidence equivalent to that of the others, the object is adjudicated to all in common property. For instance, *A* proves that he has bought an object, *B* that it has been donated to him and that he has taken possession, *C* that he has inherited it from his father, *D* that he has received it as a charitable gift and has taken possession; then one-quarter is adjudicated to each. In cases like this, instead of a decision being given in favour of one of several mutually exclusive claims, they are partially recognized although they cannot all be true; this shows the formalistic character of the Islamic law of procedure and evidence very clearly.

Judgment (*ḳaḍā'*) must be given according to the doctrine of the school of law to which the *ḳāḍī* belongs; should he deviate from it, the validity of his judgment is contested. The *ḳāḍī* cannot revoke his judgment once he has given it. If, in the example of the two pairs of witnesses who testify to a killing (above, p. 194), those who testify to the killing in Mecca appear first and judgment is given, and those who testify to the killing in Kufa appear afterwards, only the second testimony is invalid. A judgment given on the basis of false testimony is valid, at least before the *forum externum*, sometimes even before the *forum internum*. If a woman obtains, by false evidence, the judgment that she is married to a certain man, it is lawful for her to have intercourse with him. Retractation of the testimony does not make the judgment that is based on it invalid, but the witnesses become liable for the damage caused by the judgment.[1] What is to be considered as damage is narrowly defined from case to case; repudiation after the marriage has been consummated is not included. Another *ḳāḍī* can reverse the judgment only if it amounts to a grave mistake in law, that is to say if it goes against the Koran, a recognized tradition, or the consensus.

[1] On the punishment for giving false evidence, see above, p. 187.

The *ḳāḍī* is not liable for his official acts. If he sells a slave in order to satisfy creditors, and the slave is vindicated so that the price must be returned to the buyer, but the money has been lost while it was held by the *ḳāḍī*, the creditors bear the loss.

6. *Execution and self-help.* No sharp distinction is made between execution and self-help. Islamic law still envisages the primordial method of starting an action, which consists of the plaintiff seizing the defendant and hauling him before the judge. If the plaintiff declares that he has witnesses, the *ḳāḍī* may demand a surety for the person of the defendant for three days, or alternatively the plaintiff may watch over the person of the defendant, following him wherever he goes but not entering his house with him, for the same period (this personal supervision is called *mulāzama*). If the defendant defaults, the surety is imprisoned; he on his part may have the defendant imprisoned in order to make sure of his appearance. But the defendant cannot be forced to plead; he is entitled to decline (*nukūl*) to answer questions or to take the oath, except in the cases of *li'ān* and *ḳasāma*, where a plea or the taking of the oath may be enforced by imprisonment. Still less may a confession be extracted by torture.

There is no execution *ex officio* in matters of *jināyāt*; the state merely puts its administrative agencies at the disposal of the interested parties; but the execution of the *ḥadd* punishments is a duty of the *imām*; the *ḳāḍī* is responsible for the carrying out of *ta'zīr*, and he controls the prison.

Judgments concerning the law of property and obligations are enforced by imprisonment (*ḥabs*) of the debtor until he pays; if he claims to be poor, he is imprisoned only for a debt arising out of transactions which imply the payment of a consideration, such as sale, loan, suretyship, also for *mahr* which is due for immediate payment, but for other debts only if the creditor proves that he has means. He is kept in prison until the *ḳāḍī* has become convinced that he would pay if he could. Also imprisoned is the usurper who claims that the object which he has usurped has perished, until the *ḳāḍī* has become convinced that he would surrender it if it still existed. This imprisonment is defined as a term of about two or three months, but it continues if the creditor proves that the debtor has means; if the debtor becomes ill, he is released from prison. Judicial distraint is unknown in Islamic law. If the debtor is released from prison as being unable to pay, he is declared bankrupt (*muflis*); it is contested whether this wipes out his debts, or whether the creditor or creditors may still resort to self-help by watching over his person and taking from him the surplus of his earnings.

7. *Special features of criminal procedure*. No woman may act as *ḳāḍī*, and no arbitrator may be appointed, in cases concerning *ḥadd* punishments and retaliation. Proof is made more difficult than in other matters; the evidence of women is not admitted, and in the case of *zinā* four male witnesses are required. Transfer of evidence to another *ḳāḍī* and indirect evidence are not admitted, and the appointment of a deputy to exact *ḥadd* and *ḳiṣāṣ* is impossible. Notwithstanding these features common to *jināyāt* and *ḥadd*, the general concept of a penal law does not exist in Islam. Whereas in other matters there exists, to a certain extent, the religious duty of giving evidence, in lawsuits concerning offences punishable by *ḥadd* it is considered more meritorious to cover them up than to give evidence on them, and the oath is disregarded as an element of proof. In all these matters a surety for the person of the defendant can be demanded only if at least part of the evidence has been heard. It is true that all these dispositions had little effect in providing legal protection in practice.

26

THE NATURE OF ISLAMIC LAW

1. THE nature of Islamic law is to a great extent determined by its history, and its history is dominated by the contrast between theory and practice. The remarks that follow are intended to complete from a systematic point of view the historical account of the subject.

Islamic law does not claim universal validity; it is binding for the Muslim to its full extent in the territory of the Islamic state, to a slightly lesser extent in enemy territory,[1] and for the non-Muslim only to a limited extent in Islamic territory. More important than this self-imposed limitation is the fact that Islamic law is conscious of its character as a religious ideal; it believes in a continued decadence since the time of the caliphs of Medina, 'the caliphs who followed the right course', and it takes the corruption of contemporary conditions for granted. As far as the scope of the concepts obligatory / indifferent / forbidden is concerned, Islamic law is to some extent content with mere theoretical acknowledgement; this is obvious from the existence of the two intermediate categories, recommended and reprehensible. The same tendency appears in the treatment of infringements of those religious duties which are not sanctioned by *ḥadd* punishments; no legal penalties are provided for them unless they are accompanied by a denial of their obligatory character. Nevertheless, whether the prohibitions are sanctioned by penalties, such as that of drinking wine, or not, such as that of eating pork, they are meant as injunctions to refrain. But even the *ḥadd* punishment lapses in certain cases through active repentance. On a different systematic plane stands the theory of duress; if duress is recognized, its effect is not only to remove the penal sanction but to make the act itself allowed. Still wider is the scope of the doctrine

[1] For instance, according to Ḥanafī doctrine the Muslims may conclude transactions involving *ribā* with non-Muslims in enemy territory.

that necessity dispenses Muslims from observing the strict rules of the law. Within the orbit of the concepts valid / invalid, Islamic law, it is true, claims absolute validity, but even here a hypothetical element enters with the idea that this is what things ought to be in the ideal Islamic state. The admission of the validity of legal devices (*ḥiyal*) serves to counteract, in practice, the claims of the theory.

Islamic law did not remain immune from malpractices within its own sphere of application, such as bribing of *ḳāḍī*s and witnesses, and high-handed acts of governments and individuals with which the *ḳāḍī* was powerless to deal. The degree to which this happened depended on the character and the strength of the government, and the most unblemished period in this respect probably coincided with the prime of the Ottoman Empire. The early ʿAbbāsid period, on the other hand, was distinguished by frequent acts of usurpation (*ghaṣb*), misappropriation of private property; this is why Islamic law treats of *ghaṣb* in great detail, with the tendency to protect the lawful owner as much as possible. But Islamic law takes a matter-of-fact view of other abuses when it considers valid the appointment of a *ḳāḍī* who is not *ʿadl*, 'of good character', or the judgment of the *ḳāḍī* if he accepts the evidence of a witness who is not *ʿadl*, or even the appointment of a *ḳāḍī* by a political authority which is not legitimate.

2. The central feature that makes Islamic religious law what it is, that guarantees its unity in all its diversity, is the assessing of all human acts and relationships, including those which we call legal, from the point of view of the concepts obligatory / recommended / indifferent / reprehensible / forbidden. Law proper has been thoroughly incorporated in the system of religious duties; those fundamental concepts permeate the juridical subject-matter as well. Just as in the field of worship the obligatory and indispensable acts are accompanied by others which are only recommended, the heirs are recommended but not obliged to pay the debts of the deceased, and even the next of kin who has the right to demand retaliation for intentional homicide is recommended to waive it against payment of the blood-money. It might therefore seem as if it were not correct to speak of an Islamic law at all, as if the concept of law did not exist in Islam. The term must indeed be used with

the proviso that Islamic law is part of a system of religious duties, blended with non-legal elements. But though it was incorporated into the system of religious duties, the legal subject-matter was not completely assimilated, legal relationships were not completely reduced to and expressed in terms of religious and ethical duties, the sphere of law retained a technical character of its own, and juridical reasoning could develop along its own lines. That the concepts allowed / forbidden and valid / invalid were to a great extent coextensive, made it possible for this last pair, together with the kindred concept of a legal effect, to be fitted into the system. There exists, thus, a clear distinction between the purely religious sphere and the sphere of law proper, and we are justified in using the term Islamic law of the legal subject-matter which, by being incorporated into the system of religious duties of Islam, was either materially or formally, but in any case considerably, modified. This legal subject-matter became Islamic law not merely by having considerations of a religious or moral kind introduced into it, but by the much subtler process of being organized and systematized as part of the religious duties of the Muslims. There remains a certain contrast between the legal subject-matter and the principles of its formal organization.

Islamic law is systematic, that is to say, it represents a coherent body of doctrines. Its several institutions are well put into relation with one another; the greater part of the law of contracts and obligations, for instance, is construed by analogy with the contract of sale. Furthermore, the whole of the law is permeated by religious and ethical considerations; each institution, transaction, or obligation is measured by the standards of religious and moral rules, such as the prohibition of interest, the prohibition of uncertainty, the concern for the equality of the two parties, the concern for the just mean or average (*mithl*). In theory we can distinguish these two processes of systematization, in practice they merge into each other. The reason why the several contracts resemble one another in their structure so much is largely to be found in the fact that the same concern for the same religious and moral principles pervades them all. The two processes of Islamicizing and systematizing were concurrent; religious and moral norms and a structural order were together imposed on the raw material that was to become Islamic law. It was the first legal specialists themselves who created the system of Islamic law; they did not borrow it from the pre-Islamic sources which provided many of its material elements.

3. Being a 'sacred law', Islamic law possesses certain heteronomous and irrational features, but only to a limited degree. It is heteronomous in so far as two of its official bases, the Koran and the *sunna* of the Prophet, are expressions of Allah's commands. But beside them stands the consensus of the community, and although this principle, too, is covered by divine authority,[1] it represents a transition to an autonomous law; it is also the decisive instance. It decides the interpretation of Koran and traditions, and determines which traditions are to be considered authentic; it even sanctions interpretations of Koranic passages which are at variance with their obvious meaning.[2] But from the fourth/tenth century onwards, and until the growth of legal modernism in the present generation, there has been no official scope for independent new developments, and what development there has been consists, on principle, only of interpretation and application. A very limited scope remains for the *ikhtiyār*, the 'choice' of or 'preference' for a given opinion, above all in consideration of the *fasād al-zamān*. If, for instance, in a contract of suretyship for the person, production of the debtor before the *ḳāḍī* is stipulated, the older Ḥanafī doctrine holds that production in the market-place is sufficient, but the opinion 'chosen in the present time' holds that it is not; this is based on the doctrine of Zufar (d. 158/775), who, although a prominent disciple and companion of Abū Ḥanīfa, does not belong to the triad of the highest authorities of the school (Abū Ḥanīfa, Abū Yūsuf, and Shaybānī). Extreme cases like this are rare; in most cases *ikhtiyār* is limited to the elimination of differences of opinion among earlier authorities, including those of the period after the 'closing of the gate of *ijtihād*'.

The irrational elements in Islamic law are partly of religious-

1 See above, p. 47, on its having found expression in a tradition from the Prophet: 'my community will never agree on an error'.

2 For instance, the text of sura v. 6 states quite clearly: 'O you who believe, when you rise up for worship, wash your faces and your hands up to the elbows, and wipe over your heads and your feet up to the ankles'; the law nevertheless insists on washing the feet, and this is harmonized with the text by various means. For another example, see above, p. 18 f.

Islamic and partly of pre-Islamic and magical origin. Examples are the magical formula of *ẓihār*, the Islamic procedure of *liʿān*, the ancient Arabian *ḳasāma*, and the nature and function of legal evidence in general. Even that great systematizer, Shāfiʿī, often did not succeed in rationalizing these institutions to his satisfaction. But the legal subject-matter, whatever its provenance, also contained rational elements, and, above all, it was organized, systematized, and completed not by an irrational process of continuous revelation but by the method of interpretation and application which by its very nature had to be rational. In this way Islamic law acquired its intellectualist and scholastic exterior.

It might be thought that the application of religious and moral norms, which are non-legal, to legal subject-matter would normally have led to irrational decisions. This, however, is only rarely the case, and when it happens the Muslim lawyers are generally conscious of the fact that it is an exception to the general rules, to analogy. On the contrary, the religious and moral considerations are an essential part of the systematic structure of Islamic law. Whereas Islamic law presents itself as a rational system on the basis of material considerations, its formal juridical character is little developed. Even the two formal legal concepts, valid and invalid, are continually pushed into the background by the Islamic concepts, allowed and forbidden. The aim of Islamic law is to provide concrete and material standards, and not to impose formal rules on the play of contending interests, which is the aim of secular laws. This leads to the somewhat surprising result that considerations of good faith, fairness, justice, truth, and so on, play only quite a subordinate part in the system.

4. It follows from the heteronomous and irrational side of Islamic law that its rules are valid by virtue of their mere existence and not because of their rationality. This is particularly obvious in the law of evidence, which is indeed beset with particular difficulties, but it also occurs elsewhere. If a boy is mutilated unintentionally on being circumcised, the full blood-money is to be paid, but only half the blood-money if he dies of this mutilation; half of the cause of the death is attributed to the circumcision itself, because this alone may also cause death, and only half to the mutilation; only this second half creates

liability because the performance of circumcision, which is in any case recommended (and according to the Shāfiʿī and the Ḥanbalī school even obligatory), does not in itself create liability. If the owner of a wall which threatens collapse sells it after he has been asked to demolish it, and it then collapses and kills someone, neither the seller nor the buyer is liable: not the seller because he was not the owner at the time it collapsed, and not the buyer because he had not been asked to demolish it. Islamic law allows the loan of real property, and this must necessarily be gratuitous; on the other hand, the owner is, on principle, liable for the land-tax, and the fact that he has lent the property changes nothing in that. It is no concern of the lawyers that a contract under which the owner would not only lend his property but remain liable for the land-tax, is impossible in practice, as long as they are satisfied that it does not infringe the rules of the sacred Law. The law of inheritance is particularly rich in practically impossible cases, which are discussed in detail.

The heteronomous and irrational side of Islamic law also called for the observance of the letter rather than of the spirit, and facilitated the vast development and wide recognition of legal devices, including legal fictions.

5. The opposite tendency, taking material facts into account, diverging from the formally correct decision for reasons of fairness or appropriateness, is not unknown in Islamic law; it appears in *istiḥsān* (and *istiṣlāḥ*). But this principle, both in theory and in its actual application, occupies too subordinate a position for it to be able to influence positive law to any considerable degree. However much considerations of fairness and appropriateness entered into the decisions of the earliest lawyers, in the fully developed system the principle of *istiḥsān* (and *istiṣlāḥ*) is confined to very narrow limits and never supersedes the recognized rules of the material sources (Koran and *sunna*), their recognized interpretations by the early authorities, and the unavoidable conclusions to be drawn from them; it often amounts merely to making a choice between the several opinions held by the ancient authorities, that is to say, *ikhtiyār*. Occasionally, too, custom is taken into account by *istiḥsān*. (For examples of *istiḥsān*, see above, pp. 146 n. 1, 152, 155, 157, 179, 183.)

6. Islamic law possesses an impressive number of legal concepts, both special and generic, but they are, generally speaking, broad and lacking in positive content; they are derived not from the concrete realities of legal life but from abstract thought. This has the consequence that differences between two genera are often not greater or more essential than those between several species within the same genus; instead of an antithesis between two concepts, there are graded transitions from the central core of one concept to that of another, with corresponding gradations of the legal effects. This way of thinking is typical of Islamic law. For instance, the finder may use the found property if he is poor, but not if he is rich; if he is rich, he is only entitled to make a charitable gift (*ṣadaḳa*) of it; but it is, nevertheless, not a full *ṣadaḳa* because he is entitled to give it to his poor parents or children, which he may not do if he makes a *ṣadaḳa* proper. The term is used in a still wider sense of the purpose of a *waḳf*, which may be anything not incompatible with the tenets of Islam. Another typical example is provided by the concepts of thing (*ʿayn*), *res in commercio* (*māl*), substance (*raḳaba*), and usufruct (*manfaʿa*), and by the contracts of which they may form the object.[1]

Closely connected with this way of thinking is the casuistical method, which is indeed one of the most striking features of traditional Islamic law. Islamic law concentrates not so much on disengaging the legally relevant elements of each case and subsuming it under general rules—as on establishing graded series of cases. The extreme links of two series proceeding from different concepts can closely approach and even almost coincide with each other, and then there is a sudden change in the legal effect; this is the subject of the doctrine of *furūḳ*. In particular, the following uses of casuistical method can be distinguished: (1) decisions concerning pre-Islamic or early Islamic transactions, such as the *muzābana*; (2) casuistical treatment as a literary form, where the underlying rule is implied by the juxtaposition of parallel and particularly of contrasting cases; (3) casuistical decision of as many cases as possible, including purely imaginary ones, in order to cover all possibilities when their subsumption under general norms proves impossible;

[1] Cf. also the several meanings of the terms *ṣaḥīḥ*, *muḥṣan*, and *tāmm* (above, pp. 121, 125. 152).

(4) decisions of intricate cases which are difficult to decide on the basis of recognized rules. Some of these are, in fact, problems which had arisen in practice, but mostly they are questions designed as exercises in ingenuity and systematic speculation; some of the *ḥiyal* belong to this category.

7. The way in which Islamic law, in various countries and at various times, reflected, reacted to, and influenced society has been the object of a number of studies. On the other hand, a sociological analysis of its structure has hardly been undertaken so far, and the elementary remarks which follow merely aim at providing a starting-point and showing the appropriateness of this approach to the subject.

One important criterion of the sociology of law is the degree to which the legal subject-matters are distinguished and differentiated from one another. There is no such distinction in Islamic law. This is why rules of procedure are invariably intertwined with rules of substantive law, and rules of constitutional and administrative law are scattered over the most diverse chapters of the original treatises. Public powers are, as a rule, reduced to private rights or duties, for instance the right to give a valid *amān* or safe-conduct, the duty to pay the *zakāt* or alms-tax, or the rights and duties of the persons who appoint an individual as *imām* or caliph, and the rights and duties of this last. This is all the more significant as the Arabic language possessed an abstract term for 'authority, dominion, ruling power' in the word *sulṭān*, a word which came to be used as a title only from the fourth/tenth century onwards; but Islamic law did not develop the corresponding legal concept. For the same reason, the essential institutions of the Islamic state are construed not as functions of the community of believers as such, but as duties the fulfilment of which by a sufficient number of individuals excuses the other individuals from fulfilling them; in fact, the whole concept of an institution is missing.

In the field of what, in modern terminology, is called penal law, Islamic law distinguishes between the rights of Allah and the rights of humans, and only the rights of Allah entail a penal sanction in the proper meaning of the term. Even here, in the centre of penal law, the idea of a claim on the part of Allah predominates, just as if it were a claim on the part of a human plaintiff. The lack of an office of public prosecutions is, in part, supplied by the *ḥisba*, the office of the *muḥtasib*, but it is significant that the very term *muḥtasib* denotes a person who seeks to gain religious merit by his zeal for the sacred Law. The second great division of what we should call penal law belongs to the category of 'redress of torts', a category straddling civil and penal law which Islamic law has retained from the law of pre-Islamic Arabia, where it was an archaic but by no means unique phenomenon (cf. above, pp. 6, 148, 160, 177 f.). Already the law of pre-Islamic Arabia had placed the emphasis on the civil side, and the same holds true of Islamic law.[1] Here the concept of criminal guilt hardly exists, and apart from the religious expiation of the *kaffāra* and, particularly, the *'uḳūba* of the Mālikīs, there is no fixed penalty for any infringement of the rights of a human or the inviolability of his person and property, only the exact reparation of the damage caused; monetary fines are unknown. Also the execution of the judgment in this sphere is, in principle, a matter for the party in whose favour it is given. These two great divisions of what, in modern terminology, would be the penal law of Islam, correspond closely to the two sources from which the sociology of law derives all penal law.

Covering both fields there is the *ta'zīr*; the *ḳāḍī* may punish at his discretion any act which in his opinion calls for punishment, whether it infringes the rights of Allah or the rights of humans. The *ta'zīr* belongs therefore to penal law proper, but even here Islamic law has not envisaged the imposition of fines. Sociologically speaking, the *ta'zīr* stands by itself, and it has also a separate history. It belongs neither to ancient Arabian customary law which was ratified by Islam, nor to Islamic legislation which appeared in the Koran and in the traditions from the Prophet. It was the first Muslim *ḳāḍī*s in the Umayyad period who found themselves called upon to punish, at their discretion, all kinds of acts which threatened the peaceful existence of the new Islamic society which was coming into being. The penal sanctions which had been imposed by the caliphs of Medina in the first half of the first century of Islam had served the same purpose; as far as they survived as recognized

[1] Islamic law distinguishes, however, between civil liability for a tort and civil liability arising from a breach of contract.

rules, they were incorporated in the Islamic legislation; as far as this was not the case they, too, had to be interpreted as *ta'zīr* by the theory of Islamic law. *Ta'zīr*, being an extension of the original sphere of penal law proper, filled a need that was felt in practice, and this need made itself felt sufficiently early for the first specialists of Islamic religious law to incorporate it in its official doctrine. But the needs of Islamic society did not stop there, and further extensions of penal law, and the creation of agencies which were to apply them, such as the *ḥisba* and the *naẓar fil-maẓālim*, became inevitable. At the time, however, when the specialists of Islamic law had to take notice of them, the outlines of the system had already been firmly laid down, and this is why strict theory could admit them, as it were, only on sufferance. Still later developments, such as the Ottoman *ḳānūn-nāme*s, were completely ignored by the theory. The sociological character of this portion of the reality of penal law in Islam has remained constant, although its place in the official theory of Islamic law is not uniform.

8. The sociology of law shows that there are two methods by which legal subject-matter is brought into a system, the analytical and the analogical method. Islamic law represents this latter type of systematizing in great purity. The existence of well-developed legal concepts is not typical of the first method, neither is the existence of a casuistical method typical of the second. But both the nature of the Islamic legal concepts and the nature of its casuistical method show that Islamic legal thought proceeds by parataxis and association. Above all, the method of *ḳiyās*, one of the four 'roots' or principles of Islamic law, is purely analogical. All these features are manifestations of a typical way of thinking which pervades the whole of Islamic law.

As regards the formal character of positive law, the sociology of law contrasts two extreme cases. One is that of an objective law which guarantees the subjective rights of individuals; such a law is, in the last resort, the sum total of the personal privileges of all individuals. The opposite case is that of a law which reduces itself to administration, which is the sum total of particular commands. Islamic law belongs to the first type, and this agrees with what the examination of the structure of Islamic 'public' law has shown. A typical feature which results from all this is the private and individualistic character of Islamic law. However prominent a place a programme of social reform and of improving the position of the socially weak occupied in the Koran, Islamic law, in its technical structure, is thoroughly individualistic. This shows itself, for instance, in the structure of the law of inheritance (as opposed to the social effect of its rules), where each heir becomes immediately the owner of his individual portion, or even in the institution of *wakf*, the social effects of which have been very considerable, but which, in its technical function, is strictly individualistic, in so far as the provisions laid down by the founder have the force of law. In Islamic law, as in other laws, we must distinguish between the social intentions of the legislator and the sociological character of his law.

9. Islamic law represents an extreme case of a 'jurists' law'; it was created and further developed by private specialists, a phenomenon well known to the sociology of law. There are certain parallels between the functions of these specialists in Islamic and in Roman law, but the differences are more important. In Roman law it was the growing importance of commercial life which called for the creation of corresponding legal forms; in Islamic law it was the religious zeal of a growing number of Muslims which demanded the application of religious norms to all problems of behaviour. The formation of Islamic law took place neither under the impetus of the needs of practice, nor under that of juridical technique, but under that of religious and ethical ideas. If the Roman jurists were to be useful to their clients, they had to try to predict the probable reactions of the magistrates and judges to each transaction; if the earliest Islamic lawyers (and if we are entitled to speak of an Islamic law, we are entitled to call the specialists in it lawyers) were to fulfil their religious duty as they saw it, they had to search their consciences in order to know what good Muslims were allowed or forbidden to do, which acts of the administration they ought to accept or to reject, which institutions of the customary practice they were entitled to use and which they ought to avoid. At the very time that Islamic law came into existence, its perpetual problem, that of the contrast between theory and practice, was already posed. That this contrast was not fortuitous is shown both by historical and by sociological analysis.

The way in which Islamic law reacted to practice is well illustrated by the *ḥiyal*. The *ḥiyal* offer an instructive example of what, according to the sociology of law, is one of the two primary sources of law, the 'concerted action of interested parties'. This action leads to 'typical agreements', which are the *ḥiyal*. In concluding their agreements, the interested parties calculate to a nicety the chances of their receiving 'legal sanction' by the *ḳāḍī*, and they adapt their formal engagements to 'calculated risks'. The formal engagements do not exist for their own sake, they are concluded for an ulterior purpose. The accretions to the law which were brought about by the concerted action of interested parties existed, to begin with, 'outside the law'; the guaranty of legal sanction which the official administration of justice could provide was not sufficient to assure the effectiveness of their agreements; they required an additional guaranty, and this was provided by 'convention'.

The *ḥiyal* form only part of the customary commercial law which developed, beside the ideal law of strict theory, in the Islamic countries of the Middle Ages. Because Islamic law is a jurists' law, legal science is amply documented, whereas the realities of legal life are much less known and must be laboriously reconstructed from occasional evidence. It was the 'learned jurists', the specialists in Islamic law, themselves, who by their 'creative imagination' not only invented the more complicated *ḥiyal* for their customers, the merchants, but reconciled the existing customary law with the official administration of justice by the *ḳāḍī*. One result of their activity is the Mālikī *'amal*; another exists in the works on *shurūṭ* and kindred subjects. The concept of 'precaution' dominates the literature of *ḥiyal* and *shurūṭ*, as it had dominated the activity of the earliest specialists in Islamic law. These three manifestations of legal life in Islam have little in common from the Muslim doctrinal point of view; but sociological analysis shows their inherent parallelism.

10. Islamic law provides the unique phenomenon of legal science and not the state playing the part of a legislator, of scholarly handbooks having the force of law (to the extent to which Islamic law was applied in practice). This depended on two conditions: that legal science guaranteed its own stability and continuity, and that the place of the state was taken by

another authority, high enough to impose itself on both the government and the governed. The first condition was met by the doctrine of consensus which led to a cumulative elimination of differences of opinion; what differences could not be eliminated were made innocuous by the mutual recognition of the several schools of law as equally orthodox. The second condition was met by the fact that Islamic law claimed to be based on divine authority. This claim was reinforced by the progressive reduction of the human element of personal opinion, until only the mechanical method of reasoning by analogy remained, and even the use of this method was put out of reach of the later generations by the doctrine of the 'closing of the gate of independent reasoning (*ijtihād*)'. The traditionalism of Islamic law, which is perhaps its most essential feature, is typical of a 'sacred law'.

CHRONOLOGICAL TABLE

(The first of two, where combined numbers are given, refers to the Islamic, and the second to the Christian era)

A.D. 622. Emigration (*hijra*) of Muhammad, the Prophet, from Mecca to Medina; beginning of the Islamic era.

A.D. 632. Death of Muhammad.

9/632–40/661. The caliphs of Medina: Abū Bakr, ʿUmar, ʿUthmān, ʿAlī.

41/661–132/750. The dynasty of the Umayyads.

65/685–86/705. The Umayyad caliph ʿAbd al-Malik.

95/713 or 96/715. Death of Ibrāhīm al-Nakhaʿī of Kufa; in the same and in the following decade: deaths of the 'seven lawyers of Medina'.

114/732 or 115/733. Death of ʿAṭā' of Mecca.

120/738. Death of Ḥammād ibn Abī Sulaymān of Kufa.

122/740. Death of Zayd ibn ʿAlī, alleged author of a compilation of legal traditions.

124/742. Death of Zuhrī of Hijaz.

132/750. Overthrow of the Umayyads, beginning of the dynasty of the ʿAbbāsids.

138/756. Foundation of an Umayyad principality (later caliphate) in Spain.

139/756. Murder of Ibn al-Muḳaffaʿ, a Secretary of State.

148/765. Death of Ibn Abī Laylā, *ḳāḍī* of Kufa.

150/767. Death of Abū Ḥanīfa of Kufa.

157/774. Death of Awzāʿī of Syria.

161/778. Death of Sufyān Thawrī of Kufa.

170/786–193/809. The ʿAbbāsid caliph Hārūn al-Rashīd.

179/795. Death of Mālik of Medina.

182/798. Death of Abū Yūsuf, Chief *Ḳāḍi*, Iraqian.

189/805. Death of Shaybānī, Iraqian; the Ḥanafī school established.

204/820. Death of Shāfiʿī.

240/854. Death of Saḥnūn, a follower of Mālik; the Mālikī school established.

240/854. Death of Abū Thawr, founder of a school of law.

241/855. Death of Ibn Ḥanbal, Traditionist; beginnings of the Ḥanbalī school.

264/878. Death of Muzanī, a disciple of Shāfiʿī; the Shāfiʿī school established.

270/884. Death of Dāwūd ibn Khalaf, founder of the Ẓāhirī school.

297/910. Foundation of the Fāṭimid caliphate.

310/923. Death of Ṭabarī, founder of a school of law. Gradual 'Closing of the Gate of *Ijtihād*'.

321/933. Death of Ṭaḥāwī, a Ḥanafī scholar.

c. 447/1055–541/1146. The movement of the Almoravids in north-west Africa and Spain.
456/1065. Death of Ibn Ḥazm, a Ẓāhirī scholar.
524/1130. Death of Ibn Tūmart, founder of the movement of the Almohads.
558/1163–580/1186. The Almohad ruler Abū Yaʿḳūb Yūsuf.
620/1223. Death of Muwaffaḳ al-Dīn Ibn Ḳudāma, author of an authoritative Ḥanbalī handbook.
c. 700/1300. Survival of the four remaining 'orthodox' schools of law.
728/1328. Death of Ibn Taymiyya, a Ḥanbalī scholar.
751/1350. Death of Ibn Ḳayyim al-Jawziyya, a disciple of Ibn Taymiyya.
767/1365. Death of Khalīl ibn Isḥāḳ, author of an authoritative Mālikī handbook.
1451–81. The Ottoman sultan Meḥemmed II.
1481–1512. The Ottoman sultan Bāyezīd II.
1512–20. The Ottoman sultan Selīm I.
1520–60. The Ottoman sultan Süleymān I.
952/1545–982/1574. Abul-Suʿūd, Grand Mufti (*Shaykh al-Islām*).
956/1549. Death of Ibrāhīm al-Ḥalabī, author of an authoritative Ḥanafī handbook.
975/1567. Death of Ibn Ḥajar, author of an authoritative Shāfiʿī handbook.
1006/1596. Death of Ramlī, author of an authoritative Shāfiʿī handbook.
1685–1707. The Mogul emperor Awrangzīb ʿĀlamgīr; compilation of the *Fatāwā al-ʿĀlamgīriyya* (Ḥanafī).
1772. The East India Company assumes sovereign rights; starting-point of Anglo-Muhammadan law.
1200/1786. Beginning of the agitation of ʿUthmān ibn Fūdī (Fodio), founder of the Fulānī movement.
1201/1787. Death of Muḥammad ibn ʿAbd al-Wahhāb, religious founder of the Wahhābī movement.
1808–39. The Ottoman sultan Maḥmūd II; start of the reform movement in the Ottoman Empire.
1830. French conquest of Algeria; starting-point of the *Droit musulman algérien*.
1839–61. The Ottoman sultan ʿAbdülmejīd; the *Khaṭṭ-i sherīf* of Gülhane (1839); legislation of the *Ṭanẓīmāt*.
1875. Codification of the Ḥanafī law of family and inheritance by Ḳadrī Pasha in Egypt.
1877. The *Mejelle* (Ottoman Civil Code) promulgated.
1899. *Avant-projet* of a Civil and Commercial Code (*Code Santillana*) in Tunisia.
1916. *Avant-projet de code du droit musulman algérien* (*Code Morand*) in Algeria.
1917. Ottoman Law of Family Rights.
1920. Beginning of the modernist legislative movement in Egypt; numerous acts until 1955.
1926. Abolition of Islamic law in Turkey.
1926–38. Modernist legislation in Iran.
1937. Shariat Act in British India.

1939. Dissolution of Muslim Marriages Act in British India.
1951. Jordanian Law of Family Rights.
1953. Syrian Law of Personal Status.
1956. Modernist Legislation in Tunisia; Tunisian Code of *statut personnel* and inheritance.
1957–8. The *Mudawwana* (Code of *statut personnel* and inheritance) in Morocco.
1959. Iraqian Law of Personal Status.
1961. Muslim Family Law Ordinance in Pakistan.

BIBLIOGRAPHY

CHAPTER 1

Handbooks:[1]

†Th. W. JUYNBOLL, *Handbuch des islāmischen Gesetzes*, Leiden and Leipzig 1910 (transl. G. BAVIERA, *Manuale di diritto musulmano*, Milan 1916); *Handleiding tot de kennis van de Mohammedaansche wet*, Leiden 1925 (reprinted 1930) (concentrates on the Islamic aspect, the religious duties, and those institutions which have remained of practical importance for the Muslims in Indonesia; Shāfi'ī school).

†D. SANTILLANA, *Istituzioni di diritto musulmano malichita con riguardo anche al sistema sciafiita* (i, Rome 1926), 2 vols., Rome 1938 (a detailed account of the legal subject-matter, with copious references to the Arabic sources).

M. DEL NIDO Y TORES, *Derecho musulmán*, 2nd ed., Tetuan 1927 (a treatise of private law, with particular reference to the practice in the former Spanish zone of Morocco; Mālikī school).

*J. LÓPEZ ORTIZ, *Derecho musulmán*, Barcelona and Buenos Aires 1932 (Colección Labor, no. 322) (a many-sided survey of the whole subject, including the religious duties; Mālikī school).

L. MILLIOT, *Introduction à l'étude du droit musulman*, Paris 1953 (a comprehensive work of unequal quality, to be used with caution; cf. J. SCHACHT, in *A.J.C.L.* v (1956), 133–41).

Law in the Middle East, ed. M. KHADDURI and H. J. LIEBESNY, i, Washington 1955 (a collection of contributions by various authors on the history and the doctrines of Islamic law).

*A. D'EMILIA, 'Diritto islamico', in *Le civiltà dell' oriente*, iii, Rome 1958, 493–530 (a concise outline).

For translations of Arabic sources, see below, pp. 261 ff., and also see:

*G.-H. BOUSQUET, *Précis de droit musulman*, ii: *Le Droit musulman par les textes*, 3rd ed., Algiers 1960.

Works on the History of Islamic Law:

†I. GOLDZIHER, *Vorlesungen über den Islam*, Heidelberg 1910; 2nd ed., 1925; transl. F. Arin, *Le Dogme et la loi de l'Islam*, Paris 1920 (a masterly account of the development of Islamic law within the framework of the development of Islam).

*D. S. MARGOLIOUTH, *The Early Development of Mohammedanism*, London 1914 (pp. 65–98).

J. SCHACHT, *The Origins of Muhammadan Jurisprudence*, 3rd impression, Oxford 1959.

N. J. COULSON, *A History of Islamic Law*, Edinburgh 1964; cf. J. SCHACHT, in *Middle Eastern Studies*, i/4 (1965).

[1] These handbooks and the translations of Arabic authoritative works have, as a rule, not been referred to again in the bibliography of each chapter. For abbreviations of titles of periodicals, see below, pp. 286 f.

Historical Accounts by Muslim Authors:

MUḤAMMAD AL-KHUḌRĪ, *Tārīkh al-Tashrīʿ al-Islāmī* (*History of Islamic Legislation*), 7th ed., Cairo 1961.

MUḤAMMAD IBN AL-ḤASAN AL-ḤAJWĪ, *al-Fikr al-Sāmī fī Tārīkh al-Fiḳh al-Islāmī*, 4 vols., Rabat-Fes-Tunis 1345–9/1926-31.

ʿALĪ ḤASAN ʿABD AL-ḲĀDIR, *Naẓra ʿĀmma fī Tārīkh al-Fiḳh al-Islāmī*, i, Cairo 1361/1942.

MUḤAMMAD YŪSUF MŪSĀ, *Muḥāḍarāt fī Tārīkh al-Fiḳh al-Islāmī* (*Lectures on the History of Islamic Jurisprudence*), 3 vols., Cairo 1954–6; see also the introduction to his *al-Fiḳh al-Islāmī* (below, p. 272).

ṢUBḤĪ MAḤMASĀNĪ, *Muḳaddima fī Iḥyā' ʿUlūm al-Sharīʿa* (*Introduction aux études juridiques musulmanes*), Beyrouth 1962.

MAḤMŪD SHIHĀBĪ, *Adwār-i-Fiḳh* i, Teheran 1329/1951 (Publications de l'Université de Téhéran, 84) (Shiite).

HĀSHIM MAʿRŪF AL-ḤASANĪ, *al-Mabādi' al-ʿĀmma lil-Fiḳh al-Jaʿfarī*, (Baghdad) 1964 (Shiite).

Various:

†C. SNOUCK HURGRONJE, *Verspreide Geschriften*, ii, Bonn and Leipzig 1923; also *Selected Works of C. Snouck Hurgronje*, edited in English and in French by G.-H. BOUSQUET and J. SCHACHT, Leiden 1957 (the writings of Snouck Hurgronje are fundamental for a correct understanding of the nature of Islamic law).

C. A. NALLINO, *Raccolta di scritti editi e inediti*, iv, Rome 1942.

*G. BERGSTRÄSSER, 'Zur Methode der Fiqh-Forschung', *Islamica*, iv/3 (1930), 283–94.

F. KÖPRÜLÜ, art. 'Fıkıh', in *Islâm Ansiklopedisi*, iii, Istanbul 1947.

J. SCHACHT, 'Le Droit musulman: solution de quelques problèmes relatifs à ses origines', *R.A.* 1952, 1–13.

The Encyclopaedia of Islam, 4 vols. and Supplement, Leiden and London 1913–38 (also French and German editions); *Shorter Encyclopaedia of Islam*, Leiden and London 1953 (general articles: *Fiḳh*, by I. GOLDZIHER; *Sharīʿa*, by J. SCHACHT); *The Encyclopaedia of Islam*, new edition, Leiden and London 1960 ff. (also French edition).

Bibliographical:

Revue des études islamiques, Paris 1927 ff., section 'Abstracta Islamica'.

IBLA, Tunis 1937 ff., section 'Références'.

J. D. PEARSON and JULIA AṢHTON, *Index Islamicus 1906–1955*, Cambridge 1958, 101–41; *Supplement 1956–1960*, 1962, 33–47.

See also ARMINJON, NOLDE, and WOLFF, below.

Islamic Law in Comparative Law:

É. LAMBERT, *Introduction à la fonction du droit civil comparé*, i, Paris 1903, 297–389.

Ch. Cardahi, 'Les Conditions générales de la vente en droit comparé occidental et oriental', *Annales de l'École de Droit de Beyrouth*, 1945, no. 1, 7–208.

—— 'Droit et morale, le droit moderne et la législation de l'Islam au regard de la morale', 3 vols., ibid., 1950, 1954, 1958.

—— 'Le Prêt à intérêt et l'usure . . .', *R.I.D.C.* vii (1955), 499–541.

P. Arminjon, Baron B. Nolde, and M. Wolff, *Traité de droit comparé*, 3 vols., Paris 1950–2 (especially i. 83–86; iii. 399–533; with a bibliography of all books on Islamic law published in Western languages).

A. d'Emilia, 'Roman Law and Muslim Law, a Comparative Outline', in *East and West*, iv/2, Rome (Istituto Italiano per il Medio ed Estremo Oriente) 1953.

ʿAbd al-Razzāḳ Aḥmad al-Sanhūrī, *Maṣādir al-Ḥaḳḳ fil-Fiḳh al-Islāmī, dirāsa muḳārina bil-fiḳh al-gharbī* (*The Bases of Rights in Islamic Law, a comparative study with Western law*), 6 vols., Cairo 1954–9.

M. Ghauth, 'Torts due to Negligence (a comparative study of the Islamic and English laws)', *I.C.* xxxii (1958), 153–65, 232–8.

ʿAbd al-Raḥmān al-Ṣābūnī, *Madā Ḥurriyyat al-Ẓawjayn fil-Ṭalāḳ fil-Sharīʿa al-Islāmiyya, baḥth muḳārin* (*Étendue de la liberté des époux en matière de divorce en droit islamique, étude comparée*), Damascus 1962 (not seen; cf. *IBLA*, xxvi (1963), 81).

CHAPTER 2

1 G. Jacob, *Altarabisches Beduinenleben*, 2nd ed., Berlin 1897 (pp. 209–21).

J. Wellhausen, *Reste arabischen Heidentums*, Berlin 1897 (pp. 186–95).

—— *Gemeinwesen ohne Obrigkeit*, Göttingen 1900 (pp. 9, 15) (transl. in *The Historians' History of the World*, ed. H. S. Williams, viii, New York 1904, 284–293).

2 H. Lammens, *La Mecque à la veille de l'hégire*, Beyrouth 1924 (pp. 116–89).

—— *La Cité arabe de Ṭāif à la veille de l'hégire*, Beyrouth 1922 (pp. 94–103).

G.-H. Bousquet, in F. Peltier and G.-H. Bousquet, *Les Successions agnatiques mitigées*, Paris 1935, 95 f., and in *Hespéris*, 1954, 238–41 (on the volume and the character of trade in Mecca).

C. C. Torrey, *The Commercial-theological Terms in the Koran*, Leiden 1892.

Details, for Mecca:

J. Schacht, art. 'Ribā', in *Shorter E.I.*

—— *Origins*, 159 ff. (on *khiyār al-majlis*).

Details, for Medina:

Mālik ibn Anas, *al-Muwaṭṭa'*, *Kitāb al-buyūʿ*, sections on *bayʿ al-ʿarāyā* and on *muzābana* and *muḥāḳala* (these contracts are likely to go back to the pre-Islamic period because they are also attested in South Arabia, see below, section 6); transl. F. Peltier, *Le Livre des ventes*, Algiers 1911, 19–21, 27–30; cf. J. Schacht, *Origins*, 312.

Methodological:

J. Schacht, in *J.C.L.* 1950, 3–4, 11, and in *M.A.I.D.C.* iii/4 (Rome 1955), 130 f., against C. A. Nallino (1933), *Raccolta di scritti*, iv, Rome 1942, 88 f.

3 *On the Law of Family and Marriage:*

†J. Wellhausen, 'Die Ehe bei den Arabern', *Nachr. Ges. Wiss. Göttingen*, 1893, no. 11, 431–81.

W. Robertson Smith, *Kinship and Marriage in Early Arabia*, new ed. by Stanley A. Cook, London 1903 (cf. Th. Nöldeke, *Z.D.M.G.* xl (1886), 148–87).

H. Lammens, *Le Berceau de l'Islam*, Rome 1914 (pp. 276–306).

Gertrude H. Stern, *Marriage in Early Islam*, London 1939 (pp. 57–74).

*W. Montgomery Watt, *Muhammad at Medina*, Oxford 1956 (pp. 272–4, 373–88) (important, though the use of the sources seems questionable).

On Inheritance:

*G.-H. Bousquet, in F. Peltier and G.-H. Bousquet, *Les Successions agnatiques mitigées*, Paris 1935 (pp. 83–102).

†R. Brunschvig, 'Un Système peu connu de succession agnatique dans le droit musulman', *R.H.* 1950, 23–34.

On Blood Feuds:

O. Procksch, *Über die Blutrache bei den vorislamischen Arabern*, Halle 1899.

H. Lammens, 'Le Caractère religieux du 'ṯār' ou vendetta chez les Arabes préislamites' (1925), *L'Arabie occidentale avant l'hégire*, Beyrouth 1928, 181–236.

On Political Authority:

J. Wellhausen, *Gemeinwesen ohne Obrigkeit* (above, section 1).

H. Lammens, *Le Berceau de l'Islam*, Rome 1914 (pp. 197–267).

On the ḥakam, sunna, *and the Dispensation of Justice:*

I. Goldziher, *Muhammedanische Studien*, i, Halle 1889, 10 f., 14, 41.

A. Fischer, art. 'Kāhin', in *Shorter E.I.*

H. Lammens, *Le Berceau de l'Islam*, 257 f.

É. Tyan, *Histoire de l'organisation judiciaire en pays d'Islam*, 2nd ed., Leiden 1960, 27–61; art. 'Ḥakam', in *E.I.*²

C. C. Torrey, *The Commercial-Theological Terms in the Koran*, Leiden 1892.

J. Horovitz, *Koranische Untersuchungen*, Berlin and Leipzig 1926 (p. 51 on *mīthāḳ* 'covenant', pp. 60 f. on *sharīk* 'partner').

R. Brunschvig, in *S.I.* v (1956), 29 f. (on the absence of certain ancient legal terms from the vocabulary of the Koran).

On *ajr*: J. Schacht, art. '*Adjr*', in *E.I.*²

On *rahn*: J. Schacht, *Origins*, 186; also in *J.C.L.* 1950, 3–4, 15, and in *M.A.I.D.C.* iii/4, 137 f.

On *ʿuhda*: Mālik ibn Anas, *al-Muwaṭṭaʾ*, *Kitāb al-buyūʿ*, section on *al-ʿuhda*; transl. F. Peltier, *Le Livre des ventes*, 8 f.

On *maks* and *malasā*, see the Arabic dictionaries.

On *liṣṣ*, *dallas*, and *arabūn*: J. Schacht, in *XII Convegno 'Volta'*, Rome 1957, 199 f., 210, 228 f.: on *arabūn*, &c. also Mālik ibn Anas, *al-Muwaṭṭaʾ*, *Kitāb-al-buyūʿ*, section on *bayʿ al-ʿurbān*; transl. F. Peltier, *Le Livre des ventes*, 1–6.

On written documents: F. Krenkow, in *A Volume of Oriental Studies presented to Edward G. Browne*, Cambridge 1922, 265, 266, 268; S. Fraenkel, *Die armäischen Fremdwörter im Arabischen*, Leiden 1886, 249.

There exists no comprehensive treatment of, or bibliography on the law of ancient South Arabia. See, however, the list of the writings of N. Rhodokanakis in Maria Höfner, *Altsüdarabische Grammatik*, Leipzig 1943, xxiii f.; K. Mlaker, *Die Hierodulenlisten von Maʿīn, nebst Untersuchungen zur altsüdarabischen Rechtsgeschichte und Chronologie*, Leipzig 1943; M. Höfner, 'Über einige Termini in qatabanischen Kaufurkunden', *Z.D.M.G.* cv (1955), 74–80; A. F. L. Beeston, 'The Position of Women in Pre-Islamic South Arabia' in *Proceedings XXIInd Congress of Orientalists*, ii, Leiden 1957, 101–6; the same, 'Qahtan. Studies in Old South Arabian Epigraphy, i': *The Mercantile Code of Qataban*, London 1959.

On the rule of two witnesses: J. A. Montgomery, 'The Words "law" and "witness" in the South Arabic', *J.A.O.S.* xxxvii (1917), 164 f.

On *muḥāḳala*: N. Rhodokanakis, 'Der Grundsatz der Öffentlichkeit in den südarabischen Urkunden', *Sitzungsberichte Wien*, clxxvii (1915), no. 2, pp. 17, 22.

CHAPTER 3

1 É. Tyan, *Histoire de l'organisation judiciaire en pays d'Islam*, 2nd ed., Leiden 1960, 61–72.

S. D. Goitein, 'The Birth-hour of Muslim Law?', *M.W.* l (1960), 23–29 (also in *Proceedings XXIInd Intern. Congress Orientalists*, ii, Leiden 1957, 247–53) (suggests sura v. 42–51; a different point of view).

2 R. Roberts, *The Social Laws of the Qorân*, London 1925 (unsatisfactory, cf. J. Schacht, *O.L.Z.* 1927, 48–50, but usable as a collection of the relevant passages).

On sexual morality in the time of Muhammad:

L. Caetani, *Annali dell' Islam*, iii, Rome 1910, year 17, §§ 64–86.

Sara Kohn, *Die Eheschliessung im Koran*, thesis, Leiden 1934.

Gertrude S. Stern, *Marriage in Early Islam*, London 1939.

*W. Montgomery Watt, *Muhammad at Medina*, Oxford 1956 (pp. 261–302, 389–92).

M. Gaudefroy-Demombynes, *Mahomed*, Paris 1957 (pp. 596–658).

See further the relevant sections of the artt. 'Fay' in *E.I.*[2] (F. Løkkegaard), 'Ḳatl', 'Ḳiṣās', 'Mīrāth', 'Nikāḥ', 'Ribā', 'Ṭalāḳ', in *Shorter E.I.* (J. Schacht), and *Sāriḳ*, in *E.I.*[1] (W. Heffening).

Of the several translations of the Koran, that of M. Pickthall, *The Meaning of the Glorious Koran*, London 1930, reflects most faithfully its current interpretation by orthodox Muslims, that of R. Blachère, *Le Coran*, 2 vols., Paris 1949–51, with *Introduction au Coran*, Paris 1947, the conclusions of modern scholarship.

CHAPTER 4

On administration in general:

L. CAETANI, *Annali dell' Islam*, v, Rome 1912, year 23, §§ 517–811 (now dated but not yet replaced).

W. HOENERBACH, in *Der Islam*, xxix (1950), 260–4.

R. RUBINACCI, in *A.I.U.O.N.*, N.S. v (1954), 106–21 (translation of a letter addressed by ʿAbd Allāh ibn Ibāḍ to the Umayyad caliph ʿAbd al-Malik about 76/695, on the administration of Abū Bakr, ʿUmar and ʿUthmān; from BARRĀDĪ, *K. al-Jawāhir*, Cairo 1302, 156–67).

On penal law:

A. F. L. BEESTON, 'The so-called Harlots of Ḥaḍramaut', *Oriens*, v (1952), 16–22 (cutting off the hands of women who had incited to revolt, ordered by Abū Bakr; from MUḤAMMAD IBN ḤABĪB, *K. al Muḥabbar*, Hyderabad 1942, 184–9).

I. GOLDZIHER, in *Z.D.M.G.* xlvi (1892), 17–20, 28 (punishment of the authors of satirical poems by ʿUmar and ʿUthmān).

TH. NÖLDEKE and F. SCHWALLY, *Geschichte des Qorāns*, 2nd ed., i, Leipzig 1909, 248–51 (stoning to death for unlawful intercourse); cf. L. CAETANI, *Annali*, iii, 1910, year 17, §§ 84, 86.

On the punishment for drinking wine: A. J. WENSINCK, art. 'Khamr', in *E.I.*[1]; J. SCHACHT, *Origins*, 191, n. 5

For the background: O. A. FARRUKH, *Das Bild des Frühislams in der arabischen Dichtung*, Leipzig (thesis, Erlangen) 1937, 112–27.

On arbitration and the administration of justice:

É. TYAN, *Histoire de l'organisation judiciaire en pays d'Islam*, 2nd ed., Leiden 1960, 72–82.

D. S. MARGOLIOUTH, 'Omar's Instructions to the Kadi', *J.R.A.S.* 1910, 307–26.

On ḳasāma *and highway robbery:*

E. GRÄF, 'Eine wichtige Rechtsdirektive ʿUṯmān's aus dem Jahre 30', *Oriens*, xvi (1963), 122–33.

J. SCHACHT, *Origins*, 260–8.

R. RUBINACCI, 'La purità rituale secondo gli Ibāḍiti', *A.I.U.O.N.* N.S. vi (1957), 1–41 (places the emphasis differently).

*I. GOLDZIHER, *Muhammedanische Studien*, i, Halle 1889, 10 f., 41; ii, 1890, 11–16 (transl. L. BERCHER, *Études sur la tradition islamique*, Paris 1952, 12–17).

—— 'The Principles of Law in Islam', *The Historians' History of the World*, ed. H. S. WILLIAMS, viii, New York 1904, 294–304 (p. 294 f.).

R. RUBINACCI (see above, no. 1).

J. SCHACHT, 'Sur l'expression "*sunna* du Prophète",' in *Mélanges d'orientalisme offerts à Henri Massé*, Teheran 1963, 361–5.

4 On the treatise of Ḥasan al-Baṣrī: H. RITTER, *Der Islam*, xx (1932), 67–83 (text); J. OBERMANN, 'Political Theology in Early Islam', *J.A.O.S.* lv (1935), 138–62; J. Schacht, *Origins*, 74 (comment).

J. SCHACHT, *Origins*, 188, 191, 224–7.

5 *General:*

J. SCHACHT, 'Foreign Elements in Ancient Islamic Law', *J.C.L.* 1950, nos. 3–4, 9–16; also in *M.A.I.D.C.* iii/4 (Rome 1955), 127–41.

—— 'Remarques sur la transmission de la pensée grecque aux Arabes', *Histoire de la médecine*, ii/5, Paris 1952, 11–19.

—— 'Droit byzantin et droit musulman', in *XII Convegno 'Volta'*, Rome 1957, 197–218 (with bibliography), and discussion, 219–30.

On the status of tolerated religions:

XII Convegno 'Volta', 205 f.; add to bibliography: J. DE MENASCE, 'L'Église mazdéenne dans l'Empire sassanide', *Cahiers d'histoire mondiale*, ii, 1955, 555–65 (esp. p. 560).

On taxation:

CL. CAHEN, artt. 'Ḍarība' and 'Djizya', in *E.I.*²

On emphyteusis:

D. SANTILLANA, *Istituzioni*, i. 436–40 (for the background; dated in details).

CL. CAHEN, in *Annales: Économies, Sociétés, Civilisations*, 1953, 26.

On waḳf*:*

XII Convegno 'Volta', 213–15; add to bibliography: CL. CAHEN, 'Réflexions sur le waqf ancien', *S.I.* xiv (1961), 37–56.

On the 'five religious qualifications':

S. VAN DEN BERGH, *Averroes' Tahāfut al-Tahāfut*, ii, London 1954, 117 f.; cf. also J. SCHACHT, *Origins*, 133.

On the study of Hellenistic rhetoric and law:

F. SCHULZ, *History of Roman Legal Science*, Oxford 1946, 268–70, 301 f.

On Hellenistic elements in Talmudic and Rabbinic law:

XII Convegno 'Volta', 202; add to bibliography: R. YARON, *Gifts in Contemplation of Death in Jewish and Roman Law*, Oxford 1960, index, s.v. Hellenistic; S. LIEBERMANN, *Greek in Jewish Palestine*, New York 1942, and *Hellenism in Jewish Palestine*, New York 1950 (for the background).

Further on individual features derived from Roman law:

A. VON KREMER, *Culturgeschichte des Orients*, i, Vienna 1875, 532 f. (*legitima aetas* of 25 years; cf. above, p. 125).

F. F. SCHMIDT, 'Die occupatio im islamischen Recht', *Der Islam*, i (1910), 300–53.

On adultery as an impediment to marriage:

J. SCHACHT, in *R.I.D.A.*, 2nd ser., i (1952), 105–23.

On ḳiyās, *&c.:*

I. Goldziher, 'Das Princip des istiṣḥâb in der muhammedanischen Gesetzwissenschaft', *Vienna Oriental Journal*, i (1887), 228–36.

J. Schacht, *Origins*, 99 f.

On Sassanian law and features derived from it:

A. Christensen, 'Introduction bibliographique à l'histoire du droit de l'Iran ancien', *A.H.D.O.* ii (1937), 243–57; supplement by A. Pagliaro, in *R.S.O.* xxiv (1949), 120–2.

A. Pagliaro, in *XII Convegno 'Volta'*, 220 f., 400–3.

N. Pigulevskaya, 'Die Sammlung der syrischen Rechtsurkunden des Ischobocht [*end 8th cent.*] und des Matikan', *Akten des XXIV. Intern. Orientalistenkongresses*, Wiesbaden 1959, 219–21 (important parallel).

J. Schacht, in *Orientalia*, xvii (1948), 519 (on the *kātib*); *Origins*, 95, and in *M.A.I.D.C.* iii/4, 140 (on codification), against S. D. Goitein, in *I.C.* xxiii (1949), 128.

J. Schacht, 'Vom babylonischen zum islamischen Recht', *O.L.Z.*, 1927, 664–9 (statement of the problem); cf. M. San Nicolò, *Beiträge zur Rechtsgeschichte*, &c., Oslo 1931, 159 f.

I. Goldziher, in *R.S.O.* i (1907), 209 (on the meaning of *ījāb*).

CHAPTER 5

1 G. Levi Della Vida, art. 'Umayyads', in *E.I.*[1]

2 J. Schacht, *Origins*, 190–213.
On *ḳasāma*: I. Goldziher, in *Zeitschr. vergl. Rechtswiss.* viii (1889), 412; J. Wellhausen, *Reste arabischen Heidentums*, Berlin 1897, 187; the same, *Gemeinwesen ohne Obrigkeit*, Göttingen 1900, 9; R. Brunschvig, in *S.I.* iii (1955), 69 f.

3 *On the transition from* ḥakam *to* ḳāḍī*:*

*É. Tyan, *Histoire de l'organisation judiciaire en pays d'Islam*, 2nd ed., Leiden 1960, 74–76.
J. Schacht, *Origins*, 228 f.

On the seat and wand of the judge:

C. H. Becker, in *Orientalische Studien Theodor Nöldeke . . . gewidmet*, i, Giessen 1906, 338–40, = *Islamstudien*, i, Leipzig 1924, 458–60.

On Islamic judges under the Umayyads:

*M. Gaudefroy-Demombynes, 'Sur les origines de la justice musulmane', *Mélanges syriens offerts à M. René Dussaud*, ii, Paris 1939, 819–28.
*É. Tyan, *Histoire de l'organisation judiciaire*, 83–99.
J. Schacht, *Origins*, 100–2, 167 f., 191; art. 'Al-Ashʿarī Abū Burda', in *E.I.*[2]
E. Gräf, 'Gerichtsverfassung und Gerichtsbarkeit im islamischen Recht', *Zeitschr. vergl. Rechtswiss.* lviii (1955), 48–78 (the method and the historical conclusions are questionable).

Arabic sources on the early judges in Islam:

ʿAbd al-Ḥamīd ibn Yaḥyā (d. soon after 132/750), *Risāla* addressed to ʿAbd Allāh ibn Marwān, in Ḳalḳashandī, *Ṣubḥ al-Aʿshā*, x, Cairo 1916, 217 f., and in Aḥmad Zakī Ṣafwat, *Jamharat Rasāʾil al-ʿArab*, ii, Cairo 1937, 508 f. (on the qualities demanded of a *ḳāḍī* at the end of the Umayyad period).
Wakīʿ (d. 330/941), *Akhbār al-ḳuḍāt*, ed. ʿAbd al-ʿAzīz Muṣṭafā al-Marāghī, i–iii, Cairo 1947–50.
Kindī (d. 350/961), *The Governors and Judges of Egypt*, ed. R. Guest, Leiden and London 1912 (important review by G. Bergsträsser, *Z.D.M.G.* lxviii (1914), 395–413).
On the 'inspector of the market': J. Schacht, in *Orientalia*, xvii (1948), 518.

On the judicial autonomy of the non-Muslims:

N. Edelby, 'L'Autonomie législative des Chrétiens en terre d'Islam', *A.H.D.O.* v (1950–1), 307–51.
A. Fattal, *Le Statut légal des non-Musulmans en pays d'Islam*, Beyrouth 1958.

4 J. Schacht, in *Revue africaine*, xcvi (1952), 322 f.
On Rajāʾ and Abū Ḳilāba: J. Wellhausen, *Das arabische Reich und sein Sturz*, Berlin 1902, 165 (transl. Margaret G. Weir, *The Arab Kingdom*

and its Fall, Calcutta 1927, 264 f.); IBN SAʿD (d. 230/845), *Kitāb al-Ṭabaḳāt al-Kabīr*, vii/i, Leiden 1915, 133–5.

On Ibrāhīm al-Nakhaʿī and his contemporaries in Iraq: J. SCHACHT, *Origins*, 229–31, 233–7.

CHAPTER 6

1 J. SCHACHT, *Origins*, 6–10, 213–23.

†R. BRUNSCHVIG, 'Considérations sociologiques sur le droit musulman ancien', *S.I.* iii (1955), 61–73.

2 J. SCHACHT, *Origins*, 224–7.

3 †R. BRUNSCHVIG, 'Polémiques médiévales autour du rite de Mālik', *Al-Andalus*, xv (1950), 377–435.

J. SCHACHT, *Origins*, 58–97.

4 J. SCHACHT, *Origins*, 231–40, 243–8, 249–52.

—— art. "ʿAṭā'," in *E.I.*².

A list of authorities, mostly of the second century, in IBN ḤAZM (d. 456/1065), *al-Iḥkām fī Uṣūl al-Aḥkām*, chap. xxviii (ed. Cairo, 1345–8, v, 95–104).

5 J. SCHACHT, *Origins*, 73 f., 76.

6 J. SCHACHT, *Origins*, 240–2, 248 f.

7 †I. GOLDZIHER, *Muhammedanische Studien*, ii, Halle 1890, 1–274 (transl. L. BERCHER, *Études sur la tradition islamique*, Paris 1952) (fundamental).

A. GUILLAUME, *The Traditions of Islam*, Oxford 1924 (based mainly on Goldziher).

†R. BRUNSCHVIG (see above, no. 3).

J. SCHACHT, *Origins*, 253–7.

—— artt. 'Ahl al-Ḥadīth' and 'Aṣḥāb al-Ra'y,' in *E.I.*²

J. FÜCK, 'Die Rolle des Traditionalismus im Islam', *Z.D.M.G.* xciii (1939), 1–32 (uncritical).

J. ROBSON, *Muslim Traditions: the Question of Authenticity*, Manchester 1952 (reprinted from *Memoirs and Proceedings of the Manchester Literary and Philosophical Society*).

—— art. 'Ḥadīth', in *E.I.*²

On ancient polemics concerning traditions:

I. GOLDZIHER, 'Kämpfe um die Stellung des Ḥadīṯ im Islam', *Z.D.M.G.* lxi (1907), 860–72; summary in French by G. H. BOUSQUET, in *Arabica*, vii (1960), 4–8.

J. SCHACHT, *Origins*, 21–57, 59 f., 63 f., 128–32.

Methodological:

R. BRUNSCHVIG, 'Ibn ʿAbdalh'akam et la conquête de l'Afrique du Nord par les Arabes', *A.I.E.O.* vi (1942–7), 108–55.

J. SCHACHT, 'A Revaluation of Islamic Traditions', *J.R.A.S.* 1949, 143–54.

—— 'Le Droit musulman: solution de quelques problèmes relatifs à ses origines', *R.A.* 1952, 1–13.

—— *Origins*, 138–79.

Collections of traditions are extremely numerous, and the so-called 'six books', the works of Bukhārī, Muslim, Ibn Māja, Abū Dāwūd, Tirmidhī, and Nasā'ī, which date from the second half of the third century of the hijra, are regarded as particularly authoritative in orthodox Islam, although they are not source books of Islamic law.

Translations of the *Ṣaḥīḥ* of Bukhārī (d. 256/870): O. HOUDAS and W. MARÇAIS, *Les Traditions islamiques*, i–iv, Paris 1903–14; F. PELTIER, *Le Livre des testaments*, Algiers 1909; the same, *Le Livre des ventes . . . suivi du livre de la vente à terme et du livre du retrait*, Algiers 1910; the same *Œuvres diverses*, Algiers 1949, 5–71 (*Livres de l'ensemencement et de la mousaqat*); G.-H. BOUSQUET and KH. TAKARLI, 'Le Livre des successions', *R.A.* 1933, 208–38; G.-H. BOUSQUET, *L'Authentique tradition musulmane*, Paris 1964 (a selection).

A. J. WENSINCK, *A Handbook of Early Muhammadan Tradition*, Leiden 1927 (subject index of the 'six books' and of other ancient works, including the *Musnad* of Ibn Ḥanbal and the relevant parts of Mālik's *Muwaṭṭa'* and of the Zaydī *Majmūʿ al-Fiḳh*).

—— and others, *Concordance et indices de la tradition musulmane*, i– , Leiden 1933– (in progress; in Arabic).

Other important collections:

BAYHAḲĪ (d. 458/1066), *al-Sunan al-Kubrā*.

MUTTAḲĪ AL-HINDĪ (d. 975/1567), *Kanz al-ʿUmmāl*.

SHAWKĀNĪ (d. 1250/1832; a Zaydī Shiite author, using Sunnı material), *Nayl al-Awṭār*.

CHAPTER 7

1 †G. Bergsträsser, *Anfänge und Charakter des juristischen Denkens im Islam*, in *Der Islam*, xiv (1925), 76–81 (important, though partly dated).
*I. Goldziher, *Die Zâhiriten*, Leipzig 1884, 3–20, 89–94 (still important).
J. Schacht, *Origins*, 98–119.

2 On legal 'puzzles': J. Schacht, *Origins*, 241.
On legal adages: J. Schacht, *Origins*, 180–9; R. Brunschvig, in *R.H.* 1950, 29–31; the same, in *Unity and Variety in Muslim Civilization*, ed. G. E. Von Grunebaum, Chicago 1955, 85.

3 J. Schacht, *Origins*, 269–87.

Important Arabic sources for the second century:

Mālik (d. 179/795), *al-Muwaṭṭa'*, also in the version of Shaybānī; part transl. by F. Peltier, *Le Livre des ventes du Mouaṭṭā de Mālik Ben Anas*, Algiers 1911.

Saḥnūn (d. 240/854), *al-Mudawwana* (for opinions of the Medinese); key to the contents by G.-H. Bousquet, in *A.I.E.O.* xvi–xx (1958–62), and in *R.A.* 1958–61; transl. of the *Kitāb al-ḥabs*, by Almenouar Kellal, *R.A.* 1936, 186–207; cf. ibid. 1937, 149–55.

Abū Yūsuf (d. 182/798), *al-Radd ʿalā Siyar al-Awzāʿī.*

—— *Ikhtilāf Abī Ḥanīfa wa-bn Abī Laylā.*

—— *Kitāb al-Āthār.*

Shaybānī (d. 189/804), *Kitāb al-Ḥujaj.*

—— *Kitāb al-Āthār.*

—— *Kitāb al-Aṣl*; transl. of the chapter on 'defects' (above, p. 152 f.) in G. Wiedensohler, *Mängel beim Kauf* (below, p. 276).

—— *al-Jāmiʿ al-Kabīr.*

—— *al-Jāmiʿ al-Ṣaghīr*; part transl. and commentary by I. Dimitroff, *M.S.O.S.* xi/2 (1908), 60–206 (the introduction is dated).

—— version of Mālik's *al-Muwaṭṭa'*.

Shāfiʿī (d. 204/820), *Kitāb al-Umm*, containing also nine, mostly polemical *Treatises*.

—— *Ikhtilāf al-Ḥadīth.*

—— *al-Risāla*; detailed digest by L. I. Graf, *Al-Shāfiʿī's Verhandeling over de 'Wortelen' van den Fiḳh*, thesis, Leiden 1934; transl. M. Khadduri, *Treatise on Moslem Jurisprudence*, Baltimore 1961.

Muzanī (a disciple of Shāfiʿī; d. 264/878), *Kitāb al-Amr wal-Nahy*; ed. and transl. by R. Brunschvig, *B.E.O.* xi (1945–6), 145–96.

—— *al-Mukhtaṣar.*

Ṭabarī (d. 310/923), *Kitāb Ikhtilāf al-Fuḳahā'* (cf. below, p. 265).

Majmūʿ al-Fiḳh, attributed to Zayd b. ʿAlī (d. 122/740; a Zaydī Shiite work, based on Iraqian doctrines; cf. G. Bergsträsser, *O.L.Z.* 1922, 114–24; R. Strothmann, *Der Islam*, xiii (1923), 27–40, 49; part transl. G.-H. Bousquet and J. Berque, *Recueil de la loi musulmane*, Algiers 1941.

4 J. Schacht, *Origins*, 288-314; artt. 'Abū Ḥanīfa al-Nuʿmān', 'Abū Thawr', 'Abū Yūsuf', 'al-Awzāʿī', in *E.I.*[2]; 'Mālik b. Anas', in *Shorter E.I.*

W. Heffening, art. 'al-Shaibānī', in *Shorter E.I.*

J. Schacht, *Origins*, 11–20, 77–80, 88–94, 120–8, 134–7, 315–28 and in *Classicisme et déclin culturel dans l'histoire de l'Islam*, Paris 1957, 145–7.

W. Heffening, art. 'al-Shāfiʿī', in *Shorter E.I.*; J. Schacht, 'On Shāfiʿī's Life and Personality', in *Studia Orientalia Ioanni Pedersen . . . Dicata*, Copenhagen 1953, 318–26.

R. Brunschvig, in *Arabica*, i (1954), 359 f.

CHAPTER 8

1 B. LEWIS, art. 'ʿAbbāsids', in *E.I.*²
ABŪ YŪSUF (d. 182/798), *Kitāb al-Kharāj*, transl. E. FAGNAN, *Le Livre de l'impôt foncier*, Paris 1921.
2 G. GABRIELI, *Il 'cadi' o giudice musulmano*, Rome 1913 (separately printed from *Rivista coloniale*, viii/2, fasc. 3 and 4).
†É. TYAN, *Histoire de l'organisation judiciaire en pays d'Islam*, 2nd ed., Leiden 1960 (cf. M. GAUDEFROY-DEMOMBYNES, *R.E.I.* 1939, 109–47, and *J.A.* ccxxxv (1946–7), 123–32).
G. WIET, *Matériaux pour un Corpus Inscriptionum Arabicarum*, 1/2 (*Mémoires publiés par les membres de l'Institut français d'archéologie orientale*), Cairo 1930, 50–62 (on *shurṭa*).
A. CHRISTENSEN, *L'Iran sous les Sassanides*, 2nd ed., Copenhagen 1944, 300–3 (on the Iranian model of the *naẓar fil-maẓālim*).
W. BJÖRKMAN, *Die Bittschriften im* dīwān al-inšā', *Der Islam*, xviii (1929), 207–12 (suggests a hellenistic model for the *naẓar fil-maẓālim* in medieval Egypt).
S. M. STERN, 'Three Petitions of the Fāṭimid Period', *Oriens*, xv (1962), 172–209 (on *naẓar fil-maẓālim*).

On the administration of justice in the middle ages:

*G. BERGSTRÄSSER, in *Z.D.M.G.* lxviii (1914), 395–417 (on Egypt during the first four centuries of Islam).
*A. MEZ, *Die Renaissance des Islâms*, Heidelberg 1922, chap. 15; transl. S. KHUDA BUKHSH and D. S. MARGOLIOUTH, *The Renaissance of Islam*, London 1937 (reprinted from *I.C.* ii–vii, 1928–33); transl. S. VILA, *El renacimiento del Islâm*, Madrid 1936.
E. LÉVI-PROVENÇAL, *L'Espagne musulmane au Xème siècle*, Paris 1932, chap. 3.
*—— *Histoire de l'Espagne musulmane*, iii, Paris 1953, chap. 10; transl. E. GARCÍA GÓMEZ, *Historia de España*, ed. R. M. PIDAL, vol. v, Madrid 1957, chap. 3.
J. F. HOPKINS, *Medieval Muslim Government in Barbary*, London 1958, 112–47.
H. R. IDRIS, *La Berbérie orientale sous les Zīrīdes*, Paris 1962, ii, 548–72.
†R. BRUNSCHVIG, *La Berbérie orientale sous les Ḥafṣides*, ii, Paris 1947, 113–53; 'Justice religieuse et justice laïque en Tunisie, sous les Deys et les Beys, jusqu'au milieu du XIXᵉ siècle', *S.I.* xxiii.
A. SCHIMMEL, *Kalif und Kadi im spät-mittelalterlichen Agypten*, Leipzig 1943 (separately printed from *W.I.* xxiv (1942), 1–128).
*A. K. S. LAMBTON, 'Quis custodiet custodes?' Some Reflections on the Persian Theory of Government', *S.I.* v (1956), 125–48; vi (1956), 125–46.
S. R. SHARMA, *Mughal Government and Administration*, Bombay 1951, chaps. xii and xiii.
I. H. QURESHI, *The Administration of the Sultanate of Delhi*, 4th ed., Lahore 1958, 157–74.

Arabic sources on the administration of justice:

AL-MĀWARDĪ (d. 350/1058), *al-Aḥkām al-Sulṭāniyya*; transl. E. FAGNAN, *Les Statuts gouvernementaux*, Algiers 1915; cf. also H. F. AMEDROZ, 'The Office of Kadi', 'The Mazalim Jurisdiction', and 'The Hisba Jurisdiction in the Ahkam Sultaniyya of Mawardi', *J.R.A.S.* 1910, 761–96; 1911, 635–74; 1916, 77–101, 287–314.

ABŪ YAʿLĀ (d. 458/1065), *al-Aḥkām al-Sulṭāniyya*.

NUWAYRĪ (d. 732/1332), *Nihāyat al-Arab fī Funūn al-Adab*, vi, Cairo 1926, 248–315.

IBN JAMĀʿA (d. 733/1333), *Taḥrīr al-Aḥkām fī Tadbīr Millat al-Islām*; ed. and transl. H. KOFLER, *Handbuch des islamischen Staats- und Verwaltungsrechtes*, *Islamica*, vi/4 (1934), 349–414; vii/1 (1935), 1–64; *Abh. f. d. Kunde des Morgenl.* xxiii/6 (1938), 18–129.

TĀJ AL-DĪN SUBKĪ (d. 771/1370), *Muʿīd al-Niʿam wa-Mubīd al-Nikam*; German abbreviated transl. O. Rescher, Istanbul 1925.

IBN KHALDŪN (d. 808/1406) *al-Muḳaddima, faṣl* 3, § 31; transl. MAC GUCKIN DE SLANE, *Les Prolégomènes*, i, reprint Paris 1934, 447–60; transl. F. ROSENTHAL, *The Muqaddimah*, i, New York 1958, 448–65.

ḲALḲASHANDĪ (d. 821/1418), *Ṣubḥ al-Aʿshā*: W. BJÖRKMAN, *Beiträge zur Geschichte der Staatskanzlei im islamischen Ägypten*, index, s.vv. *qāḍī*, *maẓālim*, *ḥāğib*, *šurṭa*, *muḥtasib*.

WANSHARĪSĪ (d. 914/1508), *Kitāb al-Wilāyāt*; ed. and transl. H. BRUNO and M. GAUDEFROY-DEMOMBYNES, *Le Livre des magistratures*, Rabat 1937.

On ḥisba *in particular:*

C. CAHEN and M. TALBI, art. 'Ḥisba' in *E.I.*²

YAḤYĀ IBN ʿUMAR KINĀNĪ (d. 289/901), *Aḥkām al-Sūḳ*, extracts ed. Maḥmūd ʿAlī Makkī, in *R.I.E.E.I.* iv (1956), 59–151 (Arabic section); transl. E. GARCÍA GÓMEZ, in *Al-Andalus*, xxii (1957), 253–316.

W. BEHRNAUER, *Mémoire sur les institutions de police chez les Arabes, les Persans et les Turcs*, Paris 1861 (separately printed from *J.A.*, 5th ser., xv–xvii (1860–1); contains a translation of SHAYZARĪ (d. 589/1193), *Nihāyat al-Rutba fī Ṭalab al-Ḥisba*, on which cf. J. SAUVAGET, *J.A.* ccxxxvi (1948), 309–11); text ed. AL-ʿARĪNĪ and M. M. ZIYĀDA, Cairo 1946.

SAḲAṬĪ (about 500/c.1100), ed. G.-S. COLIN and E. LÉVI-PROVENÇAL, *Un Manuel hispanique de ḥisba*, Paris 1931.

IBN ʿABDŪN (about 500/c. 1100), ed. E. LÉVI-PPROVENÇAL, in *J.A.* ccxxiv (1934), 177–299; transl. F. GABRIELI, 'Il trattato censorio di Ibn ʿAbdūn', *Rendiconti Accademia Lincei*, 6th ser., xi (1935), 878–935; transl. LÉVI-PROVENÇAL, *Séville musulmane au début du XIIᵉ siècle*, Paris 1947; LÉVI-PROVENÇAL and E. GARCÍA GÓMEZ, *Sevilla musulmana a comienzos del siglo XII*, Madrid 1948.

E. LÉVI-PROVENÇAL, *Trois traités hispaniques de ḥisba*, Cairo 1955, containing the treatises of Ibn ʿAbdūn (above), of Ibn ʿAbd al-Raʾūf, and of Jarsīfī; this last transl. G. M. WICKENS, *I.Q.* iii. (1956), 176–87; the second and the third transl. RACHEL ARIÉ, *Hespéris-Tamuda*, i (1960), 5–38, 199–214, 349–86.

IBN SAʿDŪN (d. 567/1172), *Aḥkām al-Sūḳ*, ed. Maḥmūd ʿAlī Makkī, *R.I.E.E.I.* iv (1956), 59–152 (Arabic part); a collection of *fatwās*.

IBN TAYMIYYA (d. 728/1328), *Risālat al-Ḥisba fil-Islām*; cf. H. LAOUST, *Essai* (below, p. 237), index, s.v. *ḥisba*.

IBN UKHUWWA (d. 729/1330), *Maʿālim al-Ḳurba fī Aḥkām al-Ḥisba*, ed. R. LEVY, London 1938 (E. J. W. Gibb Memorial, N.S., xii) (cf. M. GAUDEFROY-DEMOMBYNES, *J.A.* ccxxx (1938), 449–57).

R. B. SERJEANT, 'A Zaidī Manual of Ḥisbah of the 3rd Century (H)', *R.S.O.* xxviii (1953), 1–34.

N. ZIYĀDA, *al-Ḥisba wal-Muḥtasib fil-Islām*, Beyrouth 1963 (contains extracts from Arabic sources).

3 É. TYAN, *Histoire de l'organisation judiciaire*, 446–51.

—— in *S.I.* x (1959), 101–8.

IBN FARḤŪN (d. 799/1397), *Tabṣirat al-Ḥukkām* (section 3); cf. N. J. COULSON, 'The State and the Individual in Islamic Law', *I.C.L.Q.* vi (1957), 49–60 (the conclusions of this paper need qualification).

IBN TAYMIYYA (d. 728/1328), *al-Siyāsa al-Sharʿiyya*; transl. H. LAOUST, *Le Traité de droit public d'Ibn Taimīya*, Beyrouth 1948.

IBN ḲAYYIM AL-JAWZIYYA (d. 751/1350), *al-Ṭuruḳ al-Ḥukmiyya fil-Siyāsa al-Sharʿiyya*.

A. N. POLIAK, in *R.E.I.* 1935, 235 f., and in *B.S.O.A.S.* x (1942), 862, 875 (on Mamlūk *siyāsa*).

4 J. SCHACHT, *Origins*, index, s.v. Ibn Muqaffaʿ.

S. GOITEIN, 'A Turning Point in the History of the Muslim State', *I.C.* xxiii (1949), 120–35.

On the control of religious law possible for a Shiite *imām*, cf. J. SCHACHT, in *Classicisme et déclin culturel dans l'histoire de l'Islam*, Paris 1957, 144 f.

CHAPTER 9

J. SCHACHT, *Origins*, 6 f., 9, 321.

On the *Muwaṭṭa'* and the *Mudawwana*, see above, p. 228; F. KRENKOW, art. 'Saḥnūn', in *E.I.*[1].

W. HEFFENING, art. 'al-Muzanī', in *E.I.*[1]; cf. also above, p. 228.

M. PLESSNER, art. 'Sufyān al-Thawrī', in *E.I.*[1]; J. SCHACHT, *Origins*, 242.

See the bibliography on *uṣūl al-fiḳh* below, pp. 266 ff.

On the gradual emergence of the group of four *uṣūl*, cf. J. SCHACHT, *Origins*, 134–6; F. KERN, 'Ṭabarīs Iḫtilāf alfuqahā'', *Z.D.M.G.* lv (1901), 61–95.

R. PARET, art. 'Istiḥsān and istiṣlāḥ', in *Shorter E.I.*; J. SCHACHT, *Origins*, 111 f., 118 f.; É. TYAN, in *S.I.* x (1959), 84–101.

I. GOLDZIHER, 'Über iǵmā'', *Nachr. Ges. Wiss. Göttingen*, Phil.-hist. Kl., 1916, 81–85; summary in French by G.-H. BOUSQUET, in *Arabica*, vii (1960), 15f.

G. F. HOURANI, 'The Basis of Authority of Consensus in Sunnite Islam', *S.I.* xxi (1964), 13–60.

MUṢṬAFĀ ZAYD, *al-Maṣlaḥa fil-Tashrīʿ al-Islāmī*, 2nd ed., Cairo 1384/1964.

On Mālikī 'amal*:*

†J. BERQUE, art. 'Amal' (3), in *E.I.*[2] (with bibliography).

†L. MILLIOT, *Démembrements du habous*, Paris 1918, 23–30, 109–17.

†—— *Recueil de jurisprudence chérifienne*, i–iii, Paris 1920–3 (especially introduction to vol. i, section iv); vol. iv, by J. LAPANNE-JOINVILLE, Paris 1952 (especially preface by Milliot, v–xix).

*—— *Introduction* 167–78.

*O. PESLE, *Le Contrat de Safqa au Maroc*, Rabat 1932 (cf. R. CHARLES, in *R.A.* 1933, 57–114).

*R. BRUNSCHVIG, 'Contribution à l'histoire du contrat de khamessat en Afrique du Nord', *R.A.* 1938, 17–21.

†J. BERQUE, *Essai sur la méthode juridique maghrébine*, Rabat 1944, 33–49, 63–77, 126–9.

Translations of Arabic sources:

ZAḲḲĀḲ (d. 912/1506), *al-Lāmiyya*, ed. and transl. Merad ben Ali, Casablanca 1927.

WANSHARĪSĪ (d. 914/1508), *al-Miʿyār*, transl. of extracts by É. AMAR, *La Pierre de touche des fetwas*, 2 vols., Paris 1908–9 (cf. F. CODERA, in *Boletín de la Real Academia de la Historia*, liv (1909), 345–55; lvi (1910), 378–86).

ʿABD AL-RAḤMĀN AL-FĀSĪ (d. 1095/1695), *al-ʿAmal al-Fāsī*; V. LOUBIGNAC, 'La Vente çafqa dans la jurisprudence des cadis de Fez', 1933, 62–114; the same, 'Le Chapitre de la préemption', *Hespéris*, xxvi (1939), 191–239; F. GUAY and M. BEN DAOUD, 'Le Mariage dans la jurisprudence des cadis de Fès', *R.A.* 1933, 178–207.

AḤMAD ʿABBĀSĪ (d. 1152/1739): J. BERQUE, 'Les *Ajwiba* d'al-ʿAbbâsî', *R.A.* 1950, 94–104.

TĀWUDĪ IBN SŪDA (d. 1209/1795): E. PRÖBSTER, 'Die *Aǵwiba* des Tāudī Ibn Sōda', *Islamica*, ii/3 (1926), 430–8.

Wazzānī (d. 1342/1923), *al-Miʿyar al-Jadīd*; J. Berque, *Les Nawâzil el muzâraʿa du Miʿyâr Al Wazzânî*, Rabat 1940; P. Mispoulet, in *R.M.M.* xxiv (1913), 298–310 (table of contents).

On *ʿurf* and *ʿāda* in Islamic law:
I. Goldziher, *Die Zâhiriten*, Leipzig 1884, 204–6.
C. Snouck Hurgronje (1884), *Verspreide Geschriften*, ii. 72–74.
—— *Selected Works*, 57.
D. Santillana, *Istituzioni*, i. 48 f. (needs qualification).
J. Berque, *Essai sur la méthode juridique maghrébine*, 72 f. (same remark).
J. Schacht, in *Classicisme et déclin culturel dans l'histoire de l'Islam*, Paris 1957, 141–51.
F. J. Ziadeh, 'ʿ*Urf* and Law in Islam', in *The World of Islam*, ed. J. Kritzeck and R. B. Winder, London 1959, 60–67.
N. J. Coulson, 'Muslim Custom and Case-Law', *W. I.*, n.s. vi (1959), 13–24.
Aḥmad Fahmī Abū Sinna, *al-ʿUrf wal-ʿĀda fī Raʾy al-Fuḳahāʾ*, Cairo 1959 (influenced by modernist thought).

4 On the chapter-headings of Bukhārī: I. Goldziher, *Muhammedanische Studien*, ii, Halle 1890, 234–6 (transl. L. Bercher, *Études sur la tradition islamique*, Paris 1952, 294–6); the same, *Die Zāhiriten*, 103–7.
*H. Laoust, art. 'Aḥmad b. Ḥanbal', in *E.I.*[2].
Aḥmad ibn Ḥanbal, *Kitāb al-Masāʾil* (only one of the several versions has been printed so far); the same, *Kitāb al-Waraʿ* (*The Book of Religious Scrupulousness*): transl. of extracts by G.-H. Bousquet and Paule Charles-Dominique, *Hespéris*, xxxix (1952), 97–119.
Later Ḥanbalī *uṣūl* in ʿAbd Allāh ibn Aḥmad ibn Ḳudāma (d. 620/1223), *Rawḍat al-Nāẓir*; cf. R. Deniel, *R.E.I.* xxxi (1963), 33–47.
†On the doctrines of Ibn Taymiyya, see the works of H. Laoust, below, p. 237; also Sirajul Haq, 'Ibn Taimiyya's Conception of Analogy and Consensus', *I.C.* xvii (1943), 77–87 (to be used with caution).

5 †I. Goldziher, *Die Zâhiriten*, Leipzig 1884 (fundamental; cf. C. Snouck Hurgronje, *Verspreide Geschriften*, vi, 19–29).
*R. Strothmann, art. '*Ẓāhiriya*', in *Shorter E.I.*
J. Schacht, art. 'Dāwūd b. Khalaf', in *E.I.*[2]
*C. van Arendonk, art. 'Ibn Ḥazm', in *Shorter E.I.*
*M. Asín Palacios, *Abenházam de Córdoba*, vol. i, Madrid 1927.
†R. Arnaldez, *Grammaire et théologie chez Ibn Ḥazm de Cordoue*, Paris 1959, 163–93, 217–48.
—— 'Les Biens en droit musulman à travers les idées d'Ibn Hazm de Cordoue', *Les Mardis de Dar el-Salam 1956–57*, 1959, 147–86.
—— 'La Guerre sainte selon Ibn Ḥazm', *Études d'orientalisme . . . Lévi-Provençal*, Paris 1962, ii, 445–59.
*Y. Linant de Bellefonds, 'Ibn Ḥazm et le zahirisme juridique', *R.A.* 1960, 1–43.

On the legal thought of the Muʿtazila, cf. J. Schacht, *Origins*, 128, 258 f.

On Ibn Tūmart and the Almohads:
I. Goldziher, *Die Zâhiriten*, 173–5.

†—— 'Materialien zur Kenntnis der Almohadenbewegung', *Z.D.M.G.* li (1887), 30–140 (especially pp. 85–100).
†—— *Le Livre de Mohammed Ibn Toumert*, Introduction, Algiers 1903.
R. Brunschvig, 'Sur la doctrine du Mahdī Ibn Tūmart', *Arabica*, ii (1955), 137–49 (also in *Ignace Goldziher Memorial Volume*, ii, Jerusalem 1958, 1–13); the same, in *Études d'orientalisme . . . Lévi-Provençal*, i, 38, 67.
J. Schacht, art. 'Abū Thawr', in *E.I.*².
R. Paret, art. 'al-Ṭabarī', in *Shorter E.I.*

Spread and distribution of the schools of law:

On the spread of Islam itself and the present distribution of Muslims see:

Sir Thomas W. Arnold, *The Preaching of Islam*², London 1913.
La Documentation française, no. 1642 (Série Internationale, cclxxiii), Paris, 9 August 1952: *Les Musulmans dans le monde* (with map).
H. W. Hazard and others, *Atlas of Islamic History*, 3rd ed., Princeton 1954 (concerned with the political rather than with the religious expansion of Islam).
H. A. R. Gibb, *Mohammedanism*², London 1953 (Home University Library), 1–22.
R. Roolvink and others, *Historical Atlas of the Muslim Peoples*, Amsterdam 1957.

A. Mez, *Die Renaissance des Islâms*, Heidelberg 1922, chap. 14; for translations, see above, p. 230.
Aḥmad Taymūr (Pasha), *Naẓra Tārīkhiyya fī ḥudūth al-madhāhib al-arbaʿa wa-ntishārihā*, Cairo 1344 (1926) (*Historical Survey of the Origin and Spread of the four Schools of Law*). 2nd ed., Cairo 1384/1965.
Muḥammad Abū Zahra, *Tārīkh al-Madhāhib al-Islāmiyya*, Cairo 1963.
L. Massignon, *Annuaire du monde musulman*, 4th ed., Paris 1955.
J. Schacht, art. 'Ḥanafiyya', in *E.I.*²
W. Heffening, art. 'Mālikīs', in *Shorter E.I.*
M. B. Vincent, *Études sur la loi musulmane* (*Rit* [*sic*] *de Malek*). *Législation criminelle*, Paris 1842 (the first part, Préliminaire, contains a still useful account of the early spread of the Mālikī school and of its literature).
Ahmed Bakir, *Histoire de l'école malikite en orient jusqu'à la fin du moyen âge*, Tunis 1962.
J. López Ortiz, *La recepción de la escuela malequí en España*, Madrid 1931 (separately printed from *Anuario de Historia del Derecho Español*).
H. Monés, '*Le Rôle des hommes de religion dans l'histoire de l'Espagne musulmane*', *S.I.* xx (1964), 47–88.
E. Lévi-Provençal, 'Le Malikisme andalou et les apports doctrinaux de l'Orient', *R.I.E.E.I.* i (1953), 156–71.
Maḥmūd ʿAlī Makkī, Ensayo sobre las aportaciones orientales en la España musulmana (i), *R.I.E.E.I.* ix–x (1961–62), 65–231.
J. Berque, 'Ville et université. Aperçu sur l'histoire de l'école de Fès', *R.H.* 1949, 64–117.
A. Demeerseman, 'Recherches tunisiennes sur le mâlikisme ifrîqiyen', *IBLA*, xxvi (1963), 1–12 (a review of recent publications).

W. HEFFENING, art. 'al-Shāfiʿī', in *Shorter E.I.* (at the end), and art. 'al-Nawawī', ibid.

I. GOLDZIHER, art. 'Aḥmad b. Muḥammad b. Ḥanbal', in *Shorter E.I.* (at the end).

—— 'Zur Geschichte der ḥanbalitischen Bewegungen', *Z.D.M.G.* lxii (1908), 1–28; summary in French by G.-H. BOUSQUET, in *Arabica*, vii (1960), 135–9.

H. LAOUST, *Le Précis de droit d'Ibn Qudāma*, Beyrouth 1950, introduction; 'Le Hanbalisme sous le califat de Baghdad', *R.E.I.* 1959, 67–128; 'Le Hanbalisme sous les Mamlouks Bahrides', *R.E.J.* 1960, 1–72; art. 'Ḥanabila', in *E.I.*[2]

7 *On* ikhtilāf*:*

J. SCHACHT, *Origins*, 95–97.

I. GOLDZIHER, art. 'Ikhtilāf', in *Shorter E.I.*

CHAPTER 10

D. B. Macdonald, art. 'Idjtihād', in *Shorter E.I.*

J. Schacht, art. 'Taḳlīd', in *Shorter E.I.*

—— in *Classicisme et déclin culturel dans l'histoire de l'Islam*, Paris 1957, 146 f.

Th. W. Juynboll, *Handleiding*, 23–26, 370–2.

Mirza Kazem Beg, 'Notice sur la marche et les progrès de la jurisprudence', &c., *J.A.* 4th ser. xv (1850), 158–214 (pp. 181–214 on degrees of *ijtihād* and *taḳlīd*; the rest of the paper is quite out of date).

On authoritative works of the several schools, see the bibliography below, pp. 261 ff.

On later developments of doctrine:

C. A. Nallino, 'Delle assicurazioni in diritto musulmano hanafita' (1927), *Raccolta di scritti*, iv, 1942, 62–84.

—— 'Intorno al divieto romano imperiale dell' affratellamento e ad alcuni paralleli arabi' (1936), ibid. 585–631 (pp. 626–9: Ibn Taymiyya's decision on a custom of mercenaries).

*R. Brunschvig, 'Théorie générale de la capacité chez les Hanafites médiévaux', *R.I.D.A.* ii (1949), 157–72.

*—— 'De l'acquisition du legs dans le droit musulman orthodoxe', *M.A.I.D.C.* iii/4 (Rome 1955), 95–110.

*—— 'Variations sur le thème du doute dans le fiqh', *Studi orientalistici in onore di Giorgio Levi Della Vida*, i, Rome 1956, 61–82.

J. Schacht, 'Sur la transmission de la doctrine dans les écoles juridiques de l'Islam', *A.I.E.O.* x (1952), 399–419.

Th. W. Juynboll, *Handleiding*, 372 f.

On the Ẓāhirīs and the Almohads, see the bibliography above, pp. 234 f.

M. Ben Cheneb, art. 'Ibn Taimīya', in *Shorter E.I.*

†H. Laoust, *Essai sur les doctrines sociales et politiques de . . . B. Taimīya*, Cairo 1939.

†—— *Contribution à une étude de la méthodologie canonique de . . . B. Taimīya*, Cairo 1939.

—— 'La biographie d'Ibn Taimīya d'après Ibn Kaṯīr', *B.E.O.* ix (1942), 115–62.

On reformers and modernists:

*H. Laoust, 'Le réformisme orthodoxe des "Salafiya" ', *R.E.I.* 1932, 175–224.

—— *Le Califat dans la doctrine de Rašīd Riḍā*, Beyrouth 1938, index s.vv. *iğtihād* and *taqlīd*.

—— 'Le réformisme musulman dans la littérature arabe contemporaine', *Orient*, iii (1959), no. 10, 81–108.

*C. C. Adams, *Islam and Modernism in Egypt*, London 1953 (sub-title: A study of the modern reform movement . . .).

J. Berque, *Essai sur la méthode juridique maghrébine*, Rabat 1944, 89–137.

*W. C. Smith, *Modern Islām in India*, revised ed., London 1946.

*H. A. R. Gibb, *Modern Trends in Islam*, Chicago 1947.

M. D. RAHBAR, 'Shāh Walī Ullāh [d. 1176/1762] and Ijtihād', *M.W.* xlv (1955), 346–58.

F. RAHMAN, 'Muslim Modernism in the Indo-Pakistan Subcontinent', *B.S.O.A.S.* xxi (1958), 82–99.

MUINUDDIN AHMAD KHAN, 'Shah Walī-Allah's Conception of Ijtihād', *J.P.H.S.* vii (1959), 165–94.

M. KERR, 'Rashīd Riḍā and Islamic Legal Reform', *M.W.* l (1960), 99–108, 170–81.

E. J. J. ROSENTHAL, 'Some Reflections on the Separation of Religion and Politics in Modern Islam', *Islamic Studies*, iii (1964), 249–84.

4 E. NUNÈ, 'Il parere giuridico ("fatwā") del "muftī" nel diritto musulmano', *O.M.* xxiv (1944), 27–35.

É. TYAN, *Histoire de l'organisation judiciaire en pays d'Islam*, 2nd ed., Leiden 1960, 219–30.

—— art. 'Fatwā', in *E.I.*²

R. BRUNSCHVIG, *La Berbérie orientale sous les Ḥafṣides*, ii, Paris 1947, 138–43.

—— 'La preuve en droit musulman', in *Recueils de la Société Jean Bodin*, xviii, Brussels 1964, 169–86.

J. LÓPEZ ORTIZ, 'Fatwas granadinas de los siglos XIV y XV', *Al-Andalus*, vi (1941), 73–127 (with an historical introduction on *fatwās* and *muftīs* in Islamic Spain).

L. SECO DE LUCENA PAREDES, *Dos fatwas de Ibn Manẓūr* (wrote 864/1460), *Miscelánea de estudios arabes y hebraicos*, v (1956), 5–17.

E. MICHAUX-BELLAIRE and others, ed. and transl. of Bāyaʿḳūbī al-Malwī (19th cent.), *Tuḥfat al-Ḳuḍāt bi-baʿḍ masāʾil al-ruʿāt*', *Archives marocaines*, xv (1909), 289–430, i–xxxi (on questions concerning shepherds).

For other examples of *fatwās* in translation, see É. AMAR, *La Pierre de touche des fetwas* (above, p. 233); P. HORSTER, *Zur Anwendung des islamischen Rechts im 16. Jahrhundert* (below, p. 246), and *Index Islamicus* (above, p. 216), 106.

5 J. SCHACHT, 'Classicisme, traditionalisme et ankylose dans la loi religieuse de l'Islam', *Classicisme et déclin culturel dans l'histoire de l'Islam*, Paris 1957, 141–61 and 162–6 (discussion).

CHAPTER 11

†C. Snouck Hurgronje, *Verspreide Geschriften,* vols. ii and iv/1, 2; index (vol. vi), s.v. *ʿadat, ʿadatrecht* (fundamental).
*—— *Selected Works,* 290–5.
*G.-H. Bousquet, *Du droit musulman et de son application effective dans le monde,* Algiers 1949.
N. J. Coulson, 'Doctrine and Practice in Islamic Law', *B.S.O.A.S.* xviii (1956), 211–26 (to be used with caution).
—— 'Muslim Custom and Case-Law', *W.I.* n.s. vi (1959), 13–24 (a balanced general survey).
†G.-H. Bousquet, S. T. Lokhandwalla, and J. Prins, art. 'ʿĀda', in *E.I.*², with important bibliography.

Supplement to the bibliography of the art. 'ʿĀda', in *E.I.*²
R. Levy, *The Social Structure of Islam,* Cambridge 1957, 242–70 (a popular general account).
G.-H. Bousquet, 'Islamic Law and Customary Law in French North Africa', *J.C.L.* 1950, parts 3–4, 57–65.
L. Milliot, *Introduction,* 158–67: 'Étude spéciale de la coutume en Afrique du Nord'.
†G. Marcy, 'Le Problème du droit coutumier berbère', *R.A.* 1954, 127–70.
E. Pröbster, 'Streifzüge durch das maghribinische Recht', *Islamica,* iii/3 (1927), 342–62.
†J. Berque, *Structures Sociales du Haut-Atlas,* Paris 1955, 237–397.
—— art. 'Djamāʿa', in *E.I.*²
*G.-H. Bousquet, 'Le droit coutumier des Aït Haddidou des Assif Melloul et Isselaten', *A.I.E.O.* xiv (1956), 113–230.
P. Gros, 'Deux ḳanouns marocains du XVIᵉ siècle', *Hespéris,* xviii (1934), 64–75 (the earliest examples of codification of customary penal law in Moroccan tribes; with bibliography).
A. Plantey, *La réforme de la justice marocaine. La justice makhzen et la justice berbère,* Paris 1962.
J. Richarte and A. Leriche, 'L'organisation judiciaire musulmane et le procès en Mauritanie', *R.A.* 1953, 13–34.
A. Leriche, 'Des châtiments prévus par la loi musulmane et de leur application en Mauritanie', *Bulletin de l'Institut Français d'Afrique Noire,* series B, fasc. xix (1957), 446–63.
R. Brunschvig, *La Berbérie orientale sous les Ḥafṣides,* ii, Paris 1947, 295–8.
†A. Goguyer, *Choix splendide de préceptes cueillis dans la loi.* Petit manuel de droit immobilier suivant les deux rites musulmans orthodoxes de la Régence de Tunis, Paris and Tunis 1885 (annotated transl. of two Arabic treatises).
J. Abribat, *Essai sur les contrats de quasi-aliénation et de location perpétuelle auxquels l'institution du hobous a donné naissance,* Algiers 1902 (with particular reference to Tunisia).
Muḥammad al- Sanūsī, *Maṭlaʿ al-Darārī* (French title: '*Le Lever des planètes*' *ou Recherches sur la conformité de la jurisprudence musulmane avec la loi immobilière*), Tunis 1888.

The Future of Customary Law in Africa (International Colloquium of Amsterdam), Leiden 1956.

J. N. D. ANDERSON, *Islamic Law in Africa* (Being a Survey of the application of Islamic law in the British Col nial Territories in Africa and in the Colony and Protectorate of Aden), London 1954.

—— 'Law and Custom in Muslim Areas in Africa. Recent Developments in Nigeria', *Civilizations*, vii (1957), 17–31.

—— 'Conflict of Laws in Northern Nigeria: a New Start', *I.C.L.Q.* viii (1959), 442–56.

—— 'Judicial and Legal Developments in the Northern Region', ibid. xii (1963), 282–94.

J. SCHACHT, 'La Justice en Nigéria du Nord et le droit musulman', *R.A.* 1951, 37–43.

—— 'L'Administration de la justice musulmane en Afrique Occidentale française et britannique', *Symposium Intercolonial*, Bordeaux 1954, 82–89.

—— 'Islam in Northern Nigeria', *S.I.* viii (1957), 123–46.

A. ABEL, *Les Musulmans noirs du Maniéma*, Brussels, 1960, 44–55, 91–94.

E. CERULLI, *Somalia*, i, Rome 1957, 149 f., 152 (= art. 'Somaliland', in *E.I.*[1]); 206–10: Diritto musulmano e diritto consuetudinario somalo (reprinted from *R.S.O.* x (1923–5), 32–36); vol. ii, 1959, *passim*.

Bibliography of further publications on Somali customary law by I. M. LEWIS, in *B.S.O.A.S.* xviii (1956), 159 f.

C. VELTEN, *Sitten und Gebräuche der Suaheli, nebst einem Anhang über Rechtsgewohnheiten der Suaheli*, Göttingen 1903.

P. GUY, 'Les Musulmans châféites de l'archipel des Comores et leur droit', *R.A.* 1951, 59–64; 'Le Mariage en droit comorien', *R.J.P.U.F.* ix (1955), 799–830; x (1956), 307–46; xii (1958), 653–90; *Traité de droit musulman comorien*, i/1, Algiers 1952, i/2 (cyclostyled), Diégo-Suarez 1956; *Cours de droit musulman à l'usage des candidats à l'emploi de cadi dans le Territoire des Comores* (cyclostyled), Antananarivo (Centre d'Études de Droit Privé et d'Histoire des Coutumes, École Supérieure de Droit) 1961.

†ALBENGO, *Lois et coutumes suivies dans le Pachalik de Jérusalem*, traduites de l'arabe et annotées, Paris 1860.

R. KNOX-MAWAR, 'Islamic Domestic Law in the Colony of Aden', *I.C.L.Q.* v (1956), 511–18.

Punjab Customary Law, revised ed., 14 vols., Calcutta 1923–8.

M. B. AHMAD, 'Theory and Practice of Law in Islam', in *J.P.H.S.* viii (1960), 184–205, 271–86, ix (1961), 8–22.

R. O. WINSTEDT, 'Old Malay Legal Digests and Malay Customary Law', *J.R.A.S.* 1945, 17–29.

—— *The Malays, A Cultural History*, Singapore 1947, 79–102.

J. N. MATSON, 'The Conflict of Legal Systems in the Federation of Malaya and Singapore', *I.C.L.Q.* vi (1957), 243–62.

P. E. DE JOSSELIN DE JONG, 'Islam versus Adat in Negri Sembilan (Malaya)', *Bijdragen tot de Taal-, Land- en Volkenkunde*, cxvi (1960), 158–203 (with bibliography).

See, further, *Index Islamicus* (above, p. 216), 116–19; *Supplement 1956–60*, 38.

On the customary law of the Bedouins:

*E. GRÄF, *Das Rechtswesen der heutigen Beduinen*, Walldorf-Hessen [1952] (digest of the previous publications, with bibliography).

J. HENNINGER, 'Das Eigentumsrecht bei den heutigen Beduinen Arabiens', *Zeitschr. vergl. Rechtswiss.* lxi (1959), 6–56.

M. J. L. HARDY, *Blood Feuds and the Payment of Blood Money in the Middle East*, Leiden 1963.

On ḥawz *and* manʿ (ṭāghūt):

B. THOMAS, *Arabia Felix*, London 1932, 57, 82 f., 86 f.; and in *J.R.A.S.* 1931, 978–81.

*E. ROSSI, 'Il diritto consuetudinario delle tribù arabe del Yemen', *R.S.O.* xxiii (1948), 1–36.

C. RATHJENS, *Tâghût gegen scherî'a*, Heidelberg 1951 (separately printed from *Jahrbuch des Linden-Museums, Stuttgart*, i (1951), 172–187).

R. B. SERJEANT, 'Materials for South Arabian History. Notes on New MSS. from Ḥaḍramawt', *B.S.O.A.S.* xiii (1949–50) (pp. 589–93: Law and Custom).

—— 'Two Tribal Law Cases (Documents)', *J.R.A.S.* 1951, 33–47, 156–69.

On taxation in Islamic law:

N. P. AGHNIDES, *Mohammedan Theories of Finance*, New York 1916 (reprinted Lahore 1961); Th. W. JUYNBOLL, art. 'Kharādj', A. GROHMANN, art. ''Ushr', J. SCHACHT, art. 'Zakāt', in *Shorter E.I.*; CL. CAHEN, artt. 'Darība (i)' and 'Djizya', in *E.I.*².

E. BUSSI, 'Del concetto di commercio e di commerciante nel pensiero giuridico musulmano in relazione alla storia generale del diritto', in *Studi in Memoria di Aldo Albertoni*, iii, Padua 1938, 7–53.

On *bayʿ al-wafāʾ* or *bayʿ al-ʿuhda*: A. GOGUYER (see above), pp. 54 ff.; R. B. SERJEANT, in *B.S.O.A.S.* xiii (1949–50), 591–3.

On *suftaja* and *ḥawāla*: R. GRASSHOFF, *Das Wechselrecht der Araber*, Berlin 1899 (also thesis, Königsberg: *Die suftaǵa and ḥawâla der Araber*); G. JACOB, 'Die ältesten Spuren des Wechsels', *M.S.O.S.* xxviii/2 (1925), 280 f.; MĀLIK B. ANAS, *al-Muwaṭṭaʾ*, *Kitāb al-buyūʿ*, section on *al-ʿīna*; transl. F. PELTIER, *Le Livre des ventes*, Algiers 1911, 52 f. (older than the passage translated by Jacob).

On banking in Islam: W. J. FISCHEL, art. 'Djahbadh', in *E.I.*² (with bibliography); S. LABIB, 'Geld und Kredit. Studien zur Wirtschaftsgeschichte Ägyptens im Mittelalter', *Journal of the Economic and Social History of the Orient*, ii (1959), 225–46 (pp. 238–42 on banking); A. K. S. LAMBTON, 'The Merchant in Medieval Islam', in *A Locust's Leg, Studies in honour of S. H. Taqizadeh*, London 1962, 121–30.

On the 'law merchant': L. GOLDSCHMIDT, 'Ursprünge des Handelsrechts. Insbesondere: Sensal', *Zeitschr. ges. Handelsrecht*, xxviii (1882), 115–30; S. FRÄNKEL, *Die aramäischen Fremdwörter im Arabischen*, Leiden 1886, 186 (on *simsār*); W. G. BEWES, *The Romance of the Law Merchant*, London 1923; E. Bussi, 'Contractus mohatrae', *Rivista di storia del diritto italiano*, v (1932), 492–519; *Max Weber on Law in Economy and Society*, ed. M. RHEINSTEIN,

Cambridge Mass. 1954, 241 (the doubts expressed by M. RHEINSTEIN in n. 60 are unfounded); J. SCHACHT in *XII Convegno 'Volta'*, Rome 1957, 215 (pp. 215–18 on the sporadic influences of Islamic law on other laws).

3 J. SCHACHT, editions of Khaṣṣāf, *Kitāb al-Ḥiyal wal-Makhārij*, Hanover 1923; of Ḳazwīnī, *Kitāb al-Ḥiyal fil-Fiḳh*, Hanover 1924; and of Shaybānī, *Kitāb al-Makhārij fil-Ḥiyal*, Leipzig 1930.

—— 'Die arabische ḥijal-Literatur', *Der Islam*, xv (1926), 211–32; further in *Der Islam*, xxii (1935), 220, and in *Revue Africaine*, xcvi (1952), 322–7.

H. LAMMENS, 'Les Ḥial dans le droit musulman' (in Arabic), *Al-Machriq*, xxix (1931), 641–6.

J. BAZ, *Essai sur la fraude à la loi en droit musulman*, Paris 1938.

G. W. J. DREWES, *De ḥila in het geding*, separately printed from *Gedenkboek . . . van het Rechtswetenschappelijk Hoger Onderwijs in Indonesië*, Groningen and Djakarta 1949.

On evasions of the prohibition of interest in particular:

MĀLIK B. ANAS, *al-Muwaṭṭa'*, *Kitāb al-buyūʿ*, section on *bayʿ al-ʿurbān*; transl. F. Peltier, 5 f.; cf. *Lisān al-ʿArab*, s.v. *ʿīna*.

C. SNOUCK HURGRONJE, *Mekka in the latter part of the 19th century*, transl. J. H. Monahan, Leyden and London 1931, 4 f.

Th. W. JUYNBOLL, *Handbuch*, 274–6; *Handleiding*, 288–90.

M. S. A. KHAN, 'Mohammedan Laws against Usury and how they are evaded', *J.C.L.* 1929, 233–44.

D. SANTILLANA, *Istituzioni*, ii, 392–7.

O. TURAN, 'A Legal Document concerning Money-lending for Interest in Seljukian Turkey', *Professor Muhammad Shafi Presentation Volume*, Lahore 1955, 255–65 (a document concerning the pledging of real property as security for a loan, entitling the creditor to use part of it, drawn up by the *ḳāḍī* of Amasya in 697/1298).

On the evasion of obligations under oath, cf. I. GOLDZIHER, *Streitschrift des Ġazālī gegen die Bāṭinijja- Sekte*, Leiden 1916, 73–80 (Arabic part, 54–58).

On fictitious actions:

A. LATTES, 'Beni vacuf e procedimenti fittizi', *Scritti giuridici dedicati ed offerti a Giampietro Chironi*, iii, Turin 1915, 75–82.

4,5 †É. TYAN, 'Le notariat et le régime de la preuve par écrit dans la pratique du droit musulman', *Annales de l'École Française de Droit de Beyrouth*, 1945, no. 2; reprinted, Beyrouth 1959 (cf. J. SCHACHT, *Orientalia*, N.S. xvii (1948), 519–22).

J. LÓPEZ ORTIZ, 'Formularios notariales de la España musulmana', *La Ciudad de Dios*, cxlv (1926), 260–75.

—— *La jurisprudencia y el estilo de los tribunales musulmanes de España*, Madrid 1933 (separately printed from *Anuario de historia del derecho español*).

R. BRUNSCHVIG, *La Berbérie orientale sous les Ḥafṣides*, ii, Paris 1947, 135–8 (on *ʿudūl*).

F. ROSENTHAL, 'Significant Uses of Arabic Writing', *Ars Orientalis*, iv (1961), 15–23 (pp. 22 f.).

On the literature of shurūṭ; *selection of editions and translations:*

I. Goldziher, *Muhammedanische Studien* ii, Halle 1890, 233, 253 (transl. L. Bercher, *Études sur la tradition islamique*, Paris 1952, 292, 316).

Ḥanafī authors:

Shaybānī (d. 189/804): his *Kitāb al-Shurūṭ* exists in extracts, incorporated in the comments of Sarakhsī (d. 483/1090), in the *Mabsūṭ* of this last (vol. xxx, Cairo 1331, 167–209).

Khaṣṣāf (d. 261/874), who also wrote on *ḥiyal*, *adab al-ḳāḍī*, *waḳf*, and *nafaḳāt*, composed three works on *shurūṭ* (*Kitāb al-Fihrist*, 206).

Aḥmad ibn Zayd (another author of the 3rd/10th century), called Shurūṭī because of his special interest in the subject, likewise wrote three works on *shurūṭ* (*Kitāb al-Fihrist*, 208).

Ṭaḥāwī (d. 321/933), too, one of the great authorities of his school, is the author of three works on *shurūṭ*, of which the most concise and parts of the most detailed have survived (two parts ed. J. Schacht in *Sitzungsber. Heidelberger Akad. Wiss.*, Phil.-hist. Klasse, 1926/27, no. 4, and 1929/30, no. 5).

al-Fatāwā al-ʿĀlamgīriyya (11th/17th century; cf. above, p. 94): this work contains, in two extensive chapters, numerous extracts on *shurūṭ* from the authoritative works of the school (vol. vi, Būlāḳ 1310, 160–248: *Kitāb al-maḥāḍir wal-sijillāt*; 248–389: *Kitāb al-shurūṭ*).

S. Rousseau, *A Dictionary of Mohammedan Law* [technical terms 'used in the East Indies'] . . . to which is added an appendix containing forms of . . . instruments and contracts of law, London 1802.

Mālikī authors:

Ibn Mughīth (d. 459/1067), *al-Muḳniʿ*, transl. S. Vila, *Abenmoguit*, *'Formulario Notarial'*, *Capítulo del matrimonio*, Madrid 1931 (separately printed from *Anuario de historia del derecho español*).

A. González Palencia, *Los Mozárabes de Toledo en los siglos XII y XIII*, i–iii and volumen preliminar, Madrid 1926–30 (Mozarabic documents drawn up in the technical forms of *wathāʾiḳ*; cf. J. Schacht, *Der Islam*, xix (1931), 172–7; W. Hoenerbach, 'Some Notes on the Legal Language of Christian and Islamic Deeds', *J.A.O.S.* lxxxi (1961), 34–38).

—— 'Documentos árabes del Cenete (siglos XII–XV)', *Al-Andalus*, v (1940), 301–82 (cf. ibid. vi (1941), 477–80).

L. Seco de Lucena Paredes, 'Documentos árabes granadinos', ibid. viii (1943), 415–29; ix (1944), 121–40.

—— 'Actas notariales arábigogranadinas', *Miscelánea de estudios árabes y hebraicos*, ii (1953), 99–107.

—— *Documentos arábigo-granadinos*, Madrid 1961 (documents of the 9th/15th century).

J. Bosch Vilá, 'Los documentos árabes del archivo catedral de Huesca', *R.I.E.E.I.* v (1957), 1–48 (documents of the 6th/12th and the 7th/13th centuries).

Ibn Salmūn (d. 767/1365), *al-ʿIḳd al-Munaẓẓam lil-Ḥukkām*: J. López Ortiz,

Algunos capítulos del formulario notarial de Abensalmún de Granada, Madrid 1928 (separately printed from *Anuario de historia del derecho español*).

IBN FARḤŪN (d. 799/1397), *Tabṣirat al-Ḥukkām*; cf. WANSHARĪSĪ, *Kitāb al-Wilāyāt*, ed. and transl. Bruno and Gaudefroy-Demombynes (above, (p. 231), Appendixes I and II.

IBN ʿARḌŪN (d. 992/1584), *Kitāb al-Lāʾiḳ li-Muʿallim al-Wathāʾiḳ*; cf. G. S. COLIN, *J.A.* ccxxii (1933), 207.

MUḤAMMAD BANNĀNĪ FIRʿAWN (d. 1281–82/1865; cf. *E.I.*², s.v. *Bannānī*), *Kitāb al-Wathāʾiḳ*, transl. under the direction of F. GUAY, 'Formulaire des actes juridiques', *R.A.* 1932, 205–22; 1933, 272–338.

MUḤAMMAD TUWĀTĪ, *Majmūʿ al-Ifāda fī ʿIlm al-Shahāda*, transl. J. ABRIBAT, *Recueil de notions de droit musulman et d'actes notariés*, 1896.

European works on Mālikī wathāʾiḳ*:*

L.-J. BRESNIER, *Extrait de la chréstomathie arabe vulgaire*, troisième partie: Actes judiciaires, Algiers 1846.

E. LAUNE, *Formulaire arabe d'actes de procédure*, Oran 1890.

P. VASSEL, 'Über marokkanische Processpraxis', *M.S.O.S.* v/2 (1902), 1–63.

E. VIALA and MOHAMMED GENNADY, *Guide du traducteur*, Casablanca 1924.

E. ZEYS and MOHAMMED OULD SIDI SAÏD, *Recueil d'actes et de jugements arabes*, avec la traduction française, 2nd ed. by H. Pérès, Algiers 1946.

A. GUIRAUD, *Jurisprudence et procédure musulmanes*, Casablanca 1925, Tunis 1948.

J. LAPANNE JOINVILLE, 'L'action en pétition d'hérédité', *R.M.D.* ii (1950), 65–69 (on 'pratique judiciaire et notariale').

Shāfiʿī and other authors:

SHĀFIʿĪ (d. 204/820) wrote a *Kitāb al-Shurūṭ* (*Kitāb al-Fihrist*, 210), and two original documents of his have been incorporated in his *Kitāb al-Umm*; cf. F. KERN, 'Zwei Urkunden vom Imām aš Šāfiʿī', *M.S.O.S.* vii/2 (1904), 53–68.

ABŪ THAWR (d. 240/854), MUZANĪ (d. 264/878), DĀWŪD IBN KHALAF (d. 270/887), and ṬABARĪ (d. 310/923) likewise wrote works on *shurūṭ* (*Kitāb al-Fihrist*, 212, 217, 234; ḤĀJJĪ KHALĪFA *Lexicon*, iv, 46 f.).

NUWAYRĪ (d. 732/1332), *Nihāyat al-Arab fī Funūn al-Adab*: this work contains a section on *shurūṭ* (vol. ix, Cairo 1333, 1–160) which is based on the *Mukhtaṣar al-Mukātabāt al-Badīʿa* of the Shāfiʿī author Muḥammad ibn ʿAbd Allāh al-Ṣayrafī (d. 330/942).

Among the numerous editions and translations of original documents, those of collections of papyri deserve special mention; cf., for instance, A. GROHMANN, *Arabic Papyri in the Egyptian Library*, i ff., Cairo 1934 ff.; A. DIETRICH, 'Die arabischen Urkunden', *Zum gegenwärtigen Stand der juristischen Papyrusforschung*, *Zeitschr. vergl. Rechtswiss.* lx (1957), 211–37.

6 J. SCHACHT, in *Der Islam*, xx (1932), 209–14, and in *S.I.* xii (1960), 101–4.

J. H. KRAMERS, 'Droit de l'Islam et droit islamique', *A.H.D.O.* i (1937), 401–14.

CHAPTER 12

G. Marçais, *La Berbérie musulmane et l'Orient au Moyen Âge*, Paris 1946, 238–45.

J. Bosch Vilá, *Los Almorávides*, Tetuan 1956.

See the bibliography on Northern Nigeria, above, p. 240.

On legal developments in Northern Nigeria since independence, see J. N. D. Anderson, 'Northern Nigerian Law: Judicial and Legal Developments in the Northern Region', *I.C.L.Q.* xii (1963), 282–94.

C. A. Nallino, *L'Arabia Saʿūdiana*, vol. i of *Raccolta di scritti*, Rome 1939, 75–80, 96–108, 123.

J. P. M. Mensing, *De bepaalde straffen in het ḥanbalietische recht*, Leiden 1936.

J. Schacht, in *A.J.C.L.* viii (1959), 136 f.

On the project of codification of Ibn Saud: *O.M.* viii (1928), 36–38; J. Schacht, loc. cit., 146 f.

On the Ordinance on Commerce: A. d'Emilia, 'Intorno al codice di commercio dell' Arabia Saudiana', *O.M.* xxxii (1952), 316–25.

P. T. Hart, 'Application of Hanbalite and Decree Law to Foreigners in Saudi Arabia', *George Washington Law Review*, xxii (1953), 165–75.

On Yemen: G. W. Bury, *Arabia Infelix*, London 1915, index, s.v. *Islamic code*.

C. van H. Engert, *A Report on Afghanistan*, Washington 1924 (Department of State, Division of Publications, Series C, no. 53), 75 f., 97–99.

S. Beck, *Das Afghanische Strafgesetzbuch vom Jahre 1924 mit dem Zusatz vom Jahre 1925*, Berlin 1928 (separately printed from *W.I.* 1928, 67–157).

S. Beck and F. Grobba, in *Rechtsvergleichendes Handwörterbuch*, ed. F. Schlegelberger, i, Berlin 1929, 289–310.

G.-H. Bousquet, *Du droit musulman et de son application effective dans le monde*, Algiers 1949, 17.

ADDENDA TO CHAPTER 11

for p. 240: J. N. D. Anderson, 'The Future of Islamic Law in British Commonwealth Territories in Africa', in *African Law*, Duke University School of Law, Durham, N.C. 1962, 617–31.

for p. 241, §2: S. D. Goitein, 'Commercial and Family Partnerships in the Countries of Medieval Islam', *Islamic Studies*, iii (1964), 315–37.

CHAPTER 13

1 *H. A. R. Gibb and H. Bowen, *Islamic Society and the West*, i/1, 2, London 1950–7 (particularly part 1, 19–25, part 2, 70–138, and indexes s.vv. *ḳaḍâ, ḳâḍî, ḳânûn, ḳânûn-nâme, muftî, muḥtesib, şerîʿa, şeyḫü'l-Islâm, şubaşî, ʿulemâ*.

P. Wittek, 'Devshirme and Sharīʿa', *B.S.O.A.S.* xvii (1955), 271–8; cf. V. L. Ménage, ibid. xviii (1956), 181–3.

V. L. Ménage, art. 'Devshirme', in *E.I.*²

B. Lewis, art. 'ʿArūs Resmi', in *E.I.*²

2 J. H. Kramers, art. 'Shaikh al-Islām', in *Shorter E.I.*; J. R. Walsh, art. 'Fatwā (ii)', in *E.I.*²

J. Schacht, art. 'Abu 'l-Suʿūd', in *E.I.*²

*M. Hartmann, in *Der Islam*, viii (1918), 313–17 (report on an important anonymous publication in *Milli Tetebbüler Mecmuasî*, i (1331/1915), 49–112, 305–48).

On Abu'l-Suʿūd *and land law:*

P. Lemerle and P. Wittek, 'Recherches sur l'histoire et le statut des monastères athonites sous la domination turque', *A.H.D.O.* iii (1948), 411–72 (pp. 427–30, 466–8); cf. J. Schacht, in *Classicisme et déclin culturel dans l'histoire de l'Islam*, Paris 1947, 151.

On restrictions of the competence of the *ḳāḍīs* and the Ottoman statute of limitation, cf. É. Tyan, *Histoire de l'organisation judiciaire en pays d'Islam*, 2nd ed., Leiden 1960, 353–6; J. Schacht, in *S.I.* xii (1960), 102 f.

P. Horster, *Zur Anwendung des islamischen Rechts im 16. Jahrhundert*, Stuttgart 1935 (edition and translation of a collection of *fatwās* of Abu'l-Suʿūd; unsatisfactory).

G. D. Galabov and H. W. Duda, *Die Protokollbücher des Kadiamtes Sofia*, Munich 1960.

F. Selle, *Prozessrecht des 16. Jahrhunderts im osmanischen Reich*, Wiesbaden 1962 (edition and part translation of a collection of *fatwās* of Abu'l-Suʿūd and others).

3 J. Schacht, in *Der Islam*, xx (1932), 211 f.

J. Deny, art. 'Tīmār', in *E.I.*¹

J. Sauvaget, *Introduction à l'histoire de l'Orient musulman*, 2nd ed. by Cl. Cahen, Paris 1961, 198 (additional bibliography on *ḳānūn-nāmes*).

*Ömer Lûtfi Barkan, *Kanunlar*, Istanbul 1945 (with an important introduction).

H. Inalcîk, 'Osmanlî hukukuna giriç: örfi-sultani hukuk ve Fatih'in kanunlarî', in *Siyasal Birgiler Fakültesi Dergisi*, xiii/2 (Ankara 1958), 102–26.

*U. Heyd, *Ottoman Documents on Palestine 1552–1615*, Oxford 1960, 59–61; artt. 'Djazā (ii)' and 'Djurm', in *E.I.*² (on penal law).

On the *ḳānūns* (*ḳānūn-nāmes*) of the predecessors of the Ottomans, cf. B. Lewis, in *B.S.O.A.S.* xvi (1954), 599; V. Minorsky, ibid. xvii (1955), 449 f.

On the supervision of public morals and the muḥtasib:

G. Jacob, in *Der Islam*, ix (1919), 252 f.; the same, 'Türkische Sittenpolizei im 16. Jahrhundert', ibid. xi (1921), 254–9.

On later Ottoman developments:

*I. Mouradgea d'Ohsson, *Tableau général de l'Empire ottoman*, in 3 vols., Paris 1787–1820, in 7 vols., 1788–1824 (vols. 5 and 6 contain an account of the actual legal system, based on the *Multaḳa 'l-Abḥur* [below, p. 261]).

G. Jäschke, 'Türkische Gesetzsammlungen', *W.I.* n.s. iii (1954), 225–34 (bibliography on all periods).

J. H. Kramers, art. 'Tanẓīmāt', in *E.I.*[1]

J. Schacht, art. 'Meḥkeme', in *E.I.*[1], *Suppl.*

D. Gatteschi, *Manuale di diritto pubblico e privato ottomano*, Alexandria 1865 (part iii, section 2, on 'civil law', reflects conditions before the introduction of the *Mejelle*).

E. Schmidt, 'Entwickelung und jetzige Verfassung der ordentlichen Gerichte . . . in der Türkei', *M.S.O.S.* i/2 (1898), 91–123.

J. Krcsmárik, 'Beiträge zur Beleuchtung des islamitischen Strafrechts, mit Rücksicht auf Theorie und Praxis in der Türkei', *Z.D.M.G.* lviii (1904), 69–113, 316–62, 539–81.

G. Baer, 'Tanzimat in Egypt—the penal code', *B.S.O.A.S.* xxvi (1963), 29–49.

A. Heidborn, *Manuel de droit public et administratif de l'Empire ottoman*, i, Vienna and Leipzig 1908.

Hîfzî Veldet, *Kanunlaştîrma hareketleri ve tanzimat*, Istanbul 1940 (separately printed from *Tanzimat*, i, 139–209; other papers in this collective volume are also relevant).

E. Pritsch, 'Tanfīḏ al-aḥkām', *Z.D.M.G.* xcviii (1944), 238–81.

M. J. L. Hardy, *Blood Feuds*, &c. (above, p. 241).

On the Mejelle, *translations:*

G. Aristarchi Bey, *Législation ottomane*, v and vi, Constantinople 1881–8.

Salīm ibn Rustam Bāz, Arabic translation with commentary, *Sharḥ al-Majalla*, 2 vols., Beyrouth 1888–89; there are other Arabic translations and commentaries.

W. E. Grigsby, *The Medjellè*, translated into English, London 1895; Sir Charles Tyser and others, *The Mejelle translated*, Nicosia 1901.

G. Young, *Corps de droit ottoman*, vi, Oxford 1906.

C. A. Hooper, *The Civil Law of Palestine and Trans-Jordan*, i, Jerusalem 1933, reprinted London 1934; ii, Jerusalem 1936 (commentary).

Studies:

C. Snouck Hurgronje (1911), *Verspreide Geschriften*, iv/2, 260–6 (on codification in general).

J. H. Kramers, art. 'Medjelle', in *E.I.*[1]

E. Bussi, 'Alcune moderne "codificazioni" o "compilazioni" del diritto musulmano', *O.M.* xx (1940), 251–61.

—— 'Introduzione ad una indagine comparativa fra il così detto "codice civile ottomano" e la compilazione privata di Muhammed Qadri Pascia', *A.H.D.O.* iii (1948), 473–84.

S. S. Onar, 'La codification d'une partie du droit musulman dans l'Empire ottoman (Le Medjelle)', *A.F.D.I.* iii (1954), 90–128.

—— *The Majalla*, in M. Khadduri and H. J. Liebesny (edd.), *Law in the Middle East*, i, Washington 1955, 292–308.

S. D. Goitein, in S. D. Goitein and A. Ben Shemesh, *Muslim Law in Israel*, Jerusalem 1957, 108–22 (in Hebrew).

Şerif Arif Mardin, 'Some Explanatory Notes on the Origins of the "Mecelle"', *W.I.* li (1961), 189–96, 274–9.

There are numerous technical studies of the provisions of the *Mejelle* as a secular code, e.g.:

Ch. Cardahi, 'La possession en droit ottoman', *Revue critique de législation et de jurisprudence*, xlvi (1926), 201–38.

—— 'Théorie générale des actions en droit musulman', *Bulletin de la Société de Législation Comparée*, lviii (1929), 379–99.

F. M. Goadby, 'The Moslem Law of Civil Delict as illustrated by the Mejelle', *J.C.L.* 1939, 62–74.

5 L. Ostrorog, *The Angora Reform*, London 1927.

*G. Jäschke, *Der Islam in der Neuen Türkei. Eine rechtsgeschichtliche Untersuchung*, Leiden 1951 = *W.I.* n.s. i/1–2; 'Berichtigungen und Nachträge', ibid. ii (1952), 278–87.

—— 'Zur Form der Eheschließung in der Türkei. Eine rechtsvergleichende Untersuchung', *W.I.* n.s. ii, (1952), 142–214.

—— 'Die "Imām-Ehe" in der Türkei', *W.I.* n.s. iv (1955), 164–201; cf. ibid. vi (1959), 139.

**Annales de la Faculté de Droit d'Istanbul*, v/6 (1956): *Le Colloque d'Istanbul* (*Septembre 1955*) (collection of important papers).

G.-H. Bousquet, 'Note sur les réformes de l'Islam albanais', *R.E.I.* 1935, 399–410.

—— 'Un exemple de laïcisation du droit musulman: le code civil albanais', *Introduction à l'étude du droit comparé . . . en l'honneur d'Édouard Lambert*, ii, Paris 1938, 643–6.

M. Begovitch, *De l'évolution du droit musulman en Yougoslavie*, thesis, Algiers, 1930; cf. G.-H. Bousquet, in *R.A.* 1930, 203–6, and 1932, 202–4.

M. Begović, *Vakufi u Yugoslaviyi* (*Les Waqfs en Jougoslavie*) (with summary in French), Belgrade 1963.

F. Bajraktarević, in *Archiv Orientální*, iii (1931), 503 (bibliography of publications on Islamic law in Yugoslavia).

On the later developments in Yugoslavia: G.-H. Bousquet, in *R.A.* 1952, 14, and M. Begović, ibid. 1958, 12–17.

'Statuto della Communità religiosa islamica nella Repubblica Federativa Popolare Jugoslava', *O.M.* xliii (1963), 662–74.

Ch. N. Fragistas, 'Le droit musulman en Grèce', *A.F.D.I.* iii/4 (1954), 129–41.

On the gradual abolition of Islamic law in Central Asia, see A. G. Park, *Bolshevism in Turkestan 1917–1927*, New York 1957, 221–37.

CHAPTER 14

A. S. Bazmee Ansari, art. 'al-Fatāwā al-ʿĀlamgīriyya', in *E.I.*[2]

Partial translations of the *Fatāwā al-ʿĀlamgīriyya*: N. B. E. Baillie, *The Moohummudan Law of Sale*, London 1850; *The Land Tax of India*, London 1853; *A Digest of Moohummedan Law*, i, London 1875, 2nd ed., 1887 (on the 'statut personnel' and connected subjects); 3rd impression: Lahore 1957 (with a supplement on sale, &c.); Mahomed Ullah ibn S. Jung, 'The Muslim Law of Pre-emption', in *Allahabad University Studies*, vii/1 (1931), 1–334.

Sir Thomas W. Arnold, art. 'India', section 4, in *E.I.*[1]

Sir Charles Fawcett, *The First Century of British Justice in India*, London 1934 (on the period 1661–1773).

*Abul Husain, *The History of Development of Muslim Law in British India*, Calcutta 1934.

*Sir Benjamin Lindsay, in *Modern India and the West*, ed. L. S. S. O'Malley, London 1941, 107–37 (lacking a bibliography).

Sir George Claus Rankin, *Background to Indian Law*, Cambridge 1946.

G.-H. Bousquet, *Du droit musulman et de son application effective dans le monde*, Algiers 1949, 50–65.

†W. H. Macnaghten, *Reports of Cases determined in the Court of Nizamut Adawlut*, 2 vols., Calcutta 1827.

†—— *Principles and Precedents of Moohummudan Law*, Calcutta 1825; 3rd ed., with additional notes, &c., by W. Sloan, Madras 1864; *Principles of Muhammadan Law* (without the Precedents, with additional material), compiled by Prosunno Coomar Sen, Calcutta 1881.

†N. B. E. Baillie, *The Moohummudan Law of Sale*, and *The Land Tax of India* (above, 1), introductions.

†Sir Roland Knyvet Wilson, *An Introduction to the Study of Anglo-Muhammadan Law*, London 1894.

I. Mahmud, *Muslim Law of Succession and Administration*, Karachi 1958 (on the divergence of Anglo-Muhammadan from strict Islamic Law).

A. A. A. Fyzee, 'Muhammadan Law in India', *Comparative Studies in Society and History*, v (1963), 401–15.

There are numerous handbooks of Anglo-Muhammadan Law; among the most important are:

Mahomed Yusoof, *Mahomedan Law relating to Marriage, Dower, Divorce, Legitimacy and Guardianship of Minors*, 3 vols., Calcutta and London 1895–8 (with translations from Arabic texts).

A. F. M. Abdur Rahman, *Institutes of Mussalman law: a Treatise on Personal Law*, Calcutta 1907 (with extracts from Arabic texts); inspired by the work of Ḳadrī Pasha, below, p. 252.

Sir R. K. Wilson, *Anglo-Muhammadan Law*, 6th ed., London 1930.

F. B. Tyabji, *Muhammadan Law*, 3rd ed., Bombay 1940.

D. F. Mulla, *Principles of Mahomedan Law*, 14th ed., Calcutta 1955.

*A. A. A. Fyzee, *Outlines of Muhammadan Law*, 3rd ed., London 1964 (the most elementary but the most scholarly of these handbooks; with bibliography).

AZIZ AHMAD, *Islamic Law in Theory and Practice*, Lahore 1956.

K. P. SAKSENA, *Muslim Law as administered in India and Pakistan*, 4th ed., Lucknow 1963.

BABU RAM VERNA, *Mohammedan Law in India and Pakistan*, 3rd ed., Allahabad 1959.

See further HAMID ALI, 'The Customary and Statutory Laws of the Muslims in India', *I.C.* xi (1937), 354–69, 444–54.

ZEKIYE EGLAR, *A Punjabi Village in Pakistan*, New York 1960, 6 f., 45, 186–90.

4 On 'family *wakfs*' in Anglo-Muhammadan law, see the handbooks.

A. A. A. FYZEE, 'The Impact of English Law on the Shariat in India', *Review of International Law*, xviii (Cairo 1962), 1–27.

KAMILA TYABJI, *Limited Interests in Muhammadan Law*, London 1949.

S. VESEY-FITZGERALD, *Muhammadan Law*, London 1931 (Islamic law as administered in the (former) British tropical African dependencies).

G. W. BARTHOLOMEW, 'Authority of Privy Council Decisions', *I.C.L.Q.* i (1952), 392–9.

J. N. D. ANDERSON, 'The Religious Element in Waqf Endowments', *J.R.C.A.S.* 1951, 292–9.

—— *Islamic Law in Africa*, London 1954.

—— 'Waqfs in East Africa', *J.A.L.* iii (1959), 152–64.

5 *On the organization of justice in Algeria:*

M. MORAND, *Les Institutions judiciaires*, pp. 157–200, in L. MILLIOT and others, *L'Œuvre législative de la France en Algérie*, Paris 1930 (Collection du Centenaire de l'Algérie).

E. NORÈS, *L'Œuvre de la France en Algérie. La Justice*, Paris 1931 (Collection du Centenaire de l'Algérie),

J. ROUSSIER-THÉAUX, 'Le droit musulman en Algérie', *M.A.I.D.C.* iii/3, Rome 1953, 189-99.

H. J. LIEBESNY, *The Government of French North Africa*, Philadelphia 1943, especially pp. 105–21: Legal systems in the African Dependencies, and pp. 122–4: Guide to legal sources.

A. KNOERTZER, 'Des réformes accomplies en Algérie . . . dans le domaine de la justice musulmane', *R.A.* 1943–5, 1–38.

J. LAMBERT, *Manuel de législation algérienne*, Algiers 1952.

A. CANAC, 'L'évolution de l'organisation judiciaire en Algérie', *R.A.* 1956, 191–210.

J. ROUSSIER, 'L'application du chraʿ au Maghrib en 1959', *W.I.* N.S. vi (1961), 25–55.

J.-P. CHARNAY, 'Le Rôle du juge français dans l'élaboration du droit musulman algérien', *R.I.D.C.* xv (1963), 705–21.

La Vie musulmane en Algérie d'après la jurisprudence de la première moitié du XXe siècle, Paris 1965.

The handbooks and studies of *Droit musulman algérien* are extremely numerous; among the most important are:

SAUTAYRA and E. CHERBONNEAU, *Droit musulman. Du statut personnel et des successions*, 2 vols., Paris 1873–4.

E. Zeys, *Traité élémentaire de droit musulman algérien*, 2 vols., Algiers 1885–6.

M. Morand, *Études de droit musulman algérien*, Algiers 1910.

—— *Introduction à l'étude du droit musulman algérien*, Algiers 1921.

—— *Études de droit musulman et de droit coutumier berbère*, Algiers 1931.

F. Dulout, *Traité de droit musulman et algérien*, 4 vols., Algiers 1948–49 (on French case-law or *jurisprudence*).

*G.-H. Bousquet, *Précis de droit musulman principalement mâlékite et algérien*, i, 3rd ed., Algiers 1959, with supplement, 1960 (the most elementary but the most scholarly of these handbooks); for vol. ii, see above, p. 215.

The *Revue algérienne* (*tunisienne et marocaine*) *de législation et de jurisprudence*, Algiers 1885 ff., is indispensable for the study of the subject.

On recent legislation:

J. Roussier-Théaux, 'La neutralisation du droit de djebr', *Revue africaine*, lxxxi (1937), 1–8.

—— 'Déclaration à l'état civil et preuve du mariage conclu "more islamico" en Algérie', *R.A.* 1958, 1–11.

—— 'Le mariage du mineur de statut musulman', *R.A.* 1959, 51–67.

A. Colomer, 'La réforme du régime des tutelles et de l'absence en droit musulman algérien', *R.A.*, 1959, 97–196.

—— 'La tutelle des mineurs en droit musulman algérien', *R.I.D.C.* xii (1960), 117–33.

Ordinance of 4 February 1959, and regulations: text in *R.A.* 1959/iii/1, 9 f., 25–30; *O.M.* xxxix (1959), 141 f. (text of the ordinance), 474 f., 567 f. (reactions).

*J. Roussier, *Le Mariage et sa dissolution dans le statut civil local algérien*, Algiers 1960.

—— 'Mariage et divorce en Algérie', *W.I.* n.s. vi (1961), 248–54.

On the 'Code Morand':

M. Morand, *Avant-Projet de code du droit musulman algérien*, Algiers 1916 (with a detailed annotation).

A. Bel, 'La codification du droit musulman en Algérie', *Revue de l'histoire des religions*, xcvi (1927), 175–92.

CHAPTER 15

1 On Islamic modernism in general, see the bibliography above, pp. 237 f.

2 E. Bussi, 'Alcune moderne "codificazioni" o "compilazioni" del diritto musulmano', *O.M.* xx (1940), 251–61.

—— 'Introduzione ad una indagine comparativa fra il così detto "codice civile ottomano" e la compilazione privata di Muhammed Qadri Pascia', *A.H.D.O.* iii (1948), 473–84.

Hifzi Veldet Velidedeoğlu, 'Le mouvement de codification dans les pays musulmans. Ses rapports avec les mouvements juridiques occidentaux', *A.F.D.I.* viii (1959), 1–55.

(Muḥammad Ḳadrī Pasha), *al-Aḥkām al-Sharʿiyya fil-Aḥwāl al-Shakhṣiyya*; official French translation: *Droit musulman. Du statut personnel et des successions d'après le rite hanafite*, Alexandria 1875; official Italian translation, Alexandria 1875; French translation also in E. Clavel, *Droit musulman. Du statut personnel et des successions*, Paris 1895, ii, 261–424; *Code of Mohammedan Personal Law* by Mohammed Kadri Pasha, transl. by (Sir) Wasey Sterry and N. Abcarius, printed for the Sudan Government, London 1914; Arabic text and English translation also in A. F. M. Abdur Rahman, *Institutes of Mussalman Law*, Calcutta 1907; commentary by Muḥammad Zayd al-Ibyānī Bey, *Sharḥ al-Aḥkām al-Sharʿiyya*, &c., 3 vols., Cairo 1342/1924.

—— *Murshid al-Ḥayrān ilā Maʿrifat Aḥwāl al-Insān fil-Muʿāmalāt al-Sharʿiyya*; Muhammad Kadri Pasha, *Droit musalman. Statut réel*, traduit de l'arabe par Abdulaziz Kahil Bey, Cairo 1893.

—— *Ḳānūn al-ʿAdl wal-Inṣāf lil-Ḳaḍāʾ ʿalā Mushkilāt al-Awḳāf*; Muhammad Kadri Pasha, *Du wakf*, traduit de l'arabe par Abdulaziz Kahil Bey, Cairo 1896; U. Pace and V. Sistro, *Code annoté du wakf*, Alexandria 1946.

ʿAbd al-Karīm al-Ḥillī, *al-Aḥkām al-Jaʿfariyya fil-Aḥwāl al-Shakhṣiyya*, Baghdad 1342/1923–4 (a private codification of 'Twelver' Shiite law, inspired by Ḳadrī Pasha).

On the organization of the *ḳāḍīs*' tribunals: J. Schacht, art. 'Meḥkemeh', in *E.I.*[1], *Suppl.*; A. von Kremer, *Aegypten*, Leipzig 1863, ii. 72–75; M. MacIlwraith, 'The Mohammedan Law-Courts in Egypt', *The Nineteenth Century and after*, lxxx (1916), 740–54; L. Mercier, 'Réorganisation égyptienne de la "justice du chraa"', *R.E.J.* 1931, 125–37; G.-H. Bousquet, *Du droit musulman et de son application effective dans le monde*, Algiers 1949.

3–12 *General studies and analyses:*

J. Schacht, 'Šarīʿa und Qānūn im modernen Ägypten', *Der Islam*, xx (1932), 209–36; shortened French version: 'L'évolution moderne du droit musulman en Égypte', in *Mélanges Maspéro*, iii, Cairo 1935–40, 323–34.

Ch. Cardahi, 'Les infiltrations occidentales dans un domaine réservé: le statut personnel musulman', in *Introduction à l'étude du droit comparé . . . en l'honneur d'Édouard Lambert*, Paris 1938, ii, 604–20.

H. J. LIEBESNY, 'Religious Law and Westernization in the Moslem Near East', *A.J.C.L.* ii (1953), 492–504.
—— 'Impact of Western Law in the Countries of the Near East', *George Washington Law Review*, xxii (1953), 127–41.
J. SCHACHT, in *Classicisme et déclin culturel dans l'histoire de l'Islam*, Paris 1957, 151–8.
J. N. D. ANDERSON, *Islamic Law in the Modern World*, London 1959; 'The Significance of Islamic Law in the World Today', *A.J.C.L.* ix (1960), 187–98 (popular accounts).
J. SCHACHT, 'Islamic Law in Contemporary States', *A.J.C.L.* viii (1959), 133–47.
—— 'Problems of Modern Islamic Legislation', *S.I.* xii (1960), 99–129.
Y. LINANT DE BELLEFONDS, 'A propos d'un livre récent du recteur d'al-Azhar', *Orient*, v (1961), no. 19, 27–42 (on MAḤMŪD SHALTŪT, *al-Islām, ʿAḳīda wa-Sharīʿa*, Cairo 1959).
On modernist opinions concerning fasting: *O.M.* xxxv (1955), 249, 346; J. JOMIER and J. CORBON, in *Mélanges de l'Institut Dominicain d'études orientales du Caire*, iii (1956), 46–48; F. HOURS, 'A propos du jeûne du mois de Ramadan en Tunisie', *Orient*, iv (1960), no. 13, 43–52; G. OMAN, 'La questione del digiuno di Ramaḍān in Tunisia', *O.M.* xl (1960), 763–74; J. GENTZ, 'Tunesische Fatwās über das Fasten im Ramaḍān', *W.I.* N.S. vii (1961), 39–66.

Regional bibliographies:

Several countries:

*G.-H. BOUSQUET, *Du droit musulman et de son application effective dans le monde*, Algiers 1949.
G. BUSSON DE JANSSENS, 'Les Wakfs dans l'Islam contemporain', *R.E.I.* 1951, 1–72.
J. N. D. ANDERSON, 'The Shariʿa Today', *J.C.L.* xxxi (1949), nos. 3–4, 18–25.
*—— 'Recent Developments in Sharīʿa Law', i–ix, *M.W.* xl–xlii (1950–2).
—— 'Recent Reforms in Family Law in the Arab World', *Zeitschr. vergl. Rechtswiss.* lxv (1963), 1–17.
CH. CARDAHI, 'La réception du droit occidental dans les systèmes juridiques orientaux', *M.A.I.D.C.* iii/3, Rome 1953, 147–67.
ʿABD AL-RAZZĀḲ AḤMAD AL-SANHŪRĪ, 'al-Ḳānūn al-Madanī al-ʿArabī (The Arab Civil Code)', in *al-ʿĀlam al-ʿArabī*, ii, Cairo 1953, 5–29.
A. D'EMILIA, 'Intorno alla moderna attività legislativa di alcuni paesi musulmani nel campo del diritto privato', *O.M.* xxxiii (1953), 301–21.
—— 'Intorno agli elementi costitutivi della compravendita secondo i vigenti codici di alcuni paesi musulmani', *A.D.C.S.L.* xxxii (1957), 82–117.
ṢUBḤĪ MAḤMASĀNĪ, *Al-Awḍāʾ al-Tashrīʿiyya fil-Ḍuwal al-ʿArabiyya Māḍīhā wa-Ḥāḍiruhā* (*Legal Systems in the Arab States. Past and Present*), Beyrouth 1957.
É. TYAN, 'Les rapports entre droit musulman et droit européen occidental, en matière de droit civil', in *Al-Andalus*, xxvi (1961), 323–36.

Y. Linant de Bellefonds, 'La répudiation dans l'Islam d'aujourd'hui', *R.I.D.C.* xiv (1962), 521–48.

M. J. L. Hardy, *Blood Feuds*, &c. (above, p. 241).

M. Borrmans, 'Codes de statut personnel et évolution sociale en certains pays musulmans', *IBLA*, xxvi (1963), 205–60.

Ottoman Law of Family Rights:

French (shortened) translation: L. Bouvat, 'Le code familial ottoman de 1917', *R.M.M.* xliii (1921), 5–26; French translation also in Abdul Karim Hussami, *Le Mariage et le divorce en droit musulman et particulièrement dans son application en Syrie* (thesis, Geneva) Lyons 1931, 219–36; Arabic translation in S. D. Goitein and A. Ben Shemesh, *Muslim Law in Israel*, Jerusalem 1957, 292–311; also printed separately for the Israel Ministry of Religious Affairs, *Ḳānūn Ḳarār Ḥuḳūḳ al-ʿĀʾila*, Jerusalem 1957.

Ziyaeddin Fahri, *Essai sur la transformation du code familial en Turquie*, Paris 1936 (thesis, Strasbourg 1935).

Egypt:

J. Schacht, 'Šarīʿa und Qānūn im modernen Ägypten' (above p. 252).

A. Sékaly, 'Le problème des wakfs en Égypte', *R.E.I.* 1929, 75–126, 277–337, 395–454, 601–59.

Abdel Fattah el Sayed Bey, 'La situation de la femme mariée égyptienne après douze ans de réformes législatives', *Revue Al Qanoun wal Iqtisad*, xi (1932), no. 2, 65–82.

A. Sanhouri, 'Le droit musulman comme élément de refonte du droit civil égyptien', *Introduction à l'étude du droit comparé*, ii, 621–42.

É. de Szàszy, *Droit international privé comparé. Traité de législation comparée avec référence spéciale au droit égyptien et musulman*, Alexandria and Paris 1940.

J. N. D. Anderson, 'The Problem of Divorce in the Sharīʿa Law of Islam. Measures of Reform in Modern Egypt', *J.R.C.A.S.* xxxvii (1950), 169–85.

—— 'The Sharīʿa and Civil Law', *I.Q.* i (1954), 29–46 (on Egypt and Syria).

R. Brunschvig, in *M.A.I.D.C.* iii/4, Rome 1955, 107–9 (on the law no. 71 of 1946 on legacies).

Y. Linant de Bellefonds, 'Immutabilité du droit musulman et réformes législatives en Égypte', *R.I.D.C.* vii (1955), 1–34.

—— 'La suppression des juridictions de statut personnel en Égypte', ibid. viii (1956), 412–25.

German translation of the act no. 462 of 1955: *W.I.* n.s. v (1958), 254–9; for a further bibliography on this act, see *S.I.* xii (1960), 114, n. 1.

A. d'Emilia, 'Il diritto musulmano e il nuovo codice civile egiziano', *A.D.C.S.L.* xxxi (1956), 114–36.

Y. Linant de Bellefonds, 'Le droit musulman et le nouveau code civil égyptien', *R.A.* 1956, 211–22.

G. M. Badr, 'The New Egyptian Civil Code and the Unification of the Laws of the Arab Countries', *Tulane Law Review*, xxx (1956), 299–324.

On the project of 1956: N. Tomiche, in *Orient*, i (1957), no. 3, 111–18.

On the draft Code of Personal Status of 1962: *al-Ahrām* (Cairo) of 1 March 1962 (cf. *Muslim Bulletin*, Muslim and Druze Division of the Israel Ministry of Religious Affairs, viii (1963), nos. 3–4, 46 f.).

*J. Brugman, *De betekenis van het Mohammedaanse recht in het hedendaagse Egypte* (*The Place of Islamic Law in Contemporary Egypt*), (thesis, Leiden), The Hague 1960.

Selected technical studies of institutions of Islamic law as applied in Egypt :

Aziz Bey Hanki, *Du wakf. Recueil de jurisprudence des Tribunaux Mixtes, Indigènes et Mehkémehs Charichs*, Cairo 1914.

Abd el-Hamid Badawi Bey, 'Du principe qu'en droit musulman la succession n'est ouverte qu'après acquittement des dettes', *L'Égypte contemporaine*, v (1914), 14–40.

Mahmoud Fahmy, *De la préemption immobilière en droit égyptien*, thesis, Paris 1928.

A. K. Sabbagh, *Les Méglis hasbys et la protection des biens des mineurs en Égypte*, thesis, Paris 1931.

Abd el-Fattah el-Sayed Bey, *La Filiation en droit égyptien*, Paris 1932.

S. Cadéménos, 'De l'acquisition du bien wakf par la prescription', *L'Égypte contemporaine*, xxv (1934), 543–80.

Aziz Bey Hanki, 'Effet de la divergence de pays sur le droit à la succession', *R.E.I.* 1935, 179–86 (on Egypt and other countries in the Near East).

El-Said Mostafa el-Said, *De l'étendue et de l'exercice des droits conjugaux. Étude de droit musulman et de droit égyptien moderne*, Cairo 1936 (a document of modernist aims).

Muḥammad Aḥmad Faraj al-Sanhūrī, *Majmūʿat al-Ḳawānīn al-Miṣriyya al-Mukhtāra min al-Fiḳh al-Islāmī* (*Corpus of the Egyptian Laws derived from Islamic Jurisprudence*), iii (*The Law of Waḳf*), 2 vols., Cairo 1949.

Sudan:

J. N. D. Anderson, 'Recent Developments in Shariʿa Law in the Sudan', *Sudan Notes and Records*, xxxi (1950), 82–104.

—— 'The Modernization of Islamic Law in the Sudan', *Sudan Law Journal and Reports*, 1960, 292–312.

E. Guttmann, 'The Reception of the Common Law in the Sudan', *I.C.L.Q.* vi (1957), 401–17.

P. S. Atiyah, 'Some Problems of Family Law in the Sudan Republic', *Sudan Notes and Records*, xxxix (1958), 88–100.

Muhammad Aku Rannat, 'The Relationship between Islamic and Customary Law in the Sudan', *J.A.L.* iv (1960), 9–16.

Palestine, Transjordan, Israel:

F. M. Goadby, *International and Inter-Religious Private Law in Palestine*, Jerusalem 1926.

—— 'Palestinian Law, Sources and Judicial Organization', *Travaux de l'Académie Internationale de Droit Comparé*, i/1, Berlin 1929, 39–52.

C. A. Hooper, *The Civil Law of Palestine and Transjordan*, above, p. 247.

J. Sussmann, 'Law and Judicial Practice in Israel', *J.C.L.* xxxii (1950), nos. 3–4, 29–31.

S. D. Goitein and A. Ben Shemesh, *Muslim Law in Israel*, Jerusalem 1957 (in Hebrew).

'Zum Eherecht der Muslims in Israel', *W.I.* n.s. v (1958), 269 f.

Jordan:

J. N. D. Anderson, 'Recent Developments in Sharīʿa Law, VIII. The Jordanian Law of Family Rights 1951', *M.W.* xlii (1952), 190–206.

E. T. Mogannam, 'The Practical Application of the Law in certain Arab States', *George Washington Law Review*, xxii (1953), 142–55 (on Jordan and Syria).

Lebanon:

Ch. Cardahi, *Le Code des obligations du Liban*, Paris 1932.

A. d'Emilia, 'Le varie spezie di obbligazioni nel codice libanese delle obbligazioni e dei contratti del 1932', *O.M.* xxvii (1947), 225–32.

B. Tabbah, 'Le wakf', *Annales de l'École Française de Droit de Beyrouth*, iii (1947), no. 1, 67–129 (reprinted in his *Propriété privée et registre foncier*, i, Paris 1947).

—— 'La préemption ou chefaʿa', *Annales de l'École Française de Droit de Beyrouth*, v (1949), 5–84 (reprinted in his *Propriété privée et registre foncier*, ii).

P. Gannagé, 'La compétence des juridictions confessionnelles au Liban et en Syrie', *Annales de l'École Française de Droit de Beyrouth*, iv (1948), nos. 1–2, 199–247.

Text of the law of 1951 on the competence of the confessional jurisdictions in *O.M.* xxxvi (1956), 14–17, and in *C.O.C.* viii (1951), 13–16.

N. Edelby, 'A propos de la loi libanaise . . . sur la compétence des juridictions religieuses', *Proche-Orient chrétien*, ii (1952), 58–68.

J. N. D. Anderson, 'The Personal Law of the Druze Community', *W.I.* n.s. ii (1952), 1–9, 83–94.

É. Tyan, *Notes sommaires sur le nouveau régime successoral au Liban*, Paris 1960 (*Annales de la Faculté de Droit, Université St.-Joseph, Beyrouth*) (on the law of 1959); shorter version in *Mélanges en l'honneur de Paul Roubier*, Paris 1961, ii, 249–81.

Syria:

A. Kouatly, *Étude comparative du droit de préemption . . . et son évolution en droit syrien*, Damascus 1948.

On the legislation of 1949: *C.O.C.* vi (1949), 160, 162; vii (1950), 15, n. 2.

Muṣṭafā Aḥmad al-Zarḳā', *al-Madkhal al-Fiḳhī al-ʿĀmm ilal-Ḥuḳūḳ al-Madaniyya* (*General Introduction to the Civil Law of Islamic Jurisprudence*), Damascus 1952.

E. T. Mogannam, *The Practical Application of the Law in certain Arab States* (see above, under *Jordan*).

J. N. D. Anderson, *The Sharīʿa and Civil Law* (see above, under *Egypt*).

—— 'The Syrian Law of Personal Status', *B.S.O.A.S.* xvii (1955), 34–49.

G. M. Badr, *The New Egyptian Civil Code* . . . (see above, under *Egypt*).

Cyprus:

J. N. D. Anderson, 'The Family Law of the Turkish Cypriots', *W.I.* n.s. v (1958), 161–87.

Iraq:

Z. E. Jwaideh, 'The New Civil Code of Iraq', *George Washington Law Review*, 1953, 176–86 (with an historical introduction).

J. N. D. Anderson, 'A Draft Code of Personal Law for ʿIrāq', *B.S.O.A.S.* xv (1953), 43–60.

—— 'A Law of Personal Status for Iraq', *I.C.L.Q.* ix (1960), 542–63.

——'Changes in the Law of Personal Status in Iraq', *I.C.L.Q.* xii (1963), 1026–31.

Y. Linant de Bellefonds, 'Le code du statut personnel irakien du 30 décembre 1959, *S.I.* xiii (1960), 79–135.

G. Krotkoff, 'Beduinenrecht und gesatztes Recht', *Wiener Zeitschrift für die Kunde des Morgenlandes*, lvi (1960), 99–108 (on the special regulations concerning Bedouins, 1916–58).

N. F. Küppers, 'Das irakische Zivilgesetzbuch', *Zeitschr. vergl. Rechtswiss.* lxii (1960), 181–98, lxiii (1961), 1–44.

Iran:

R. Aghababian, *Législation iranienne actuelle intéressant les étrangers et les Iraniens à l'étranger*, Teheran 1939 (a survey of the constitution, the sources of civil law, the administration of justice, penal law, and the law of family and succession).

—— *Législation iranienne actuelle. Lois constitutionnelles, code civil iranien, statuts particuliers*, Paris 1951.

On the law of 1931 on marriage and repudiation: *O.M.* xi (1931), 494–7.

M. Habib, 'The Administration of justice in Modern Persia', *I.C.* vii (1933), 234–48, 410–16, 573–82.

J. Greenfield, 'Die geistlichen Schariagerichte in Persien und die moderne Gesetzgebung', *Zeitschr. vergl. Rechtswiss.* xlviii (1934), 157–67; also in *Rechtsvergleichendes Handwörterbuch*, ed. F. Schlegelberger, i, Berlin 1929, 427–65.

A. Amir-Soleymani, *La Formation et les effets des contrats en droit iranien*, Paris 1936 (also thesis, Paris: *Étude comparative sur la formation* . . .)(with an introduction on the history and the sources of the Civil Code of Iran).

A. Bassidji, *La Situation juridique de la femme en Iran*, thesis, Paris 1936 (with translation, in an appendix, of the relevant sections of the Civil Code of Iran).

Djalal Abdoh, *L'Élément psychologique dans les contrats suivant la conception iranienne*, thesis, Paris 1937 (with an introduction on the history of the Civil Code of Iran).

A.-M. Amirian, *Le Mouvement législatif en Iran et le mariage en droit et en fait*, Paris 1937.

—— *Le Mariage en droits iranien et musulman*, i: *Formation*. Paris 1938 (also thesis, Paris: *La Formation du mariage* . . .) (with translations from Iranian laws in an appendix).

M. Amid, *Le Divorce en droit iranien*, thesis, Paris 1939.

Ibrahim Docteur-Zadeh, *De la validité des contrats sur la chose d'autrui en droit positif iranien*, Paris 1939 (to be used with caution).

L. Lockhart, 'The Constitutional Laws of Persia', *M.E.J.* xiii (1959), 372–88 (pp. 380 f. on the committee of *ʿulamā*').

A. D'Emilia, in *O.M.* xliv (1964), 308.

Pakistan:

Documents:

Abdur Rahim, *The Principles of Muhammadan Jurisprudence*, London and Madras 1911, 168–92 (reprinted Lahore 1958).

S. Khuda Bukhsh, *Essays Indian and Islamic*, London 1912, 287–95.

S. ʿAbdur-Rahmān, *Eine kritische Prüfung der Quellen des Islamitischen Rechts*, Oxford University Press 1914 (cf. H. P. Smith, in *American Journal of Semitic Languages and Literatures*, xxxvi (1920), 302–9).

K. A. Faruki, *Ijma and the Gate of Ijtihad*, Karachi 1954 (cf. J. Schacht, in *Classicisme et déclin culturel*, 153–5).

—— *Islamic Jurisprudence*, Karachi 1962.

Abul Aʿla Maudoodi, *Islamic Law and Constitution*, Karachi 1955.

—— *The Islamic Law and its Introduction in Pakistan*, Karachi 1955.

—— *The Limits of Legislation in Islam and the Place of Ijtihād in it* (in Urdū), in *International Islamic Colloquium December 29, 1957 – January 8, 1958*, Lahore 1960, Appendix ii, 21–28.

Muslim Family Law Ordinance of 1961: text in *Dawn* (Karachi) of 3 March 1961; French transl. in *R.A.* 1961, 73–78.

Studies:

N. J. Coulson, 'Reform of Family Law in Pakistan', *S.I.* vii (1956), 133–55.

K. J. Newman, *Essays on the Constitution of Pakistan*, Dacca 1956.

A. Chapy, 'L'Islam dans la constitution du Pakistan', *Orient*, i (1957), no. 3, 120–7.

A. Gledhill, *Pakistan. The Development of its Law and Constitution*, London 1957.

J. Roussier, 'L'ordonnance du 2 mars 1961 sur le droit de famille au Pakistan', *R.I.D.C.* xiii (1961), 799–808.

Manzooruddin Ahmed, 'Islamic Aspects of the New Constitution of Pakistan', *Islamic Studies*, ii (1963), 249–86.

A. d'Emilia, 'L'Islām e la costituzione pakistana del 1962', *O.M.* xliii (1963), 415–26.

Indonesia:

J. Prins, art. 'ʿĀda (iv)', in *E.I.*²

Libya:

E. Bussi, 'Alcune moderne "codificazioni" o "compilazioni" del diritto musulmano', *O.M.* xx (1940), 251–61 (on the *Mulakhkhaṣ al-Aḥkām al-Sharʿiyya*, a private codification of Mālikī law by the Libyan author Muḥammad ʿĀmir, 1937–8).

C. A. Nallino, *Cadi* (1937), *Raccolta di scritti*, ii, 1942, 27–39 (31–34 on Libya, 34–39 on Eritrea and Somalia).

V. Cattaneo, *La 'scefaa' nel diritto coloniale italiano*, Padua 1944.

A. d'Emilia, 'La giurisprudenza del Tribunale superiore sciaraitico della Libia in materia di fidanzamento matrimonio e divorzio (1929–1941)', *R.S.O.* xxi (1946), 15–50.

—— 'Per il nuovo diritto libico delle obbligazioni', *Atti del Terzo Convegno di Studi Africani*, Florence 1948, 156–72.

A. M. Qasem, 'A Judicial Experiment in Libya: Unification of Civil and Shariat Courts', *I.C.L.Q.* iii (1954), 134–7.

G. M. Badr, *The New Egyptian Civil Code* . . . (see above, under *Egypt*).

Tunisia:

B. Guiga, *Essai sur l'évolution du chrâa et son application judiciaire en Tunisie*, thesis, Paris 1930.

R. Scemama, *Essai théorique et pratique sur le droit de chefaa en Tunisie*, (thesis, Paris) Tunis 1934.

On the political events of 1950: *O.M.* xxxiii (1953), 216.

G. N. Sfeir (transl.), 'The Tunisian Code of Personal Status', *M.E.J.* xi (1957), 309–18.

A. Colomer, 'Le code du statut personnel tunisien', *R.A.* 1957, 115–239 (translation with detailed commentary).

J. Roussier, 'Le code tunisien du statut personnel', *R.J.P.U.F.* xi (1957), 213–30.

J. N. D. Anderson, 'The Tunisian Law of Personal Status', *I.C.L.Q.* vii (1958), 262–79.

J. Magnin, 'Réformes juridiques en Tunisie', *IBLA*, xxi (1958), 77–92.

E. Pritsch, 'Das tunesische Personenstandsgesetz', *W.I.* n.s. v (1958), 188–205.

On an interpretative law of 1958: *W.I.* n.s. vi (1959), 130–3.

J. Roussier, 'Le mariage du mineur de statut musulman' (above, p. 251).

—— 'Dispositions nouvelles dans le statut successoral en droit tunisien', *S.I.* xii (1960), 131–44.

—— 'Le livre du testament dans le nouveau code tunisien du statut personnel', *S.I.* xv (1961), 89–124.

—— 'L'application du chraʿ au Maghrib en 1959' (above, p. 250).

R. Jambu-Merlin, *Le Droit privé en Tunisie*, Paris 1960.

M. Borrmans, 'Le Code tunisien de statut personnel et ses dernières modifications', *IBLA*, xxvii (1964), 63–71.

Morocco:

R. Marty, 'La justice civile musulmane au Maroc', *R.E.I.* 1931, 341–538, 1933, 185–294.

On the *dahir* of 16 May 1930: *O.M.* x (1930), 462 f. (text); 463–7 (reactions).

O. Pesle, *L'Organisation de la justice du chrâa par le Makhzen*, Casablanca 1941.

J. Berque, *Essai sur la méthode juridique maghrébine*, Rabat 1944 (with Appendix, pp. 111–37: *Le 'tajdîd al-fiqh' selon un juriste marocain moderne*

[Muḥammad ibn al-Ḥasan al-Ḥajwī, *al-Fikr al-Sāmī*, above, p. 216]).

J. Caillé, *Organisation judiciaire et procédure marocaines*, Paris 1948.

J. Lapanne-Joinville, 'L'émancipation des mineurs de 25 ans en droit malékite', *R.M.D.* v (1953), 158–66 (on the *dahir* of 14 March 1938).

J. Lapanne-Joinville, 'Les mesures conservatoires devant les juridictions du Chraa', ibid. ix (1957), 197–229.

Official French translation of the Moroccan *Mudawwana* in *R.A.* 1958/iii/2, 25–36, 38–44, 1959/iii/2, 1–11, 160 (also in *R.M.D.* x (1958), 254–70, 399–406; xi (1959), 49–56, 126–30).

J. N. D. Anderson, *Reforms in Family Law in Morocco, J.A.L.* ii (1958), 146–59.

J. Lapanne-Joinville, 'Le code marocain du statut personnel', *R.M.D.* xi (1959), 97–125 (also in *Revue juridique et politique d'outre-mer*, n.s. xiii (1959), 75–99).

J. Roussier, 'Le mariage du mineur de statut musulman', (above, p. 251).

—— 'L'application du chraʿ au Maghrib en 1959' (above, p. 250).

A. Colomer, 'Le code du statut personnel marocain', *R.A.* 1961, 79–217 (also printed separately, together with the Arabic text, as *Droit musulman*, i, Rabat 1964).

—— 'La tutelle des mineurs dans la Moudawwana ou code du statut personnel marocain', *R.I.D.C.* xiii (1961), 327–37.

ADDENDA

for pp. 253 f. Several countries:

J. N. D. Anderson, 'Recent Reforms in the Islamic Law of Inheritance', *I.C.L.Q.* xiv (1965), 349–65.

A. D'Emilia, 'Intorno alle Costituzioni provvisorie repubblicane del Yemen', *O.M.* xliv (1964), 301–12.

Orientalisches Recht, Leiden and Cologne 1964 (Handbuch der Orientalistik, Erste Abteilung, Ergänzungsband III), 344–440 (contributions by É. Tyan and J. Baz on Lebanon and Syria, Chafik Chehata on Egypt, Ch. Samaran on Tunisia, J. Roussier on Algeria, J. Lapanne-Joinville on Morocco).

for p. 258. Malaysia:

Ahmad Bin Mohamed Ibrahim, 'The Status of Muslim Women in Family Law in Malaysia and Brunei', *Malaya Law Review*, v (1963), 313–37; vi (1964), 40–82, 353–86.

—— 'The Legal Position of the Muslims in Singapore', *World Muslim League* [*Magazine*], i/1–6 (Singapore 1963–64).

—— 'The Administration of Muslim Family Law in Malaysia', *ibid.*, ii/3– (1965–).

Mrs. M. Siraj, 'The Shariah Court, Singapore', *ibid.*, i/1 (1963).

CHAPTER 16

Selected Authoritative Handbooks of Islamic Law (for the earliest texts, see above, p. 228; for a general bibliography, see C. Brockelmann, *Geschichte der arabischen Litteratur*², 2 vols., Leiden 1943–9; *Supplementbände*, 3 vols., Leiden 1937–42).

Ḥanafī works:

KUDŪRĪ (d. 428/1036), *al-Mukhtaṣar*; part transl. G.-H. BOUSQUET and L. BERCHER, *Le Statut personnel en droit musulman hanefite*, Paris (1952).

SARAKHSĪ (d. 483/1090), *al-Mabsūṭ*.

KĀSĀNĪ (d. 587/1191), *Badā'iʿ al-Ṣanā'iʿ*.

MARGHĪNĀNĪ (d. 593/1196), *al-Hidāya*, with numerous commentaries, particularly the *Wiḳāyat al-Riwāya* by BURHĀN AL-DĪN MAḤMŪD AL-MAḤBŪBĪ (7th/13th century); transl. CHARLES HAMILTON, *The Hedaya*, 4 vols., London 1791, 2nd ed. 1870, reprinted Lahore 1957, 1963 (to be used with caution).

ABUL-BARAKĀT AL-NASAFĪ (d. 710/1310), *Kanz al-Daḳā'iḳ*, with numerous commentaries, particularly *al-Baḥr al-Rā'iḳ* by IBN NUJAYM (d. 970/1563.)

MAWLĀ KHUSRAW (d. 885/1480), *Ghurar al-Aḥkām*, and his own commentary *Durar al-Ḥukkām*.

IBRĀHĪM AL-ḤALABĪ (d. 956/1549), *Multaḳa 'l-Abḥur*; commentary *Majmaʿ al-Anhur* by SHAYKHZĀDE (d. 1087/1667); part transl. (chapters on sale, money-changing, suretyship) by H. SAUVAIRE, *Le Moultaqa el abheur, avec commentaire abrégé du Madjma el anheur*, Marseilles 1882 (Académie des Sciences, Belles-Lettres et Arts de Marseille) (the systematic part of the present book is based on this work).

al-Fatāwā al-ʿĀlamgīriyya (above, pp. 94, 249).

IBN ʿĀBIDĪN (d. 1252/1836), *Radd al-Muḥtār ʿala 'l-Durr al-Mukhtār*.

ÖMER NASUHÎ BILMEN (*muftī* of Istanbul), *Hukukı İslâmiyye ve Istılahatı Fıkhiyye Kamusu*, 6 vols., Istanbul 1950–5 (a detailed contemporary handbook).

Collections of *fatwās* by Ḳāḍīkhān (d. 592/1196), Kardarī (d. 827/1414; *al-Fatāwā al-Bazzāziyya*), Ḳōnawī (d. 985/1577; *al-Fatāwā al-Ḥāmidiyya*), and Anḳirawī (d. 1098/1687).

Mālikī works:

IBN ABĪ ZAYD AL-ḲAYRAWĀNĪ (d. 386/996), *al-Risāla*; transl. E. Fagnan, Paris 1914; L. BERCHER, Algiers 1945.

KHALĪL IBN ISḤĀḲ (d. 767/1365), *al-Mukhtaṣar*, with numerous commentaries, e.g. by Ḥaṭṭāb (d. 954/1547), Khirshī (d. 1101/1689), and Dardīr (d. 1201/1786), with a gloss by Dasūḳī (d. 1230/1815); transl. I. GUIDI and D. SANTILLANA, *Sommario del Diritto Malechita*, 2 vols., Milan 1919 (a standard work); G.-H. BOUSQUET, *Abrégé de la loi musulmane selon le rite de l'imâm Mâlek*, 4 vols., Algiers 1956–62 (supersedes the previous French translations); E. FAGNAN, *Concordances arabes*, Algiers 1889.

IBN ʿĀṢIM (d. 829/1427), *Tuḥfat al-Ḥukkām*; transl. L. BERCHER, Algiers 1958.

ʿAbd Allāh Gannūn, *Muḥādhi 'l-Zaḳḳāḳiyya*, ed. and transl. B. de Parfentief, *En suivant la Zaqqāqiya*, Paris 1958 (a contemporary beginners' manual).

Fatwās of Muḥammad ʿIllīsh (d. 1299/1881), *Fatḥ al-ʿAlī al-Mālik*.

Shāfiʿī works:

Shīrāzī (d. 476/1083), *al-Tanbīh*; transl. G.-H. Bousquet, 4 vols., Algiers 1949–52.

Ghazzālī (d. 505/1111), *al-Wajīz*.

Abū Shujāʿ (d. 593/1196), *al-Taḳrīb*; transl. G.-H. Bousquet, *Abrégé de la loi musulmane selon le rite de l'imâm El-Châfi'î*, separately printed from *R.A.* 1935.

Nawawī (d. 676/1277), *Minhāj al-Ṭālibīn*; transl. L. W. C. van den Berg, *Le Guide des zélés croyants*, 3 vols., Batavia 1882–1884 (very unsatisfactory; corrections in Bousquet's translation of Shīrāzī).

—— *al-Majmūʿ*, a commentary on another work of Shīrāzī, *al-Muhadhdhab*; much more detailed but less authoritative than the *Minhāj*; completed by Taḳī al-Dīn al-Subkī (d. 756/1355), *Takmilat al-Majmūʿ*.

Ibn Ḳāsim al-Ghazzī (d. 918/1512), *Fatḥ al-Ḳarīb*, a commentary on Abū Shujāʿ, *al-Taḳrīb*; transl. L. W. C. van den Berg, *La Révélation de l'Omniprésent*, Leiden 1895 (unsatisfactory; corrections in Bousquet's translation of Shīrāzī).

Ibn Ḥajar (d. 975/1567), *Tuḥfat al-Muḥtāj*, and

Ramlī (d. 1006/1596), *Nihājat al-Muḥtāj*; these two commentaries on Nawawī's *Minhāj* are the standard texts for the doctrine of the Shāfiʿī school.

Ibrāhīm al-Bājūrī (d. 1276/1860), a *ḥāshiya* (supercommentary) on the *Fatḥ al-Ḳarīb* of Ibn Ḳāsim al-Ghazzī; partly digested (omitting the chapters on religious duties, the holy war, &c.) by E. Sachau, *Muhammedanisches Recht nach schafiitischer Lehre*, Stuttgart and Berlin 1897 (cf. C. Snouck Hurgronje, in *Z.D.M.G.* liii (1899), 125–67; reprinted in *Verspreide Geschriften*, ii. 367–414).

Ali bin Hemedi el Buhriy, *Mirathi, a Handbook of the Mahomedan Law of Inheritance*, transl. (Sir) Philip E. Mitchell, Nairobi (Government Printer) 1923, reprinted 1949; *Nikahi, a Handbook of the Law of Marriage in Islam*, transl. J. W. T. Allen, Dar es Salaam (Government Printer) 1959 (translations from the Swahili of contemporary beginners' manuals).

Collections of *fatwās* by Taḳī al-Dīn al-Subkī, Ibn Ḥajar, and Ramlī.

Ḥanbalī works:

Khiraḳī (d. 334/945), *al-Mukhtaṣar*.

Muwaffaḳ al-Dīn Ibn Ḳudāma (d. 620/1223), *al-Mughnī*, formally a commentary on the *Mukhtaṣar* of Khiraḳī; an encyclopaedic work.

—— *al-ʿUmda*, a concise treatise; transl. H. Laoust, *Le Précis de droit d'Ibn Qudāma*, Beyrouth 1950 (with a valuable introduction).

Shams al-Dīn Ibn Ḳudāma (d. 682/1284), *al-Sharḥ al-Kabīr*, a commentary on a more detailed handbook of Muwaffaḳ al-Dīn, *al-Muḳniʿ*.

Ḥijāwī (d. 968/1560), *al-Iḳnāʿ* (or *Zād al-Mustaḳniʿ*).

Marʿī ibn Yūsuf (d. 1033/1624), *Dalīl al-Ṭālib*; commentary by Ibrāhīm

IBN MUḤAMMAD IBN DŪYĀN (d. 1353/1934), *Manār al- Sabīl*, part transl. G. M. BAROODY, *Crime and Punishment under Hanbali Law*, privately printed 1962.

BAHŪTĪ (d. 1051/1641), *Sharḥ al-Muntahā*.

—— *al-Rawḍ al-Murbiʿ*, a commentary on the *Iḳnāʿ* of Ḥijāwī; the four last works are prescribed textbooks in Saudi Arabia.

Ẓāhirī work:

IBN ḤAZM (d. 456/1065), *al-Muḥallā*.

Ibāḍī works:

ʿALĪ IBN MUḤAMMAD BASYĀNĪ (or Basyūnī; middle of the 5th/11th century), *al-Mukhtaṣar*; E. SACHAU, *Muhammedanisches Erbrecht nach der Lehre der Ibaditischen Araber von Zanzibar und Ostafrika, Sitzungsber. Preuss. Akad. Wiss.*, Phil.-hist. Kl., 1894, viii.

ʿĀMIR IBN ʿALĪ AL-SHAMMĀKHĪ (d. 792/1389–90), *al-Īḍāḥ*; extract translated by Mercier, below.

ʿABD AL-ʿAZĪZ IBN IBRĀHĪM AL-MUṢʿABĪ (d. 1223/1808), *al-Nīl*; part transl. E. ZEYS, *Droit mozabite. Le Nil. Du mariage et de sa dissolution*, Algiers 1891 (separately printed from *R.A.* 1887, 1888, 1890); HUREAUX, *Droit mozabite. De la tutelle*, Algiers 1882; extract translated by Mercier, below.

MUḤAMMAD IBN YŪSUF AṬFIYĀSH (d. 1332/1914), *Sharḥ al-Nīl*, a commentary on the preceding work; extract translated by Mercier, below.

M. MERCIER, *Étude sur le waqf abadhite et ses applications au Mzab*, Algiers 1927.

Zaydī Shiite work:

ḤUSAYN IBN AḤMAD AL-SIYĀGHĪ (d. 1221/1806), *al-Rawḍ al-Naḍīr*, a commentary on the *Majmūʿ al-Fiḳh* attributed to Zayd ibn ʿAlī (above, p. 228).

'Twelver' Shiite work:

MUḤAḲḲIḲ AL-ḤILLĪ (d. 676/1277), *Sharāʾiʿ al-Islām*; part transl. N. B. E. BAILLIE, *A Digest of Moohummudan Law*, ii, London 1869, reprinted Lahore 1958 (on the 'statut personnel' and connected subjects); transl. A. QUERRY, *Droit musulman. Recueil de lois concernant les Musulmans schyites*, 2 vols., Paris 1871–2.

Ismāʿīlī Shiite work:

AL-ḲĀḌĪ NUʿMĀN (d. 363/974), *Daʿāʾim al-Islām*; part transl. A.A.A. FYZEE, *The Ismaili Law of Wills*, London 1933.

Other lists of authoritative works:

*J. H. HARINGTON, *Remarks upon the Authorities of Mosulman Law*, in *Asiatick Researches: or Transactions of the Society Instituted in Bengal*, x (Calcutta 1808), 475–512 (on Ḥanafī works used in India).

*N. P. AGHNIDES, *Mohammedan Theories of Finance, with . . . a Bibliography*, New York 1916, 177–94 (reprinted Lahore 1961).

TH. W. JUYNBOLL, *Handleiding*, 29–32, 373–8.

E. PRÖBSTER, in *Islamica*, iii/3 (1927), 352–4 (on Mālikī works used in Morocco).

LÓPEZ ORTIZ, *Derecho musulmán*, 36–41 (on Mālikī works used in Spain).

*H. Laoust, *Le Précis de droit d'Ibn Qudāma*, introduction.
Cf. also Ibn Khaldūn (d. 808/1406), *al-Muḳaddima*, *faṣl* 6, §§ 7 (on *fiḳh*), 8 (on *farāʾiḍ*), 9 (on *uṣūl*); transl. Mac Guckin de Slane, *Les Prolégomènes*, iii, reprinted Paris 1938, 1–38; transl. F. Rosenthal, *The Muqaddimah*, iii, New York 1958, 3–30.

2 †G. Bergsträsser, *Zur Methode der* Fiqh-*Forschung*, Islamica, iv/3 (1930), 283/94.

3 W. Heffening, *Zum Aufbau der islamischen Rechtswerke*, in Studien . . . *Paul Kahle . . . überreicht*, Leiden 1935, 101–18 (but see J. Schacht, in *XII Convegno 'Volta'*, Rome 1957, 208).

On reasonings explaining the traditional order of subjects, cf. Snouck Hurgronje, *Verspreide Geschriften*, ii. 395, n. 1; Santillana, *Istituzioni*, i. vii–ix.

Works on farāʾiḍ :

Ibn al-Mutaḳḳina (d. 579/1183), *Bughyat al-Bāḥith* (or *al-Raḥbiyya*), ed. and transl. William Jones, *The Mahomedan Law of Succession*, London 1782 (Ḥanafī).

Sirāj al-Dīn al-Sajāwandī (end of the 6th/12th century), *al-Sirājiyya*, ed. and transl. W. Jones, Calcutta 1792; the transl. often reprinted, e.g. with additions by A. Rumsey, London 1869, Lahore 1959; text and transl. in Mahomed-Ullah ibn S. Jung, *The Muslim Law of Inheritance*, Allahabad 1934 (Allahabad University Studies, x); digest, with extracts from the text, by N. B. E. Baillie, *The Moohummudan Law of Inheritance*, Calcutta 1832 (Ḥanafī).

Ibrāhīm al-Tilimsānī (d. 690/1291), *al-Manzūma al-Tilimsāniyya*; digest by G. I. Faure-Biguet, *Abrégé des successions*, Valence 1912 (Mālikī).

Shaykh ʿAbd al-Ḳādir (wrote 1304/1886), *al-Nahr al-Fāʾiḍ fī Ilm al-Farāʾiḍ*, ed. and transl. L. Hirsch, *Der überfliessende Strom in der Wissenschaft des Erbrechts*, Leipzig 1891; text and transl., *Treatise on the Muhammedan Law*, entitled '*The Overflowing River of the Science of Inheritance and Patrimony*', &c., 2nd ed., Aden 1899 (Ḥanafī and Shāfiʿī).

Works on waḳf (*Ḥanafī*):

Hilāl al-Raʾy (d. 245/859), *Aḥkām al-Waḳf*.

Khaṣṣāf (d. 261/874), *Aḥkām al-Waḳf*.

Ibrāhīm ibn Mūsā al-Ṭarābulusī (d. 922/1516), *al-Isʿāf fī Aḥkām al-Awḳāf* (based on the two preceding works); part transl. in B. Adda and E. D. Ghaliounghi, *Droit Musulman. Le wakf*, Alexandria 1893.

Practical handbooks for the ḳāḍī:

Ḥanafī:

Ṭarsūsī (d. 758/1356), *Anfaʿ al-Wasāʾil ilā Taḥrīr al-Masāʾil*.

ʿAlī ibn Khalīl al-Ṭarābulusī (d. 844/1440), *Muʿīn al-Ḥukkām fīmā yataraddad bayn al-Khaṣmayn min al-Aḥkām*.

Ibn al-Shiḥna (d. 921/1515), *Lisān al-Ḥukkām fī Maʿrifat al-Aḥkām*.

Mālikī:

Ibn Farḥūn (d. 799/1397), *Tabṣirat al-Ḥukkām fī Uṣūl al-Aḳḍiya wa-Manāhij al-Aḥkām*.

Works on furūḳ:

J. Schacht, *Aus zwei arabischen* Furūq-*Büchern*, *Islamica*, ii/4 (1927), 505–37 (extracts from one Ḥanafī and one Ḥanbalī work, with an introduction on the literature of *furūḳ*).

Mālikī:

Ḳarāfī (d. 684/1285), *Anwār al-Burūḳ fī Anwā' al-Furūḳ*.
Wansharīsī (d. 914/1508), *'Uddat al-Furūḳ*

Works on ashbāh wa-naẓā'ir, ḳawā'id:

Ibn Nujaym (d. 970/1563), *Kitāb al-Ashbāh wal-Naẓā'ir* (Ḥanafī).
Suyūṭī (d. 911/1505), *Kitāb al-Ashbāh wal-Naẓā'ir* (Shāfi'ī).
Ibn Rajab (d. 795/1393), *al-Ḳawā'id* (Ḥanbalī).

Works on technical terms:

Abul-Ḥafṣ al-Nasafī (d. 537/1142), *Ṭalibat al-Ṭalaba* (Ḥanafī).
Ibn 'Arafa (d. 803/1401), *Kitāb al-Ḥudūd al-Fiḳhiyya* (Mālikī).
Nawawī (d. 676/1277), *Tahdhīb al-Asmā' wal-Lughāt* (second part; the first part is a dictionary of proper names occurring in works of Islamic Law) (Shāfi'ī).
Tahānawī (wrote 1158), *Kashf* (or *Kashshāf*) *Iṣṭilāḥāt al-Funūn* (a general dictionary of technical terms).

Works on ikhtilāf:

Abu Yūsuf (d. 182/798), *al-Radd 'alā Siyar al-Awzā'ī*, and *Ikhtilāf Abī Ḥanīfa wa-bn Abī Laylā* (polemical).
Shaybānī (d. 189/804), *Kitāb al-Ḥujaj* (polemical).
Ṭabarī (d. 310/923), *Kitāb Ikhtilāf al-Fuḳahā'* (consisting mostly of extracts from the works of his predecessors; only two fragments of this very extensive work have survived).
Ṭaḥāwī (d. 321/933), *Sharḥ Ma'āni 'l-Āthār* (the author argues from the Ḥanafī point of view).
'Abd al-Wahhāb al-Baghdādī (d. 422/1031), *al-Ishrāf 'alā Masā'il al-Khilāf* (a Mālikī handbook).
Ibn Rushd al-Ḥafīd (Averroes, the philosopher; d. 595/1198), *Bidāyat al-Mujtahid* (cf. R. Brunschvig, 'Averroès juriste', in *Études d'orientalisme . . . Lévi-Provençal*, i, Paris 1962, 35–68); part translations: A. Laïmèche, *Du mariage et de sa dissolution*, Algiers 1926; the same, *Des donations, des testaments, des successions, des jugements*, Algiers 1928; the same, *Livre des échanges*, Algiers 1940; G.-H. Bousquet, 'Le livre de l'interdiction', *R.A.* 1949, 41–49.
Sha'rānī (d. 973/1565), *al-Mīzān al-Kubrā* (derived from Muḥammad ibn 'Abd al-Raḥmān al-Dimashḳī [wrote 780/1378], *Raḥmat al-Umma*, a Shāfi'ī handbook); transl. M. Perron, *Balance de la loi musulmane*, Algiers 1898.
Kitāb al-Fiḳh 'ala 'l-Madhāhib al-Arba'a (a modern handbook; i², published by the Egyptian Ministry of Wakfs, Cairo 1931; ii²–iv, by 'Abd al-Raḥmān al-Jazīrī, Cairo 1933–8; has not been completed).

STUDIES: I. GOLDZIHER, *Die Zâhiriten*, Leipzig, 1884, 37–39; the same, 'Zur Litteratur des Ichtilâf al-madzâhib', *Z.D.M.G.* xxxviii (1884), 669–82; F. KERN, 'Ṭabarî's Iḫtilāf al-fuqahā'', ibid. lv (1901), 61–95.

Works of ṭabaḳāt*:*

An important early source is the *Kitāb al-Fihrist* of Ibn al-Nadīm (wrote 377/987), the sixth section of which deals with the *fuḳahā'* and their writings.

Ḥanafī ṭabaḳāt

ʿABD AL-ḲĀDIR IBN MUḤAMMAD (d. 775/1373), *al-Jawāhir al-Muḍīʾa.*

MUḤAMMAD ʿABD AL-ḤAYY AL-LAKNAWĪ (d. 1304/1886), *al-Fawāʾid al-Bahiyya.*

G. FLÜGEL, 'Die Classen der hanefitischen Rechtsgelehrten', *Abh. Kgl. Sächs. Ges. Wiss.* viii (1860), 267–358.

Mālikī ṭabaḳāt*:*

IBN FARḤŪN (d. 799/1397), *al-Dībāj al-Mudhahhab*; cf. E. FAGNAN, 'Les tabakāt malekites', *Homenaje a D. Francisco Codera*, Saragossa 1904, 105–13.

AḤMAD BĀBĀ AL-TUMBUKTĪ (d. 1036/1627), *Nayl al-Ibtihāj* (a supplement to the preceding work).

MUḤAMMAD MAKHLŪF, *Shajarat al-Nūr al-Zakiyya*, 2 vols., Cairo 1349/1930–1350/1931.

R. CASTEJÓN CALDERÓN, *Los juristas hispano-musulmanes*, Madrid 1948.

Shāfiʿī ṭabaḳāt*:*

TĀJ AL-DĪN AL-SUBKĪ (d. 771/1370), *Ṭabaḳāt al-Shāfiʿiyya al-Kubrā* (cf. G. MAKDISI, *S.I.* xvii (1962), 57–80).

F. WÜSTENFELD, *Der Imâm al-Schâfiʿí und seine Anhänger*, i–iii, Göttingen 1890–91 (separately printed from *Abh. Ges. Wiss. Göttingen*, xxxvi–xxxvii).

Ḥanbalī ṭabaḳāt*:*

IBN ABĪ YAʿLĀ (d. 526/1133), *Ṭabaḳāt al-Ḥanābila.*

IBN RAJAB (d. 795/1392), *Ṭabaḳāt al-Ḥanābila* (a supplement to the preceding work).

Collections of biographies of *ḳāḍīs* are numerous; see the works of Wakīʿ and Kindī, above p. 224, and further:

KHUSHANĪ (d. 371/981), *Kitāb al-Ḳuḍāt bi-Ḳurṭuba.*

NUBĀHĪ (8th/14th century), *Tārīkh Ḳuḍāt al-Andalus*, ed. E. Lévi-Provençal, Cairo 1948.

IBN ḤAJAR AL-ʿASḲALĀNĪ (d. 852/1449), *Rafʿ al-Iṣr ʿan Ḳuḍāt Miṣr.*

IBN ṬŪLŪN (d. 953/1546), *Ḳuḍāt Dimashḳ*, ed. Ṣalāḥ al-Dīn al-Munajjid, Damascus 1956.

5 *Selected Sources on* uṣūl*:*

Ḥanafī works:

PAZDAWĪ (d. 482/1089), *Kanz al-Wuṣūl ilā Maʿrifat al-Uṣūl.*

ABUL-BARAKĀT AL-NASAFĪ (d. 710/1310), *Manār al-Anwār.*

Ṣadr al-Sharīʿa al-Thānī (d. 747/1346), *Tanḳīḥ al-Uṣūl*, with the author's own commentary, *al-Tawḍīḥ*.

Ibn al-Humām (d. 861/1457), *al-Taḥrīr*.

Mullā Khusraw (d. 885/1480), *Mirḳāt al-Wuṣūl ilā ʿIlm al-Uṣūl*, with the author's own commentary, *Mir'āt al-Uṣūl*.

Mālikī works:

Ibn Rushd al-Ḥafīd (d. 595/1198), preface to the *Bidāyat al-Mujtahid* (above, p. 265), transl. L. Bercher, *Revue Tunisienne de Droit*. 1954, no. 3/4, 30–37 (cf. R. Brunschvig, in *Études d'orientalisme . . . Lévi-Provençal*, i. 44–56).

Ibn al-Ḥājib (d. 646/1249), *Mukhtaṣar al-Muntahā*.

Ḳarāfī (d. 684/1285), *Sharḥ Tanḳīḥ al-Fuṣūl*.

Shāṭibī (d. 790/1388), *al-Muwāfaḳāt*.

Shāfiʿī works:

Shāfiʿī (d. 204/820), *al-Risāla* (the first treatise written on *uṣūl*); digest by L. I. Graf, *Al-Shāfiʿī's verhandeling over de 'wortelen' van den fiḳh*, thesis, Leiden 1934; transl. M. Khadduri, *Treatise on Moslem Jurisprudence*, Baltimore 1961; cf. also K. I. Semaan, *Ash-Shafʿi's Risalah: Basic Ideas*, Lahore 1961 (with transl. of the sections on repeal).

Muzanī (d. 264/878), *Kitāb al-Amr wal-Nahy*, ed. and transl. R. Brunschvig, ' "Le Livre de l'ordre et de la défense" d'al-Muzanī', *B.E.O.* xi (1945–6), 145–96.

Imām al-Ḥaramayn (d. 478/1085), *Kitāb al-Waraḳāt*; transl. L. Bercher (with notes drawn from commentaries), *Revue Tunisienne*, n.s. i (1930), 93–105, 185–214.

Ghazzālī (d. 505/1111), *al-Mustaṣfā*.

Tāj al-Dīn al-Subkī (d. 771/1369), *Jamʿ al-Jawāmiʿ* (commented upon by Shāfiʿī and by Mālikī authors).

Ḥanbalī works:

Muwaffaḳ al-Dīn ibn Ḳudāma (d. 620/1223), *Rawḍat al-Nāẓir*.

Ibn Taymiyya (d. 728/1328), *Maʿārij al-Wuṣūl*, and *al-Ḳiyās fil-Sharʿ al-Islāmī*; transl. H. Laoust, *Contribution à une étude de la méthodologie canonique de . . . B. Taimīya*, Cairo 1939.

Ibn Ḳayyim al-Jawziyya (d. 751/1350), *Iʿlām al-Muwaḳḳiʿīn*.

Ibn Badarān (d. 1346/1927–28), *al-Madkhal ilā Madhhab al-Imām Aḥmad ibn Ḥanbal*.

Ẓāhirī work:

Ibn Ḥazm (d. 456/1065), *Kitāb al-Iḥkām fī Uṣūl al-Aḥkām*.

Muʿtazilī work:

Ḳāḍī ʿAbd al-Jabbār (d. 415/1024), *al-Mughnī*, section xvii: *al-Sharʿiyyāt*.

Almohads:

Ibn Tūmart (d. 524/1130), *Le Livre de Mohammed Ibn Toumert*, introduction by I. Goldziher, Algiers 1903.

Works by modern Muslim authors:

ṢUBḤĪ MAḤMASĀNĪ, *Falsafat al-Tashrīʿ fil-Islām* (*The Philosophy of Jurisprudence in Islam*), Beirut 1946; English transl. F. J. ZIADEH, *Falsafat al-Tashrī fi al-Islām*, Leiden 1961.

MUḤAMMAD ṬĀHIR IBN ʿĀSHŪR, *Maḳāṣid al-Sharīʿa al-Islāmiyya* (*The Aims of Islamic Law*), Tunis 1366/1947.

ʿABD AL-WAHHĀB KHALLĀF, *ʿIlm Uṣūl al-Fiḳh*, 5th ed., Cairo 1952.

——*Maṣādir al-Tashrīʿ al-Islāmī fīmā lā Naṣṣ fīh* (*Bases of Islamic Legislation in the Absence of Material Sources*), Cairo 1955.

MUṢṬAFĀ AḤMAD AL-ZARḲĀʾ, *al-Madkhal al-Fiḳhī al-ʿĀmm ilal-Ḥuḳūḳ al-Madaniyya* (*General Introduction to the Civil Law of Islamic Jurisprudence*), Damascus 1952.

ʿABD AL-RAZZĀḲ AḤMAD AL-SANHŪRĪ, *Maṣādir al-Ḥaḳḳ fil-Fiḳh al-Islāmī* (*The Bases of Rights in Islamic Law*), i–vi, Cairo 1954–9.

ʿALĪ AL-KHAFĪF, *Asbāb Ikhtilāf al-Fuḳahāʾ* (*Grounds of Disagreement of the Lawyers*), Cairo 1956.

Digests:

C. SNOUCK HURGRONJE, *Selected Works*, 215–44, 268–89.

ABDUR RAHIM, *The Principles of Muhammadan Jurisprudence*, London and Madras 1911 (reprinted Lahore 1958) (modernist).

N. P. AGHNIDES, *Mohammedan Theories of Finance with an Introduction to Mohammedan Law and a Bibliography*, New York 1916, 23–156 (reprinted Lahore 1961) (the author's own remarks are to be used with caution).

B. DUCATI, *Sintesi del diritto musulmano*, Bologna 1926, 91–127.

O. PESLE, *Les Fondements du droit musulman*, Casablanca n.d.

L. MILLIOT, *Introduction*, 103–55 (lacks references to the sources).

D. SANTILLANA, *Istituzioni*, i. 51–81.

A detailed account of the contents of one of the great classical works on *uṣūl* is still lacking.

Studies:

Shorter E.I., artt. 'Idjmāʿ', 'Idjtihād' (D. B. Macdonald), 'Istiḥsān and Istiṣlāḥ' (R. Paret), 'Khaṭaʾ' (J. Schacht), 'Ḳiyās', 'Sunna' (this last now partly out of date) (A. J. Wensinck), 'Taḳlīd', 'Uṣūl' (J. Schacht).

I. GOLDZIHER, 'Das Prinzip des istiṣḥâb in der muhammedanischen Gesetzwissenschaft', *Vienna Oriental Journal*, i (1887), 228–36; summary in French by G.-H. BOUSQUET, in *Arabica*, vii (1960), 12–15.

—— 'Über iǵmāʿ' (above, p. 233).

J. LAPANNE-JOINVILLE, 'L'istiṣḥāb', *Travaux de la Semaine Internationale de Droit Musulman*, Paris 1953, 80–99 (to be used with caution).

R. BRUNSCHVIG, 'Sur la doctrine de Mahdī Ibn Tūmart', *Arabica*, ii (1955), 137–49 (also in *Ignace Goldziher Memorial Volume*, ii, Jerusalem 1958, 1–13).

—— 'Variations sur le thème du doute dans le fiqh', in *Studi orientalistici in onore di Giorgio Levi Della Vida*, Rome 1956, i. 61–82.

—— art. 'Barāʾa', in *E.I.*²

—— in *Études d'orientalisme . . . Lévi-Provençal*, i. 44–56.

É. TYAN, 'Méthodologie et sources du droit en Islam (*Istiḥsān*, *Istiṣlāḥ*, *Siyāsa šar'iyya*)', *S.I.* x (1959), 79–109.
K. I. SEMAAN, 'Al-Nāsikh wa-al-Mansūkh. Abrogation and its Application in Islam', *I.Q.* vi/1–2 (1961), 11–29 (see also above, *Shāfi'ī works*).
T. KOÇYIĞIT, 'Kitap ve sunnette nesh meselesi' (*The Question of Abrogation in Koran and Sunna*), *İlâhiyat Fakültesi Dergisi*, xi (Ankara 1963), 93–108.

On 'Twelver' Shiite uṣūl*:*

C. FRANK, 'Über den schiitischen Mudschtahid', *Islamica*, ii/2 (1926), 171–92.
G. SCARCIA, in *A.I.U.O.N.* N.S. vii (1957), 103–15.
—— 'Intorno alle controversie tra Aḫbārī e Uṣūlī presso gli Imāmiti di Persia', *R.S.O.* xxxiii (1958), 211–50.
A. K. S. LAMBTON, 'A Reconsideration of the Position of the *Marja' al-Taqlīd* and the Religious Institution', *S.I.* xx (1964), 115–35.

On Ibāḍī uṣūl*:*

M. M. MORENO, in *A.I.U.O.N.* N.S. iii (1949), 300–2.

ADDENDA

for p. 262. Shāfi'ī works:
NAWAWĪ (d. 676/1277), *Minhāj al-Ṭālibīn*; transl. into English from the French by E. C. Howard, London 1914.
for p. 263. Other lists of authoritative works:
Orientalisches Recht, Leiden and Cologne 1964 (Handbuch der Orientalistik, Erste Abteilung, Ergänzungsband III), 237–70 (by the late E. PRITSCH and O. SPIES).
for p. 264. Practical handbooks for the ḳāḍī: Mālikī:
ZAḲḲĀḲ (d. 912/1506), *al-Lāmiyya* (see above, p. 233).
p. 267. Mu'tazilī works on uṣūl:
ABUL-ḤUSAYN MUḤAMMAD IBN 'ALĪ IBN AL-ṬAYYIB AL-BAṢRĪ (d. 436/1044), *al-Mu'tamad fī Uṣūl al-Fiḳh*.
for p. 268. Works on uṣūl *by modern Muslim authors:*
MUḤAMMAD AL-KHUḌRĪ, *Uṣūl al-Fiḳh*, Cairo 1962.
MUḤAMMAD ADĪB ṢĀLIḤ, *Tafsīr al-Nuṣūṣ fil-Fiḳh al-Islāmī* (*The Interpretation of Material Sources in Islamic Law*), Damascus 1964.

CHAPTER 17

1 A. J. WENSINCK, art. 'Nīya', in *Shorter E. I.*

CHOUKRI CARDAHI, 'La valeur juridique du silence en droit musulman et en droit libanais', *Mélanges à la mémoire de Paul Huvelin*, Paris 1938, 47–74.

P. DIB, *Essai sur une théorie des mobiles en droit civil ḥanafite*, Beyrouth 1952.

Y. LINANT DE BELLEFONDS, 'Volonté interne et volonté déclarée en droit musulman', *R.I.D.C.* x (1958), 510–21.

—— art. 'Ḍarūra', in *E.I.*[2]

W. MANSBACH, '"Laesio enormis" in Muhammadan Law', *B.S.O.A.S.* x (1940–2), 877–85.

Z. A. RIFAÏ, *Le Consentement et les vices du consentement en droit musulman hanafite*, thesis, Nancy 1933.

ṢUBḤĪ MAḤMASĀNĪ, *al-Naẓariyya al-ʿĀmma lil-Mūjabāt wal-ʿUḳūd fil-Sharīʿa al-Islāmiyya* (*The General Theory of the Law of Obligations and Contracts under Muhammadan Jurisprudence*), 2 vols., Beyrouth 1948.

I. GOLDZIHER, 'Das Prinzip der taḳijja im Islam', *Z.D.M.G.* lx (1906), 213–26 (summary in French by G.-H. BOUSQUET, in *Arabica*, vii (1960), 131–5).

R. STROTHMANN, art. 'Taḳīya', in *Shorter E.I.*

2 L. R., *De l'absence en droit musulman*, Paris 1897.

4 I. GOLDZIHER, *Die Ẓâhiriten*, Leipzig 1884, 66–69.

I. GUIDI, *Sunnah e nadb presso i giuristi malechiti*, in *Festschrift Eduard Sachau*, Berlin 1915, 333–7.

J. SCHACHT, art. 'Aḥkām', in *E.I.*[2]

—— art. 'Bāṭil', in *Shorter E.I.*

Y. LINANT DE BELLEFONDS, 'Les actes juridiques valables et les actes nuls en droit musulman', *R.A.* 1959, 1–24.

—— art. 'Fāsid wa-Bāṭil', in *E.I.*[2]

O. SPIES, 'Das System der Nichtigkeit im islamischen Recht', in *Deutsche Landesreferate zum VI. Internationalen Kongress für Rechtsvergleichung 1962*, Berlin and Tübingen 1962, 87–99.

R. BRUNSCHVIG, 'Variations sur le thème du doute' (above p. 268), 64 f.

Ch. CHEHATA, art. 'Djā'iz', in *E.I.*[2]

CHAPTER 18

†R. Brunschvig, 'Théorie générale de la capacité chez les Hanafites médiévaux', *R.I.D.A.* ii (1949), 157–72.

Almenouar Kellal, 'De l'émancipation des mineurs en droit musulman', *R.A.* 1935, 53–70.

[J. Schacht], art. 'Bāligh', in *E.I.*²; the same, art. 'Hadjr', *ibid.*

W. Heffening, art. 'Shāhid', in *Shorter E.I.*

É. Tyan, art. ' 'Adl', in *E.I.*²; the same, '*Iflās* . . .' (below p. 283).

Th. W. Juynboll, art. 'Fāsiḳ', in *Shorter E.I.*

N. J. Coulson, art. 'Bayt al-Māl (ii)', in *E.I.*²

*W. Heffening, art. 'Waḳf', in *Shorter E.I.* (with important bibliography).

*L. Milliot, *Démembrements du habous*, Paris 1918.

G. Busson de Janssens, 'Les waḳfs dans l'Islam contemporain', *R.E.I.* 1951, 1–120; 1953, 43–76.

A. d'Emilia, 'Il *waqf ahlī* secondo la dottrina di Abū Yūsuf', *Pubbl. Ist. di Diritto Romano . . . dell' Università di Roma*, ix, Milan 1938, 67–87.

—— 'Per una comparazione fra le *piae causae* nel diritto canonico, il *charitable trust* nel diritto inglese e il *waqf khairi* nel diritto musulmano', *Atti del Primo Congresso di Diritto Comparato*, i, Rome 1953, 187–230.

J. Luccioni, *Le Habous ou Wakf* (*rites malékite et hanéfite*), thesis, Algiers 1942.

O. Pesle, *La Théorie et la pratique des habous dans le rite malékite*, Casablanca 1941.

R. Brunschvig, in *Classicisme et déclin culturel dans l'histoire de l'Islam*, Paris 1957, 166 (cf. D. Santillana, *Istituzioni*, i. 443 ff., ii. 446) (on *waḳf*).

W. Heffening, art. 'Wilāya', in *Shorter E.I.* (on guardianship).

O. Pesle, *La Tutelle dans le chra et dans les législations nord-africaines*, Casablanca 1945.

I. Dimitroff, 'Die Stellung der Frauen nach mohammedanisch-hanafitischem Rechte', *Zeitschr. vergl. Rechtswiss.* xxiv (1910), 1–99.

O. Pesle, *La Femme musulmane dans le droit, la religion et les mœurs*, Rabat 1946.

†R. Brunschvig, art. ''Abd', in *E.I.*²

A. J. Wensinck, artt. 'Mamlūk' and 'Mawlā', in *Shorter E.I.*

J. Schacht, art. 'Umm al-Walad', in *Shorter E.I.*

L. Gardet, *La Cité musulmane*, 2nd ed., Paris 1961, 69–79.

W. Björkman, art. 'Kāfir', in *Shorter E.I.*

A. Abel, artt. 'Dār al-ḥarb' and 'Dār al-Islām', É. Tyan, art. 'Djihād', and M. Khadduri, art. 'Ḥarb', in *E.I.*²

M. Khadduri, *War and Peace in the Law of Islam*, Baltimore 1955.

A. Fattal, *Le Statut légal des non-Musulmans en pays d'Islam*, Beyrouth 1958.

I. Goldziher, art. 'Ahl al-Kitāb', in *Shorter E.I.*

G. Vajda, art. 'Ahl al-Kitāb', in *E.I.*²

*Cl. Cahen, artt. 'Dhimma' and 'Djizya', in *E.I.*²

W. Heffening, *Das islamische Fremdenrecht*, Hanover 1925.

J. Schacht, art. 'Amān', in *E.I.*²

E. Pröbster, 'Fragen des islamischen Kollisionsrechts nach malikitischem Ritus', *Zeitschr. vergl. Rechtswiss.*, lv (1942–4), 147–62 (153–9 on *dhimmīs*).

CHAPTER 19

1 Muḥammad Yūsuf Mūsā, *al-Fiḳh al-Islāmī. Mudkhal li-Dirāsatih. Niẓām al-Muʿāmalāt fīh*, 3rd ed., Cairo 1958 (on property and obligations).

L. Gardet, *La Cité musulmane*, 2nd ed., Paris 1961, 79–90.

R. Arnaldez, 'Les biens en droit musulman à travers les idées d'Ibn Ḥazm de Cordoue', *Les Mardis de Dar el-Salam*, 1959, 147–80.

J. Schacht, art. 'Maita', in *Shorter E.I.*

2 J. Roussier-Théaux, 'La possession', *R.A.* 1935, 147–92.

R. Brunschvig, 'Sur la possession dans l'histoire du droit musulman', *R.A.* 1936, 33–40.

A. d'Emilia, 'Una comparazione fra diritto bizantino e musulmano in materia possessoria', *Studi in onore di Vincenzo Arangio-Ruiz*, iii, Naples 1952, 391–413.

*F. F. Schmidt, 'Die occupatio im islamischen Recht', *Der Islam*, i (1910), 300–53.

F. Løkkegaard, art. 'Ghanīma', in *E.I.*[2]

O. Pesle, *Le Crédit dans l'Islam malékite*, Casablanca 1942 (part i, chap. 4, on *luḳaṭa*).

J. Schacht, art. 'Luḳaṭa', in *Shorter E.I.*

O. Spies, 'Verarbeitung und Verbindung nach den Lehrmeinungen des islamischen Rechts', *Zeitschr. vergl. Rechtswiss.* xliv (1929), 41–128 (cf. G. Bergsträsser, in *Islamica*, iv/3 (1930), 289 f.).

*C. Snouck Hurgronje, 'Iets over verjaring in het moehammedaansche recht' (1897), *Verspreide Geschriften*, ii. 329–48.

F. Guay, 'La nature juridique de la prescription en droit musulman malekite', *R.M.D.* ii, (1949), 186–92.

J. Lapanne-Joinville, 'L'action en revendication et la prescription en droit malékite', *R.A.* 1951, 195–240; 1952, 16–57.

L. Milliot, 'La preuve du droit de propriété', *Travaux de la Semaine Internationale de Droit Musulman*, Paris 1953, 46–67 (= *Introduction*, 618–37).

Ch. Chehata, 'L'acte translatif de propriété en droit musulman hanafite', *Travaux de la Semaine*, 36–43.

†R. Brunschvig, 'De l'acquisition du legs dans le droit musulman orthodoxe', *M.A.I.D.C.* iii/4, Rome 1955, 95–110.

3 J. Schacht, art. 'Rahn', in *E.I.*[2]

O. Pesle, *Le crédit* (part ii, chap. 3).

4 *Selected publications:*

*E. Pröbster, 'Privateigentum und Kollektivismus im muhammedanischen Liegenschaftsrecht insbesondere des Maghrib', *Islamica*, iv/4 (1931), 343–511 (cf. J. Schacht, in *Der Islam*, xx (1932), 263–70).

Y. Linant de Bellefonds, 'Un problème de sociologie juridique. Les terres "communes" en pays d'Islam', *S.I.* x (1959), 111–36.

F. F. Schmidt, *Die occupatio* (above 1; on *iḥyāʾ al-mawāt*).

O. Spies, 'Islamisches Nachbarrecht nach schafiitischer Lehre', *Zeitschr. vergl. Rechtswiss.* xlii (1927), 393–421.

*R. Brunschvig, 'Urbanisme médiéval et droit musulman', *R.E.I.* 1947, 127–55.

J. Schacht, in *A.J.C.L.* viii (1959), 141 f. (on expropriation), 142 f. (on *abus des droits*) (with bibliography).

F. Arin, 'Essai sur les démembrements de la propriété foncière en droit musulman, *R.M.M.* xxvi (1914), 277–317.

J. Roussier-Théaux, 'L'établissement des servitudes', *R.A.* 1938, 40–46.

Selected publications :

H. Bruno, *Contribution à l'étude du régime des eaux en droit musulman*, thesis, Paris 1913.

R. Tresse, 'L'irrigation dans la Ghouta de Damas', *R.E.I.* 1929, 459–573.

J. Lapanne-Joinville, 'Le régime des eaux en droit musulman (rite malékite)', *R.A.* 1956, 12–61, 63–90.

D. A. Caponera, *Water laws in Moslem countries*, Rome 1954 (F.A.O. Development Paper, Agriculture, no. 43).

R. B. Serjeant, 'Some Irrigation Systems in Ḥaḍramawt', *B.S.O.A.S.* xxvii (1964), 33–76.

CHAPTER 20

1 R. Grasshoff, *Das schâfiʿitische Obligationenrecht*, i, Göttingen 1895 (also thesis, Königsberg: *Die allgemeinen Lehren des Obligationenrechts . . . sowie die Lehre vom Kauf-, Vollmachts-, Gesellschaftsvertrage und von den Realcontrakten*).

2 *Chafik T. Chehata, *Essai d'une théorie générale de l'obligation en droit musulman*, i, Cairo 1936 (cf. E. Volterra and C. A. Nallino, in *S.D.H.I.* iv (1938), 563–71).

—— artt. 'ʿAḳd' and 'Dhimma', in *E.I.*²

Ṣubḥī Maḥmaṣānī, *al-Naẓariyya al-ʿĀmma lil-Mūjabāt wal-ʿUḳūd fil-Sharīʿa al-Islāmiyya* (*The General Theory of the Law of Obligations and Contracts under Muhammadan Jurisprudence*), 2 vols., Beirut 1948.

Muṣṭafā Aḥmad al-Zarḳā', *al-Madkhal al-Fiḳhī al-ʿĀmm ilal-Ḥuḳūḳ al-Madaniyya* (*General Introduction to the Civil Law of Islamic Jurisprudence*), Damascus 1952.

Muḥammad Yūsuf Mūsā, *Al-Fiḳh al-Islāmī. Mudkhal li-Dirāsatih. Niẓām al-Muʿāmalāt fīh*, 3rd ed., Cairo 1958 (on property and obligations).

*—— 'The Liberty of the Individual in Contracts and Conditions according to Muslim Law', *I.Q.* ii (1955), 79–85, 252–63.

'Abd al-Razzāḳ Aḥmad al-Sanhūrī, *Maṣādir al-Ḥaḳḳ fil-Fiḳh al-Islāmī* (*The Bases of Rights in Islamic Law*), i–vi, Cairo 1954–9.

Z. A. Rifaï, *Le Consentement et les vices du consentement en droit musulman hanafite*, thesis, Nancy 1933.

Y. Linant de Bellefonds, 'L'autonomie de la volonté en droit musulman', *R.A.* 1958, 87–111.

3 F. Arin, *Recherches historiques sur les opérations usuraires et aléatoires en droit musulman*, thesis, Paris 1909.

J. Schacht, art. 'Ribā', in *Shorter E.I.*

Ch. Cardahi, 'Le prêt à intérêt et l'usure . . .', *R.I.D.C.* vii (1955), 499–541 [527–34 on Islamic law].

4 B. Carra de Vaux, art. 'Maisir', in *Shorter E.I.*

C. A. Nallino, 'Delle assicurazioni in diritto musulmano ḥanafito' (1927), *Raccolta di scritti*, iv. 62–84.

5 É. Tyan, *Le Système de responsabilité délictuelle en droit musulman*, thesis, Lyons 1926, pp. 149–261.

Abd el Rahman Sanhouri Bey, 'La responsibilité civile et pénale en droit musulman', *Revue al Qanun wal Iqtisad*, xv (1945), 1–26.

E. Schram-Nielsen, *Studier over Erstatningslæren i Islamisk Ret* (*Études sur la doctrine des dommages-intérêts en droit islamique*) (with summary in French), Copenhagen 1945.

J. Lapanne-Joinville, 'La théorie des risques en droit musulman (rite malékite)', *R.A.* 1955, 1–24, 51–75.

O. Spies, 'Die Lehre von der Haftung für Gefahr im islamischen Recht', *Zeitschr. vergl. Rechtswiss.* lviii, 1955, 79–95.

[J. Schacht], art. 'Ḍamān', in *E.I.*²

J. El-Hakim, 'Le Dommage de source délictuelle en droit musulman',

Paris 1964 (Université St-Joseph, *Annales de la Faculté de Droit et des Sciences Humaines*, xl).

R. GRASSHOFF, *Das Wechselrecht der Araber*, Berlin, 1899 (also thesis, Königsberg: *Die suftağa und ḥawâla der Araber*).

D. SANTILLANA, *Code civil et commercial tunisien. Avant-projet*, Tunis 1899, notes on artt. 1964, 1965, 1970, 2011, 2016.

A. CHÉRON and M. S. FAHMY BEY, 'Le transport de dette . . . en droit musulman', *L'Égypte Contemporaine*, xxii (1931), 137–190 [= *Bulletin de la Société de Droit Comparé*, lix (1930), 571–622].

É. TYAN, 'Cession de dette et cession de créance dans la théorie et la pratique du droit musulman (d'après le Madhab hanafite)', *Annales de l'École Française de Droit de Beyrouth*, ii, 1946, no. 3–4, 23–37.

A. DIETRICH, art. 'Ḥawāla', in *E.I.*[2]

CH. CHEHATA, art. 'Faskh', in *E.I.*[2]

CHAPTER 21

2 †I. Dimitroff, 'Asch-Schaibānī' (transl., with commentary, of the section on sale in Shaybānī's *al-Jāmiʿ al-Ṣaghīr*), *M.S.O.S.* ii/2 (1908), 60–206.

O. Pesle, *La Vente dans la doctrine malékite*, Rabat 1940.

Ch. Cardahi, 'Les conditions générales de la vente en droit comparé occidental et oriental', *Annales de l'École de Droit de Beyrouth* i (1945), 7–208.

Ch. Chehata, 'L'acte translatif de la propriété en droit musulman hanafite', *Travaux de la Semaine*, 36–45.

J. Schacht, art. 'Bayʿ', in *E.I.*²

W. Heffening, artt. 'Ṣarf' and 'Tidjāra', in *E.I.*¹

J. Schacht, art. 'Khiyār', in *Shorter E.I.*

A. d'Emilia, 'La struttura della vendita sottoposta a *ḫiyār* secondo la *sedes materiae* dell' *Al-Mudawwanah*', *O.M.* 1941, 86–98.

—— 'La compravendita con patto d'opzione secondo alcune fonti del diritto musulmano malikita', *S.D.H.I.* x (1944), 167–83.

—— 'Il patto d'opzione applicato alla compravendita secondo la codificazione turca di diritto musulmano hanafito', *S.D.H.I.* xi (1945), 225–36.

—— 'Il *baiʿ al-ḫiyār* nella *Mudawwanah*', *R.S.O.* xxiv (1949), 45–58.

—— 'Il *Ḫiyār aš-Šart* nel *Aṣl* di Šaibānī', *R.S.O.* xxxii (1957), 633–40.

G. Wiedensohler, *Mängel beim Kauf nach islamischem Recht*, Walldorf-Hessen 1960.

R. Brunschvig, art. 'Barāʾa', in *E.I.*²

3 O. Pesle, *Les Contrats de louage chez les Malékites de l'Afrique du Nord*, Rabat 1938.

E. Pritsch and O. Spies, 'Der islamische Werklieferungsvertrag nach al-Kāsānī', *Zeitschr. vergl. Rechtswiss.* lvi, 1953, 47–75.

4 W. Heffening, art. 'Shirka', in *E.I.*¹

O. Pesle, *La Société et le partage dans le rite malékite*, Casablanca 1948.

5 O. Spies, 'Das Depositum nach islamischem Recht', *Zeitschr. vergl. Rechtswiss.* xlv, 1930, 241–300.

—— art. 'Wadīʿa', in *E.I.*¹

O. Pesle, *Le Crédit dans l'Islam malékite*, Casablanca 1942 (part i, chap. 3).

6 O. Pesle, *Le Crédit* (part i, chaps. 1 and 2).

Th. W. Juynboll and J. Schacht, art. 'ʿĀriyya', in *E.I.*²

7 O. Pesle, *La Donation dans le droit musulman (rite malékite)*, Rabat 1933.

Y. Linant de Bellefonds, *Des donations en droit musulman* (thesis, Paris), Cairo and Paris 1935.

—— art. 'Hiba', in *E.I.*²

F. Rosenthall, 'Gifts and Bribes: the Muslim View', *Proceedings of the American Philosophical Society*, cviii (1964), 135–44.

8 O. Pesle, *Le Crédit* (part ii, chap. 2).

J. Gentz, 'Die Bürgschaft im islamischen Recht nach al-Kāsānī', *Zeitschr. vergl. Rechtswiss.* lxii (1960), 85–180 (also printed separately, Walldorf 1961).

9 Johs. Pedersen, *Der Eid bei den Semiten*, Strasbourg 1914.

—— art. 'Ḳasam', in *Shorter E.I.*

On obligations arising from torts and crimes in general, see the bibliography of chap. 20, section 5 (above, p. 274).

On *ghaṣb* in particular:

O. Spies, 'Verarbeitung und Verbindung' (above, p. 272).
art. 'Ghasb', in *E.I.*[2]

J. Lapanne-Joinville, 'Les actions possessoires en droit musulman , *R.M.D.* i (1948–9), 13–24, 36–52, 63–78.

A. d'Emilia, 'Il *Kitāb al-Ġaṣb* nella *Mudawwanah* di Saḥnūn', *R.S.O.* xxviii (1953), 79–98.

CHAPTER 22

1 J. Lecerf, art. '‘Ā'ila' in *E.I.*² (with bibliography).

—— 'Note sur la famille dans le monde arabe et islamique', *Arabica*, iii (1956), 31–60.

—— Sir Hamilton Gibb, 'Women and the Law', *Colloque sur la sociologie musulmane* 11–14 *Septembre* 1961, Brussels 1962 (Correspondence d'Orient, no. 5), 233–45.

P. Paquignon, *Le Traité du mariage et de l'éducation d'Ibn Ardoun* (cf. *G.A.L.* S II, 693), *R.M.M.* xv (1911), 1–59.

H. Bauer, *Islamische Ethik*, ii: *Von der Ehe*, Halle 1917 (translation of a section of Ghazzālī, *Iḥyā' ‘Ulūm al-Dīn*).

L. Bercher and G.-H. Bousquet, *Ghazâlî, Le Livre des bons usages en matière de mariage*, Paris and Oxford 1953.

G.-H. Bousquet, *La Morale de l'Islam et son éthique sexuelle*, Paris 1953.

2 J. Schacht, art. 'Nikāḥ', in *Shorter E.I.*

I. Dimitroff, 'Die Stellung der Frauen, &c. Mit einem Anhang: Schaibanis Eherecht', *Zeitschr. vergl. Rechtswiss.* xxiv (1910), 1–99.

O. Pesle, *Le Mariage chez les Malékites de l'Afrique du Nord*, Rabat 1936.

P. García Barriuso, *Derecho matrimonial islámico y matrimonios de Musulmanes en Marruecos*, Madrid 1952.

F. J. Ziadeh, 'Equality (*Kafā'ah*) in the Muslim Law of Marriage', *A.J.C.L.* vi (1957), 503–17.

J. Schacht, art. 'Raḍā'', in *Shorter E.I.*

J. Lapanne-Joinville, 'Les conventions annexes au contrat de mariage (*tatawwu'at*) en droit musulman malékite', *R.A.* 1954, 112–25.

W. Heffening, art. 'Mut‘a', in *Shorter E.I.*

On *fāsid* and *bāṭil* marriages:

J. N. D. Anderson, 'Invalid and Void Marriages in Hanafi Law', *B.S.O.A.S.* xiii (1950), 357–66.

J. Lapanne-Joinville, 'La théorie des nullités de mariage en droit musulman malékite', *R.A.* 1951, 92–102.

N. U. A. Siddiqui, *Studies in Muslim Law*, i: *Batil and Fasid Marriages*, Dacca 1955 (modernist).

Y. Linant de Bellefonds, art. 'Fāsid wa-Bāṭil', in *E.I.*²

3 J. Schacht, art. 'Ṭalāḳ', in *Shorter E.I.* (on all kinds of divorce).

O. Pesle, *La Répudiation chez les Malékites de l'Afrique du Nord*, Rabat 1937.

J. Lapanne-Joinville, 'La rescission du mariage en droit musulman malékite', *R.M.D.* iv (1952), 431–50.

C. Snouck Hurgronje, *The Achehnese*, Leiden and London 1906, 349–56 (on *ta‘līḳ al-ṭalāḳ*).

*H. Laoust, 'Une *risāla* d'Ibn Taimīya sur le serment de répudiation', *B.E.O.* vii–viii (1938), 215–36.

G.-H. Bousquet and H. Jahier, 'Les vices rédhibitoires de la femme en droit musulman: remarques juridico-médicales', *R.A.* 1951, 52–58 (and correction by G.-H. Bousquet, ibid. 1952, 68).

4 G.-H. Bousquet and H. Jahier, 'L'enfant endormi. Notes juridiques, ethnographiques et obstétricales', *R.A.* 1941, 17–36.

J. LAPANNE-JOINVILLE, 'La reconnaissance de paternité de l'enfant issu du concubinat légal', *R.M.D.* iv (1952), 153–68.

O. PESLE, *L'adoption en droit musulman*, Algiers 1919.

C. SNOUCK HURGRONJE, 'Rechtstoestand van kinderen, buiten huwelijk geboren uit inlandsche vrouwen, die den mohammedaanschen godsdienst belijden' (1897–98), *Verspreide Geschriften*, ii. 351–62.

J. LAPANNE-JOINVILLE, 'La filiation maternelle naturelle en droit musulman malékite', *R.M.D.* iv (1952), 256–67.

†R. BRUNSCHVIG, 'De la filiation maternelle en droit musulman', *S.I.* ix (1958), 49–59.

E. PRITSCH and O. SPIES, 'Das Findelkind im islamischen Recht nach al-Kāsānī', *Zeitschr. vergl. Rechtswiss*, lvii, 1954, 74–101.

W. HEFFENING, art. 'Wilāya', in *Shorter E.I.* (on parental authority).

O. PESLE, *La Tutelle dans le chra et dans les législations nord-africaines*, Casablanca 1945.

Y. LINANT DE BELLEFONDS, art. 'Ḥaḍāna', in *E.I.*²

J. SCHACHT, art. 'Yatīm', in *Shorter E.I.* (on the orphan).

J. LAPANNE-JOINVILLE, 'Le régime des biens entre époux (dans le rite malékite)', *R.M.D.* ii (1950), 394–406.

O. SPIES, art. 'Mahr', in *Shorter E.I.*

J. LAPANNE-JOINVILLE, 'L'obligation d'entretien (*nafaqa*) de l'épouse (dans le rite malékite)', *R.M.D.* iii (1951), 102–14.

CHAPTER 23

1 ABD EL-HAMID BADAWI BEY, 'Du principe qu'en droit musulman la succession n'est ouverte qu'après acquittement des dettes', *L'Égypte Contemporaine*, v (1914), 14–40.

2 *Analytical studies and digests*:

J. SCHACHT, art. 'Mīrāth', in *Shorter E.I.*

*W. MARÇAIS, *Des Parents et alliés successibles en droit musulman*, thesis, Rennes 1898.

A. D. RUSSELL and A. M. SUHRAWARDY, *An Historical Introduction to the Law of Inheritance*, London n.d. (a compilation of traditional and other material).

*F. PELTIER and G.-H. BOUSQUET, *Les Successions agnatiques mitigées*, Paris 1935.

†R. BRUNSCHVIG, 'Un système peu connu de succession agnatique dans le droit musulman', *R.H.* 1950, 23–34.

G.-H. BOUSQUET, 'Plaidoyer pour les faraïdhs', *R.A.* 1951, 1–14 (reprinted in *M.A.I.D.C.*, iii/4, Rome 1955, 81–93).

J. SCHACHT, art. ''Awl'. in *E.I.*[2]

J. LAPANNE-JOINVILLE, 'La filiation maternelle naturelle en droit musulman malékite', *R.M.D.*, iv (1952), 256–67.

—— 'Les principes fondamentaux du droit de succession musulmane', *M.A.I.D.C.*, iii/3 (1953), 1–20.

E. PRITSCH, 'Grundzüge des islamischen Intestaterbrechts', ibid. 21–42.

M. TIAR, 'De la vocation héréditaire du Beït-el-mal', *R.A.* 1955, 109–12.

I. MAHMUD, *Muslim Law of Succession and Administration*, Karachi 1958.

†R. BRUNSCHVIG, 'De la filiation maternelle en droit musulman', *S.I.* ix (1968), 49–59.

Descriptive:

N. B. E. BAILLIE, *The Moohummudan Law of Inheritance according to Aboo Huneefa and his Followers*, London 1874.

J. D. LUCIANI, *Traité des successions musulmanes (ab intestat)*, Paris 1890.

G. FAUVELLE, *Traité théorique et pratique de dévolution des successions musulmanes (rite malékite)*, Sétif 1905.

J. A. SÁNCHEZ PÉREZ, *Partición de herencias entre los musulmanes del Rito Malequí*, Madrid 1914.

O. PESLE, *Exposé pratique des successions dans le rite malékite*, Casablanca 1940.

V. LOUBIGNAC, 'Du partage des successions musulmanes', *R.A.* 1929, 1–32 (on the traditional methods of calculation in the Maghrib).

M. TEFFAHI, *Traité de successions musulmanes d'après le rite malékite*, Saint-Louis (Senegal) 1948 (Études Mauritaniennes, i).

C. H. WITHERS PAYNE, *The Mahommedan Law of Inheritance according to the School of Shafii*, Singapore 1932.

A. A. A. FYZEE, 'The Fatimid Law of Inheritance', *S.I.* ix (1958), 61–69.

E. SACHAU, 'Muhammedanisches Erbrecht nach der Lehre der Ibaditischen Araber von Zanzibar und Ostafrika' (above p. 263).

See also the bibliography of translations, above, p. 264.

J. SCHACHT, art. 'Waṣīya', in *Shorter E.I.*

M. ABDEL GAWAD, *L'Exécution testamentaire en droit musulman, rite hanafite*, Paris 1926.

O. PESLE, *Le Testament dans le droit musulman* (*rite malékite*), Rabat 1932.

†R. BRUNSCHVIG, 'De l'acquisition du legs dans le droit musulman orthodoxe', *M.A.I.D.C.*, iii/4 (1955), 95–110.

CHAPTER 24

1 TH. MOMMSEN, *Zum ältesten Strafrecht der Kulturvölker. Fragen zur Rechtsvergleichung*, Leipzig 1905; section v: TH. NÖLDEKE, *Arabisch* (pp. 87–89); section vi: J. WELLHAUSEN, *Arabisch-israelitisch* (pp. 91–99); section vii: I. GOLDZIHER, *Islam* (pp. 101–12).

J. KRCZMÁRIK, 'Beiträge zur Beleuchtung des islamitischen Strafrechts', *Z.D.M.G.* lviii (1904), 69–113, 316–60, 539–81.

L. BERCHER, *Les Délits et les peines de droit commun prévus par le Coran*, thesis, Paris 1926.

R. ARÉVALO, *Derecho penal islámico, Escuela Malekita*, Tangiers 1939.

*W. HEFFENING, art. 'Taʿzīr', in *Shorter E. I.*

J. SCHACHT, in *A.J.C.L.* viii (1959), 140 f. (on the absence of fines).

2 J. SCHACHT, art. 'Zināʾ', in *Shorter E.I.*

TH. W. JUYNBOLL, art. 'Ḳadhf', in *Shorter E.I.*

*A. J. WENSINCK, artt. 'Khamr' and 'Nabīdh', in *Shorter E.I.*

W. HEFFENING, art. 'Sāriḳ', in *E.I.*[1]

J. SCHACHT, art. 'Ḳatl', in *Shorter E.I.* (section ii/4, on *ḳaṭʿ al-ṭarīḳ*).

J. P. M. MENSING, *De bepaalde straffen in het ḥanbalietische recht*, thesis, Leiden 1936.

3 J. SCHACHT, artt. 'Ḳatl' and 'Ḳiṣāṣ' in *Shorter E.I.*

É. TYAN, *Le Système de responsibilité délictuelle en droit musulman*, thesis, Lyons 1926, pp. 11–147.

—— art. 'Diya', in *E.I.*[2]

†R. BRUNSCHVIG, art. 'ʿĀḳila', in *E.I.*[2]

J. N. D. ANDERSON, 'Homicide in Islamic Law', *B.S.O.A.S.* xiii (1951), 811–28.

E. GRÄF, 'Probleme der Todesstrafe im Islam', *Zeitschr. vergl. Rechtswiss.* lix (1957), 83–122.

OMAR BEY LOUTFI, *Note sur la légitime défense d'après le droit musulman*, 2nd ed., Paris 1909.

4 J. SCHACHT, art. 'Ḳatl', in *Shorter E.I.* (section ii/7, on *bughāt*; section ii/6, on neglect of ritual prayer).

W. HEFFENING, art. 'Murtadd', in *Shorter E.I.*

L. BERCHER, 'L'apostasie, le blasphème et la rébellion en droit musulman malékite', *Revue Tunisienne*, 1923, 115–30.

S. M. ZWEMER, *The Law of Apostasy in Islam*, New York 1916.

—— 'The Law of Apostasy', *M.W.* xiv (1924), 373–91.

CHAPTER 25

Th. W. Juynboll, art. 'Ḳāḍī', in *Shorter E.I.*

†É. Tyan, *Histoire de l'organisation judiciaire en pays d'Islam*, 2nd ed., Leiden 1960 (cf. M. Gaudefroy-Demombynes, *R.E.I.* 1939, 109–47, and *J.A.* ccxxxv (1946–7), 123–32).

O. Pesle, *La Judicature, la procédure, les preuves dans l'Islam malékite*, Casablanca 1942.

E. Pritsch, in *Z.D.M.G.* xcviii (1944), 256–66.

E. Gräf, 'Gerichtsverfassung und Gerichtsbarkeit im islamischen Recht', *Zeitschr. vergl. Rechtswiss.* lviii (1955), 48–78.

É. Tyan, 'La procédure du "défaut" en droit musulman', *S.I.* vii (1957), 115–34.

——art. 'Hiba', in *E.I.*[2]

F. Rosenthal, 'Gifts and Bribes . . .' (above, p. 276).

É. Tyan, art. 'Daʿwā', in *E.I.*[2]

E. Pröbster, 'Die Anwaltschaft im islamischen Recht', *Islamica*, v/5 (1932), 545–55.

P. Vassel, 'Über marokkanische Proceßpraxis', *M.S.O.S.* v/ii (1902), 1–63.

O. Pesle, 'Le réalisme du droit musulman', *R.A.* 1934, 92–110 (on limits of presumptions).

J. Lapanne-Joinville, 'Études de droit musulman malékite: les présomptions', *R.A.* 1957, 99–114.

R. Brunschvig, art. 'Bayyina', in *E.I.*[2]

†—— 'Le Système de la preuve en droit musulman', in *Recueils de la Société Jean Bodin*, xviii, Brussels 1964, 169–86.

W. Heffening, art. 'Shāhid', in *Shorter E.I.*

Almenouar Kellal, 'Le serment en droit musulman (école malékite)', *R.A.* 1958, 18–53.

É. Tyan, 'L'autorité de la chose jugée en droit musulman', *S.I.* xvii (1962), 81–90.

O. Pesle, *Le Crédit dans l'Islam malékite*, Casablanca 1942 (part ii, chap. 1 on execution, chap. 4 on bankruptcy).

R. Bouvet, *De la faillite en droit musulman*, thesis, Paris 1913.

É. Tyan, '*Iflās* et procédure d'exécution sur les biens en droit musulman (maḏhab hanafite)', *S.I.* xxi (1964), 145–66.

N. J. Coulson, 'The State and the Individual in Islamic Law', *I.C.L.Q.* vi (1957), 49–60 (needs qualification).

CHAPTER 26

1,2 *C. Snouck Hurgronje, *Selected Works*, 256–67.
J. Schacht, *Origins*, 283–7.
R. Brunschvig, in *S.I.*, i (1953), 12 f. (English transl. in *Unity and Variety in Muslim Civilization*, ed. G. E. Von Grunebaum, Chicago 1955, 52 f.).
—— in *M.A.I.D.C.* iii/4 (Rome 1955), 110 (on the autonomy of legal reasoning in Islamic law).

3 J. Schacht, *Origins*, 320.

7 *On Islamic law and society (selection of recent publications):*
D. de Santillana, 'Law and Society', in *The Legacy of Islam*, ed. Sir Thomas Arnold and A. Guillaume, Oxford 1931, 284–310.
F. I. Schechter, 'A Study in Comparative Trade Morals and Control', *Virginia Law Review*, xix (1933), 794–845 (pp. 795–822 on Islamic law; based on secondary material but competent, except for the omission of *ḥiyal*).
B. Tabbah, *Du heurt à l'harmonie des droits. Essai . . . suivi d'exemples tirés des systèmes juridiques du Levant*, Paris 1936 (also thesis, Lyons 1935).
E. Bussi, 'Del concetto di commercio e di commerciante nel pensiero giuridico musulmano in relazione alla storia generale del diritto', in *Studi in memoria di Aldo Albertoni*, iii, Padua 1938, 7–53.
*R. Brunschvig, 'Urbanisme médiéval et droit musulman', *R.E.I.* 1947, 127–55.
—— 'Considérations sociologiques sur le droit musulman ancien', *S.I.* iii (1955), 61–73.
—— in *S.I.* ix (1958), 59.
J. Berque, 'Petits documents d'histoire sociale marocaine', *R.A.* 1948, 53–62.
*—— 'Problèmes initiaux de la sociologie juridique en Afrique du Nord *S.I.* i (1953), 137–62.
*—— *Structures sociales du Haut-Atlas*, Paris 1955, 242–5, 323–97.
Cl. Cahen, 'L'histoire économique et sociale du monde musulman médiéval', *S.I.* iii (1955), 93–115.
—— 'Réflexions sur le waqf ancien', *S.I.* xiv (1961), 37–56.
S. D. Goitein, 'The Rise of the Near Eastern Bourgeoisie in Early Islamic Times', *Cahiers d'Histoire Mondiale*, iii (1957), 583–604.
N. J. Coulson, The State and the Individual in Islamic Law, *I.C.L.Q.* vi (1957), 49–60 (needs qualification).
J. Schacht, 'Islamic Law in Contemporary States', *A.J.C.L.*, viii (1959), 133–47.
*L. Gardet, *La Cité musulmane*, 2nd ed., Paris 1961.

7–9 *On the sociology of Islamic law :*
Max Weber on Law in Economy and Society, transl. E. Shils and M. Rheinstein, Cambridge (Massachusetts) 1954; the ideas of Max Weber are fundamental, but the special section on Islamic law (pp. 237–44) is highly unsatisfactory; for an application of Weber's ideas to Islamic law, see J. Schacht, 'Zur soziologischen Betrachtung des islamischen Rechts', *Der Islam*, xxii (1935), 207–38.

J. Schacht, 'Notes sur la sociologie du droit musulman', *Revue Africaine*, xcvi (1952), 311–29.

A. d'Emilia, 'Correlazioni fra sistemi giuridici e coscienza sociale', *A.D.C.S.L.* xiii (1938), 185–96.

—— 'Il diritto musulmano comparato con il bizantino dal punto di vista della tipologia del diritto', *S.I.* iv (1955), 57–76.

—— 'Intorno ad alcuni caratteri dell'esperienza giuridica medievale sunnita', in *A Francesco Gabrieli*, Rome 1964, 95–113.

J.-P. Charnay, 'Pluralisme normatif et ambiguïté dans le Fiqh', *S.I.* xix (1963), 65–82.

A. A. Schiller, 'Jurists' Law', *Columbia Law Review*, lviii (1958), 1226–38 (on Roman law).

A d'Emilia, 'Sulla dottrina quale fonte del diritto, *S.D.H.I.* xi (1945), 19–36.

—— 'Forma e sostanza della "interpretatio prudentium" nell' Islam medievale sunnita', in *Studi in onore di Emilio Betti*, i, Rome 1961, 95–115.

E. Gräf, *Jagdbeute und Schlachttier im islamischen Recht*, Bonn 1959, 340–9 (on the function of Islamic jurisprudence in the intellectual life of Islam; the rest of the book is to be used with caution, cf. J. Schacht, in *Der Islam*, xxxvii (1961), 268–76).

J. Schacht, 'Classicisme, traditionalisme et ankylose dans la loi religieuse de l'Islam', in *Classicisme et déclin culturel dans l'histoire de l'Islam*, Paris 1957, 141–61 (pp. 162–6, discussion).

LIST OF ABBREVIATIONS

A.D.C.S.L.	*Annuario di Diritto Comparato e di Studi Legislativi.*
A.F.D.I.	*Annales de la Faculté de Droit d'Istanbul.*
A.H.D.O.	*Archives d'Histoire du Droit Oriental.*
A.I.E.O.	*Annales de l'Institut d'Études Orientales* (Algiers).
A.I.U.O.N.	*Annali dell' Istituto Universitario Orientale di Napoli.*
A.J.C.L.	*American Journal of Comparative Law.*
B.E.O.	*Bulletin d'Études Orientales* (Institut Français de Damas).
B.S.O.A.S.	*Bulletin of the School of Oriental and African Studies.*
C.O.C.	*Cahiers de l'Orient Contemporain.*
E.I.	*The Encyclopaedia of Islam* (see p. 216).
G.A.L.	C. Brockelmann, *Geschichte der arabischen Literatur* (see p. 261).
IBLA	*Revue IBLA* (Institut des Belles Lettres Arabes, Tunis).
I.C.	*Islamic Culture.*
I.C.L.Q.	*International and Comparative Law Quarterly.*
I.Q.	*The Islamic Quarterly.*
J.A.	*Journal Asiatique.*
J.A.L.	*Journal of African Law.*
J.A.O.S.	*Journal of the American Oriental Society.*
J.C.L.	*Journal of Comparative Law.*
J.P.H.S.	*Journal of the Pakistan Historical Society.*
J.R.A.S.	*Journal of the Royal Asiatic Society.*
J.R.C.A.S.	*Journal of the Royal Central Asian Society.*
M.A.I.D.C.	*Mémoires de l'Académie Internationale de Droit Comparé.*
M.E.J.	*The Middle East Journal.*
M.S.O.S.	*Mitteilungen des Seminars für Orientalische Sprachen.*
M.W.	*The Muslim World.*
O.L.Z.	*Orientalistische Literaturzeitung.*
O.M.	*Oriente Moderno.*
R.A.	*Revue Algérienne, Tunisienne et Marocaine de Législation et de Jurisprudence* (unless otherwise indicated, the references are to Section i: Doctrine).
R.E.I.	*Revue des Études Islamiques.*
R.H.	*Revue Historique de Droit Français et Étranger.*
R.I.D.A.	*Revue Internationale des Droits de l'Antiquité.*
R.I.D.C.	*Revue Internationale de Droit Comparé.*

R.I.E.E.I.	*Revista del Instituto Egipcio de Estudios Islámicos.*
R.M.D.	*Revue Marocaine de Droit.*
R.M.M.	*Revue du Monde Musulman.*
R.J.P.U.F.	*Revue Juridique et Politique de l'Union Française.*
R.S.O.	*Rivista degli Studi Orientali.*
S.D.H.I.	*Studia et Documenta Historiae et Iuris.*
S.I.	*Studia Islamica.*
W.I.	*Die Welt des Islams.*
Z.D.M.G.	*Zeitschrift der Deutschen Morgenländischen Gesellschaft.*

GENERAL INDEX

abandonment of rights, relinquishment, waiver of claims, 11, 120, 148, 168, 169 n. 3, 184.
'Abbāsids, 4, 23, 25, 49 ff., 57, 69, 200.
'Abd Allāh ibn Ibāḍ, a Khārijī leader, 18.
'Abd Allāh ibn 'Umar, son of the caliph 'Umar, an authority of the ancient school of Medina, 32.
'Abd al-Malik, Umayyad caliph, 18.
abduction, 160, 168.
'Abdülmejīd, Ottoman sultan, 92.
abeyance, 119, 130, 138.
abortion, 124, 186.
Abū Bakr, caliph of Medina, 17.
Abū Bakr ibn 'Abd al-Raḥmān, a scholar of Medina, 31.
Abū Ḥanīfa, a scholar of Kūfa, eponym of the Ḥanafī school, 38, 40 f., 44, 57, 202.
Abū Ḳilāba, an early specialist in Islamic law, 26.
Abul-Su'ūd, Grand Mufti, 90.
Abū Thawr, founder of a school of law, 65.
Abū Ya'ḳūb Yūsuf, Almohad ruler, 65.
Abū Yūsuf, a companion of Abū Ḥanīfa, 19, 40 ff., 44 f., 49, 51, 56, 57, 81, 202.
acknowledgement, 79, 144, 151, 177, 192; of paternity, 166.
acquisition of ownership, 136 ff.
administration, 24, 53 f., 55, 114.
administration of justice, subject of special works, 114.
administrative law, 112, 206.
adoption, rejected by the Koran, 14 n. 1; no adoption in Islamic law, 166.
adultery as an impediment to marriage, 21; concept of adultery missing in Islamic law, 179.
Afghanistan, 65, 88.
agency, agent, 119 f., 173, 190; unauthorized agency, 122, 159, 188.
agnates, 170, 172.
agoranome (ἀγορανόμος), 25.
Akbar, Mogul emperor, 94.
Aḳ-Ḳoyunlu, 91 n. 1.
Albania, 93.
aleatory transactions, 147.
Algeria, 4, 66 n. 1,, 97 ff.
'Alī, caliph of Medina, 33 f., 38 f.
allowed, 121 f.
Almohads, 64 f.
Almoravids, 65, 86.
alms-tax, 105, 118, 206.
analogy, systematic reasoning, 37 ff., 60, 63 f., 114, 201, 203, 208, 211.
apostasy, apostate, 118, 119, 133, 138, 165, 187.
appeal, reversal of judgment, 189, 196.
arbitrators, in pre-Islamic Arabia, 7 f.; in the Koran, 10; Muhammad as arbitrator, 10 f.; arbitrators in the first century of Islam, 15; superseded by the Islamic *ḳāḍī*, 24; in Islamic law, 189, 198.
arrha, 9.
assignment of a claim, 149.
association, 119; in property, 138; *see also* society.
'Aṭā' ibn Abī Rabāḥ, a scholar of Mecca, 31, 42.
attorney, 190.
aval (French), derived from Arabic *ḥawāla*, 78.
Awrangzīb 'Ālamgīr, Mogul emperor, 94.
Awzā'ī, a scholar of Syria, 40 ff., 43, 57, 65.

Babylonian law (?), 22.
Balādhurī, an historian, 19.
banking, 78.
bankruptcy, bankrupt, 126, 198.
barter, 146, 154.
Basra, 28, 30, 57.
Bāyezīd II, Ottoman sultan, 91.
Bedouins, their customary law, 77, 186.
bills of exchange, 78, 149.
binding, 121.
blood feuds, 7, 13, 24, 185.
blood-money,.7, 13, 16, 24, 107, 181 f., 184, 185 f., 187.

insane, insanity, 124, 126, 182.
inspector of the market, 25, 52.
intent, 124, 178, 181, 185, 201.
intention 116 f.
interdiction, 125, 126.
interest, in pre-Islamic Arabia, 6; in the Koran, 12 f.; according to the Ẓāhirīs, 63 f.; in Islamic law, 145 f.; devices for evading its prohibition, 78; envisaged in the Ottoman Code of Commerce, not envisaged in Saudi Arabia, 87 n. 1.
international law, 112.
invalid, 35, 46, 121, 152, 165.
Iran, 110; *see also* Persia.
Iraq, Iraqians, 6, 17 f., 20, 22, 28 f., 31, 33 f., 35 f., 37 ff., 40 ff., 46, 57 f., 65 f., 81, 93, 103 f., 107, 142.
Islamic law, defined, 1; its nature, 1–5, 11 f., 14, 199 ff.; its emergence in the late Umayyad period, 27; its recognition by the early ʿAbbāsids, 49 ff.; the end of its formative period, 55 f., 69; its final rigidity, 75; its reshaping by the Modernists, 100 ff.; its subject-matters, 113, 206 ff.; its validity, 199 f.; a 'sacred law', 202, 211; a 'jurists' law', 209 f.
Israel, 93, 103.
iura in re aliena, 142.

Jewish (Talmudic, Rabbinic) law, 2, 13, 15, 20 f., 79.
John of Damascus, 18 f., 25.
joint property, joint ownership, 137, 138.
Jordan, 93, 103, 105 f.
judge, 188 ff.
judgment, 196.
jurisprudence, see *uṣūl*.
juristic persons, 125.

Ḳāsim ibn Muḥammad ibn Abī Bakr, a scholar of Medina, 31.
Ḳazwīnī, Shāfiʿī author of a treatise of *ḥiyal*, 81.
Khārija ibn Zayd ibn Thābit, a scholar of Medina, 31.
Khārijīs, Khārijī law, 16 f., 21, 64, 66.
Khaṣṣāf, Ḥanafī author to whom a treatise of *ḥiyal* is attributed, 81.
Khaṭṭ-i sherīf of Gülhane, an Ottoman constitutional document, 92.
Koran, 10 ff., 18 f., 22 n. 1, 29, 38, 41 f., 47, 53, 55, 60, 63, 64, 67, 82, 114, 175, 202, 209.
Kufa, Kufians, 24, 27, 28 f., 31 f., 33 f., 38, 42, 44 f., 57.
Kuwayt, 107 n. 1.

land law, land tenure, 86, 89 f., 91, 142; *see also* real estate.
lapidation, 15.
law merchant, 78.
Lebanon, 93, 101, 103, 107.
legacy, 24, 83, 93, 103, 119, 132, 134, 135, 138, 169, 173 f.
legal maxims, 39.
legal theory, see *uṣūl*.
legislation, legislators (lawgivers, lawmakers), 5, 8, 10 f., 15, 25, 52 ff., 55, 84, 87; legislation of the Ottoman sultans, 91; modernist legislation, 73, 100 ff.
liability, 39, 137, 139, 147 f., 155, 156, 157, 158 f., 160, 173, 177 f., 180, 182 ff., 187, 196, 204, 207 n. 1; for torts caused by a slave, 128 f.; for acts of animals, 183; subject of special works, 114.
liberty of contract, 144.
Libya, 66 n. 1, 103, 107.
lien, 140.
limitation, 176 f.; *see also* prescription.
loan of fungible objects for consumption, 157.
loan of non-fungible objects for use, 134, 157, 204; its premature termination, 122, 157.
locatio conductio, 21.

Maḥmūd II, Ottoman sultan, 92.
maintenance, 83, 161, 166, 167 f., 188.
majority, 124.
Malaya, 66.
Mālik, a scholar of Medina, eponym of the Mālikī school, 19, 39, 41, 43 f., 57, 61, 73, 79.
Mālikī doctrines, 39, 59, 61 f., 81, 82, 104, 108, 127 n. 1, 132 n. 1, 172 n. 1, 185 n. 1.
Mālikī school, 57, 61, 63, 65 f., 86, 97, 98.
Mamlūks, 54, 91 n. 1.
mandate, 120.
Manṣūr, ʿAbbāsid caliph, 55 f.

INDEX AND GLOSSARY OF ARABIC TECHNICAL TERMS

dār al-Islām, the territory of the Islamic state, 132.
darak, default in ownership, 139.
ḍarūra, necessity (as a dispensing element), 84.
da'wā, claim, lawsuit, 189.
dayn, debt, claim, obligation, 134, 144 f., 146.
devshirme, a forced levy of non-Muslim children in the Ottoman Empire, 89.
dhawu l-arḥām, (roughly) the cognates, 170.
dhimma, engagement, undertaking, 130; care as a duty of conscience, obligation, 144.
dhimmīs, non-Muslims who are protected by a treaty of surrender, 130 ff., 156, 191 f., 194.
dhukr or *dhukr ḥakk* (pl. *adhkār, adhkār ḥukūḳ*), written document, 82 n. 1.
dhul-yad, possessor, 136.
dīwān, army list, 186; records of the tribunal, 189.
diya, blood-money, 185.
diyāna, conscience, *forum internum*, 123.
dukhūl, consummation (of marriage), 161.

faḍl māl bilā 'iwaḍ, unjustified enrichment, 145 f.
faḳīh (pl. *fuḳahā'*), the specialist in *fiḳh* (q.v.), 1.
farā'iḍ, the portions allotted to the heirs, succession in general, 114, 170 ff.
farḍ, duty, 121.
farḍ, fixed share of an heir, 170.
fasād al-zamān, the (ever-increasing) corruption of contemporary conditions, 84, 202.
fāsid, defective, voidable, 121, 123, 135, 146, 152, 163, 167, 178.
fāsiḳ, sinner (opp. *'adl*), 125, 179, 189.
faskh, cancellation, 121, 148, 152, 154.
fatwā, the considered legal opinion of a *muftī* (q.v.), 73 f.
fidā', 128 (q.v. for definition).
fiḳh, the science of the *sharī'a*, the sacred Law of Islam, 1.
fuḍūlī, unauthorized agent, 122, 159.
fuḳahā' (pl. of *faḳīh*), the religious lawyers of Islam, 1, 28.
furū', the 'branches', positive law, as opposed to *uṣūl* (q.v.), 59, 65.
furūḳ, legal distinctions, 205; subject of special works, 114.

ghabn fāḥish, 'grave deception', fraud, 117.
ghā'ib, absent, 188.
ghalla, proceeds, 134.
ghanīma, booty, 136.
gharar, risk, hazard, uncertainty, 135, 146 f.
ghaṣb, usurpation, 160, 168, 200.
ghāṣib, usurper, 160.
ghayr ma'lūm, not known, 135.
ghayr mamlūk, that in which there is no ownership, 134.
ghurra, indemnity for causing an abortion, 124, 186.

ḥabs, imprisonment, 175, 187, 197.
ḥabs, retention of a thing in order to secure a claim, lien, 140.
ḥaḍāna, care of the child by the mother, 167.
ḥadd (pl. *ḥudūd*), a fixed punishment for certain crimes, 38 f., 86 n. 1, 91 f., 95 n. 1, 118, 120, 132, 148, 151, 158, 163, 175 ff. (q.v. for definition), 178 ff., 184, 187, 197, 198, 199.
ḥadīth (pl. *aḥādīth*), a formal tradition deriving from the Prophet, 34.
hadr, hadar, not protected by criminal law, 184 (opp. *ma'ṣūm*).
ḥajr, interdiction, 125, 126, 129.
ḥakam, arbitrator, 7 f., 10 f., 24, 189.
ḥaḳḳ ādamī, private claim (as opposed to a right or claim of Allah), 113, 160, 176 f.
ḥaḳḳ Allāh, right or claim of Allah (as opposed to a private claim), 113, 176.
ḥalāl, not forbidden, 121.
ḥarām, forbidden, 121, 123.
ḥarbī, enemy alien, 131, 184.
ḥawāla, transfer of debts, 78, 106, 148 f., 158.
hiba, donation, 157 f.
ḥirz, custody (of things), 134, 179 f.
ḥisba, the office of the *muḥtasib* (q.v.), 52, 114, 207 f.

ḥiyal (pl. of *ḥīla*), legal devices, evasions, 78 ff., 83 f., 114, 200, 206, 210.
ḥukm (pl. *aḥkām*), 'qualification' 124; see also *al-aḥkām al-khamsa*.
ḥukm al-ḥawz, *ḥukm* (*aḥkām*) *al-man'*, or *al-man'a*, *ḥukm al-ṭāghūt*, tribal customary law of the Bedouins in Arabia, 77.
ḥukūma, a penalty for certain wounds, 186.
ḥurr, free person, 127.

ibrā', acquittance, 148.
'idda, waiting-period of a woman after termination of marriage, 118, 166, 168.
idhn, 'permission', extension of the capacity to dispose, 126.
īfā', fulfilment (of an obligation), 148.
iḥtiyāṭ, (religious) precaution, 123.
iḥyā' al-mawāt, cultivating waste land, 141.
ījāb, offer (as a constitutive element of a contract), 22, 145.
ijāra, hire and lease, 21, 22, 126, 134, 154 f., 191.
ijāza, approval, *ratihabitio*, 122.
ijmā', consensus, 30, 60 f., 64, 67, 114; *ijmā' ahl al-Madīna*, consensus of the scholars of Medina, 61.
ijtihād, 'effort', the use of individual reasoning (also *ijtihād al-ra'y*), later restricted to the use of *ḳiyās* (q.v.), 37, 46, 53, 69 ff., 102, 104, 115, 202, 211.
iḳāla, reversal (of a sale), 148, 154.
ikhtilāf, disagreement, 67, 114.
ikhtilās, 180 (q.v. for definition).
ikhtiyār, 202 (q.v. for definition), 204.
ikrāh, duress, 117 f.
iḳrār, acknowledgement, confession, 151.
īlā', oath of abstinence from intercourse by the husband, 164.
ilḳā' bil-ḥajar, an aleatory transaction, 147.
imām, leader, 17; caliph, 130, 141, 182 f., 187, 197, 206.
imām ma'ṣūm, infallible *imām*, title assumed by Ibn Tūmart, 65.
imḍā', ratification, 121, 152.
'īna, a device for evading the prohibition of interest, 79, 153.
ishāra ma'hūda, 'gesture', conclusive act, 117.
ishtirāk, joint ownership, 137.
isḳāṭ, relinquishment (of a claim), 148.
isnād, the chain of transmitters of a tradition, 34.
istibrā', waiting-period of a female slave after a change of owner, 118, 166.
istīfā', receiving (taking possession), 138.
istighlāl, acquisition of proceeds, 137.
istiḥbāb, 'preference', a synonym of *istiḥsān* (q.v.), 37.
istiḥḳāḳ, vindication, 139.
istiḥsān, 'approval', a discretionary opinion in breach of strict analogy, 37, 40, 46, 60 f., 62, 115, 146 n. 1, 152, 155, 157, 179, 183, 204.
istīlā', occupancy of a *res nullius*, 136.
istirdād, vindication, 139.
istiṣḥāb, a method of legal reasoning particular to the Shāfi'ī school and to the 'Twelver' Shiites, 21.
istiṣlāḥ, taking the public interest into account, 21, 60, 61, 62, 109, 115, 204.
istiṣnā', contract of manufacture, 155.
'itḳ, *i'tāḳ*, manumission, 129 f.
'iwaḍ, countervalue, 145, 152.

jā'iz, allowed, unobjectionable, 121 f.
jam', 162 (q.v. for definition).
jāriya, female slave, 127.
jināya (pl. *jināyāt*), tort, delict, 128, 176, 177 f., 181 ff., 197, 198.
jizya, poll-tax, 131.
ju'l, reward for bringing back a fugitive slave, 159 f.
juzāf, undetermined quantity, 147.

ḳabḍ, taking possession, 138.
ḳabūl, acceptance (as a constitutive element of a contract), 22, 145.
ḳaḍā', judgmen given by the *ḳāḍī*, *forum externum*, 123, 196.
ḳaḍā', the district, circumscription, of a *ḳāḍī*, 90.
ḳaḍā', payment (of a debt), 148.
ḳadhf, false accusation of unchastity (unlawful intercourse), 125, 166, 175, 177, 179 (see also 13, 14 n. 1).

ḳāḍī, the Islamic judge, 4, 10, 16, 21, 24 ff., 37, 44, 50 ff., 54, 56, 74 f., 83, 84, 86 ff., 90 ff., 93, 95, 97, 103, 106 f., 108, 110, 114, 122 f., 125, 127, 130, 133, 139, 161, 165, 168, 173, 175, 177, 188 ff., 193 ff., 200, 207, 210.

ḳāḍi l-jamāʿa, a judicial office in Islamic Spain, 55 n. 1.

ḳāḍi l-ḳuḍāt, the chief *ḳāḍī*, 50 f., 55 n. 1.

kafāʾa, equality by birth, 162.

kafāla, suretyship, 158.

kaffāra, religious expiation, 129, 159, 165, 181 f., 183, 185, 207.

kafīl, guarantor, surety, 158.

kāfir, unbeliever, 131.

kāhin, soothsayer, 8, 10.

ḳānūn, 'law', used of secular acts, 87; the administrative law of the Ottoman Empire, 90.

ḳānūn-nāme, a text containing one or several *ḳānūns*, 54, 84, 91, 208.

ḳarḍ, loan of fungible objects for consumption, 157.

ḳasāma, a kind of compurgation, 24 n. 2, 184, 192, 197, 203.

ḳaṣd, aim, purpose, 181.

ḳāsim, divider of inheritances, 189.

ḳaṭʿ al-ṭarīḳ, highway robbery, 9, 175, 180.

kātib, secretary of the *ḳāḍī*, 'clerk of the court', 21, 25, 189.

ḳatl, homicide, 181.

ḳawad, retaliation, 181.

ḳawāʿid, 'rules', the technical principles of positive law, subject of special works, 114.

khalwa, privacy (between husband and wife), 161.

kharāj, land-tax, 131.

khārij, 'stranger', third party, 139, 194.

khaṣm, party to a lawsuit, 190.

khaṭaʾ, mistake, 181 f., 187.

khiyāna, embezzlement, 180.

khiyār, *optio*, right of rescission, 118, 121, 145, 148, 152 f., 154, 155, 169.

khiyār al-sharṭ, stipulated right of cancellation, 106, 153.

khulʿ, a form of divorce, 164.

khuṣūma, litigation, 189.

ḳīma, value, 152.

ḳīmī, non-fungible, 136.

kināya, 'allusion', implicit declaration, 116.

ḳiṣāṣ, retaliation, 120, 181, 184, 198.

ḳisma, division, 139.

ḳiyās, analogy, parity of reasoning, 21, 37, 46, 60, 114, 157, 208.

laḳīṭ, foundling, 159, 166.

lāzim, binding, 121, 139.

liʿān, 165 (q.v. for definition), 168, 179, 195, 197, 203.

liṣṣ, robber, 9.

luḳaṭa, found property, 137.

madhhab (pl. *madhāhib*), 'school' of religious law, 59 n. 1.

maʾdhūn, a slave who has been given permission to trade, 128 f.

maʿdin, mine, 136.

maʿdūd mutaḳārib, things that can be counted, 136.

mafḳūd, missing person, 124.

maḥārim, see *maḥram*.

maḥḍar, minutes, the written record of proceedings before the *ḳāḍī*, 83, 189.

mahr, nuptial gift, 38 f., 161, 163, 167, 178, 191, 192, 195, 197.

'fair' or average *mahr* defined, 167.

maḥram (pl. *maḥārim*), a person related to another within the forbidden degrees, 129, 162, 167, 180, 184.

majhūl, unknown, 147.

majlis, 'session', meeting of the parties, 145, 164.

majnūn, insane, 124.

makīl, *kaylī*, things that can be measured, 136.

makrūh, reprehensible, disapproved, 121 f.

maks, market dues in pre-Islamic Arabia, 8; illegal taxes in Islamic law, 76.

maʿḳūl, 'reasonable', the result of systematic thought, 46.

māl, *res in commercio*, 134, 135, 152, 205.

māl manḳūl, *māl naḳlī*, movables, 136.

malasā, the reverse of *ʿuhda* (q.v.), 8.

mālik, owner, 136.

maʿlūm, 'known', certain, 118, 147 (opp. *ghayr maʿlūm*, *majhūl*, qq.v.).

mamlūk, male slave, 127.

mandūb, recommended, 121.

manfa'a (pl. *manāfi'*), proceeds, usufruct, 126, 134, 205.
marsūm, 'decree', used of modern, secular acts, 87.
mashrū', recognized by the law, 121.
maṣlaḥa, the public interest, 61.
mastūr, 125 (q.v. for definition).
ma'ṣūm, inviolable, protected by criminal law, 184 (opp. *hadr*).
ma'tūh, idiot, 124.
mawḳūf, in abeyance, 119.
mawlā, the patron, or the client, 40, 130, 133, 170.
mawlawī, term used in India for a Muslim scholar of religious law, 95.
mawzūn, *waznī*, things that can be weighed, 136.
maysir, a game of hazard, 12 f., 146.
mayta, animals not ritually slaughtered, 134.
mazālim, see *naẓar fil-maẓālim*.
milk, ownership (also in a wider meaning), 136, 178, 179.
milk al-'āmma, public property, 134, 141.
mithl, just mean, average, fair, 154, 167, 201.
mithlī, fungible, 136.
mu'āmala, 'transaction', euphemistic term for a device for evading the prohibition of interest, 79.
mu'āmalāt, pecuniary transactions, 145.
mu'āwaḍa māliyya, exchange of monetary assets, 119, 120, 145.
mubāḥ, indifferent (neither obligatory/recommended nor reprehensible/forbidden), 121.
mubāra'a, a form of divorce, 164.
mubham, ambiguous (declaration), 117.
mudabbar, a slave who has been manumitted by *tadbīr* (q.v.), 129, 135, 169, 186.
muḍāraba, sleeping partnership, 119, 156 f.
mudda'ā 'alayh, defendant, 189.
mudda'ī, claimant, plaintiff, 189.
mufāwaḍa, unlimited mercantile partnership, 116, 132, 156.
muflis, bankrupt, 198.
muftī, a specialist in religious law who gives an authoritative opinion, 27, 73 f., 90, 93, 95, 126.
muḥāḳala, a contract of barter in corn, 9, 146, 154.
muḥṣan, 125 (q.v. for definition), 178, 179.
muḥtakir, speculator on rising prices of food, 188.
muḥtasib, the Islamic inspector of the market, 25, 52, 55 n. 1, 84, 92, 114, 190, 207.
mujtahid, a qualified lawyer who uses *ijtihād* (q.v.), 37, 65, 71 f.
mukallaf, (fully) responsible, 124, 131, 179, 182.
muḳallid, a lawyer who uses *taḳlīd* (q.v.), 71.
mukātaba, manumission by contract, 42, 125, 129 f., 158.
mukātab, the slave who has concluded this contract, 42 f., 129 f., 135, 136, 174, 186.
mukhāṭara, a device for evading the prohibition of interest, 78 f.
mulāmasa, an aleatory transaction, 147.
mulāzama, personal supervision (of defendant by plaintiff, &c.), 197.
mumayyiz, 'intelligent', 'discriminating' minor, 125, 192.
munābadha, an aleatory transaction, 147.
murābaḥa, resale with a stated profit, 154.
murtadd, apostate, 138.
musāḳāt, a contract of lease of agricultural land, 119, 155, 156.
mushā', joint ownership, 138.
mustaḥabb, recommended, 121.
musta'min, an enemy alien who has been given an *aman* (q.v.), 131.
mut'a, temporary marriage, 163.
mut'a, indemnity payable in certain cases of repudiation, 167.
muta'ārif, customary, 144.
muwāḍa'a, 'understanding', term for a document used in connexion with *ḥiyal*, 83.
muwakkil, the principal (as opposed to the agent), 120.
muwālāt, contract of clientship, 133, 170.
muzābana, a contract of barter in dates, 40, 146, 154, 205.
muzāra'a, a contract of lease of agricultural land, 119, 155, 156.

nafaḳa, maintenance, 167.
nāfidh, operative, 121.

nafy, banishment, 187.
nahb, robbery, 180.
nā'ib, deputy in matters of worship, 119.
nasī'a, delay, 153.
naskh, repeal (*nāsikh*, the repealing passage; *mansūkh*, the repealed one), 115.
naẓar fil-maẓālim, 'investigation of complaints', 51, 54, 84, 189, 208.
nikāḥ, marriage, 161.
niyāba, proxy in worship, 119.
niyya, intent, 116 f., 118, 123.
niẓām, *niẓām-nāme*, 'ordinance', used of modern, secular regulations, 87.
nukūl, refusal (to take the oath, &c.), 190, 197.

rabb, owner, 136.
rabb al-māl, sleeping partner, 156.
raḍā', fosterage, 162.
rahn, pledge, pawn, security, 8, 12, 39, 138, 139 f.
raḳaba, substance, also the person (of a slave), 127, 129, 134, 205.
raḳīḳ, slaves, 127.
ra's al-māl, capital, 153.
rashwa, bribery, 188.
rasūl, messenger, 119.
ra'y, 'opinion', individual reasoning, 26, 37, 46, 53, 60, 70.
ribā, 'excess', interest, 12, 40, 145 ff., 153 f., 155, 157.
riḍā, consent, 117.
rikāz, treasure, 136.
rujū', withdrawal, revocation, retractation, 145, 151, 158, 177; return, 157.
ruḳbā, an archaic form of donation, 8, 158.
rukn (pl. *arkān*), essential element, 118.

ṣabī, minor, 124.
ṣadāḳ, nuptial gift, 161.
ṣadaḳa, charitable gift, 137, 158, 205.
safīh, irresponsible, 125.
ṣafḳa, 8, 145 (q.v. for definition), 146.
ṣaghīr, minor, 124.
ṣāḥib al-sūḳ, inspector of the market, 25.
ṣaḥīḥ, valid, legally effective, 121 ff., 190.
sahm, fixed share of an heir, 170.
ṣakk (pl. *ṣukūk*), written document, 78, 82 n. 1, 193.
salam, contract for delivery with prepayment, 106, 119, 147, 153, 155.
ṣarf, exchange (of money and precious metals), 154.
ṣarīḥ, explicit (declaration), 116.
sariḳa, theft, 175, 179.
sa'y, *si'āya*, 129 (q.v. for definition).
shahāda, testimony, evidence of witnesses, 192, 194.
shāhid (pl. *shuhūd*), witness, 193.
shar', *sharī'a*, the sacred Law of Islam, 1, and *passim*; opposed to *siyāsa*, administrative justice, 54 f.
sharīk, partner, 139, 155.
sharika, *shirka*, society, partnership, 119, 155 f.
sharikat māl, association in property, joint ownership, 138, 156.
sharṭ (pl. *shurūṭ*), prerequisite, condition, 118; stipulation, 145.
shaykh al-Islām, the chief *muftī* of a country, 74; in the Ottoman Empire, 90.
shibh, quasi-, 181 f., 185 n. 1.
shirā', purchase, 151.
shubha, 163, 176 (q.v. for definition), 178, 179 f.
shuf'a, pre-emption, 94, 106, 142, 192, 194.
shurb al-khamr, wine-drinking, 175, 179.
shurṭa, police, 50.
shurūṭ (pl. of *sharṭ*), 'stipulations', legal formularies, 82 n. 1, 83 f., 114, 210.
sijill, written judgment of the *ḳāḍī*, 83, 189.
simsār, broker, 78, 120.
siyāsa, 'policy', administrative justice, 54, 86 f., 91, 187.
siyāsa shar'iyya, *siyāsa* within the limits assigned to it by the *sharī'a*, 54.
subashi, chief of police in the Ottoman Empire, 90, 92.
suftaja, bill of exchange, 78, 149.
ṣulḥ, amicable settlement, 148, 181.
sulṭān, authority, dominion, ruling power, 206.
sunna, precedent, normative legal custom: in pre-Islamic Arabia, 8; in early Islam, 17; in the ancient schools of law, 30 f., 33; according

to Shāfi'ī, 47, 59; according to Ibn al-Muḳaffa', 55; according to Ibn Tūmart, 64.
sunna of the Prophet, 17 f., 33 f., 43, 47, 53, 60 f., 67, 114.
sunna of Abū Bakr and 'Umar, 18.
sunna, recommended, 121.

ta'addī, fault, illicit act, tort, 140, 147 f., 157.
ṭabaḳāt, biographies of lawyers arranged by 'classes' or generations, subject of special works, 114.
tadbīr, manumission which takes effect at the death of the owner, 129.
tafrīḳ, a dissolution of marriage, 165.
tafwīḍ, 164 (q.v. for definition).
taḥāluf, 191 (q.v. for definition).
tahātur, conflict of equivalent testimonies, 195.
tahdīd, threat, 117.
taḥlīl, a device to remove an impediment to marriage, 81 f.
tājir, trader, merchant, euphemistic term for the money-lender, 79.
taḳābuḍ, taking possession reciprocally, 138, 152.
taḳiyya, simulation, 118.
taḳlīd, reference to the Companions of the Prophet (in the ancient schools of law), 32, 47; reliance on the teaching of a master, 58 f., 65, 71 ff., 102, 115, adopting the doctrine of a school of law for a particular transaction, 68 n. 1.
ṭalāḳ, repudiation, 163 f., 165 n. 1.
talfīḳ, combining the doctrines of more than one school, 68 n. 1, 106.
ta'līḳ al-ṭalāḳ, form of conditional repudiation, 164.
tamlīk fil-ḥāl, immediate transfer of ownership, 119.
tāmm, complete, 152, 157.
tanazzuh, religious scruple, 123.
tapu, an Ottoman fiscal institution of land law, 90.
ta'rīf, 187 (q.v. for definition).
tarika, estate, 169.
tasallum, taking delivery, 138.
taṣarruf, capacity to dispose, 124; disposition, 145.
tasbīb, *bi-sabab*, indirect causation, 181, 182.
taslīm, delivery, 138.
tawba, repentance, 176.
tawliya, resale at the stated original cost, 153 f.
ta'zīr, discretionary punishment awarded by the *ḳāḍī*, 88, 91, 132, 175, 178 f., 180, 184, 187, 197, 207 f.
thaman, price, 152.
thiḳa, a trustworthy person, 83.
ṭifl, small child, babe-in-arms, 124.

'udhr, excuse (for non-fulfilment of a contract of *ijāra*), 154.
'udūl (pl. of *'adl*, q.v.), professional witnesses, 'notaries', 194.
'uhda, a guarantee against specific faults in a slave or an animal, particular to the Mālikī school, 8.
ujra, hire, rent, 154.
'uḳr, 178 (q.v. for definition).
'uḳūba, a Mālikī punishment in certain cases of homicide, 185 n. 1, 207.
'ulamā', the religious scholars of Islam, 28, 84, 87 f., 89, 102, 105, 110.
umm walad, female slave who has borne a child to her owner, 129, 135, 166, 169, 178, 186.
'umrā, donation for life, 8, 158.
'urf, custom, 62, 136.
uṣūl (sing. *aṣl*), or *uṣūl al-fiḳh*, the 'roots' or theoretical bases of Islamic law, 48, 59 ff., 71, 114 f.

wadī'a, deposit, 157.
waḍī'a, resale with a rebate, 154.
wājib, (1) obligatory, 121; (2) definite, binding, due, 22, 121 f.
wakāla, procuration, 120, 156.
waḳf, pious foundation, mortmain, 19, 76 f., 80 n. 1, 83, 90, 93, 94, 96 f., 101 f., 103, 108, 114, 125 f., 134, 142, 160, 205, 209.
wakīl, deputy, agent, proxy, 120; attorney, 190.
walā', the relationship of client and patron, 40, 130.
walī, legal guardian, 120, 161 f., 165.
walī al-dam, the next of kin who has the right to demand retaliation, 181, 184.

wara', religious scruple, 123.
wārith, heir, 170.
waṣf, the circumstances of a transaction (opp. *aṣl*), 121.
waṣī, executor and/or guardian appointed by testament, 120, 173.
waṣiyya (pl. *waṣāyā*), legacy, 173 f.
wathīḳa (pl. *wathā'iḳ*), written document, 82 n. 1, 193.
wilāya, competence, jurisdiction, 188.
wuḳūf, abeyance (of rights and legal effects), 119.
yad, possession (also in a wider meaning), 136.
yamīn, oath (undertaking), 159.

ẓāhir, the literal meaning (of Koran and traditions), 63 f.; the 'outward' state, 123 n. 1.
zakāt, alms-tax, 105, 206.
zawj, husband; *zawja*, wife, 161.
ẓihār, 165 (q.v. for definition), 203.
zinā, unchastity (unlawful intercourse), 175, 177, 178 f., 198.